AN ISLA
THE HISTORY OF
MANX EDUCATION
(Volume 1)

Hinton Bird

The publication of this book was made possible by financial assistance from the
MANX HERITAGE FOUNDATION

Dedicated to the memory of
Robert Curphey

Published by:
Hinton Bird, Rushen Vicarage, Port St. Mary, Isle of Man
with aid of the Manx Heritage Foundation

Printed in England by Ipswich Book Co.

CONTENTS

VOLUME ONE

Preface

Abbreviations

Introduction — The Isle of Man

Chapter 1   The Foundations are Laid

Chapter 2   The Age of Wilson (1) Petty Education — The Saviour Sows the Seeds of Decay.

Chapter 3   The Age of Wilson (2) The Expansion of Higher Education.

Chapter 4   The Late Eighteenth Century — The Petty Schools.

Chapter 5   The Golden Age of the Endowed Schools.

Chapter 6   The Failure of the Endowed Schools in the Early Nineteenth Century.

Chapter 7   The Explosion in Education — The Role of the Private Sector.

Chapter 8   King William's College — Fulfilment or Betrayal?

Chapter 9   Elementary Education 1800-1849. Influences from the Mainland.

Chapter 10 Elementary Education 1847-1869. The Legacy of James Kay.

ILLUSTRATIONS

Between pages 46 and 47
1 Bishopscourt in the time of Bishop Wilson
2 Castletown Grammar School
3 Bishop Wilson
4 Private boarding schools — The Villa Marina, Rushen Abbey, Oakhill, the Athol Academy, Douglas

Between pages 186 and 187
5 King William's College, the original design
6 King William's College, two early views
7 Two of Ward's 'Mountain Schools' — Sulby and Dalby
8 The Day-school Keeping Churches of Douglas 1840

Between pages 242 and 243
9 The National Schools of Douglas and Castletown
10 Episcopal enthusiasts for education — Ward and Short
11 Ramsey around 1840
12 Douglas around 1840

My thanks for permission to use illustrations are due to the Manx Museum and National Trust (1.3), Mr. Peter Kelly (4), Mr. Frank Cowin (5), The Principal of King William's College (6, 10b), the Wardens of St. Stephen's, Sulby (7), and the Ven. David Willoughby (10a).

MAPS

Manx Petty Schools 1669-1704	Opposite page 18
Manx Schools by 1800	96
Private Schools offering Secondary Education outside Douglas 1800-1860	,, page 174
'Unofficial' Elementary Schools 1820-1850	,, page 250
The Surge Towards Elementary Education for All. New 'Official' Schools 1800-1870	,, page 280

PREFACE

As might well have been expected, much of the history of education in the Isle of Man mirrored trends on the mainland, as for example in the foundation and later decline of endowed schools, the decades of triumph for private adventure schools, the influence at elementary level of the National Society, and the gradual involvement of the state in the Nineteenth Century which culminated in the Twentieth with the provision of secondary education for all. Yet there is much more to the story than a piece of the Celtic fringe lagging behind, and incidentally offering a microcosmic view on account of its compactness of some three centuries' development in education.

For to a surprising extent the Isle of Man has often led rather than followed the mainland. In the late Seventeenth Century an integrated system was developed, with compulsory elementary education in every parish leading to a free grammar school and thence to provided places at university, or the Island's own equivalent. Shortly afterwards regulations concerning universal education, free to the poor, were incorporated in a formal Act of Tynwald, the Manx Parliament. Later in the Eighteenth Century the Island government gave a grant each year to assist specialised education at one of the Island's endowed schools, long before such an idea became acceptable at any level of education on the mainland. In 1830 the founding of King William's College came at the outset of the movement in favour of 'public schools' situated in rural locations, which appealed so much to Victorian minds. While dependence upon the mainland increased markedly in the Nineteenth Century, the Island again led England in such ways as grasping the nettle of rate-aided education as early as 1851, and in the insistence that elementary education must be compulsory, not an option. In the present century, the Isle of Man developed a system of educational administration which could be claimed with some justice to be superior to that of the mainland, a process which enabled it to become the first authority in Britain to introduce a complete system of comprehensive education, although, contrary to common assumption by educational historians, there were no factors present to make this step an obvious one to take.

It is thus hoped that this study will make some contribution to the story of the development of education in the British Isles as a whole, as well as fill a gap in Manx national studies. While it might be expected that general histories of the Island make but scanty reference to education, it is rather surprising, in view of the Manx interest in their heritage, that no overall account of Manx education has been published. Again, apart from shorter articles, there is a distinct dearth of in-depth specialised writing, even in manuscript, Dr. J. E. Jenkin's detailed analysis of the 1908 Higher Education Act appearing to stand alone in this respect. Many dark corners await the casting of light upon them, and if this book encourages the exploration of some, it will have served a further purpose. Perhaps, too, the excellent local histories of Constance Radcliffe on the north of the Island will find their counterparts in the other towns and parishes. An attempt has been made to set the Island happenings in due perspective against their mainland backgrounds, with brief outlines of some educational developments in Britain where thought necessary for proper comprehension.

I would like to thank for all their help in furnishing material for this book, the librarians and staff of the Douglas Public Library; St. George's Library, Douglas; the Clerk of Tynwald's Library; the sorely-missed Isle of Man Rural Library, especially for help in obtaining books and theses from the mainland; the Main and Educational Libraries of University College, Cardiff; the Public Record Office at Kew; and above all the Manx Museum Library. I would also like to thank the Sodor and Man Diocesan Office, the Principal of King William's College for access to the Bishop Barrow Trustees' records — College too must be one of the few public schools to lack an adequate published history of itself — the Department of Education, especially Mr. Ralph Cowin, the late Robert Curphey for his kindness and encouragement at the outset of this undertaking, which was greatly appreciated, and the Minister of Education, G. V. H. Kneale, for sparing the time to look over some of this manuscript. My thanks too to Dr. David Alsobrook of Cardiff University for helping to mitigate the insularity of outlook which so easily pervades writers based on the Island.

ABBREVIATIONS

BBT	Minutes of the Bishop Barrow Trustees.
BC	Book of Charities.
BH	Bridge House Papers.
Debates	Isle of Man Times Reports of Debates in the Manx Legislature.
GO	Government Office Papers.
JHK	Journal of the House of Keys.
JMM	Journal of the Manx Museum.
Procs of IOMNHAS	Proceeddings of the Isle of Man Natural History and Antiquarian Society.
PRO	Public Record Office.
Bryce Report	Report of the Royal Commission on Secondary Education 1895.
Carson Report	The Central Education Authority. Report of its Committee on the development of Secondary Education 1921.
Hadow Report	Report of the Consultative Committee on the Education of the Adolescent 1926.
Jackson Report	Report on Secondary and Higher Elementary Education by Cyril Jackson, MA 1906.
McDonnell Report	Report of the Departmental Committee on the Constitution etc. of the Isle of Man 1912.
Norwood Report	Report of the Committee on Curriclum and Examinations in Secondary Schools 1943.
Phipps Report	Report of the Commission on Education in the Isle of Man 1933.
Spens Report	Report of the Consultative Committee on Secondary Education with Special Reference to Grammar Schools and Technical High Schools 1938.
Taunton Report	Report of the Commissioners on Education in Schools in England, not comprised within Her Majesty's two recent Commissions on Popular Education and Public Schools 1868.

INTRODUCTION
THE ISLE OF MAN

From the summit of Snaefell, at 2,034 feet the highest peak on the Isle of Man, can be seen, on a clear day, the four countries of England, Wales, Scotland and Ireland, and although English popular opinion often brackets the Island with the Isle of Wight, the period of English dominance occupies but part of the Island's history, in which all four countries have played a role. Indeed the 16 miles to Burrow Head in Galloway, Scotland, is less than half the distance to St. Bees Head, at 34 miles the nearest point in England. Ireland is a little further away, there being 40 miles to Stranford Lough in Ulster, while Wales is the most distant land, with 55 miles from Holyhead on the island county of Anglesey even to the Calf of Man, off the Manx southern coast.

The Island occupies 227 square miles, in shape quite similar to the herring for which it is so famed, with a distance of 34 miles from the northernmost point at Ayre to the Chicken's Rock just off the Calf of Man, and of 13 miles from east to west at its widest point. Yet despite the apparent compactness of the Island, the nature of the terrain is such that there was no point of easy access from all parts until the advent of the motor car. A range of rugged, high ground with ten peaks, divided by only one central valley running from east to west, separates the Island, except for the flat northern plain, a legacy of the last Ice Age. The high ground falls away almost to the sea to both east and west, making access from north to south too much more difficult than a glance at a map would suggest.

Early settlers left their megaliths and forts as permanent memorials, but the first written references to the Island are found in Latin authors, who name it variously Mona, Monaodia, Mevania and Monopia. Although the root of the name 'Mann' has been linked with Manannan, a Celtic sea-god, others find it more prosaically in the Gaelic 'monadh', maning mountain.[1] Crosius in 416 stated that the Island of Mevania was inhabited by Scots, and the first mention of language links the Island firmly with the Goidelic group of Celtic tongues, for it relates how an Irish poet, Senchan, visited the Island and was able to cap a couplet of verse given by an old woman.[2] The common language meant that the conversion of the Manx to the Christian faith by Irish missionaries was more easily undertaken, and numerous cells or keeils were built during the Age of Saints.

The first great intrusion into the Celtic way of life came from beyond the British Isles in the shape of the Vikings, who as elsewhere came first to plunder and then to settle. The strategic importance of the Isle of Man in the middle of the Irish Sea was evident, and the coastal placenames abound in Norse roots. In the years after 883, the harshness of Harald Harfager, King of Norway, led to subjects fleeing his rule, and settling overseas. For two hundred years Vikings based in Norway itself, the Orkneys and Ireland fought over the Island until in 1079 Godred Crovan established a regime destined to last two hundred years.

The Millennium celebrated in 1979 on the Island to mark a thousand years of parliamentary rule had no more basis in history than the date of 447 plucked out of the air as a foundation of the ecclesiastical see, but certainly in the Norse period the custom of the open air assemby to promulgate laws with the consent of the people took root in the Island, and its traditions continue to form the basis of the present Manx constitution. No law declared by king, lawmen, and Keys, twenty four 'worthiest men', had force without popular acclamation, and still in the Twentieth Century the Gregorian Calendar equivalent of June 24th sees the solemn ceremony of law-passing at the Tynwald or Parliament field.[3] The original twenty four Keys came from the whole of the Sudreys or Southern Islands, as opposed to the Northern Islands of Shetland and the Orkneys, but as time passed the Outer and Inner Hebrides were detached politically from the Isle of Man, and the original wide-flung Kingdom of the Isles is remembered only in the title of the see, 'Sodor and Man'. During the period of Norse rule, the Church, which had a loose connection with the English Church, was linked in 1154 with Trondheim in Norway. However, the predominant influence was the abbey of Furness in England, whose monks were given land in the sheading of Rushen to found an abbey in 1134.[4]

The Norse period ended with the death of King Magnus, who had already lost the Western Isles to Alexander III of Scotland, and paid homage for Man alone to him, and no longer to the King of Norway. For four thousand marks, the Norse gave up all claims to Man and the rest of the Sudreys in favour of Scotland, but for a hundred and fifty years the struggle for the Island between England and Scotland caused misery and confusion, with a weakened Island raided by Irish and French forces too. In 1405 Henry IV awarded Man to the Stanley family as Kings or Lords of Man, and their house ruled the Island for over three hundred years. Their regime was autocratic, yet with some respect for the traditions of the past. John II (1414-1432) had the ancient folk laws put in writing, and generally the actual governance of the Island was given to a deputy. Under Henry VIII, Thomas III (1504-1521) took the politic step of relinquishing the title of King, using Lord of Mann only. The direct Stanley line failed in 1736, and the Lordship of Man passed to James, Duke of Athol, but a more important change in the history of the Island was the Revestment Act of 1765 whereby the English government, exasperated by the use of the Island for the purpose of smuggling, bought the regalities and customs of the Island for £70,000, so that Man became a colony of the English crown. The Duke himself fixed a high price for all his rights, and a long legal dispute was not resolved until 1828, when a sum of £417,000 was paid.

The House of Keys meantime fought bitterly against the Duke's attempts to enforce their remaining manorial rights, and passed laws against the Athol interests, as well as claiming that surplus revenue should go to the Island, and not the Duke. The appointment of John, fourth Duke of Atholl, as Governor in 1793 increased the tensions, complicated by the fact that the Keys themselves could be claimed by the Duke to no more represent the people of Man than the natives of Peru.[5]

The early election of the Keys by the people of the sheadings was replaced in the Sixteenth Century by the Lord choosing his own appointees. Early Seventeen Century protests, as by Bishop John Philips in 1610, had no effect, but by 1700 the Keys themselves proffered two names to the Governor to choose one. They soon became bolder in opposition to the Governors, and also looked after their own interests to such a great degree that a Petition to the English Parliament pleaded for a new method of selection. The English 1832 Reform Act encouraged further attempts, but not until 1866 did the Keys cease to be self-electing. This was part of an agreement whereby the Island gained the right to dispose of its surplus revenue above the expenses of government, apart from £10,000 towards defence. The condition of this was the end of the self-recruitment of members of the Keys from a few leading families of the Island. Instead ten electoral districts were established, composed of each sheading and the four towns of Castletown, Douglas, Peel and Ramsey, with representation so divided as to yield the traditional twenty four members.

In the Norse traditions of Tynwald, an important part was played by the law-men or deemsters, as advisers on the law to the king. Under the Stanleys, the Lord or his resident Governor was assisted by members of his Council, the official holders of lay and ecclesiastical positions, forming an upper chamber. Even after 1866 it was very easy for the Council and a Governor armed with a veto to thwart any wishes of the Keys, and a struggle for reform did not reach any satisfactory end until 1921, when some officials were removed, giving way to two nominees of the Governor and four of the Keys. Gradually the officials, including the deemsters, were removed, and in 1984 only the Bishop remained ex-officio, the other members of the Legislative Council being nominated by the House of Keys. Further reforms are planned to make the Council directly elected by the people.

Unlike the practice in the British Parliament, both chambers meet together for business, thus forming Tynwald Court, to approve expenditure and until 1986, when a system of ministries was introduced, met to appoint Boards of Tynwald, and to accept or reject subordinate legislation made by the various boards. The joint session also acts as a forum for public debate. Although the United Kingdom represents the Island in international affairs, the aim of Tynwald as declared in a Resolution of July 14 1981 is full self-governing status.

While much of the Westminster legislation is adopted by Tynwald, with the normal channels of passing through both chambers and receiving the royal assent having the Manx addition of formal promulgation on Tynwald Hill, there is no necessity to follow Westminster. Much has not been adopted, and in education as in other areas, careful assesment of mainland law has often led to modifications which avoid problems experienced in the United Kingdom. Tynwald has also, of course, the right to pass its own independent legislation with no mainland counterpart.

This legal independence meant that bitterness over religious differences did not play any notable part in the educational and other history of the Island. Indeed in the Eighteenth Century Bishop Hildesley (1755-1772) found every person a member of the Established Church on his arrival while a little later John Wesley reported "but six paptists and no dissenters on the Island".[6] Although following Wesley's visits, Methodism spread very rapidly, services which clashed with those of the Church were not held until 1836, and the general low churchmanship of the Island, together with mutual support for such causes as the Temperance Movement, saved the Island from much sectarian strife, including the adoption of legislation which would set Church and Chapel against one another.

The absence of Manx literature also prevented language problems in education as a cause of friction. By the time the Bible and other books were printed in the Manx tongue, it had long been accepted that English must be the language of education, although it was still the tongue of two-thirds of the population. As the Nineteenth Century wore on, the old native Gaelic retreated to the hills, with the last native speakers being found in the village of Cregneish in the South in the early decades of the present century.

It has been said that for the Vikings the sea was their highroad, and this was true of the Island for many centuries. Internal communications were poor indeed, and even in the middle of the Eighteenth Century a journey from Douglas to Peel was full of uncertainty. The railways came late to the Island, and the adoption of a curious narrow gauge system did not make for speed. Although the opening of lines between Peel and Douglas in 1873, with a link to Ramsey which left the main line at St. John's in 1877, and between Douglas and Port Erin in 1877 made reasonable travel possible, times were very slow for the short distance involved by normal mainland standards. The line to Ramsey in particular was forced to make a long sickle-shaped detour up the west coast, although an electric railway finished in 1898 tackled the more severe gradients of the east coast. Well into the Twentieth Century problems of time and distance dogged the attempts to provide centralised higher education.

The central range, apart from causing access difficulties, also meant there was no central town, and the four towns mentioned earlier of Castletown, Douglas, Peel and Ramsey grew up independently, becoming centres of local feeling and pride. Castletown, dominated by the mighty walls of Castle Rushen, emerged as the recognised capital and residence of the Governors, but suffered from the handicap of a poor harbour, difficult to negotiate. Peel possessed the Cathedral of St. German, sharing the same islet as Peel Castle, but both were in ruins by the Seventeenth Century. Douglas possessed the best harbour on the Island, and although in 1726 it was only marginally larger than Castletown (810 to 785) in its population, completely outpaced it in development to the point that in 1891 it had 19,525 inhabitants to Castletown's 2,178.[7] All four towns had their fishing fleets and indeed their own flourishing boat building yards, but the links with Liverpool which Douglas developed in the Nineteenth Century proved crucial in its development. By 1860 the Governor had moved his seat from Castletown to Douglas, and the expansion of the harbour, one of the first fruits of Home Rule in 1866, enabled Douglas to attract an ever-increasing number of tourists and holiday makers from the North of England. Yet the suspicion of Douglas shown by the rest of the Island was a factor in addition to the parochial outlook which was to be expected from a rural community, and seriously hampered the progress of education on the Island.

    A. W. Moore's standard work on the history of the Isle of Man ended with a chapter on the Three Great Industries of the Island.[8] The agriculture and fishing remain, but the mining has long disappeared. Around 1850 the mines at Foxdale in the centre of the south of the Island, and at Laxey on the east coast between Douglas and Ramsey were very prosperous — in 1854 £80 shares of the Laxey Mining Company were being sold at £1,200. Yet the end of the century saw prices falling steeply: Foxdale was closed in 1911 and the mighty Isabella Wheel at Laxey turns only for tourists now. Fishing too is but a shadow of its former self, and the tourist trade has suffered greatly from the competition of package holidays offering Spanish sun to the people of Lancashire who once flocked to the Island. Generation of sufficient work has been a problem, and the continuous rise of the Nineteenth Century was reversed in the Twentieth until the 1961 figure of 48,000 was the lowest population total since 1841. Although the policy of attracting new residents with low tax rates was successful to the degree that a new record population of 64,679 was recorded in 1981, it had the effect of making the Manx for the first time a minority in their own Island, as newcomers had already replaced natives who emigrated in the Nineteen Fifties to a significant degree. A further wave of new residents with a target figure of 75,000 is now being suggested as one answer to economic difficulties. The encouragement of a wide range of financial services to establish themselves on the Island has also meant that the new residents are not composed solely of retired people.[9]

    Even if the new target figure of popuation is reached, it will amount to no more than that of a moderate English town, and the Island claim to independence may seem nothing than an anachronism. The language has gone except for a few enthusiastic revivalists: the Church is part of the Church of England, although it retains its own Convocation. Yet just as in the last century the Church fought off attempts to annexe the Island first to Carlisle and later to the new diocese of Liverpool, so the Isle of Man, proud of its distinctive history and heritage, fiercely maintains its right to rule itself, and to plot its own future course. Despite the influx of 'come-overs', the words of Canon Stenning in 1949 remain substantially true:

"... *in spite of incursions and invasions into the Island from Britain, so close at hand, (they) remain a markedly Celtic race, Celtic in outlook, in artistry, in speech, in culture, in spite of the super-imposition on them of the Scandinavian type of government and policy which they received, assimilated and absorbed from the Vikings .. They are a people who enjoy and value "Home Rule", who have worked out their destiny and constitution, often with great difficulty and against great odds, but have come through happily with their claim fully realised, and their future, as part of the British nation satisfactorily and happily under their own control.*"[10]

REFERENCES

INTRODUCTION

1 F. H. Stenning. *Isle of Man*, Robert Hale, London 1950. 4.
2 A. W. Moore. *A History of the Isle of Man*, T. Fisher Unwin, London 1900. Vol. I. 46.
3 David Craine. *Tynwald Symbol of an Ancient Kingdom*, Government Property Trustees Isle of Man 1960.
4 The six sheadings of the Isle of Man probably find their origin in the 'skeid-thing' meaning ship community, responsible for providing a certain number of boats and crew.
5 A. W. Moore. *Op. cit.*Vol. II. 541.
6 James Rosser. *The History of Wesleyan Methodism in the Isle of Man.*
7 Bishop Wilson's Census 1726. Official census 1891.
8 A. W. Moore. *Op. cit.* Vol. II. 913.
9 Fd. Tony Faragher. *Isle of Man Official Year Book 1983*. Motor in Mann Publications, Ramsey 1983. 18.
10 F. H. Stenning. *Op. cit.* 3.

CHAPTER ONE

THE FOUNDATIONS ARE LAID

Before the latter half of the Seventeenth Century, little is known in detail about education at any level in the Isle of Man apart from scattered references. An entry in the Rotuli Patentium for 1403 reveals, however, that there was in medaeval times a system of providing for Manx scholars, when Henry IV gave to Luke Macquyn

> 'of the Island of Man, Scolars, certain alms called particles, in the island aforesaid, vacant, as said, and in our gift, and which alms are appropriated to the support of certain poor scholars of the island aforesaid and which were given, confirmed, and conceded perpetually to the scholars by our predecessors, former Kings of England; to have and to hold to the said Luke the alms aforesaid, as long as he shall remain a scholar for the benefit of the Church, and shall not be promoted'.[1]

A similar system was to be a feature of Manx church life centuries later under the provisions of Bishop Barrow, but the next bishop, Richard Payl or Pully, was clearly not one to appreciate long term educational benefits. A dispute of 1429 concerning church dues found the bishop accused of having 'dealt into other uses' the particles of land 'ordained to the reliefe of poor scholars'.[2] Perhaps it was in a moment of absentmindedness that A. W. Moore referred to the arrangements about particles as being 'for the benefit of the sons of the clergy'[3] rather than suggesting that the Manx clergy generally ignored their vows of celibacy in those Pre-Reformation times. A century and a half elapses before there is any other reference to education, apart from an Abbot of Rushen sending a young man for a specialised musical education to Chester. Then in 1578 in the Ingates and Outgates of Castle Rushen there is a mention of the salary at 'iiij li per annum' of Peter ffarand, the schoolmaster. In like manner at Peel Castle in 1599 the accounts refer to 'the Sallary of the Scholar xx s', presumably the payment for a quarter.[4] While these schools might appear to be primarily for the occupants of the respective castles, the danger of assuming too hastily that there was no worthwhile education to be obtained in the Island is shown by the fact that a leading Roman Catholic exile of the early Seventeenth Century, Hugh MacCawell, consecrated as Archbishop of Armagh in 1626 after teaching theology in Salamanca, Louvain and Rome, (but dying the same year), apparently received his education in the Isle of Man from the age of fourteen, sent in 1585 from his native County Down 'in Monam Insularum'. Why and to whom, at a time when Bishop Meryck was soon to write in 1590 that the Manx people 'most readily conform without a single exception to the formularies of the Church of England', remains a matter for pure speculation.[5]

The first island-wide survey to mention schools was in the Visitation of Bishop Foster in 1634, which lumped them in the articles of enquiry with alm-houses and hospitals. Foster, appointed bishop only the year before, was especially desirous to know if there were any masters without a bishop's licence. The manuscript is much the worse for wear, but at least two parishes were able to state categorically that they contained schools. In Malew, Robert Parr replied that 'we declare yt their is noe Schoole keept in or pish but one, ye mr whereof saies he hath his licence'. One other, possibly Lezayre, claimed to be 'well used for Alme house and schooles, as for spitiles wee doe use none'. Other replies were more ambiguous. German merely reported 'no default', while Marown's reply was the same as that from Peter Thompson of Braddan; 'neither scolemaster that teacheth without licence'. Whether thee was actually a licensed master is left unclear. Others still were more decidedly negative, although at Rushen William Nores (Norris) showed a degree of caution with his 'knowe of none'. John Otte at Onchan was more forthright; 'as for scole master we have non within or parish', while another claimed 'no alseme houses kept or schools or spittles used'.[6] But was abundantly clear was what was missing. Of the great outpouring of wealth into education by the middle classes, with merchants well to the fore, traced by W. K. Jordan in *Philanthropy in England 1485-1660*, there was no echo in the Island at all.[7] Not a single school before 1660 was set up which might proportionally balance the impressive total of 1320 grammar schools listed by W. A. L. Vincent as in existence between 1600 and 1660, itself a conservative estimate without account being taken of private schools offering a similar education.[8] The Manx clergy generally received unflattering reports: "... illiterate men, brought up in the island in secular professions" and "of no better ability that to read distinctly divine service." Bishop Parr concluded in 1639 that the Island "was destitute of means of learned education."[9] However, others were less damning than the bishop, who even claimed that many could not preach. James Chaloner in 1656 made cautious allowance. "Considering the Ministers here are generally natives, and have had their whole education in the Isle, it is marvailous to here what good preachers there be."[10] William Blundell in the same year had no reservation. "Their ministers truly are not unlearned. I did not converse with anyone, but that I found him both a scholar and discreet."[11]

Yet although little effect could be discerned in Man, the great growth in interest in education on the mainland in the first part of the Seventeenth Century was soon to bear fruit. James, Seventh Earl of Derby, who as Lord Strange began to rule the Island in 1627 in his father's lifetime, and later left such an impression on the Manx that he was known as Yn Stanlagh Mooar, the Great Stanley, had informally brought the Island into contact with higher education by giving promising youths the chance to study at university. The Liber Irrotulamentorum in 1631 included the payment "unto Wm Langley sone unto my servant Matthias Langley, Constable of my Castle of Rushen, ye yearlie pay or pencoon of six pounds towards his education in ye University of Cambridge." Soon Derby was thinking terms of providing a higher education on the Island itself.

> "I had design, and God may enable me, to set up a university, without much charge (as I have contrived it) which may much oblige the nations round about us. It may get friends in the country, and enrich this land."[12]

However the Battle of Worcester 1651 led to the execution of the Earl soon after, and by the end of that year, the surrender of his widow to the invading forces of Parliament meant that its grant of the Lordship of Man in September 1649 to Thomas Fairfax was now a meaningful reality. Derby's dream was probably inspired by the precedent of the founding of Trinity College, Dublin, in 1591 — "The first colonial university institution."[13]

The change of rule ended such grandiose plans, but had less impact otherwise than might have been expected, for there had been no bishop since 1645, and the secular power already controlled the bishop's revenues. While military expenses were the obvious use, Blundell asserts that Derby himself used some of the revenues to maintain four free schools.[14] Indeed interest in education transcended the political divisions, and the Puritans gave a high place to the education of the young. The new governor, James Chaloner, may therefore have only been preserving the status quo, when part of the revenus was used "for the maintaining of Free-Schooles, i.e. at Castletown, Peel, Douglas and Ramsey" or may have been following the lead of the Commissioners for the Propagation of the Gospel in Wales and the North of England, who established new schools in the early Sixteen Fifties, over sixty of them in Wales alone.[15] Chaloner's own word "maintaining" suggests the former interpretation is the more correct.[16]

THE WORK OF BISHOP BARROW

THE FIRST TIER OF EDUCATION — THE PETTY SCHOOLS

The Restoration in England brought to an end there thoughts of a complete national system of schooling, although new grammar schools were founded in large numbers. On the contrary, in the Island such ideas were actually put into practice through the vigour of Bishop Isaac Barrow (1663-69), "a man of public spirit and great designs for the good of the Church, to whose industry is owing all that little learning amongst us, and to whose prudence and charity the poor clergy owe the bread they eat."[17] A former Fellow of Peterhouse before moving to Oxford as Chaplain of New College, he was described by John Keble as being "as thorough a disciple in the school of Laud as any that could well be named," and spent the period of the Commonwealth in the country. His appointment to the see to succeed Samuel Rutter, who survived his installation by only six months, was rapidly followed by his appointment as the governor of the Island. This continuance of a pattern which put the powers of both church and state under one man, added to the limited and clearly defined area of the Island which made effective supervision a real possibility, allowed dreams shelved in England to be pursued with energy and success.

John Comenius, a Bohemian exiled in Poland, had written in 1632 *The Great Didactic*, proposing Vernacular Schools for every village, with the more able passing to a Latin School to be set up in each city. He, together with another enthusiast for education, John Drury from Denmark, were invited to England in the early days of the Long Parliament, when a scheme for national education appeared to be in the offing. Although such ideas were more usually propounded by Puritan writers such as James Harrington, whose *The Commonwealth of Oceana* favoured free and compulsory schooling with inspection and supervision by magistrates, a committed Royalist such as Barrow could still agree that education properly structured could be an effective tool for promoting Godliness and civilised behaviour. Indeed, not far from the shores of Man, the example of Scotland showed what could be attempted. The First Book of Discipline desired that every parish should have a school, and while the dream of John Knox that there should be an ascending chain of schools, including Higher Grammar Schools leading to university, was not realised, a serious attempt was made in 1616 to ensure that each parish had its school. While this and legislation to the same end in 1633 and 1646 was not totally effective, many parish schools acted both as elementary and grammar schools, and sent pupils direct to university.[18]

As far as Barrow was concerned, the need in man was overwhelming.

> "At my coming into the island, I found the people for the most part loose and vicious in their lives, rude and barbarous in their behaviour; and — which I suppose the cause of this disorder — without any true sense of religion, and indeed, in a condition almost incapable of being bettered; for they had no means of instruction, or of being acquainted with the very principles of Christianity. Their ministers, it is true, took upon them to preach; but were themselves much fitter to be taught, being very ignorant and wholly illiterate; having had no other education than what that rude place afforded them; not many books, which came rarely thither . . . This being their condition, I suppose the best way of Cure would be to acquaint them with the English tongue, so that they might be in a capacity of reading Catechisms and books of devotion: and for this purpose to set up an English school in every parish: and withal, to fit the children for higher learning in a Grammar School, which was also wanting."[19]

The wisdom of making English the language of all levels has been questioned, but in the short term Barrow had little choice. He himself pointed out "there is nothing either written or printed in their language, which is peculiar to themselves; neither can they who speak it best write to one another in it, having no character or letter among them."[20] Although Bishop Phillips (1605-33) had in fact translated the Prayer Book into Manx in 1610, it remained unpublished, and translation and publication of the Bible and other books would take many years, even if started at once. There were simply no Manx tools in existence for education. Practical reasons thus strongly reinforced probable prejudice against Celtic tongues, for the spread of English was often regarded as a mark of progress and light. In the same way English parochial schools were urged upon Ireland from 1537 onwards.[21]

Barrow acted with vigour to construct a system of education which would make the Island self-sufficient in training its own clergy to the required level. He recognised the present clergy could not be expected to buy books on stipends of five or six pounds, and the need to make ends meet prevented them from giving time to study, as they strove "even in keeping of ale-houses, to procure a living."[22] Barrow thundered against clergy who

> "disgrace their Callinge and prostitute yer houses ... to Irregular and disorderly meetings by vending ayle and beere and keeping victuallinge Houses. These are to require all Ministers within the Isle aforesaid to forebare this unhansome and undecent Course ... so contrary to that studious retirement they are obliged to by it."[23]

Suspension for a first offence was followed by being made "incapable of any spiritual preferment in this Island."[24] Yet Barrow realised that financial help was essential too, and raised a large sum of money by subscriptions which he hoped would alleviate present distress and build for the future. A list of benefactors in the 1669 entries of the Liber Causarum gave a total of £916-8-4, while a list found in Jurby dated the following year made the sum up to £1,041-8-4 and listed three objects:— the "erection of a Free School in the said Island, and of an English School in the several parishes thereof; and also for the augmentations of stipends to the poor livings in that Island."[25] Barrow's good standing with Charles II also gained a further nominal £100 a year, but this Royal Bounty proved elusive when it came to payment. Even by 1670, "the arrears of His Majesty's gift of £100 per annum for three years past" was mentioned, which would have made up the £1,041 to £1,341.[26]

The substantial sum obtained through subscriptions was used by Barrow to obtain a lease of 10,000 years on the tithes which had formally belonged to Rushen Abbey, but which had passed through royal hands to William, Sixth Earl of Derby, in 1609 by gift of James I.[27] The terms were the payment of one thousand pounds, certain reserved rents, and a fine of £130 English every thirty years. Yearly meetings of the Bishop, Archdeacon and two other trustees nominated by the Earl would "distribute and dispose" of the tithes. The trust's objects were listed as

> "... for the encrease and augmentation of the maintenance, and better support and livlihood of the Ministers of the Gospel settled and exercising their functions within the said Isle of Man; and for or towards the erection of a Free School with the same Isle, or to the maintenance of some Schoolmasters there ..."[28]

Of the donors, Dr. Brough, Dean of Gloucester, and Mrs. Hall, the widow of the Bishop of Chester, were the most generous, each giving £100, but nearly all the bishops and most deans gave something. Dr. Ingelo, a former colleague of Barrow at Eton College had already given £15 for teaching of schools before the appeal was started.

From the outset Barrow made it clear that increased stipends and schools were to be interlinked, the Jurby list of subscriptions having a note added that 'every Minister is obliged to teach an English school in his parish', by the increase of his stipend, which was the work intended, and the Royal Bounty similarly as 'distributed to the Ministers for teaching an English school in their several parishes.'[29] Although the Act of Tynwald passed in 1704 has attracted great attention, the year 1669 may well be considered the most significant of all the landmarks in Manx educational history, for in that year Barrow put into effect his plans for a complete system of parochial schooling, which formed the basis for all future developments. His instructions to his Vicar-General dated July 15th indicated his determination that even if some of the clergy failed in their duty, the provision of schooling would continue

> "... have a special care to see that ye severall Schooles of this Island be diligently kept and observed, and if they find any neglect in any of ye Schoolmasters by the testimony of severall Churchwardens or any others, that can make just proof thereof, that Mr Deemster Norris upon notice given by the Vic's Genrll shall stopp their Salary and they appoint another to fill upon for that period, and to have Salary until my returne into the County, which Salary I leave to their discretion'.[30]

At the same time careful enquiry was made to see if a start had been in each parish. The Bishop's order to this end had been posted in each church, as is indicated in the reply from Santan. The chapter-quest, men chosen to report to the Vicar-Generals all those who had transgressed against the rules of the Church, confirmed that 'the minister of the parish keeps a constant schoole ... according to our honourable Lord's order lately set up in the parish church of Kk St Anne.'[31] The reply from Ballaugh hinted with a touch of smugness that other parishes were less virtuous in this respect than their own.

> 'We ye old chapter quest for the Lord Bops half year doo certifie that divine service is constantly read and a schoole kept all the year through not only for our own parish but as for such as come from Kk Michael and Kk Christ Lezer'.

In the east of the Island the routine report from Onchan that a school was 'kept and observed by ye minister' is far less interesing than the case of the Parish of Lonan. There the minster appeared to be going through the motions of saying the right things on Sundays but doing nothing about it during the week.

> 'We whose names are subscribed ... do declare and give in writing whether there be a schoole kept in ye parish or noe do give our answer that ye minister hath given calls and doth each Sunday admonish his parishioners to send their children to him to be taught and still ingaging himselfe to them that their children should be diligently taught and have good usage to the parents content, yett none send any to schoole for that there is none kept; ye reason aledged is yt they cannot spare their children, and this we certifie.'[32]

Although it was not clear whether minister or parents were more to blame, the Vicar-General came down severely against both parties. The duty of the minister to teach was balanced by a duty of the parents to send children to school. Decades before the law of 1704, the principle of compulsory education was being established, with financial sanctions imposed for failure to comply.

> 'If any minister fayle in his duty of schoole keeping or ye parrents in sending their children, he shall lose 20s allowed by his augmentation and they pay ...'

A precise sum may have been mentioned, but at this point the entry in the Liber Causarum tantalisingly slips below the binding. Clearly further enquiry was made, for the following month on August 30 the chapter-quest gave a further report which might have aroused a little sympathy for the pleading minister.

> '... ye minister doth continue his course as formerly in desiring ye prshoners to send their children to him to be taught, and that they should have good usage and be diligently taught and this with admonitions thereto he hath done very oft yet ye pishoners send none to him.'[33]

No sympathy however was shown: as far as the Vicar-Generals were concerned the report was a complaint which needed strong action

> 'The minister enjoined to teach and attend the schoole daily for ye future and if any saying or further complaint against him in this behalfe, a considerable part of ye augmentacon shall be given to another schoolemr and those of the prshioners who are able and will not send their children to schoole, shall be made lyable to a certain allowance to ye maintenance of ye Schoolmr as well as if they did send their child to School.'

How quickly this case at Lonan was resolved is not known, but already the basis of Manx elementary education was established. Every child was to receive an education, and a duty imposed on both parent and incumbent to see that this was performed, with fees expected from those who could afford to pay. Nothing was to be left, as in England, to the chance forces of supply and demand.

Although doubtlessly very imperfect in application, the new system differed little in this respect from later laws. The parents who could not spare their children for school were to be a feature even of the last decades of the Nineteenth Century. Moreover, to cavil at the application of the term 'compulsory education' because as yet Tynwald had not become involved would be to misunderstand completely the role of the Church in society in the Isle of Man at the time of Barrow. The 'discipline', the application of its spiritual laws, involved powers far more extensive than those of the Church courts of the mainland, controlling rigidly many areas of life which today would be regarded as secular, and offenders who were 'presented' by chapter-quest or churchwardens faced imprisonment for a whole range of offences. Grinding corn on the Sabbath, to take one example, could involve fourteen days in prison. Barrow had ordered the spiritual laws to be written down in 1667, just before the arrangements for education were put into effect, but this did not prevent other regulations from being added. Such was the acceptance of the role of the Church that no confirmation of the 1667 collection was ever sought from Tynwald. A. W. Moore pithily summed up the prevailing state of affairs in the late Seventeenth Century with the words 'The Church was in fact omnipotent'.[34] In any case effective secular power was in the hands of Barrow as governor and above all in the hands of the Lord of Man, Earl Charles, who strongly supported the efforts of his governor-bishop in 1672 by repeating the demands for parents to send children to school and aiding his own threat of all positions of trust being closed to those who had not attended the schools

> 'All farmers and other tenants in my Isle of Mann of what degree or quality soever doe and shall send their eldest sonnes and all other their children to such pettie schools as they are capable wherin if any doe faile or be remiss . . . shall not onely be fined severely, but their children made incapable of bearing any office or place of trust . . . for want of such literature and education'.[35]

The pattern of schools on the Island was complicated by the relationship of the parishes and the four towns. The Manx Church was essentially a Celtic Church, the parish churches built on the sites of selected ancient keeils with little consideration being given to proximity to the populace, who themselves lived in scattered homesteads quite unlike the neat compact English village snuggling around its church. The growth of the four towns led to modifications in the structure of the parishes. In the case of Peel, where the town grew up in the shelter of St. Patrick's Isle, none was needed, but the other three towns were provided with chapels and chaplains only. Thus the parish church for Douglas continued to be that of Braddan, two miles away; for Ramsey the ancient site at Maughold; for Castletown, even though it was the capital of the Island, that of Malew. The use of the incumbents of the parishes as schoolmasters failed to provide for the needs of the towns, with the added complication that lay schoolmasters there were probably still continuing the schools set up by Derby or Fairfax. A certain Samuel Robinson is mentioned as schoolmaster of Castletown in the Malew Parish Register for 1660, while at Ramsey the following year Robert Ferguson swore on oath of allegiance to the King, fidelity to the Lord and conformity to Church laws. Although one obvious step would have been to allow the curates or chaplains of the towns to receive a share in the Royal Bounty and/or the Impropriate Fund, no such step was taken until 1842. Barrow appears to have left the parish minister to be reponsible from his own pocket for the town although a former bishop, Richard Parr, had in 1640 expected the people of Ramsey themselves to find the salary for a master. In 1670 Edward Nelson complained that he had 'taught Schoole in the Chapple of Ramsey's' since 1663 for a pittance of twenty shillings a year from the Vicar of Maughold. Barrow responded to the petition by increasing the salary to thirty shillings, but gave the Chaplain of Ramsey, Richard Fox, the task of finding not only the extra for the future, but also arrears from the past.[36] Fox decided that his best course was to undertake the Schoolmaster's job himself — possibly a move of great significance in the development of advanced education in the North of the Island. Eventually the solution adopted was to attach a small income to the school itself, thereby affording a measure of flexibility as to whether the masters in the towns should be ordained or lay people.

The presence of the towns also affected the nomenclature attached to the schools. Although a later age would describe them as 'elementary', this term was not used. Normally they were referred to as 'petty' schools from the French word for small, being for the 'petits' or young ones. The vast majority were also parochial schools, but the existence of schools in the towns prevented the terms 'petty' and 'parochial' being completely interchangeable. All of them were also 'English Schools', a term which not only denoted that the medium for education was the English language and not the native Manx tongue, but also contrasted with a 'Grammar School', a term strictly confined to one where Latin, if not Greek, was taught.

It would be misleading to think of a fixed steady income available annually for the parishes in these early years. For decades to come there was considerable uncertainty about when the Royal Bounty would actually be paid, while the full benefit of the Impropriate Tithes would not be secured until well into the next century when the current leases finally fell in. Until then there would be a gradual build-up from a modest start. An entry in the Ecclesiastical Wills dated July 4 1672 referred to the accumulation of the Impropriate Funds in the hands of Deemster Norris. Barrow had been translated to St. Asaph in 1669, but was allowed to remain Bishop of Sodor and Man in commendam until 1671. His successor, Henry Bridgman (1671-82) did not set foot in the Island until 1675, and was content to leave the running of the affairs of the Manx Church to the Vicars-General. Without an assured income for their efforts and lacking the supervision of a very firm resident bishop, it was not surprising that the embryonic system showed distinct signs of strain.

This in fact helped to resolve a conflict of interest for the three Vicar-Generals during these years. Barrow apparently had promised them three pounds a year each for their 'diligent, conscientious and impartial executing of the ecclesiastical laws', but they nobly put the path of duty first

> 'Notwithstanding such we thought it meet that such schoolmasters as did canonically and diligently teach youth in every respective parish should be first paid their respective salaries according to the intention of the Benefactors.'

However, by penalising those who had failed to perform their duties thoroughly, enough was saved from the fines to let them have their three pounds apiece.

Of the shortcomings in the system, only one was really educational in that some schoolmasters failed to teach throughout the year as intended.

> 'Now whereas it is too manifest that several of the sd schoolmasters have not ... Nor have taught the same diligently and entirely the whole year, but some only a half year and some but a quarter.'

With proof of guilt provided by the testimony of the church wardens the Vicars-General stopped the salaries due to be paid the schoolmasters 'proportionately to the respective Demerits and Defects for the last year' of the wilful offenders.[37]

On the positive side it appeared that each parish did now have an established school, even if it did not operate for the length of time which was considered necessary to earn the full amount of money allotted from the funds. There was no mention of any parish which had failed still to provide a school; presumably the appeals of the Vicar of Lonan had been received more favourably by his parishioners in the six years since 1669.

The other shortcoming of the masters which concerned the Vicars-General related to church discipline more than education. A number of them had failed to secure the official licence to teach, obtainable only from the Bishop or his delegated officers, the Vicars-

General. It was recognised that these were technical offices against Canon 77 of church law, and the Vicars-General promised to show 'careful justice with favour unto such as were defective in their duties only through ignorance'. Some of the clergy may well have assumed that their position as incumbent was sufficient in itself and rendered unnecessary any further documentation about their fitness to teach. Yet the authorities of the time felt it an important principle to uphold that none should presume to teach without the bishop's licence, not so much as to uphold the standards of education but rather to ensure that the minds of the children were not corrupted by teaching that ran counter to the doctrines and practices of the Church.

On the mainland, Acts of Parliament following the Restoration tried to ensure that Dissenters would play no part in education. The 'Clarendon Code' forbad them to act as schoolmasters or even instruct youths in any private house or family.[38] Attempts at the Savoy Conference to reconcile religious differences had failed, and when traditional Church of England doctrines and rites were reimposed once more instead, a thousand incumbents surrendered their livings in the 'Great Ejectment' of 1662 rather than give up their Puritan beliefs and practices. But the unorthodoxy of such men and the rest of the main Noncomformist bodies paled into insignificance compared with that of the sect known as the Quakers. Their refusal to see the need for religious ministers, to attend church or pay tithes, might arouse the admiration of Voltaire in his Lettres Philosophiques in sixty years time, but their views seemed to virtually everyone at the time to endanger the stability of society itself, a view which was hardened by the rising under Thomas Venner in 1661 to establish the Kingdom of Jesus. Even in 1912 when *'The Ejectment of 1662 and the Free Churches'* was published to celebrate the two hundred and fiftieth anniversary of that event, the editor explained that although an essay from each of the main Nonconformist bodies had been solicited, the Quakers were so far removed from mainstream Nonconformity that it had not been felt right to include them in the volume. To deal with them in England a special Quakers' Act was passed, imposing severe penalties for meeting together, with transportation for a third offence.

In the Isle of Man the main Noncomformist bodies scarcely made an appearance until the Nineteenth Century, but there were Quakers in the time of Fairfax, who himself gave them short shrift, and Barrow prosecuted them vigorously.[39] A note in the Ecclesiastical Wills for 1664 reveals Vicar-General John Harrison fearful of the infection of Quaker ideas, and the strict enforcement of the rule permitting no teachers other than those who held the Bishop's licence was intended above all to curtail the spread of dangerous ideas. Yet neither on the mainland nor the Isle of Man were the Quakers daunted by prosecution or willing to give heed to any laws passed against them. (Although strictly speaking the series of Acts which compose the Clarendon Code were not applicable to the Island, the Vicars-General in 1675 cited the Act of Uniformity as authority that the schoolmasters must hold the Bishop's licence.) W. C. Braithwaite demonstrated how in England the Quakers set up their own schools in the reign of Charles II irrespective of what Parliament had enacted. Similarly on the Isle of Man the Quakers in the Ramsey area cared little for canonical demands. Richard Fox, Chaplain of Ramsey, was reprimanded in 1670 was allowing 'Richard Cunards neice' to teach, but a decade later five people were represented in 1681 who were clearly Quakers. 'William Casemt., Patricke Kneale, Thomas Freer and wife, Robt Fletcher for keeping scoole and not having licences from the ordinarie, and for not coming to church, and professing another religion that the Church allowes.' Presumably only one of them, probably the first named, actually ran a school, but all five were fined ten shillings, a considerable sum for the time.[4]

For those more respectful of the law, the possession of the Bishop's licence gave official status, especially valuable to a lay schoolmaster, and prevented his efforts being damaged by the establishment of rival schools which drained away his income from parental fees. For over a century unofficial teachers were the subject of complaints and presentments. Yet although episcopal dignity might be affronted and the licensed master exasperated, such later disobedience never threatened the very fabric of society in the way the Quaker schools appeared to do.

The years 1675 and 1676 also the first attempt to organise satisfactorily the proportion of the Royal Bounty (supplemented by the Impropriate Fund) allocated to each schoolmaster. The Jurby list of 1670 had referred to the Royal Bounty as 'distributed to the Ministers for teaching an English School in their several parishes' without any line drawn between rich and poor livings. Nor was there any such distinction in the stated purposes of the Impropriate Fund, although the preface to the lease clearly had the poorer livings in mind with the mention of small revenues 'by reason whereof, many of the ministers in the said Isle are enforced to live in mean conditions, far unbecoming their callings, and likewise are necessitated, for the gaining and obtaining of a livelyhood for themselves and their families, to betake themselves to mean and inferior employments, to the diminution of their function and profession.' However, in 1675 what was before implied was now made explicit when the source of income was changed. Hitherto the Royal Bounty came from 'His Majesty's Rents from Abbey Lands in the Island', but the hundred pounds a year was to be paid in future to the Earl of Derby, Thomas Cholmondeley of Cheshire and William Banks of Lancashire from the excise duties on beer, ale and other liquors, and the Letters Patent expressly stated that the income should be 'from time to time employed and disposed towards the maintenance of such poor ministers in the Isle of Man as shall be found to stand most in need thereof'.[41]

While at first sight this declaration of priorities appeared just and equitable, it meant in practice that the richer livings on the Island, the three rectories of Ballaugh, Bride and Andreas would receive nothing from the funds, and their incumbents would lose any financial incentive to hold a school in their parishes. Nor, as has been noted, would this arrangement help to secure the position of the town schools. The following year these problems were largely resolved by a further directive from Whitehall which gave very precise instructions as to the division of the King's Bounty. An income of three pounds a year was attached to the three town schools which were a distance from their parish church, at Castletown, Douglas and Ramsey, and also to the petty schools of the three rectories. By this somewhat artificial device, the richer livings were not benefiting quite as obviously from the Royal Bounty as much as were the poorer vicarages. This royal directive has often been misconstrued as evidence of schools being founded in the six places specified, as though a complete system of town and parochial schools were not already in existence, but its purpose was simply to find a reasonable balance between the financial needs of the poor clergy and the actual educational needs of the Island. The rest of the hundred pounds was then applied to the other parishes of the diocese in a way that made them worth around seventeen pounds per annum. Eleven of the fourteen parishes benefited in varying degrees from £82. Lezayre for instance received the handsome addition of thirteen pounds to its miserable four, while Maughold needed only one pound to bring it to the approval total of seventeen pounds. There still remained anomalies, for three parishes, Michael, Patrick and Malew, already had incomes of seventeen pounds and in the short term had less incentive to run English schools than the rich rectories. However, as the amount raised from the Impropriate Fund part of the income would increase, there would be an incentive for two of these parishes as well. The main cause of the failure of modern writers to distinguish between foundation of schools and arrangements for allotting funds to them may probably be traced to a reference in the royal warrant to 'six petty schools in the most convenient places in the said Island', which were to receive the three pounds each. Yet a glance at a map of the Island will show that they were not the most convenient places in the geographical sense; the tight northern cluster of no less than four out of six would be hard to justify. The 'inconvenient places' were selected on criteria of financial need by existing schools which otherwise were difficult to fit into a system geared to improving the lot of poor clergy. They were not chosen as starting points for a future system of parochial schools, for that was already in existence.(42)

The arrangements made in 1676 assumed that a full hundred pounds would be available from the Royal Bounty, but in practice exchequer fees and agent's commission reduced the amount to £93, so that some alteration in amounts was needed. It appears that the two richest livings lost for the time being the three pounds allocated to

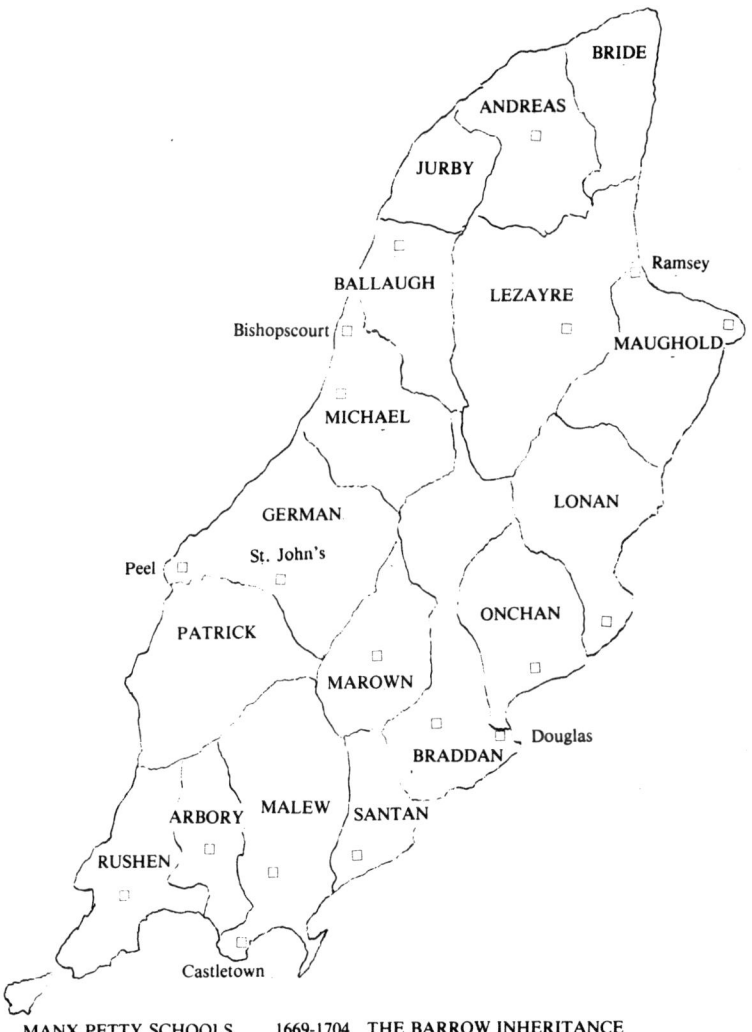

MANX PETTY SCHOOLS   1669-1704   THE BARROW INHERITANCE

their schools, and the ministers who taught at Andreas and Bride looked for some compensation from the money accumulated from the Impropriation Fund. It was recorded at the 1683 Convocation that

'whereas Parson Jon Harrison Rector of Kirk Braddan and Jon Christian Curate of Kirk Andreas have made complains this day that they have caused a constant and diligent Schoole to be kept in their respective Parish Churches for the space of five years last past and have noe allowance or satisfaction for the same out of the King's Anuity unto the Clergy, but still had their dependence of being satisfied of those Impropriacions when they would come in and be accounted for, therefore it is consented unto by the said Clergy, and accordingly ordered that the said Parson Harrison and Mr John Christian be paid each of them the sum of ten pounds . . . out of the above awards as their allowance and Satisfaction for their said Schools (Wch is confirmed by several of the Clergy to be constantly and duely kept) And for the time to come they are to be taken to further Consideration'.

The claims of the clergy schoolmasters to the Impropriate Fund came second to those of the Vicar-Generals, who used this source of income to ensure that their three pounds a year promised by Barrow was not lost to them, despite being left out of the Royal Warrant of 1676. They were joined in 1683 by the Bishop's Registrar, John Parr, who upon complaint that his trouble was a great as that of the two Vicar-Generals, was awarded an annual sum of twenty shillings. Indeed the Impropriate Fund was seen as a source of relief by those who considered themselves underpaid. In 1676 Edward Nosson, complained that his vicar, William Oates, had deserted his living of Marown and left him in charge for four years, but paid him only three pounds a year. He acordingly sought relief from the Impropriate Fund, although his petition made no mention of schooling provided by him.

In 1678 all the clergy assented to the decision that Robert Fletcher, 'ludimagister' (schoolmaster) of Douglas should be provided with Letters Testamonial for a petition to the Bishop. The clergy praised his life and moral integrity, after long acquaintance, and noted his 'diligent effort in his duties'. The reason for the petition is obscure: the key phrase of the document, drawn up in Latin, is 'Concedi petevit', possibly best translated as 'he has sought to be pardoned'. The matter in hand is vaguely referred to as 'certain causes'. One of the early acts of Bishop Wilson, in 1702, was to defrock a Robert Fletcher, then Vicar of Braddan, for his immoral life, although the stress in the latter part of the document on Fletcher's orthodoxy, may suggest that his early errors were theological rather than carnal. If the two Robert Fletchers were the same person, the incident at least shows that in this early period, the town schools were taught by persons of reasonable education, who could proceed to holy orders.

Not much is known of individual schools during this period, yet the continuation of the schools at Andreas and Bride without any immediate financial reward for five years suggests that the system was fast establishing itself as an accepted part of Island life. In the presentments of the Chapter Quests which are found scattered among the records, sometimes in places like the Archidiaconal Wills, or the Liber Causarum, sometimes in collections of the presentments only, the parishes of Santan and Marown were very regular in affirming that a 'constant schoole' was kept by the minster, although other parishes did not bother to give this information. The Island's support of education was all the more praiseworthy considering the lack of episcopal attention after the departure of Barrow. Henry Bridgeman followed his visit of 1675 with only one other, five years later, while John Lake, soon to achieve fame when he had become Bishop of Chichester, as one of the seven bishops imprisoned in the Tower of London by James II, came to the Island only once to preside over Convocation in 1683. His instruction given there made no mention of the petty schools; he may possibly have had reservations about English schools for the Manx, or even about the whole notion of educating the masses at day school. He was content to insist on the traditional Sunday afternoon instruction in 'ye Lord's Prayer, the Beleefe, Tenn Commandments, and the Catechisme' and perhaps significantly 'in such tongue as they are capable to learn the same. Those neglecting this to be proceeded against by imprisont or other punisht as the law provides'. Certainly when it came to enforcement, there was a willingness to present those who neglected to send their children and servants for catechism, whereas, despite the dire threats of Barrow and the Earl of Derby himself, there appears to be no example of presentment for failure to send a child to school surviving in the records from 1669 to 1685.

In contrast to Lake, his successor Baptist Levinz (1684-1693) not only took a keen interest in education, but also sought to enforce the instructions concerning compulsory education, both for clergy and parents. In his Regulations at Convocation 1685 Levinz ordered under his ninth heading that

"Every minister that receives augmentation from his Maties Benefaction, or the Impropriacon money, be obliged to teach an English schoole constantly in his respective parish. Parents who do not send their children to be presented.
Lastly let all these orders be forthwith putt in execution under paine of suspencon or sequestracon, except the Ordinary see just cause to dispense.' (Liber)[43]

The ever reliable Chapter Quest at Santan reported that their minister still kept his constant school, and 'allso hath given a call in the Church to the parishioners to send their children to the Schoole and if they do not they shall be presented the next Court Day'.[44] Not all incumbents were so conscientious, and the parishioners of the parish of Arbory complained 'there is noe Schoole taught in ye parish of this Island according to the Rt. Rev. Ordinary's injunctions, and yr own obligation upon receipt of ye augmentacon.' The offender, Samuel Robinson, was ordered to give notice to his parishioners that after November 22 'a constant and also good schoole would be kept in the parish by himself 'or assure y'self that upon Complaint of ye failure we will duly place some fitt pson to take care of the same'.

Levinz was also strict when it came to the matter of licences. An order was issued on September 1st 1685 to 'enjoyne all and every the ministers with my Diocese of Mann that they take out Lycenses for preaching and teaching of Schooles within their respective Parish Churches according to the Cannons of the Church, under ye payne of suspension'. Levinz left instructions that he had signed and sealed the licences before departing from the Island, and the clergy could obtain them from the Episcopal Registrar at a cost of half a crown. Lay masters were required too 'to take out Lycence for schoole' at the lesser cost of one shilling. The use of lay masters was given further scope when Levinz did not hesitate to use the severe sanction of suspension for other matters. Samuel Robinson, Vicar of Arbory, was suspended in September 1685 for his scandalous mode of life, and the following year Robert Fletcher, the former schoolmaster of Douglas, suffered the same fate for officiating at a clandestine marriage in his parish of Marown.

The Convocation of August 1685 succeeded too in settling for the rest of the century the distribution of the King's Bounty, augmented on a regular basis by the Impropriate Fund to make a total of £114. The sum of £17 considered a decade before to be a reasonable stipend was retained, priority being given to the clergy rather than to the schools, reversing the order of 1676. 'And because the labour and trouble of the 2 Vicars Genll. and the Bpp's Regr is great, the fees little or nothing answerable to their paines, nor indeed their charges, and yet their use necessary and indispensable', the three officials had their ad hoc payments from the Impropriation Fund established on a permanent basis. The three rectories continued to have their allowance of three pounds each carefully marked as being 'for Shoolkeeping', but were joined in this respect by the benefices of Patrick and German, now held in plurality, whose incumbent received six pounds for keeping two schools. The parish of Michael, which ten years before had an income of seventeen pounds, now for some reason needed three pounds from the fund to reach this figure. The three town petty schools kept the allowance attached to them, although in the case of Castletown the amount was raised from three to five pounds a year. Approval of this distribution as 'just and equal' was given to Levinz's scheme not only by the clergy, but also by the Earl of Derby himself and the Governor, Robert Heywood.

Four clergy appended their names to the distribution document— the Bishop; William Urquart, D.D. (the Archdeacon) and the two Vicar-Generals, John Christian and Thomas Parr. However, the last named, who had been Vicar of Malew since the time of Charles I, was the only beneficed clergyman who received nothing for teaching from the combined fund. By an arrangement peculiar to Malew, the incumbent was supposed to receive half the tithes in lieu of any stipend, but Thomas Parr found he had continual battles at law, as many of the parishioners claimed exemptions or 'prescriptions'. It is not clear whether until this time Parr had kept a parochial school distinct from the Castletown Petty School which lay within his parish boundaries, but certainly in 1689 he found himself presented by the Enquest, a feature of the Manx constitution whereby twelve men from each sheading, returned by the coroner for the area, were charged by the deemster to present all men who had transgressed. As with the presentments made by the Chapter Quest, the list of offences covered many areas, from taking the Lord's wreck to exporting cattle without licence, and included the failure of officials to perform their duties properly. Failure by an incumbent of a parish to keep a school was now added, although in the case of Malew the actual teaching, it was conceded, might be performed by another. The charge was that there was no school taught in the Parish Church 'either by himselfe or another in his behalfe'.[45] The decision, nevertheless, was given in favour of Parr. 'In regard he hath no part of the augmentation money as other ministers in the Isle hath ... are of opinion that he is not obliged'.[46]

Malew appeared to be the exception which proved the rule. Only the nearby parish of Rushen in 1689 joined Santan and Marown in declaring that the parochial school was being duly kept by their incumbent, in this case Mr. Thompson, as a regular feature of their presentments,[47] but Levinz had shown sufficient determination already in stamping his authority on the diocese, to make the Barrow intention of a school in every parish more likely to be a reality than not. One other document from the time, shows the appointment in 1687 of Horatio Darling, Sergeant at Law, as attorney on behalf of Thomas Cholmondeley, a move which may well have expedited the payment of the Royal Bounty, continued by James II after the death of his brother. The episcopate of Levinz amply demonstrated once again the great advantage for education in having a bishop who took his responsibilities for the Island seriously. Moreover in one very special case, it showed the benefits of the Island having a voice in London and access to places which even the most diligent of Manx Vicar-Generals could scarcely penetrate.

THE SPECIAL CASE OF PEEL

For what was to prove to be the soundest base for elementary education in the Isle lay outside the main system, and became the Island's sole link with the mercantile wealth of the mainland, which did so much for education there. The connection came through a Manx boy, Philip Christian, who was born at 'Hollan Towne', Peel in 1593, but went to London to serve his apprenticeship in the woollen trade under another Manxman, John Garrett. After his seven years, he was admitted a freeman of the 'Clothworkers' Company, one of the 'Twelve Great Companies' among the total of nearly a hundred guilds and fraternities known as the Livery Companies. The Clothworkers' traced their incorporation back to 1482, in the reign of Edward IV, when they were known as the Shermen, (Cloth-sheerers). In 1582 they united with the Fullers and the joint fraternity took the name of Clothworkers, with their privileges confirmed by further charters of Elizabeth I and Charles I. Their hierarchy consisted of a Master, four Wardens, and thirty three assistants. After being admitted to the livery in 1639, Christian achieved the honour of being elected Renter

Warden in August 1653, but unfortunately died within the year. He attended the Company's Court in January 1654 for the last time, and had been replaced by April on account of his death. In his will of December 6 1653, proved in March 1655, he did not forget the town of Peel.

Five pounds in the hands of his cousin, Capt. William Christian, was to be applied at a pound a year for five years for buying 'small books, pen, inke and paper, or what shall be thought most fit by the Minister and the Schoolemaster of the towne of Peele, in the Isle of Man', with their use strictly confined to 'the poorest men's sons and daughters of the said town of Peele, inhabiting there, and not otherwise.' This was, of course, in the Commonwealth period, when four free schools were maintained from the Bishop's revenues, and the existence of a school at Peel is clearly known to Christian.

He also desired to encourage Manx boys to follow in his own footsteps, and left in trust to the Clothworkers' Company his two houses 'in Lovell's Inn, in Pater Noster Rowe in the Parish of St Faith, under Paule's Church, London', so that the rents and profits from them might support two poor youths as apprentices, at ten pounds a year. His order of priority was his own family, those of the name of Christian, natives of the Island whose poverty was duly attested, and lastly boys in London whose parents were Manx born. If, however, 'it shall happen that there be nor a free schoole maintained for the teaching of children in the towne of Peel', then the payments to apprentices should cease, and the Clothworkers apply the money to the school at Peel. Of the twenty pounds, eighteen were to provide the salary of the master, and the other two used as in the earlier part of the will, for books, pen, ink and paper for poor scholars. All this was only to come into effect 'after the departure of my said loveing wife, Rebecca, out of this present world'.[48]

There was thus to be no immediate effect upon Peel, as while the one contingency of Mrs. Christian's death might arise at any time, the failure of the school at Peel was less likely to happen when such an enthusiast for education as Bishop Barrow was taking pains to estalish and maintain schools in every parish of the Island, with the four towns already established as the obvious key places. A further unexpected complication was the Great Fire of London in 1666, which consumed the two houses 'under Paule's Church' in its wake: there was no longer any twenty pounds a year rent for anyone to use.

Yet the potential benefits to Peel seem to have been known. The Court Book of the Clothworkers' Company recorded that in January 1682, the new Bishop of Sodor and Man, John Lake, announced his attention of 'endeavouring the settlement of the free school for the maintenance whereof the Company was concerned and at his return he would give the Court a true account how he found it and how he left it and in what hands he entrusted the management of that affair'.[49] This appears to be a frank admission that a school at Peel was still in existence, thereby making void the strict wording of the will, while it was hoped that some arrangement could be made whereby Peel would receive the benefit of the contingent bequest. It was certainly the impression in the Clothworkers' Company at the end of the Nineteenth Century that the way out had been found by letting the school become vacant, and technically ceasing to be. Accordingly in 1684, the Archdeacon of Sodor and Man, Dr. Harcourt (Urquhart), and other Manx representatives presented a petition from the Island to the Company, asking them to pay the allowance to the school. The Court of the Company promised to make payments 'as soon as a master shall be settled as he ought to do'. For their part in this act of collusion the Company offered each year ten pounds — only half the amount stipulated in Christian's will. The matter was regulated by a legal decree on a suit by arrangement. The Attorney-General on behalf of the people of Peel asked for an account from the Company, setting out their claim that Rebecca, the widow, had died in 1666, and that the Clothworkers had received rents to the value of £350. The Company stated that Rebecca Christian had been remarried to a Mr. Parker, and had not died until 1671: that Mr. Parker had not rebuilt the houses after the Great Fire, but that the Company had been forced to spend £80 rebuilding them through the requisition of the Commissioners for rebuilding the City of London: and that after the property came into their hands in 1671, it had been let on a lease of 71 years at only £15 a year. They had received in all £230, of which they offered two-thirds, together with two-thirds of all future rents. The court heard the case on Bill and Answer, with no further evidence being given. On July 16th, 1686, Lord Chancellor Jeffreys decreed concerning 'the charity established for building a school at Peel' that the Company's account was to stand as the settled account, that the Company was entitled to keep their £80 out of £230 received, and that two-thirds of the residue, afterLcosts, was to be paid to the attorney of the Bishop of Sodor and Man, by now Baptista Levinz. In addition, two-thirds of future rents were to be paid to the bishop, the obvious choice, as a permanent official in charge of education on the Island. While it became settled law that the two-thirds rule should apply if the founder apportioned the whole income of the charity as it stood on the date of the foundation, the future history of education in Peel should have made Jeffreys looked upon there in a more kindly light than history normally accords to the hanging judge of the Monmouth Rebellion. The attorney in the case, none other than the Bishop's own brother, Sir Cresswell Levinz, informed the Bishop of the outcome and the long association of the Clothworkers' Company with the town of Peel was now established. A deed of October 2nd 1688 recorded how William Gell sold premises to Baptista, Lord Bishop

> 'for the use and benefit of the Free Schoole now erected and settled in the said Towne of Peel, and Endowed with a yearly salary out of the Benefaction of our dear countryman, Mr. Philip Christian, late of London deceased, to be paid by the Worpl Company of Clothworkers in the said City of London, as they, by his Will and other Writings more at large appeareth.'

After legal costs had been met, the two-thirds of the residue of £150 still mysteriously amounted to the full hundred pounds. A document in the Liber Causarum dated January 22nd, 1689, recorded how Levinz presented a Bill of Charges for his endeavours for £38, but as it was felt that this modest charge was in no way proportionate to the true cost of three journeys to London, he was awarded a further £20 for his efforts. Ten pounds was allowed for the first year's salary for the master and twenty pounds for the purchase of the schoolhouse, leaving twelve pounds to be laid out at interest for the benefit of the schoolmaster. The signatories, the inhabitants of Peel, declared themselves to be sufficiently satisfied and contented, and exonerated, acquitted and discharged the Bishop from further responsibility, with confirmation and countersigning by Governor Heyward and his officers, with their thanks.[50]

Unfortunately for the Island 'his Lopps great zeal' hailed in the document evaporated quickly. After securing a prebend's stall at Winchester, having described the Island as a 'poor desolate place', he returned only once, for Tynwald in 1691, before his death in January 1693. Yet as far as Peel was concerned, the efforts of Bishops Lake and Levinz had been sufficient to create a link with the Clothworkers' Company which would last for well over two hundred years. Possibly one Jo Young was the first master at the linked school, but certainly John Woods was appointed in 1691. The Liber Causa entry for August 1693 complained that Mr. Wattleworth, the Registrar, was loathe to pay Woods eight pounds 'wch we (Governor Sacheverell and Archdeacon Lomax) verbally ordered to him lately at Peel town in Consideration of his small sallary for teaching schoole there these two years past.'[51] They ordered Wattleworth, or whoever held the twelve pounds which remained in hand from the hundred pounds recovered by Levinz, to pay Woods eight and the remainder to Jo Young. (Woods, by 1721 one of the Island's senior clergy, swore in that year, that despite the Governor's order, he had received only four pounds.)

The 'Small sallary' mentioned by Sacheverell seems a strange description if the ten pounds per annum was actually being paid as agreed. Although only nearly half the amount intended by William Christian, the salary still compared very favourably with other petty schools on the Island, with their three pounds from the Royal Bounty. By 1685 the master at Castletown was receiving five pounds instead of the original three, but this still left him half as well off as his colleague at Peel. In practice during the early Sixteen Nineties the situation was far worse for the other schoolmasters on the Island. After the death of Levinz, the diocese was, according to Sacheverell, deliberately left vacant so that funds might be accumulated to pay for the repair, in particular the re-roofing, of the Cathedral on St. Patrick's Isle, Peel. Without the powerful voice of the bishop to assist the cause of the Island, the Royal Bounty was not paid. The parochial clergy were severely affected, with incomes falling back to the level of the days of Barrow's arrival. Governor Sacheverell wrote in 1696 to the Archbishop of Canterbury of the difficulty in retaining clergy.

'... three of the hopefullest of our young men that the Island bred' had left the because of the fear that livings worth a pittance would be thrust upon them'.[52] Yet schools run by lay masters dependent entirely upon the Royal Bounty were hit even harder; Castletown Petty School for instance is known to have been without a master at this time.

A forward looking system of popular education started by Bishop Barrow was being threatened by lack of supervision from a resident bishop and the breakdown of financial arrangements. A vigorous and determined effort was needed to restore the system to effective working order. The tragedy for the Island was to be that the bringer of discipline and order so modified Barrow's system that the deleterious effects of the changes were felt for nearly two hundred years.

THE SECOND TIER OF EDUCATION — THE GRAMMAR SCHOOL

The breakdown in arrangements at the end of the Seventeenth Century in what would later be described as 'elementary education' was mirrored by a similar situation at the higher levels of education which Barrow proposed for the Island. A very important part of the parochial school system was its provision of candidates for the Free Grammar School in Castletown; 'and withal to fit the children for learning, in a Grammar School which was also wanting', as Barrow himself put it.[53]

The Free School mentioned in the Impropriate Fund indenture of 1666 was thus clearly intended to be a higher school, which need not, as many mainland grammar schools did, provide its own training through elementary stages.[54] The inclusion of primary subjects was particularly marked in late Stuart foundations, but the Manx system was carefully designed through its feeder schools to prevent the state of affairs mentioned by Charles Hoole, that children were brought to Latin before they could read well, or that the primary stage was left at the "meanest and the worst".[55] The level of the Free Schools of the Commonwealth period is uncertain; had they been advanced rather than petty schools, it is more likely that Barrow would have retained the pattern of one in each town, rather than centralising all in Castletown.

The exact meaning of 'free' caused problems in the Isle of Man as on the mainland, being interpreted as meaning open to all, subject to no authority other than its governors, or free from tuition charges. The Nineteenth Century desire to restrict schools to the fee-paying classes led to a stress on the first two meanings as opposed to the third, but W. A. L. Vincent contends that grammar schools with the title 'free school' all originally intended at least some scholars to be taught without payment of fees.[56] Whether fees of any sort should be charged was a question to be posed before too long on the Island. It was obvious from the references to the Grammar School that it was intended to serve all the Island, but in days of extremely poor communications it was evident that the chosen site would draw its pupils especially from the petty schools nearby, a fact that Barrow recognised when he sited the Free School at the capital, Castletown, "for the benefit of the sd town and adjacent parishes in Espetial."

The method of payment for a master was for the money to be given by undertakers, to whom the Impropriate Tithes of Kirk Christ, Rushen, the most south westerly parish on the Island, were assigned. In the Agreement of February 8th 1667, Barrow expressed his confidence in the success of his arrangements: if they failed, then Richard Stephenson and his fellow undertakers were free of all obligations.[57] The value of the tithes, and thus the amount paid to the master, was £30 a year. By the standards of the time, this was quite a handsome amount. If Castletown is inserted into place in the fifty English schools whose salaries can be gleaned from the Wase manuscripts, it would emerge as joint eighth — a commendable position for a poor island — and near double half the schools recorded by Wase.[58] Of English counties, the highest salaries were in Warwickshire, at Birmingham, Sutton Coldfield, Nuneaton and Rugby, but according to Samuel Frankland in 1675 the other score of grammar schools in the country rarely paid more than £20. This was not just a case of time eroding a salary once quite generous, for a number of Post-Restoration foundations paid no more than this.

Yet although the salary was respectable, the failure to anticipate future contingencies by providing adequate funds for repairs or pensions meant that like so many other grammar schools, Castletown would suffer by having masters cling to office when they should have long retired, and by having to endure dilapidated buildings which eventually had to be shut up for lengthy repair. One other point which eventually was settled by the Court of Chancery was the nature of the income for the Free School: was it linked with the value of Rushen tithes, or was it a fixed sum of thirty pounds?

These problems for Castletown still lay in the future. For the time being the arrangements were satisfactory, far better than for those clergy who could never depend on prompt and regular payment of the Royal Bounty. The undertakers seem to have done their part satisfactorily. A note in Malew Parish Register records "Tho Parr his Lott for the Tythes for Castletown School is for in Sorby at the rate of £4-3-0 being with mutual consent done by the Undertakers of the free school and Order from the Govr."[59]

The premises used for the Grammar School seem from the start to have been the Thirteenth Century Chapel of St Mary, whose dedication in 1257 is recorded in the Chronicle of Man and the Sudreys.[60] This building may have been used in the past for education; a reference in the Manorial Roll of 1584 to "Chamb. peatae Mariae Vocat Scole house" is probably to the chapel. If so, it would suggest itself naturally as a place which would avoid both the costs and delays of a new building, allowing Barrow's plan to put into effect with the minimum of delay. (The ground for F. M. Cubbon's assertion that the Grammar School was not in the Chapel until 1698 is not clear.[61])

The registers of Malew Parish refer to schoolmasters George Harrison in 1660 and Samuel Robinson in 1668, but they seem masters of the Petty School, and for the first specific mention of the Grammar School occured in 1671 when the name of Henry Lowcay is recorded.[62] His tenure lasted until 1686 according to Ballaugh Parish Register, and in that year a refeence to Gilbert Holt, "now Schoolemaster at the sd Town", in connection with more advanced teaching he was able to give, to be considered shortly, would indicate that he was master of the Free School at that time. A more certain and direct reference occurred in the early Nineties to "Mr. David Genkins schoolmaster of the ffree school."[63] and likely to be the person mentioned by Bishop Levinz in 1690.

> "I am preparing to send a new Schoolmaster and Accademique Teacher to Castletown and I hope I may compass to send a very ingenious man, a Master of Arts of this University and distinguished neighbour to Mr Columondley thither by Christmas next."[64]

The last clear reference to Genkins is in June 1693, and in 1695 the Governor, William Sacheverell, found himself with the task of finding a new master, as the see was vacant from 1693 until 1698, and there was no archdeacon either. John Woods, of Peel, was selected to act as a temporary stop-gap.

> "Whereas ye place of Schoolmaster of the free school and Chaplain at Castletown are to present vacant the care of them (sede vacante) having devolved on me, I doo hereby authorise and impower Mr John Woods to ye said free School and officiate ye said Chaplain's place.[65]

Although a temporary arrangement, this appointment was significant as it marked the success of a third level of educational provision in Barrow's scheme for the Island.

While Castletown was the Island's official Grammar School, from the North of the Island only boarders could possibly attend there, a fact which would have been as obvious to Barrow as to others. The earliest stages of grammar school education in Douglas and Ramsey seem to have been unofficial and gradual developments of the petty schools there, in just the same way as the parish schools of Scotland combined elementary and higher education in one building.[66] Educated chaplain/schoolmasters passed on some of their more advanced learning to brighter pupils. The drawback with such a system was that it depended too much on the individual teacher; a lay successor could not manage the standard of work in the same degree. Constance Radcliffe has unearthed a typical example dating from Ramsey in 1680. 'There has been noe Grammar Schoole kept in our Town since May last but now Miss Hannah Bennett is keeping an English schoole'.[67] While Miss Bennett — a very early example of a female in charge of a Manx school — was felt by the people of Ramsey as deserving the Royal Bounty of three pounds set apart for Ramsey, she clearly could offer no Latin to her charges. It is quite possible that Barrow himself earmarked Ramsey as a centre for higher education. Around the time of his departure from the Island, £200 was put into the hands of Thomas Cholmondeley, although by 1720 it was not remembered whether it had been by Barrow directly or through Bishop Bridgeman by Barrow's direction. While as has been seen Ramsey School was one of 'the most convenient places' in 1675 to receive the Royal Bounty of three pounds[68] and was listed in 1685 as having received its due from that source, Bishop Levinz clearly believed that Ramsey deserved special consideration. He wrote to Cholmondely in October 1687 asking one more favour for the inhabitants of the Island, requesting that the £200 in his hands might 'be put to use for theyre benefitt, which will bring in some 10£ a yer and this may be set aside as a salary to provide a schoolmaster for Ramsey.[69] Whether this idea was entirely Levinz's own , or there was an understanding dating back to Barrow that money should be used for Ramsey is uncertain. Levinz pursued the matter in person, although at this stage it appeared that Douglas might have a share too. 'I hope to wayte upon ye at Vale Royal and desire ye salary for the schoolmasters at Ramsey and ye preacher and schoolmaster at Doglas may be ready for me to carry over to them. 'Yet shortly afterwards in 1690, all the income from the two hundred pounds at five per cent interest was destined for Ramsey alone. Levinz told John Christian of Andreas, his Archdeacon that he had written to Cholmondeley about Ramsey School, and that 'he is willing to continue the 10£ Salary to ye schoolmaster.'[70] With an income of thirteen pounds a year plus quarterage, the Ramsey master was not handsomely paid compared with the endowment of Castletown Grammar School, or those of the future grammar schools at Peel and Douglas, but was still better off than a number of undoubted grammar schools in Vincent's list. The endowment may well have marked a recognised widening in the scope of the school at Ramsey. While direct evidence of higher education at this time does not appear to have come to light, it may be very significant that in the records of the Impropriate Fund for the years 1694-96, the word 'Petty' was no longer applied to Ramsey as it was still for Castletown and Douglas Petty Schools; Ramsey was simply 'Ramsey School'. Although L. W. Williamson in her pamphlet history of the school made not such claim until 1743. John Keble certainly in his Life of Bishop Wilson talked guardedly of 'a sort of grammar school' in these early days.[71]

Unlike Peel, but in common with the parochial schools of the Island, Ramsey's school was kept in the place of worship, in this case the Chapel of Ballure, rebuilt by Bishop Richard Parr in 1640, but needing repair by the end of the century. Ballure was a chapel of ease for the parish church at Maughold, which Parr still expected the townfolk to attend for major feasts. Apparently Maughold people in general and Ramsey in particular were notorious for their indecent behaviour in church. Perhaps it was with some degree of relief that Chaplains such as John Parr (1688-91) moved on to take his first living at Rushen. Nevertheless it appears that a second centre of grammar school education was slowly taking shape in the north of the Island, although lacking the declared status of the school at Castletown, which was also the home of a still higher level of education.

THE THIRD TIER OF EDUCATION — THE ACADEMIC SCHOOL

Just as the notion of petty schools feeding grammar schools found favour on the Island after the Restoration, when such ideas faded on the mainland, so it was with attempts to provide higher learning. The interest expressed by the Earl of Derby in a university has already been noted, but again such ideas were more prominent in Puritan thought. In 1641 both Manchester and York had petitioned Parliament to establish a university in the North of England, and a College at Durham for a short time before the Restoration became a reality.[72] Barrow himself thought in terms of an 'Academic School' although realism prevented any grandiose thought that the Island could sustain the full blown Academy which Milton wished to see in the provinces, with a hundred and thirty students and twenty staff, outlined in the treatise "Of Education".[73] Shortly after settling the affairs of the free grammar school, Barrow turned his attention to providing education for those who had advanced beyond the level of the grammar school.

His first step was to see there would be an immediate start to securing learned clergy for the Island, and provision made for study "at the University or College of Dublin", for two scholars from the Free School of Castletown, "Or wheresoever it shall be in the Island who I resolve shall be of the ablest Scholars, and most capable of the service of the Ministry".[74] Twenty pounds a year were allocated for their education and maintenance a year for five years, "supposing they continue civill, and studious, and industrious to fitt themselves for the service intended and not otherwise." In case the students, having enjoyed their university education at Manx expense, felt tempted to look for preferment alsewhere, Barrow laid down that bonds with security should ensure that all moneys expended upon them should be paid back in full. Any such sums would be spent on further scholars at Dublin, "till the supply be thought sufficient for the Island, and then to what other publicke work or charity shall by my trustees be thought most profitable for the Island."

Barrow also expressly reserved to himself "a liberty, during my life, of disposing of the sd yearly rent of twenty pounds, to any other use in the Island." After his death, "that this my guist may go on and succeed for all ages," Trustees were to be appointed, the Bishop, Archdeacon (or in their absence the Vicars-General and the Official) the Governor and three other "Chief Temporal Officers", whose duty it would be to maintain the two scholars. The actual "Nomuacon, examinacon, and approbacon" was to be left in the hands of bishop and archdeacon, but in their absence to those appointed by the trustees in their discretion, whether "clergie or others". (The regulations about bonds did not always achieve the intended effect. With the Royal Bounty a hazardous thing to rely upon, some still chose to leave the island service rather than accept poor Island livings).

According to Bishop Wilson, the great generosity of Barrow was the source of this provision.

> "And by his own charity private, he purchased two estates in land, worth twenty pounds a year, for the support of such young persons as should be designed for the ministry. So that the name and good deeds of that excellent prelate will be remembered with gratitude, so long as any sense of piety remains among them."[75]

Canon Stenning thought the phrase 'blatant confiscation' more appropriate, for the occupier of one of the two farms which provided the rents of twenty pounds had his right to Hango Hill totally ignored. The hapless Lace family had in the earlier years of the Seventeenth Century fought successfully to maintain their rights, but this time the support of the Keys was of no avail, they themselves being summoned to England to be denounced for "insolent and exorbitant behaviour" in protesting against a clandestine court which awarded rights to the bishop-governor without the name of Lace even being mentioned. The Lace family continued a legal fight until 1786 but poverty hindered the successful prosecution of their case.[76] Nevertheless, whether hero or villain, Barrow had set up another link in his educational chain, albeit one in practice confined to the future clergy of the Island.

Barrow pressed on rapidly with his scheme to make the Island self-sufficient regarding clergy. The Jurby document of 1670 stated that after paying the Earl of Derby eleven hundred pounds for the Importation Tithes, there remained a surplus of contributions whose application was already decided.

> "And at the translation of that Bishop from that Bishoprick unto St. Asaph, in the year 1670, there remained to be disposed of £241 8s 4d:
> Which, with what shall be given by others, whose charitable minds God shall raise up to so good a work, is intended for the erection of a School in the Island for academical learning."[77]

Paradoxically a substantial boost came with the departure of Barrow, for during the interregnum before the arrival of Bishop Bridgeman, the profits of the see were applied to a fund designed to erect an academical school on the Island.

> "Whereas there is a full accord between the bishops of St Asaph and the Isle of Man concerning the profits belonging to the bishoprick of the island from the time of its vacancy, and all disputes and differences between them about any concerns in the Island being concluded. And whereas it is agreed between them with my consent and approbation that the whole profits for the year 1671 shall be placed in the hands of Willam Banks of Winstanley in the Co: of Lancaster, Esq., till we can meet with convenient purchase for the erection of a public school for academical learning. These are to require you (the Deputy-Governor) to collect the profits aforesaid . . . that it may be fixed and employed according to the agreement between us. Given my hand at Knowly, the 8 June 1672
> Signed Derby-Man
> In the presence of Isaac Asaph
> Henric Sodorens [78]

Although Barrow had left the Island, he never lost his interest in his schemes, and seems to have kept his own control over the £241 surplus. Together with the money collected by Banks, there was £500 which was invested in Ireland, using the offices of James, Duke of

Ormonde, who had ruled Ireland in the Sixties but was not actually Lord Lieutenant between 1670 and 1677.[79] Interest would be paid to the two bishops and archdeacon until he could secure

> "to the Trustees intended for the Academic Schoole for soelong time as I shall have the sayd five hundred pounds in my hands, fifty pounds yearly rent, to be paid half yearly, and to be secured by, and to be issuing out of, certayne lands near Dublin, in Ireland, of one hundred pounds per annum value att ye least, of a good title and free from incumbrances."[80]

Although a time limit of six months was laid down, the agreement with the Trustees, William Banks of Winstanley, and Thomas Cholmondeley of Vale Royal, Cheshire, was not actually made until two years later in May 1676, by which time the sum available for investment had grown to £600 through the addition of the two amounts of £50 mentioned by the Duke. Lands in Meath and other parts of Ireland then brought in £60 a year to be used by the Trustees to maintain "a person of Sufficient Learning and Ability to Exercise and discharge the place, Imployment and duty of a publick reader of Logick, Philosophy and History within the Isle of Man and Dominion of Man."[81] It is to be noted that just as in the case of the grammar school, the whole of the money was devoted to the salary, in this case of the reader.

Lack of sufficient funding meant that the Academic School, itself as intended by Barrow a very modest version of the Miltonic Academy, would be further drastically reduced in practice. Although educating the clergy was its primary function, the Academic School was not in the bishops' eyes to be confined to that purpose. "An illustrious School for the instruction of youth (especially such as are . . . designed for the sacred function of the Ministeriall office)" was Bishop Bridgeman's ambition when he asked for the aid of Governor and Keys in the labour of building one.[82] Rushen Abbey, a Cistercian foundation, (and far less likely to have been a general centre of education than is popularly imagined for that reason,) was purchased from the Deemster Charles Moore for renovation, but soon the cost of the venture caused Bridgeman to have second thoughts, and he was relieved to sell back the Abbey buildings to Moore for the same price.[83]

Nevertheless the bishops soon "with joynt consent elected, approved, and appointed Willam Gostwike, Mr of Arts and fellow of Trinty College at Cambridge, to be our first reader in the academicall school aforesaid."[84] Indeed Gostwike entered into his duties in March 1676 before the formal deed which arranged his salary, so that the bishops applied in September 1676 for half a year's salary for him, "hee producing the said Bishop of Manns lycence for his instructing and teaching of youth in the academical scholl aforesaid, and certificate of his performance of the same."[85] For Gostwike had been "at a great expense of payne and time and money in pursuance of the said undertaking." As William Banks had died and "Thomas Cholmondeley not yet assumed the said trust upon him," the bishops applied directly to Ormonde for payment.

Although the reference to performance suggests that the academical school was already in existence, the document earlier spoke in terms of the future.

> "... an able reader of academicall learning in the Isle of Man, where a College of Gymnasium is intended by the present Bishop of Mann (and he is already in some forwardness to that purpose) ..."

Clearly the appointment of the reader was not by itself to be considered as establishing the College, even if he were already at work. This interpretation receives support from Barrow's will dated December 14th 1679, where the existence of the Academic School is still regarded as future and uncertain: "at the Academical School when it shall be there settled; and in case there be no such School within twelve months of my death ..."[86]

Although the reader with salary was available, the proposed school was without premises, and its most obvious intended pupils were in receipt of grants enabling them to study at Dublin, but not on the Island. Bishop Barrow corrected this anomaly in his will of 1679. As noted already, his deed had in 1668 expressly reserved a liberty of disposing the twenty pounds in question to any other use in the Island. This was now to be applied "towards the maintenance of three Boys at the Academical School, when it shall there be settled" but Barrow imposed a time limit.

> "and in case there be no such School within twelve months of my death, then to go towards the maintenance of two boys of most pregnant parts at some University abroad; in the meantime to be employed as it is.[87]

Barrow did not long survive the making of his will, and Thomas Cholmondeley, the surviving trustee of the Reader's money, was faced with the choice of prompt action or seeing the intended pupils at the Academic School continue to study beyond the seas, the will giving a wider scope by replacing the explicit mention of Dublin by "some University abroad". The only action known to have been taken was the appointment of a new Reader. Gostwike had clearly vacated the position but appears to have remained in the vicinity, as the death of Professor Gostwike is recorded some years later in Malew Parish Register. In March 1680 John Shaw, Clerke, Master of Arts, was appointed

> "To teach, read, inform and instruct, in the study and reading of logick, philosophy, and history, all and every person and persons within the said Isle of Man who shall, from time to time, and at all times hereafter ... be willing or desirous to study, read, be informed or instructed in the same ..."[88]

Was this action sufficient to found the Academical School? As the appointment of Shaw differed from that of Gostwicke only in that the legal formalities were more nicely observed, hardly enough for Barrow to have made it a crucial distinction, it is difficult to avoid the conclusion that appointing Shaw made no real difference, and the twelve month deadline for bringing the Academical School into being had not been met. This was certainly the view held in the Nineteenth Century. On the other hand, those who lived at the end of the Seventeenth Century were in no shadow of doubt that the Academical School was a living reality, and the failure of the grand plan to use

Rushen Abbey or a similar building was only of secondary importance. R. E. Curphey in his paper, as yet unpublished, on *Bishop Barrow's Trusts* argued that the provision of a master and pupils to study can in themselves be reckoned as constituting a school, although it must be admitted that the Gostwike appointment seriously weakens this argument, which depends on the appointment of Shaw being a new departure.[89]

It is hard to escape the conclusion that what Barrow saw as the Academical School and what people in the decades following saw as the Academical School were radically different institutions, and that Barrow's School did not materialise as the bishop had intended. The call to all people willing and desirous to study faded away. A handful of ordinands which should have been the nucleus of the School became instead its only membership, and the Derby dream of the University and Barrow's dream of an Academical School saw the light of day only as a shadow.

The earliest years of Academic School reveal a confusing state of affairs and bristle with difficulties. Shaw presumably arrived and fulfilled the terms of his appointment, for his executor in 1705 was claiming arrears of salary, possibly the cause of his and Gostwike's leaving the position. A similar claim from the Reader's or Academic Master's Fund as it became known as more usually, came from Henry Lowcay, Master of the Grammar School. His claim would rule out any theory that Shaw was claiming money for his acceptance of a post which did not come into existence. It appears that the trustees decided that the appending of the tasks of the Academic Master to those of the Grammar School Master was a convenient solution to the problem of finding a home for the Academic School such as it was, and at the same time the problem of finding a master. This state of affairs prevailed for most of the time until the momentous changes of the Eighteen Thirties. But whom did Shaw and Lowcay teach in their capacity of Academic Master? The obvious answer that it was the Academic Students relies heavily on the dating of the Denton manuscript to 1681. A well known passage described the Castletown situation.

"There is a large Chappel in the town, and a school at the end thereof. The Schoolmaster has £60 a year sallery allowed by the Earl of Derby for reading prayers every morning at 11 of ye clock and teaching a Grammar School, and for reading logick and phylosophy to four Academick Scollars, who are habited in black wide-sleeved gowns and square caps and have lodging in the castle and a salary of £10 a piece by a new foundation of the present Earl and Lord of Man."[90]

If, however, a Resolution of the Tustees of the Academic Students' Fund of August 24th 1686 is read without any presuppositions, the clear impression is gained that for the very first time the Academic Scholars were ordered to study within the confines of the Island. There is no trace of a hint that the practice of sending students to Dublin had been interrupted at any time.

"Whereas there hath been an allowance made of twenty pounds per annum, for the maintenance of two Schoolers out of this Island, at the University of

34

Dublin, and that to be raised and paid out of the profitts of the Tenements of Ballagilley and Hango Hill, which hath for some years past been bestowed that way; and now that we, the Tustees appointed for the management of that concern, haveing taken into our considerations that it is not altogether so convenient to cntinue ye said allowance to send those of our Schoolers abroad, whiles they may now have the opportunity of attaining unto academical learning, under the Tuition of Mr Gilbert Holt, Schoolmaster in this Isle, whom wee have now obliged to the discharge of that duty."[91]

Barrow's Deed of 1668 had mentioned a course of five years, and a couple of years might be accounted for by the reluctance of the Trustees to interrupt students halfway through their course, rather than bring them home on the appointment of a reader. There would still remain years when the Reader was in Castletown and the students in Dublin. Shaw and Lowcay may have had pupils not destined for the church, or if they were, those who had failed to gain the Barrow Studentships of ten pounds, but still hoped to take holy orders. The suggestion of Robert Curphey that Shaw and Lowray had taught the students who held the Barrow places, and that the Trustees had then reverted to Dublin would imply that Lowray, although in Castletown until 1685, had rapidly been found wanting and his services no longer required; the phrase "for some years past" excludes any temporary interregnum arrangement. Had this been the case, some allusion might have been expected. The Denton manuscript which would support Curphey's suggestion if the date of 1681 is accepted has been dated by Curphey himself as belonging to 1687-89.

One fact is reasonably certain; that when Denton wrote the Academical School consisted only of four Barrow Scholars, the demand by others having dropped right away, if it ever existed. Perhaps the trustees of the Students' Fund had hoped that proposed School would begin to take shape under the Reader before they risked moving the students from Dublin, and finding that it did not, then decided to use the local teaching as it was there, although the School as hoped had not become a reality. The terms of the sending of students to Holt indicate a certain freedom on the part of the Trustees; catching the spirit of the will, although its strict provisions had not materialised in the shape of the Academic School — "we have therefore thought it very fitting..."[92]

Assuming Denton's figures to be correct, the Trustees of the Master's Fund did not feel that the master exercising the dual role of grammar school master and academic teacher should receive the full £90 to which the combined salaries came. Nevertheless the salary of £60 per year would put Holt near the very top of grammar school earnings, assuming that the salary was paid. Barrow's will had indicated that three could be educated in the Island for the cost of two in Dublin, and clearly the Trustees of the Students' Fund felt this could be stretched to four, Henry Halsall and Jon. Woods being joined by two others. The dress which Denton described, "that suitable and decent equipage and apparell", as the Resolution of 1686 put it, was aimed "to distinguish them as students in this quality and condicon..." This provision of training at Castletown was not felt by the Trustees of the Students' Fund to preclude them from sending students on the foundation to university overseas, as frequent examples showed.

By 1690 the story of the Academic Master or Reader was that of two special appointments, Gostwike and Shaw, and the use of two Grammar School masters, Lowcay and Holt. There were clearly difficulties over payment from the Master's Fund, as in 1705, three of the four, Shaw Lowcay and Holt had claims outstanding for arrears of pay.[93] In 1690 the failure of the independent Reader was sufficiently clear to have the appointment of David Genkins explicity combining the two posts of "Schoolmaster and Accademique Teacher", marking acceptance of the fact that Academic School would not be the separate entity which Barrow and Bridgeman had hoped it would be, altough Levinz ensure that in this way the Grammar School would have the services of a Master of Arts.

However, even this compromise solution was in danger of breaking down, chiefly due to financial troubles. Genkins was clearly not at all happy

"... man who at present officiates is a very ingenious seems determined to leave except some are to be taken for a more convenient subsistence."[94]

This letter of Governor Sacheverell also reveals that the transitions between masters had not been smooth, as frequent changes meant "ye school hath been much neglected". They had not "been able to fix any proper persons among us as whether by the discouragement in devideing the sallery as for want of a convenient house." A further problem was the bottleneck as Academic Students had to wait for preferment on the Island, Sacheverell's own solution being to widen the scheme to embrace two lawyers, if "not forrain to ye intent of ye donor." Genkins carried out his threat to leave, and both the second and third levels of Barrow's scheme appeared in danger of breaking down.

It was in this crisis that Sacheverell was forced to take advantage of the offer of John Woods, to do duty "at the school until a new bishop made a formal appt... at present the school and services of the Chapell stand still to the great prejudice of the youth of the Island."[95] Woods, a non-graduate, was offered a salary of £35, the chaplain's duties worth £5 being paid by the Lord's exchequor. Woods hardly qualified as "a person of sufficient learning and ability to execute the place, imployment and duty of a publique reader of logick, philosophy and history" as the 1676 deed demanded, but possibly acted informally as academic master to the best of his ability. Despite all the current difficulties, the fact that one of the Academic Students of 1686 was acting head of the Grammar School did mark the successful achievement of one of Barrow's main aims, that the Island should be able to educate its own clergy to a reasonable degree.

CONCLUSION

The uniting of the powers of church and state in the capable hands of Isaac Barrow had led to the Isle of Man being the locus of a remarkable experiment in education, with every child not only provided with basic education, at his parish church, but told in no uncertain terms that this was compulsory, and that action would be taken if parents failed in this respect. The scheme had been given the approval of the Lord of the Isle, the Earl of Derby, who added the weight of his own threats, but was notably less forthcoming as far as money was concerned. The Derby family do not appear to have given a single penny to education during the whole period of their Lordship of Man. The free grammar school and the Academic School were intended to provide further ascending levels of education, which would allow promising Manx pupils the opportunity of enjoying an Island equivalent of a university education. By the end of the Seventeenth Century, these ambitious schemes had met with mixed success. The system of parochial schools had been successfully launched, but the provision of seperate Grammar and Academic Schools had never really been achieved. In the last decade of the century indeed, all three levels of educational provision seemed to be at the point of collapse. If the Island's brave experiments were not to be as ephemeral almost as some of those of the Commonwealth period, firm leadership from the new bishop was not merely desirable, it was absolutely essential.

THE FOUNDATIONS ARE LAID
REFERENCES

1 Rot Pat Manx Society Vol. VII, 225-226.
2 *Statutes of the Isle of Man* Vol. I, 24.
3 A. W. Moore. *A History of the Isle of Man* Vol. I, 346.
4 William Cubbon. *Early Schools and Scholarship in Mann* Procs. of IOMNHAS Vol. III, 106
5 Moore *Op cit* Vol. I, 353.
6 Visitation of Bishop Foster 1634.
7 W. K. Jordan. *Philanthropy in England 1485-1660* London 1959.
8 W. L. Vincent. *The State and Social Education 1640-1660*. SPCK 1950. Appendix A.
9 A. W. Moore *Op cit* 361.
10 James Chaloner. *A Short Treatise of the Isle of Man* 1656 Manx Society Vol. X, 18.
11 William Blundell. *A History of the Isle of Man* 1656 Manx Society Vol. XVII, 167.
12 James Stanley. *History and Antiquities of the Isle of Man* 1648 Manx Society Vol. III, 19.
13 Norman Atkinson. *Irish Education — A History of Educational Institutions*. Allen Figgis, Dublin 1969, 35-41.
14 Blundell *Op cit*, 48.
15 W. A. L. Vincent. *The Grammar Schools 1660-1714*. John Murray 1969, 14.
16 Chaloner *Op cit*, 18.
17 William Sacheverell. *An Account of the Isle of Man 1708*. Manx Society I, 91.
18 J. Strong. *History of Secondary Education in Scotland* OUP 1909, 106. (Rosemary O'Day, *Scotland — Education and Society* Longmans 1982 stresses that the needs of the Kirk was the paramount concern, as were those of the Church with Barrow).
19 Weedon Butler. *Hildesley's Memoirs — The Memoirs of Mark Hildesley DD*, 1799, 304-305.
20 Ibid.
21 28 Hen VIII C 15 (T. Corcoran. *State Policy in Irish Education* 1536-1816 Longmans 1916.
22 *Hildesley's Memoirs*, 304.
23 Malew Parish Register, July 29, 1667.
24 *Hildesley's Memoirs*, 304.
25 MS 44 Ib.
26 Ibid.
27 A. W. Moore, *Op. cit* Vol. I 351.
28 BC II.

29. MS 44 Ib.
30. Ecc Wills July 15 1669.
31. Liber Causarum July 15 1669.
32. Ibid.
33. Ibid Aug 30 1669.
34. A. W. Moore. *Sodor and Man (Diocesan Histories)* SPCK 1893, 172.
35. A. W. Moore. *A History of the Isle of Man* Vol. I, 472.
36. Constance Radcliffe. *Ramsey 1600-1800*, 1986, 93.
37. MD 436 17/3 June 4 1675.
38. G. N. Clark. *The Later Stuarts* OUP 1934, 22.
39. A. W. Moore. *Op cit* Vol. I 474-475.
40. William and Constance Radcliffe. *A History of Kirk Maughold*, Manx Museum 1979, 123.
41. BC 6 April 19 1675.
42. Ibid 7 Feb 15 1676.
43. Liber Causarum 1685.
44. Ibid.
45. Liber Plitor 1690.
46. MS 3928.
47. Presentments June 23 1689.
40. BC 63.
49. D426/I/3(8).
50. Liber Causarum Jan 22 1689.
51. Ibid Aug 4 1693.
52. William Sacheverell Op cit.
53. Hildesley's Memoirs 305.
54. R. S. Thompson. *Classics or Charity?* Manchester UP 1971, 21.
55. Charles Hoole. *A New Discovery of the Old Art of Teaching Schools* 1660.
56. W. A. L. Vincent. *Op cit* 41.
57. Athol Papers 136/2.
58. W. A. L. Vincent. *Op cit*, 5170-171.
59. Malew Parish Register Feb 5 1689.
60. William Cubbon. *Island Heritage*. George Faulkner, Manchester 1952, 33.
61. Ibid Proceedings of the IOMNHAS Vol. III, 120.
62. Malew Parish Register, March 7 1671.
63. Ibid, June 5 1692.
64. *Ramsey Church Magazine*. Sept. 1897.
65. Liber Causarum, June 21 1695.
66. J. Strong. *The History of Secondary Education in Scotland*. OUP 1909, 106.

67 Constance Radcliffe. *Ramsey 1600-1800*. Nelson Press 1986. 93.
68 BC 7.
69 Oct 13 1687. Quoted more fully. L. E. Williams. *A Short History of Ramsy Grammar School*, Ramsey 1977.
70 MD 436 20/5 Nov 5 1690.
71 Thomas Willson. *Memoranda*. Quoted John Keble, Life of the Right Reverend Father in God Thomas Wilson, DD Vol. 2, 864.
72 Godfrey Davies. *The Early Stuarts 1603-1660* OUP 1937, 348.
73 David Daiches. *Milton*, Arrow Books, London 1957, 120.
74 Athol Papers 136/3 Deed of July 7 1668.
75 Thomas Wilson. *History of the Isle of Man*. In edited works, R. Cruttwell, Bath 1782 Vol. I, 369.
76 MS 2025c. See E. H. Stenning. *The Original Lands of the Bishop Barrow Trusts* IOMNHAS Vol. V 122-145.
77 MS 44BI.
78 Liber Scacc 1673.
79 Edmond Curtiss. *A History of Ireland*, Methuen 1961, 257-265.
80 BC 24 May 1674.
81 MS 841a May 23 1676.
82 A. W. Moore. *Documents from the Notes and Records of the Isle of Man*, Manx Sun 1904.
83 Liber Cancell Deed, Oct 26 1675.
84 Historical Manuscript Commission, Ormonde Papers. Appendix 6, 776.
85 Ibid.
86 MS 482c.
87 Ibid.
88 MS 1507c March 25 1680.
89 Robert Curphey. *Bishop Barrow's Trust* (unpublished) 1982.
90 MS 1438c. Thomas Denton. *A description of the Isle of Man*.
91 MS 1507c.
92 MS 482c.
93 MS 1507c.
94 Derby MS 1719/28. Sacheverell to Cholmondeley Aug 4 1693.
95 Ibid 1719/4. Sacheverell to Derby.

CHAPTER TWO

PETTY EDUCATION IN THE AGE OF WILSON: THE SAVIOUR SOWS THE SEEDS OF DECAY

THE NEW BROOM

The long interregnum in the diocese since 1693 was ended eventually by the appointment of Thomas Wilson, the most famous and revered of all Manx bishops, and one whose interest in education equalled that of Barrow. Born in Cheshire in 1663, and educated at a school near Chester, he received his university education in Dublin. Although ordained as deacon in Kildare, his first curacy was back in Cheshire at Winwick. In 1692 he became tutor to James, son of the Earl of Derby, and three years later Sacheverell hoped he would fill the gap at Castletown. The purpose of his letter of May 1695 was to prevail on Lord Derby to speak to Mr. Wilson if he would accept of the post, as there was need, with the Academy now void, of a man of merit who would "Reside perpetually in the Island". He recommended "if the Island may not be so happy", a kinsman of his own who had the approval of the Bishop of Oxford, and he himself would give a residence.[1] Both hopes came to nothing, but when Wilson was offered the bishopric itself in 1698, he accepted, although apparently with considerable reluctance.[2]

His episcopate saw the last real effort to put into practice the three-tiered system of education which Barrow had planned, and which had only partly been fulfilled.

As Barrow had seen the need to have a sound base for education, so too did Wilson. The first essential to preserve the very structure of elementary education was to secure the Royal Bounty arrears. Even the Impropriate Fund depended upon the success of this, for if the agreed fine every thirty years to the Earl of Derby were not paid, the whole contract negotiated by Barrow would fall to the ground before the Island had ever enjoyed the full fruits of the agreement. In July 1698 Wilson was able to report to the clergy assembled at Peel his success in these matters, and to arrange with mutual consent a distribution of both funds for the years 1694 to 1696. Those schools expressly designated as Royal Bounty schools each received £6.11.6, with the exception of Castletown, which had £10.19.2 allocated to it. While the clergy were asked to wait until the money from the impropriations for 1697 was actually received, greater consideration was shown for 'Such persons as are hired to teach English schools, and have their dependence on their salaries.' They were to be paid 'for their present supply', the money being stopped from the general share-out when it occurred.

The next step was to ensure that the schools were functioning as intended, and that masters were appointed where necessary. The terms of one of the earliest of his licences are interesting as foreshadowing the arrangements for payment soon to be applied to the whole island. Castletown seems to have been bereft of any schoolmaster at any level once John Woods was appointed to the benefice of Malew, so that John Watterson was given freedom in September 1698 to act as Grammar School master as well as for the Petty School.

> 'Whereas we are given to understand that there is great necessity of an English School being diligently kept in the town of Castletown. This is therefore to authorise you to teach Schoole in the old Chapell of Castletown and to instruct ye young children of the said township in learning and good manners. And for your encouragement you shall receive yearly ye sum of five pounds, as also for each child you instruct (whose parents are of ability to pay it) you are hereby empowered to demand six pence for each quarter. If any of the children you teach have occasion to be instructed in the Latin tongue, or in writing and casting account, you are empowered to demand ninepence a quarter from all such ... (Sept. 23 1698).[3]

Slack incumbents and lazy schoolmasters found themselves presented by chapter courts and enquests and forced to provide schooling. Mr. Graham, schoolmaster of Kirk Braddan, was accused in 1699 of 'neglecting his school by ye deposicions taken',[4] but the mending of ways was short-lived for in June 1703 the Liber Placitorum records him being presented for the same offence. (This time it was decided that the case should be brought to the attention of the Bishop himself.) In the north of the Island, John Curghy appeared in October 1699 charged with failing to keep a constant school, in the parish of Andreas,[5] and even the Vicar of Malew found his former dispensation was no longer considered valid. When John Woods was presented in the same month, October 1699, the Malew tithe arrangement appeared to be considered as equivalent to a share in the Impropriate Fund, and Woods was forced to offer 'the allowance to a schoolmaster who would work the school.[6]

The use of lay schoolmasters was encouraged by Wilson from the start of his episcopate, but realising that their allowances from the incumbents were meagre indeed, he sought to supplement their salaries with extra payments. The Bishop's generosity was outstanding, and the Liber Causarum for 1701-1702 contains a long list of the beneficiaries of his kindness including nearly a dozen schoolmasters. Robert Dykes at Arbory received fifteen shillings, the highest amount given at one time for a master, but the other petty school teachers received ten shillings, supplemented later by a further five shillings. John Graham of Braddan School was evidently considered a reformed character, although it is surprising to find him receiving a further payment in 1703, the year of his second presentation for neglecting his school. Also singled out then for extra payments were Dykes of Arbory, John Kewley of Kk. Michael, and William Crow of Ballasalla. The last named was bracketed with Susan Aspinal in the original list and received a mere five shillings, listed as being from Ballasalla, and contrasted apparently with John McLaughland of Malew. In 1703, however, he is named simply as of Malew. Susan Aspinal was not the only woman to feature in the list; a Mrs Flaxney of Douglas also appeared. With the Christian School established at Peel, the parochial school for German was already centred at St. John's Chapel instead, with a William Quilliam as master. The other three masters awarded payments were Christopher Cowl of Santan, John Garrot of Lezayre and John Killip of Lonan. Wilson sought to involve his clergy in this charitable activity, organising a monthly meeting together at which voluntary contributions were collected, destined primarily 'For the encouragement of such poor Schoolmasters as were observed to be diligent in their duty', with the plight of those stranded in the Island by bad weather and poor housekeepers as subsidiary objects. Wilson recognised that the amounts involved would not be large; 'No great matter can be expected, considering the poverty of the Place and Circumstances of the Clergy'.[7]

Like Barrow and Levinz before him, Wilson sought also to make parents send their children to school. However, this proverbial new broom swept more cleanly than his predecessors. Whereas Barrow, Derby himself and Levinz had uttered threats against those who failed to send children to school, there does not appear to be in the records any case before Wilson of parents being presented for deficiency in this respect. But in the early years of Wilson's episcopate the threats were actually translated into hefty fines. At Castle Rushen court on May 7th 1698, Thomas Moor, of Patrick, was fined seven shillings for not sending his eldest son to school.[8] At Lonan the following year the Great Enquest presented seven persons for 'not sending their children to Schoole'. Daniel Looney, James Corrin, Daniel Cowne, William Looney, Philip Collister, Gilbert Brown and William Kelly were duly fined two shillings.[9] Wilson followed the earlier precedent set out in theory at least of making parental negligence rebound to the advantage of the schoolmaster; 'the moar (the collector of the Lord's rates) is to collect and pay to the schoolmaster of the parish for his encouragement pursuant to our Rt. Honourable Lord's leave for fines of that nature'. A similar order was made in the case of John Clarke and Robert Kegg of Arbory on June 2 1701. It is important to note that this enforcement of compulsory education was based purely upon past arrangements without Wilson needing to assume any further powers, and certainly without invoking the aid of the legislature.

Nevertheless, Wilson clearly felt that there was an advantage to be gained by having the ecclesiastical and educational regulations which he drew up for Convocation in February 1704 (1703 in the old reckoning) passed and promulgated as full Acts of Tynwald in June. Such recourse to law, as has been noted, was taken in Scotland in 1616, 1633 and 1646, and not long before Wilson's move in this direction, a further Scottish Act 'for the Settling of Schools' had made it harder for the heritors, or local landowners, who varied in number from three to thirty depending on size of estate found in the parishes, to evade their legal responsibility of providing school, master, and salary. Now, if they failed in their duty, commissioners of supply would do the work and charge the expenses to the heritors. Any falling into arrears was punished by double payment after a fixed period of time had lapsed.[10] In New England, the Puritans there had also sought to make setting up of schools a matter of legal obligation. In 1674 for instance in Massachusetts every fifty households were required to hire a schoolmaster 'to teach all such children as shall resort to him to read and write', with each hundred households providing a grammar school to fit them for university. (Harvard College had been founded in 1636). Other states had similar legislation — Connecticut in 1650, New Hampshire in 1689 and Plymouth in 1671.[11] While Wilson did not enjoy any secular power as Barrow had wielded as both Bishop and Governor, the Erastian ideal of total integration of Church and State was now a reality on the Island as far as education was concerned. The passing of detailed clauses making education at the petty school level an obligation upon parents put the Island in this matter in advance of the mainland, even Scotland, by the best part of two centuries, and made it the leader of the English-speaking world.

This has been hailed, rightly, as a notable achievement well in advance of its time. Yet, if the vital question is asked 'What difference did this adoption by Tynwald of the principle of 1669 make to education on the Isle of Man?' the truthful answer would seem to be 'Absolutely nothing'. Scottish experience throughout the Eighteenth Century, when presbyteries fought with varying degrees of success to make heritors fulfil their legal duties and provide schools for each parish, revealed that passing a statute did not mean that its provisions would be universally observed, even where the legislative body had provided for sanctions aginst defaulters. In the Island the parochial system was an established fact, and under the vigorous young bishop, existing church laws had already been applied to punish defaulting parents. Wilson's canons of 1704 went into further detail than those of Levinz, but their adoption by Tynwald in practical terms added nothing at all. The agency of enforcement continued to be presentment under the traditional church discipline, and it appears to have petered out, as far as compelling parents to send their children went, within a year or two, long before the church's discipline as a whole began to lose its power. The first instance of enforcement after the Act was passed was in the Parish of Marown where William Cottier, Nick Kewley, William Kelly, James Kelly, Gilbert Kelly, William Moore and Jon Moore were ordered 'To reform forthwith subpoena five shillings a piece ad usum domini' after being presented 'for not sending their children to schoole according to the Act of Convocation'.[12] A year later in the Parish of Rushen the Presentments for 1705 list William Maddrell, J. Maddrell and J. Waterson 'for not sending their children to Schooll' without any explicit mention of the latest piece of legislation. They recorded that 'Jo Maddrell has obliged himself to send his son to school next winter subpoena' without mentioning the other two defendants. These two cases appear to stand out in isolation and they were certainly not followed by a flood of others. (No member of the Chapter Quest or Rushen Warden was able to sign his own name, only make his mark). Perhaps Wilson lost something of his reforming zeal after the first flush of enthusiasm or found local Chapter Quests reluctant to expose local people to financial penalties for what must have seemed a very novel offence. The same difficulty was felt right up to the end of the Nineteenth Century when the importance of education had been recognised for many decades in theory, but employers and parents alike preferred nimble young fingers in the fields to enforcing laws demanding compulsory school attendance. Wilson, when presenting his detailed provisions concerning church discipline and education to Convocation in 1704, expressed the belief that they needed the 'Authority of the Civil Power to make them effectual'.[13] There is no evidence that his wishes were fulfilled as regards effectiveness once the authority of Tynwald had been added to his canons. Indeed as far as education was concerned, the act passed in 1697 which forbad absence of bishop, archdeacon and other clergy from the Island for more than four months in any year, would turn out in the long run to be of greater importance and benefit to education. While the civil power hailed the Ecclesiastical Constitutions of 1704 as 'very reasonable, just and necessary' as the preamble to the Act of Tynwald put it, they were considered very much matters of and for the church. The 'instruction of the growing age in Christian learning and good manners' lay alongside the aim to 'by all laudable means promote the conversion of sinners'. As with the Scottish systems of parish and burgh schools, the aim of education was provision of religious training for the masses, with the eventual goal of securing learned ministers of religion. The Manx system alone specifically allowed no normal exceptions.

> "For the promotion of religion, learning and good manners all persons shall be obliged to send their children, as soon as they are capable of receiving instruction, to some petty school, and to continue them there until the said children can read English distinctly, unless the parents can give a just cause to the ordinary to excuse themselves, approved of by the Ordinary in open court;'[14]

This ninth canon was extended carefully to thwart those who would have sent their children for a token number of times only, as well as imposing fixed penalties for non-attendance.

> 'And that such persons who shall neglect sending their children to be so taught shall be fined one shilling per quarter to the use of the schoolmaster, who may refuse to teach those children who do not come constantly to school (unless for such causes as shall be approved of by the Minister of the parish), and their parents shall be fined as if they did altogether refuse to send them to school.'

It was custom that fees were paid by those who could afford them but Canon X laid down fixed amounts to augment the small increases in stipend or the small salaries already given for holding a school.

> 'And for the further encouragement of the schoolmasters, they shall respectively receive, over and above the salaries already allowed them, sixpence quarterly from the parents of every child that shall be taught by them to read English, and ninepence quarterly from such as shall be taught to write : which sums being refuded, the sumner shall be' ordered to require punctual payment within fourteen days; and upon default thereof they are to be committed till they submit to law.'

For those accustomed to think of basic education in terms of the 'Three Rs', the omission of simple arithmetic might be puzzling, but in the Eighteenth Century, reading, writing and arithmetic were very much in ascending order as the higher fee for writing indicated in Wilson's scheme. The stringent penalties for failure to pay the fees were of no avail in the case of those too poor to pay the fees in the first place. Although the statutes to keep wages fixed at low rates were ineffective, many of the Manx were nevertheless extremely poor, and day-labourers received only twopence a day. Wilson had the choice of excluding from education those whose parents could not afford to pay, or making special provision for them. He chose the latter cause, retaining the principle of universal education by giving free education to those who could not afford to pay, wisely leaving the nomination of such people to those likely to know their particular circumstances.

> 'Notwithstanding, where the parents or relations are poor, and not able to pay as aforesaid, and this to be certified by the Ministers and Churchwardens of the parish to the Ordinary, such children are to be taught gratis.'

The loss of the income earned by children would be a heavy blow to many families if attendance were rigidly enforced at all times, and Wilson showed commendable commonsense in this matter, allowing time off at busy periods as long as some touch was kept with schooling.

> 'XII And whereas some of the poorer sort may have just cause, and their necessities require it, to keep their children at home for several weeks in the summer and harvest; such persons shall not be liable to penalties aforesaid, provided they do send such children, during such absence from school, every third Sunday to the parish church, at least one hour before evening service, there to be taught by the schoolmaster, to prevent losing their learning:'

THE WILSON CHANGES — THE ROLE OF TEACHER

While at first sight these Canons incorporated into Manx Law merely gave more detailed legal authority to the arrangements of Barrow and his sucessors, there were in fact considerable differences in the outlook of Wilson and those who went before. For Barrow and Levinz the norm was to be the teaching incumbent, with possible lay provision for the towns. Yet as early as 1704 in his Canons, Wilson saw the role of the minister not as teacher primarily, but as overseer or superintendent. The continuation of the Twelfth Canon made it very clear that the local minister was not to be regarded as the most likely schoolmaster: indeed it scarcely allowed for such a state of affairs to exist.

> ':and if any schoolmaster shall neglect his duty and complaint be made and proved, he shall be discharged, and another placed in his stead, at the discretion of the Ordinary: And every Rector, Vicar, or Curate shall the first week of every quarter visit the petty school, and take an account in a book of the improvement of every child, to be produced as often as the Ordinary shall call for it.'

Although careful supervision by the clergyman was thus called for, a quarterly visit was a far cry from the daily teaching clearly intended by Barrow and Levinz. The 1670 Jurby list had stated '... every Minister is obliged to teach an English School in his parish, by the increase of his stipend, which was the work intended', while Levinz,

Bishopscourt, 1702-1788, after Bishop Wilson's reconstruction. From a print in *Church Bells*, 1872, based on a drawing now lost, but corroborated by another sketch in J. Crigan's album, 1813.

1   Bishopscourt in the time of Bishop Wilson

2   Castletown Grammar School

3 Bishop Wilson

4 Private boarding schools — Rushen Abbey

The Villa Marina

Oakhill

The Athol Academy

as has been seen ruled that 'whatever Minister received any augmentacon should be obliged to teach a school in his parish.' Wilson was quite within his rights to depart from this practice, as neither the Letters Patent concerning the Royal Bounty, nor the indenture concerning the Impropriate Fund had explicitly linked the two functions together. The question remains — 'Was this marked shift to be commended or deplored?'

On balance it may be maintained that Wilson's removal of the clergy from the schools was deleterious, even disastrous, for the long term success of the system which had been created so far in advance of its time. A reasonable incentive to a clergyman to teach was transformed into a very small incentive if it were the sole source of income for a lay schoolmaster apart from his fees or quarterage, unlikely to attract fit and suitable men to the profession. In practice the lion's share of the Royal Bounty and Impropriate Fund was retained by the clergy, leaving only a pittance of forty shillings as salary for the schoolmasters, who were no better off than a common labourer. The status of the clergy among the Manx was extremely high; indeed one outsider, George Waldron, who lived in the Island in the Seventeen Twenties went so far as to claim that they were 'in a manner, idolised by the natives',[15] but very little of this rubbed off onto the parochial schoolmaster. For all their limitations, the clergy were men of far greater learning than the lay masters who replaced them. While doubtlessly the good bishop wished to save his clergy from the drudgery of daily elementary teaching, his action was an important contributory factor in gravely harming what he had dearly wished to establish. For over one hundred and fifty years, the Isle of Man suffered in the quality of its basic education through this mistake of Wilson. While it would be unrealistic to assume that all would have been well if the incumbents had been in direct charge of teaching, the retention of Bishop Levinz's conditions would have been very much to the benefit of Manx education. It was all very well to include provisions for the removal of negligent masters, but there was nothing at all to induce any man of skill or learning to undertake the role of parish schoolteacher until the English reforms of the mid-Nineteenth Century.

While this situation was most unsatisfactory at the best of times, in practice it was very often worse. The schools which depended on the Royal Bounty found the early Eighteenth Century as unreliable as the late Seventeenth had been. The Convocation of 1715 indemnified Wilson from misfortune after he had paid from his own pocket two years' augmentation from this source, should there be 'any miscarriage by non-payment of the Royal Bounty'. Only three years later the Royal Bounty was eighteen months in arrears, and in 1720 Convocation gave its thanks to Dr. Finch, the Dean of York, 'for his seasonal Charity to the Parish Schoolmasters and the poor children who shall be, by them, instructed in Learning and Good Manners. And as this shall be a relief to their present necessity, so we do heartily desire to testify our gratitude to the pious donor.'[16] When in 1721 the Royal Bounty was once again three years in arrears, Dr. William Walker, the Rector of Ballaugh, gave four acres of glebe by deed of April 29th for the use of the schoolmaster, a most useful and practical gift.[17] Although the Convocation records from this period refer to the Impropriate Fund as being 'for the use of ye Clergy of this Isle for the maintenance of schools etc', no-one else seems to have followed Walker's example in supplementing the meagre yearly salary of forty shillings. Instead the failure to provide an adequate salary for parochial teachers led to the custom of the schoolmaster doubling as parish clerk. A typical case was at Ballaugh where John Brideson began his long career in 1725 as licensed master, acting as clerk as well until his move to Maughold in 1757. The dual function renders more intelligible the record in the Manx Convocation Book of the schoolmaster in Lonan being asked to bring the register of births, marriages and deaths to the Chapter Court in Douglas.

FROM CHURCH TO SCHOOLHOUSE

A second major departure by Wilson from the ideas of his predecessors was his marked dislike of allowing the use of church buildings as school premises. Thomas Parr of Malew, it may be recalled, was formally presented for not keeping a school in his Parish Church, but Wilson did everything in his power to provide other secular buildings for use as schools. Not until the advent of Bishop Ward in the Eighteen Thirties were dual-purpose buildings again given episcopal approval. One of Wilson's earliest acts as bishop was in 1698 to provide Castletown with a new church used exclusively for worship, making other arrangements for the petty and grammar schools in the vacated St. Mary's Chapel. While this policy would mean that each parish and town would have two buildings instead of one to support, in practice this did not make all that much difference. There was no guarantee that even the parish church would be carefully maintained in repair, so that keeping the schools in the church buildings would not have solved any problems in that respect. The average life for a building, whether church or schoolhouse, was only something in the order of fifty years before it was proclaimed 'ruinous'. Ballure Chapel which served the town of Ramsey, was extensively restored by Wilson in 1706, but apparently needed repair as early as 1712. It was rebuilt in 1746 after a town petition described it as 'in a most ruinous condition', and yet as will be seen, in a dozen years was in bad repair once again. This was the fate of a building which served as both church and school, and undermines any argument that a community would keep one building in good condition, but not two.

Although Wilson's Canons went into considerable detail in some respects, they failed to make any provision for maintenance: 'a stitch in time saves nine' was an unheeded proverb, the neglect of which had dire consequences in Manx educational history at all levels. The custom was rather to let matters get so bad that a full scale assessment of the neighbourhood was needed — a cumbersome and unpopular procedure. Some foresight in these matters would have avoided many unnecessary crises both for schools and churches.

The reason for Wilson's dislike of schools in the churches was the lack of respect for a place of worship which would ensue. The Arbory presentments for 1705 reported that the 'windows of ye schoolehouse was crushed and broken about a foot and halfe'. It was ruled that 'ye children are to be corrected for ye same by ye master'. (This report suggests that Arbory was the first of the parishes, as opposed to the towns, to have a separate schoolhouse. Just over a century later, the same parish would stand out as the only one *not* possessing a proper school building for its children). Perhaps similar boisterous behaviour caused Wilson to have second thoughts about having the petty school and grammar school and under the same roof in Castletown. The old petty school, sold when a new church was built and the move made to the old St. Mary's Chapel to join the Grammar School, was purchased back in 1708 from Thomas Looney for £11.19.00.[18] Certainly costs for glazing appear among repairs to the old chapel a couple of years later. When a new parish church for Patrick was provided in 1714, Wilson gave explicit instructions that the new hallowed building would not suffer such indignities.

'We do likewise prohibit every Schoolmaster or other person from teaching School in the said Church or Cancel under pain of severe ecclesiastical censure and being for ever incapacitated to teach school within this Island.'[19]

Wilson's Memoranda Book recorded 'I built a new school-house at St. Patrick and recovered the Glebe', and a similar venture in the Parish of Lezayre was recorded in 1722: 'A new school-house in Kirk Christ Lezair to which I have given three pounds.'

The sole response to the Bishop's lead as far as the clergy were concerned came once again from William Walker of Ballaugh. In his will of 1729 he bequeathed '. . . towards erecting a School-house, on the piece of ground lately purchased, and given by me to the Parish of Ballaugh, the sum of four pounds'.[20] Once more Wilson played his own part, adding five pounds and providing Ballaugh with a house for the schoolmaster too, although the full advantage of such a provision took more than a century to be realised. When Walker's example was not followed by other incumbents, Wilson was left to be the initiator. A Mrs. Esmond of Onchan had left the remainder of her money in her will to 'Pious Uses' at the Bishop's discretion. Possibly to encourage further school-building, Wilson brought the matter before Convocation in June 1734, securing a resolution that the money might be

'applied towards the purchasing of a convenient place and building of a Schoolhouse thereon in the said parish if the Parishioners will put their helping hand so that the intended work may be perfected and kept in repair, wch proposal the Revd Mr Gell Vicar of the said Parish is to signify to them the next Holy Days'.[21]

Two years later, on June 17th 1736, Convocation heard that the work was finished. Around the same time Wilson's Memoranda Book in 1734 recorded that 'I gave two pounds towards building a schoolhouse in Kirk Rushen and a good one is now being built which saves the church from being abused.' Nevertheless, Wilson soon concluded that leading by patient example was not enough, and a tougher line was needed.

By November 1735 the Bishop was obviously irritated by the laggardly attitude shown by parishes to his obvious desire to confine schooling to secular buildings, and wrote a severe letter to one, or perhaps more, of his clergy.

> 'Whereas many complaints have been made to us of the Great disorder and mischiefs done to the severall churches, Both in seats and windows, by keeping the Petty Schooles in them, and there being to many other evil consequences attending such practices, particularly the Children's being Breed up in a disrespect for the House of God in which they are accustomed to play, and do many Indecent things unbecoming the sacredness of such Holy Places. You are therefore to call a Vestry of your Parishioners and signifye this to them and that they take care to have some convenient School House provided for the master to teach in as is done in other parishes, and this before Whitsuntide next year, after which time you are required to hinder the master from teaching any longer in your Church upon pain of forfeiting his Lycence and you would do well to let your people know that if they Expect to have a School kept in their parish they are and must be obliged to find a convenient place for the master to teach in. Given under our hand this 13th day of November 1735.

If this were intended as a general ultimatum, it was a signal failure. While eventually the Bishop's wishes in this respect were translated into reality, it took until the end of the century to complete the provision of separate schoolhouses in all the Island parishes.

Indeed even the provision of a schoolhouse for a parish or town did not guarantee that its problems with accommodation were over. Events at Peel exemplified the reluctance of the Manx to take care of their buildings. In the Presentments of February 1718, the Vicar and Wardens of German told of 'ye Schoole House there ruinous and very much out of repair', and secured permission to levy an assessment upon the inhabitants. The sanctions appeared formidable enough to secure obedience. The repairs were to be completed before midsummer, and if any refused, 'he is to be committed into St. German's prison there to remain until he submit and pay all fees.' If the sumner's authority were not heeded, he could call for assistance from the garrison of Peel Castle.[22] Despite this, it was clear four years later that threats had been insufficient to make the people of Peel part with their money. Work had been put in hand, and the labourers understandably were asking for their wages, yet 'the said inhabitants of Peel have absolutely refused to pay, aledging that there is Eight pounds of the money belonging to the said Schoole in the hands of the Rev Mr Woods of Castletown since he was schoolmaster in that place.' John Woods it may be recalled, had been master of Peel fully thirty years earlier in the Sixteen Nineties, and had been officially awarded the eight pounds by the Governor and Archdeacon of the day to supplement his small salary. Woods was ordered to attend court with any papers he might possess, and swore that in any case he had only ever received four pounds.[23] Again part of a letter survives from 1730 in which the petitioner referred to '... no school kept at the parish school house which is now quite obsolete and the school is kept at the Clerk's dwelling.' The parish in question was almost certainly Braddan, for a few years later a Mr. John Gelling of that parish wrote to Wilson about 'no school at the parish school house, which was purposely erected by your Lordship and the parishioners ... which is now quite obsolete'. Within twenty years the children of Braddan were being taught back inside the walls of the parish church.

Another problem facing Wilson was the fact that the system of parochial schools did not mean that every child was within easy access of a centre of education. The purpose of the Braddan petitioner of 1730 was to secure permission for one John Clark to instruct his children until they were able to travel to a better school, on the grounds that the clerk's house where the school was kept was 'a prodigious distance from the Petitioner's residence.'[24] Wilson appreciated the problems, and raised no objections when a Mr. Garret in the Parish of Lezayre offered a piece of land to build a school for Sulby, whose inhabitants 'cannot possibly have the advantage of the School kept at the Church, their parents being not of ability to maintain them abroad.' When in June 1715 the inhabitants of Sulby 'obliged themselves to build a schoolhouse and maintain a master to teach an English School'.[25] Wilson himself helped matters along with a typically generous gift of five pounds. How successful this first example of 'infilling', the supplementing of the parochial schools, turned out to be is uncertain, and the area may have failed to support a master as intended. Mrs. Margaret Christian in her will of 1725 left forty pounds British to buy land which would provide rents 'towards the maintenance of such unmarried woman, being a native of the Island, as shall be willing, and they the said Bishop, Minister Wardens for the time being shall from time to time nominate, licence and appoint to keep a school at Sulby, for the teaching of the children of the said parish of Kirk Christ to read and write, and for instructing them in the Church Catechism'.[26] It appears that as this was not an official parish school no help was given from the Impropriate Fund, nor were the set fees laid down in 1704 insisted upon. A licence has survived which was granted to Jane Curghy on October 29 1739, which apart from telling her to impart learning, good manners, the catechism and the fear of God, allowed her 'to receive from the parents or guardian such sums as you can further agree on'. The licences was given 'during our pleasure and whilst you shall behave as becometh'. Part of the land of the Milntown Estate belonging to the Christian family was bought in the same year in accordance with the will[27] but how long the school continued is not known. By 1771, when there was recorded a conveyance of land at Sulby for a school, the 1715 school was noted as being in decay.[28]

Within the growing town of Douglas, the original Petty School had, as will be seen, developed into a school which was primarily for more advanced learning, and the intention that no child should be deprived of education on the grounds of poverty appeared to be in danger of being forgotten, for there was no incentive for any private school providing a basic education to teach for no financial reward. Wilson sought to overcome this problem by utilising general bequests to the poor. The will of John Thompson of Middlesex in 1700 gave three hundred pounds to be laid out and disposed by the Bishop and Governor for the use of the poor of the Parish of Braddan, which included Douglas within its boundaries. In 1730 Bishop Wilson let it be known that any Douglas schoolmaster who taught poor and fatherless children, 'not in a condition to pay anything for their learning', would receive due consideration. One John Kissag claimed to be the sole master who took such destitute boys under his wing, 'their numbers dayly increasing'. As he had a large family to support without any financial resources apart from his teaching, he appealed for assistance under the Thompson Charity to compensate for the large amount of time he spent with his poor boys. Wilson and Governor Horton in May 1732 awarded Kissag forty shillings a year from the funds, on condition that he taught 'all the poor people's Children that come to this school.' A footnote added that poor people's children were those unable to pay for education, perhaps a superfluous remark, but went on to rule that they should be so adjudged by the Chaplain, Wardens and principal inhabitants of the town of Douglas.[29] Further provision for the poor came several years later, when the Douglas merchant, Philip Moore, directed by deed that half of a hundred pounds given by him for the use of St. Matthew's Chaplain and Schoolmaster, should go to a petty schoolmaster in return for the tuition of eight poor scholars. Certainly the Royal Bounty continued to be paid to the official school until its eventual closure in the Nineteenth Century.

However these were but teething troubles compared with a number of developments which threatened to destroy both the legal and financial foundations of the Manx educational system.

THE CHANGE IN CHURCH — STATE RELATIONSHIPS

The old unity of church and state which had been so important was shattered by a series of disputes from 1716 onwards. Detailed consideration will be left until the Free or Grammar School at Castletown is discussed, as the persons involved had more to do with higher education than the petty schools, but among the points at issue was the right of the church to enforce its law by use of soldiers. The arrival in 1725 of Governor Horton led to a fresh refusal to permit soldiers to execute the orders of ecclesiastical courts. The Earl of Derby now claimed that the spiritual laws had been invalid as early as the reign of Henry VIII when the Island became part of the Province of York, and suspended the whole code until the spiritual laws were revised. All parties had desired a measure of revision but the House of Keys pointed out that the routine life of the Island would be 'in great measure if not entirely at a stand', and appealed to the King in Council. Derby's side for their part accused the spiritual courts of 'arbitrary practices and proceedings' which overturned the rights and privileges of the people, condemning 'divers absurd arbitrary pretended practices' which were without 'authority, content, allowance of the lord or legislature of the said Island'.[30] The temporal laws were held to be sufficient for the 'body, goods and fame' of every subject. By the simple expedient of turning out eleven of its members and replacing them, the House of Keys was changed from a supporter of the Church into an opponent, and the authority of the old church discipline very much weakened. As the educational provisions had received secular approval in 1704, they were technically outside the scope of the argument, but in practice they could scarcely be other than weakened by the attacks made upon presentments, the traditional channel for enforcing the rules of the Church. With church and state at loggerheads, there was no hope of strict enforcement of laws demanding compulsory education. 'The great contempt that of late has been put upon the discipline of the church', as Wilson put it, was bound to affect regulations about schooling, whether Tynwald had once approved of them or not. As the theoretical coercion by law faded right away, all would depend upon the diligence of clergy and masters.

In February 1730 Wilson expressed his disquiet about the obvious lack of such diligence, and found the need to order Vicar-General Woods to remind the clergy of their duty under law to visit the parochial schools every quarter. 'I have reason to fear that the law has not been generally and conscientiously observed, forasmuch as several who have applied to me for books have not been able to say even the Catechism and prayers as well as might reasonable have been expected'.[31] Soon Wilson would be lucky enough to see a scheme brought to fruition which would give extra incentive to the teachers at least to perform their duties properly, through the generosity of Lady Elizabeth Hastings, who had already received the thanks of Convocation in 1732 for her kindness to clergy widows and orphans. Yet before this happened both clergy and master alike found themselves facing a new crisis which threatened to undo virtually all that had been achieved on the Island in the sphere of education.

THE GREAT EVICTION

The death of James, Earl of Derby, without male heir meant that the Lordship of Man passed to James, Duke of Atholl, who exercised his legal right to claim the tithes which formed the Impropriate Fund. As the entail had never been barred, the deed of alienation by Earl Charles at the time of Barrow was now null and void. Luckily Barrow had also had the foresight to guard against precisely such a happening, arranging 'a collateral and further security for the quiet enjoyment of all the said rectories and tithes', in the form of lands in Lancashire, the Manor of Bispham and the farm of Methop, valued at £2,000. The Stanley family were allowed to hold the lands 'until the said same Bishop and Archdeacon should be interrupted in the quiet possession of the said Rectories and tithes'.[32] When a meeting of the clergy at St. John's in August 1736 was informed that the Duke was impervious to tales of seventy years of quiet enjoyment of the tithes and had warned the clergy they could count on them no longer, thoughts turned to the collateral security. Panic set in when the relevant documents relating to the collateral could not be found. Wilson wrote to Governor Murray about the plight, not only of his clergy, but also of 'the free school in Castletown and thirteen petty schools in several parishes; which schools must be utterly laid down, there being no other provision for them.'[33] Luckily the diligent searches of Wilson's son proved fruitful in the Rolls Office in London, but even so the new Earl of Derby showed no disposition to surrender his manors as Wilson hoped. He had written with the good news of the discovery to Lady Elizabeth Hastings in Yorkshire;

'... we hope that when the Earl of Derby, who has possessed himself of the lands given in England as counter-security, knows this, he will do us the justice, without the expense and difficulty of contending with too powerful an adversary'. On the contrary, that seemed to be the hope of the Earl, that the expense of pursuing their legal rights would deter Bishop, clergy and schoolmasters from making the attempt. Some money was in the Bishop's hands already, saved up in order to pay the great fine of £130 when that fell due, but the clergy were told at the 1738 Convocation that their own contributions were also needed, and '... the several Schoolm's are to contribute towards the above charge in proportion'.[34] The Duke of Atholl agreed in the interim to pay the money from the tithes, at interest, to those who so desired, on bond to repay from the security when all was settled, but a plea to Derby from clergy and schoolmasters, 'constrained by hard necessity to become Your Lordship's most humble and distressed Petitioners', claimed 'we are given to understand that the favour is not to be continued to us much longer.[35] The Earl of Derby countered with an offer of a mere thousand pounds, rejected although Wilson admitted 'we would be content to take any reasonable consideration rather than lose all'. When the Earl claimed that the benefits had already been received, amounting to both principal and interest, Wilson pointed out that some leases had only recently expired, and until then there had been no benefit to the clergy from them. If the Earl would not honour the agreement regarding the manors, 'not only the present clergy and schools and their families, must sink under it, but the island itself will for ever lose a very considerable income'. Appeals to honour were of no avail: a bill in Chancery was eventually exhibited in 1742, and the legal mills began to grind in their notoriously tardy fashion. In the meantime, the Duke of Atholl consented to continue paying the tithe money on bond, although when matters were eventually settled in the next decade, it emerged that only a third of the money lost to the schoolmasters had been borrowed from the Duke during these years — £352 out of a total of £1,486 due.

LADY BETTY HASTINGS OFFERS SOME RELIEF

There was luckily some mitigation of their plight for the petty schoolmasters in the legacy from Lady Betty Hastings, a daughter of the Earl of Huntingdon, who was born in London in 1682, and a long-standing friend of Bishop Wilson, from whom she sought guidance from time to time concerning her charitable gifts. For instance when Wilson preached at Ledsham in Yorkshire in 1717, he had helped to draw up regulations for the schools in the West Riding, including a rule that schoolmasters must retire at 65 — one from which the Isle of Man would have benefited too. The Society for the Propagation of Christian Knowledge and Queen's College, Oxford were also recipients of her generous gifts.[36] The first reference to help for Wilson's own diocese occurs in September 1730: 'The Lady Betty Hastings by my desire has promised twenty pounds per annum after her death to the petty schools in my diocese'. Lady Betty was apparently eager and enthusiastic to help

> 'When I last saw you Lordship, you let me know that so small a things as £20 per annum to commence at my decease, applied to the petty schools in your Island, might be a very useful charity. I Beg by the first post your direction in what manner I shall bequeath it.[37]

However, despite Lady Betty's desire to know whether her gift should be left merely in general terms or drawn up in detailed provisions, six years elapsed before the matter was attended to again. The loss of the Impropriate Fund and the failure to find the documents relating to the collateral gave a new urgency to the intended bequest. Lady Betty in May 1737 again assured Wilson that he might make the detailed arrangements as he thought fit. 'I will observe your direction in regard to what I leave to your petty schools'. In September, Wilson urged the importance of having the lands which would provide the intended income in *England*. (Current and past troubles had shown the dangers of investing in Ireland). The Deed of Settlement was finally drawn up in December 1738, and enrolled in Chancery the following April, with a reference in its opening sentence to 'a calamity' which applied especially to the events of the past two years as well as geneally.

> 'The above named Lady Elizabeth Hastings being informed that several Petty Schools within the Diocese of the Isle of Man are very meanly provided for, the Masters and Mistresses having little or no encouragement to do their duty, insomuch that many of the people being poor, their children are destitute of instruction and such learning, as is even necessary for the meanest Christian; and that it would be a work of charity very acceptable to God to contribute towards remedying so great a calamity'.[38]

The twenty pounds was to be in the hands of the Bishop who would distribute the money each Easter 'to such Masters or Mistresses of Petty Schools there as do not receive the Royal Bounty, who shall produce certificates yearly'. The schools who did not receive the Royal Bounty were carefully listed, with special conditions attaching to two of them. The school for Maughold 'to be kept near the Church', but quite the opposite in the case of German — '(the School to be kept in some convenient place remote from the Town of Peel,)' As the Clothworkers' School provided for Peel already, the official parochial school for German served the purpose of filling in the gaps, the opposite of the usual practice. The certificates mentioned were to be obtained from the Incumbents, themselves reminded of their obligation to vist their schools the first week in every quarter, certifying that the schools had been duly visited as under the 1703/4 Constitution, and 'that the children there have been carefully taught, and do improve in learning and good manners, are taught to say their prayers and catechism, and do duly attend the public service of the Church'. If no such certificate were brought, duly signed by the incumbent, to the Bishop (or in his absence, to the Vicar-General) then the portion intended for that parish would be divided among the rest who had brought along their certificates. Wilson made it explicit that this increment was not to be at the expense of the other ways in which the meagre salary of the petty schoolteachers was made up in normal times.

'... this charity shall not, upon any pretence whatever, lessen the payment of the 40 shillings a year to the said Schools out of the Impropriations, whenever they or the value of them shall be recovered or restorted to the Church. Nor shall this charity be understood to excuse such parents as are able, from paying such sums quarterly as the law appoints, or shall be agreed upon betwixt the Masters or Mistresses and parents of such children.'[39]

As Wilson had suggested, Lady Betty made the payment a charge upon lands in her local area, on estates in Collingham, Shadwell and Burton Salmon in the West Riding of Yorkshire, so that there were not likely to be any problems in receiving the money due. However, the statement in A. W. Moore's History of the Isle of Man, that 'The parochial schools ... gained large additions to their endowments, chiefly through the charity of Lady Elizabeth Hastings'[40] is a very misleading. An extra £1.8.6 per annum, although undoubtedly welcome to the fourteen teachers involved, was scarcely a 'large addition' sufficient to attract teachers. With the loss of the forty shillings from the Impropriate Fund taken into account, their plight was desperate indeed, even with this new provision. There was bound to be increased reliance upon quarterage, but fewer and fewer would be able to pay. As if to confirm the saying that trouble rarely comes alone, the years from 1737 onwards were disastrous for the Island. A form of influenza swept the Island causing many deaths, followed in 1739 by the severest drought that Bishop Wilson could remember, ruining many farmers. The following year saw a poor harvest on top of a severe winter, and 'a violent epidemical flux and diarrhoea' caused many more deaths for two more years, to be followed by 'contagious fever' which wiped out whole families. Only an excellent harvest in 1742 and the ending of an embago on exports of corn from England enabled the Island to survive until normality in 1746. For those struggling to find money to pay for food at inflated prices, quarterage must have been very low in the list of priorities, and fulfilling the provisions of the law concerning compulsory education came nowhere compared with the desperate struggle to survive.

In these circumstances it was hardly surprising that it was a period of decay and depression as far as many of the petty schools were concerned, but all fourteen parishes had teachers in 1740 to sign the appeal to Derby. One lady, Rebecca Mordy of Santan joined the thirteen men (Silvester Radcliffe of Patrick, Robt Rogers of Lezayre, John Killup of Lonan, James Clagg (sic) of Marown, Robert Quayle of Malew, John Garret of Rushen , Wiiliam Kneale of Arbory, Robert Allen of Maughold, Matthew Crellin of German, John Kewley of Michael, John Stole of Braddan and William Christian of Onchan).[41]

The rules drawn up concerning the Lady Betty Hastings payments were brought before the clergy at the 1740 Convocation, with the instruction to take a copy to their petty schoolteachers, who must surely have found any sadness at the death of their patroness in that year outweighted by their sense of relief at some assured income augmenting their fees and borrowings from the Duke of Atholl.

What was less predictable was the fact that a number of parishes made the move to building a schoolhouse instead of using the church in this period. In May 1740 Bishop Wilson informed the parishioners of German that land had been offered in a spot of which he approved, and which fulfilled the condition put in the Elizabeth Hastings Deed that a parochial school must be remote from Peel in order to receive the share allotted to it. Six parishioners were to assist the curate to select a site there, while he would provide forty shillings towards a decent house. This last seems to have referred to a residence for the master for in 1743 a licence from Governor Murray dated February 11th gave the Rev. James Wilks the right to enclose waste ground at St. John's for the purpose of erecting a schoolhouse and schoolmaster's house, a progressive step that did not become widely followed until after 1850. This new parochial school also had the benefit shortly of a local endowment given under the will of John Craine of Ballnahown in 1750, who sought to ensure thereby that the small repairs often neglected would be carried out.

> 'Secondly, I leave, settle and appropriate upon the School of the Parish of Kk German the sum of twenty pounds while the School is continued in the house at the Chapel of St. John's for that purpose, the use of the said sum to be enjoyed by the successive masters for their better encouragement, they being obliged to keep the said house in all repairs except failure or decay of the wall, roof, or timber.'[42]

The Vicar and Wardens were given charge of the money, the settlement liable to be revoked and the fund kept for the heirs of Ballnahown in the case of two contingencies. First was that 'the School happen at any time hereafter to be removed from that place', but the other was more ambigious — '. . . in case the said School-house be not perfected . . .' This might suggest the building was not yet fully completed, or could be a reference to the failure of the master to adhere to the terms of the bequest and keep it in good repair. Be that as it may, the Parish of German now had two endowed schools, shortly to be joined by two more of more advanced degree.

The Parish of Maughold was also fortunate to receive a local endowment in the same period under the will of Edward Christian in 1738 who left land in the Parishes of Jurby and Bride, half for the poor of Ramsey and Maughold Parish and half 'to a Schoolmaster, to go towards the free teaching and instructing of five of the poorest children of the Parish of Kk Maughold, the same to be equally divided and distributed yearly and every year, by the Wardens of the said Parish, upon the 25th March.' Another piece of land left to his son Thomas was subject to a payment of three shillings to the schoolmaster and three to the poor. This proved over the years to be a most beneficial bequest, as in addition to normal rents, the land yielded considerable profits from the sale of peat. These were invested in land and made the parochial schoolmaster of Maughold the best paid in the Isle of Man. Yet although their value was less at the start, when the Rev. Henry Allen, Vicar of Maughold, was entered as the nominal tenant in May 1742, it was even then a valuable supplement to a low income.[43]

Maughold, again like German, received at this time its own school building, although in this case merely leaving the parish church in obedience to Wilson's wishes. The Liber Assesdationis, the rent roll containing the landowners' names and the rent paid to them, refers to a licence granted to the Vicar, Henry Allen, to enclose a parcel of waste ground for the use of a parish schoolhouse in July 1740. The researches of William and Constance have revealed the unsettled start of the new school. The building standards of Maughold Parish seem to have been extremely low, even by Manx standards. The rapid decay at Ballure Chapel in Ramsey has already been noted; a further renovation needed in the Seventeen Forties will be dealt with under higher education later. The new school for Maughold similarly needed repair well within the decade. In 1747 the Vicar reported that 'The School-house is out of repair and begs an order may be issued out to redress the sd grievance. The public assessment ordered by the Chapter Court was no more popular than usual, and many were presented in May 1748 for refusing to pay.'[44]

Another parish to establish its separate school was Marown, but in this case it appears that the bishop's injunction of 1735 not to use parish churches as schools had led to the use of a house quite a way from the church causing inconvenience to the pupils. A complaint about the competency of the schoolmistress, Ann Callin, had been made, the complainants alleging that despite pleas for someone better the Vicar had imposed her. They had submitted but now 'felt the melancholy effects thereof', and wished to make their own recommendation. After investigation Vicar-General Cosnahan found the charge to be without substance.

> 'The Vicar has not imposed upon your Lordship. Ann Callin has been publicaly examined, and is qualified to teach an English school. It appears she has been diligent beyond some schoolmasters because her scholars read well, and repeat the Catechism distinctly.'

Nevertheless Wilson concurred with the other complaint regarding remoteness, which lead to the decision to build the schoolhouse in the churchyard.[45]

> 'Mr Vicar-General was to signify to the parishioners that it is expected that a schoolhouse shall be built in a convenient place near the church within a reasonable time otherwise that the Lady Eliz (sic) Hastings her bounty cannot be paid.'

Marown in fact appears to have had two gifts of land for the education during the decade. The Vicar, the Rev. Thomas Christian, by deed of May 2 1741 granted a parcel of land by the church to Bishop Wilson, and it was this first gift, later known as Ellerslie, which was the site of the parochial school.[46] Also in 1742 Thomas Christian of Ballahutchin gave part of his estate of Ballaquinney a plot measuring seven yards by five 'on the north west side of the Ballaquinney highway, with fifty yards of the Glenbeg river, to John Kewley and John Quilliam. In trust for the use and benefit of a School-house for the said Parish'.[47]

Wherever the schools were held, conditions were not likely to be conducive to learning. In the 1743 Visitation records, Onchan school is described by Vicar-General Cosnahan is in good order, but lacking seating'. Rushen Church had 'several seats broken', while those at Malew were 'most scandously out of repair' — perhaps not unconnected with rough usage on the part of pupils that Wilson had complained about. The chancels of Andreas, Jurby and Lezayre needed extensive mending, while the same was true at Braddan of both nave and chancel.

THE DEFICIENCIES OF THE WILSON SYSTEM EMERGE

It is clear from Cosnihan's comparison with other teachers that the system of lay schoolmasters was not working as had been hoped. From the Marown desire to make their own appointment it is evident that the strict control exercised by means of the Bishop's licence thwarted the operation of laws of supply and demand. The granting of a license to a teacher in a parish gave him or her a monopoly, which could easily be abused. A glaring case occurred in the Parish of Malew, where a petition of complaint alleged

> 'Robert Quayle keeps no school, though he yearly receives the salary which they would not mind, could they but have the liberty at their own expense to put their children to one who would teach them: but when they try to do so, the said Quayle sues the other teacher at law. Would he be at pains to teach our children, and as careful to get them taught as he is to hinder their teaching, we would have a good school.'

How conscientiously Quayle kept his promise to be more diligent in future is open to question.

Something similar occurred at Maughold. Henry Allen, the Vicar reported an Irishman, William Young for holding a school without a license from the Bishop. The principle of the Bishop's control was duly upheld — 'The teaching of children by persons of unknown or suspected principles being of dangerous consequence, the Vicar is to admonish Young to forebear teaching of school until he has qualified himself according to the Laws and Constitution of this Church'. It is unlikely that Young ever managed this, as the Radcliffes' researches have uncovered him the next year accused of running a public house which diverted parishioners from attending Sunday Evensong.[48] But behind it all seemed to lie the lethargy of the official schoolmaster, the Vicar's brother, Robert, who was warned to be very regular and diligent in giving instruction 'that there be no cause for complaint.'

The paucity of suitable men offereing themselves as schoolmasters may be illustrated by the events at the Clothworkers' School in Peel. William Tear was found guilty by a Consistory Court held in his own schoolhouse of habitual drunkeness, and swore to finish teaching. Nevertheless after six months' suspension he was restored by Bishop Wilson, who commanded the Clothworkers and Wardens 'as they tended the welfare of the place, the education of their children, and our good intent', to watch Tear and report irregularities. During his absence the head scholar had tried to run the school, but the children had gone wild. John Keble was puzzled why there was not ample competition for a school offering a salary of £18 a year.[49] Although Keble over-estimated the salary at this time, the ten pounds paid was certainly far above the amount paid to any parochial schoolmaster at the best of times; even more so during the time of the loss of the Impropriate Fund. If no suitable person could be found to replace Tear, there was little hope of decent schoolmasters, who would have to work for a pittance, being found anywhere else. The figures given in documents relating to the controversy about the Impropriate Fund reveal that for all the cries of distress by the clergy, the fund furnished by this time just a useful addition to the rest of their stipends, usually amounting to no more than a third, in some cases very much less. Far different was the case of the schoolmasters who lost all their fixed income, and had every incentive to abandon their schools and seek a living in some other way. The years of distress were a further vindication of the policy of Barrow and Levinz as opposed to that of Wilson in respect of the employment of the clergy as actual teachers.

There were signs that Peel would prove at this time to be the school on the Island which would be the exception to the scenes of financial extremities. The London properties had been let for 71 years in 1671 and upon expiry of this period in 1742 hopes were high that the full £18 per annum in Philip Christian's will could now be paid. Bishop Wilson was promised that 'he would be used after the best manner' but nothing had come of it. Supposing the whole sum of £20 mentioned in the will were now to be paid, he urged his son Thomas, Rector of St. Stephen's Walworth, to request that two or three pounds might go to 'a mistress for teaching the lesser children, the town being become so populous'. The master was attempting to cope with up to 70 pupils when he could not manage more than a score. If his son let him know if the full amount were to be paid, the Bishop could write to the company more fully. The Islanders were too sanguine about the rents, and when Dr. Thomas Wilson presented in 1747 a petition from the Peel schoolmaster, still Tear apparently, stating that the school was 'in ruinous condition, needing to be taken down and rebuilt', it was pointed out that Peel had already enjoyed favourable treatment. The rents brought in only £12 a year: under the two-thirds rule, the Clothworkers' School was only entitled to receive £8 of this, but nevertheless £10 had been paid. As for the plea about the premises, the appeal to augment the collection made by Dr. Wilson among his friends did not fall upon deaf ears. Ten guineas would be voted upon completion of the work, although here again the Company pointed out that they had no connection whatsoever with the schoolhouse, and therefore no obligation.[48] Fortunately for Peel, going beyond the bounds of duty became a feature of the Company's policy over the years to come. Dr. Wilson duly returned grateful thanks for the extra payments to the master, and the generosity regarding the schoolhouse.

Bishop Wilson himself tried to give some encouragement to education in his will drawn up in February 1746, leaving ten shillings to each master amd mistress having a share in the Elizabeth Hastings charity, 'they producing such certificates and not otherwise'.[51] In a codicil to his will, added in June 1748, he left £50 to encourage a Grammar School to be established in Kirk Michael, but if this was not settled within a year of his death,

> 'then I give the said fifty pounds as follows, viz. towards a fund for a petty schoolmistress in Peel town, if not given before my death, and five pounds towards erecting a parish schoolhouse in Jurby if done within a year after my death and not otherwise'.

The time limits imposed showed Wilson's awareness of the Manx 'traa de looar', the belief there was ample time ahead and no need to hurry things along. Small financial incentives were, however, usually inadequate to conquer the ingrained tendency to procrastinate.

The last decade of Wilson's long episcopate was a sad contrast to the brisk efficiency which had characterised his earliest years. Morale among clergy and schoolmasters was low as the Earl of Derby resolutely failed to honour his obligations concerning the collateral to the Impropriate Fund, and the Bishop could do little more than exhort his clergy to play their own part diligently. In his Convocation charge of June 1747 he referred to the educational work being carried out in Wales. The Welsh had had their own equivalent to Barrow in Thomas Gouge, who established a Welsh Trust, which maintained between three and four hundred charity schools in North and South Wales, with English as the medium of instruction, although (unlike in the Isle of Man) books in the native tongue were published and distributed. After Gouge's death, the supporters of the trust transferred their activities to England, resulting in the foundation of the Society for the Propagation of Christian Knowledge in 1699, under the chairmanship of Sir John Phillips of Picton Castle, Pembrokeshire. The Society aimed at a school in every parish, and in Wales the use of Welsh was encouraged by bishops such as William Lloyd of St. Asaph, and William Thomas of St. David's, although Humphrey Lloyd of Bangor did not believe the language was worth preserving. The early Charity Schools fell into disfavour after 1715, labelled as nurseries of Jacobitism, but were given new life through the work of Griffith Jones, who had very definite views on the folly of trying to uplift a people through the medium of a foreign tongue; 'It may be suggested that it were better to set up Charity Schools for the Welsh people in the English language... To give them English schools would be the same as setting up French schools for the poor in England'.

In 1731 he founded his first 'Circulating School' which soon became extremely popular. It has been estimated that they taught 158,000 to read between 1737 and 1761, with 3,500 schools kept throughout Wales. Teaching was free, for all ages, young and old alike, and the schools were open for certain periods only, trying not to clash with busy times on farms. It has been claimed that the use in the schools of Welsh Bible and catechisms prevented the Welsh language from degenerating into a number of dialects.[52] Wilson made no effort to copy the use of the native tongue as the medium of instruction; despite some work in translation of part of the Bible into Manx, as far as schools were concerned on the Island, the policy of Barrow remained unchanged in this respect. The enthusiasm attending the Circulating School movement certainly impressed him, however, and he reported how 36,800 of all ages were taught to read in Wales. What could be done with similar zeal in the Isle of Man?

> 'If every Rector, Vicar and Curate would but spend one hour in every week in visiting his petty school, and seek how the children are taught to read, to say their Catechism ... If this were faithfully done and the masters reproved when they are lazy and negligent, there would soon be a change for the better both among the young and the old.'[53]

As it was, there was clearly room for much improvement. With regard to Lady Hasting's Charity,

> 'This will be sadly perverted if every one of us do not put his helping hand to render it more effectual: and other people will be discouraged from helping us, when they see so excellent a charity neglected or abused.
> I have had several complaints that many of the petty schools have been neglected — both those that receive the Royal Bounty, and they that have had that good lady's charity.
> I would be glad if you would let the masters know, that a very strict enquiry and visitation shall be made, that such as are found faulty may be turned out, and such as do their duty may receive further encouragement.'[54]

Formal Visitations were used infrequently by Wilson. The first, in 1719 made no mention of schools at all. The second, undertaken by Cosnahan and Moore in 1743 mentioned the existence of schoolhouses at Onchan, Ballaugh and Douglas, but passed no comment on teaching in any parish. Whether the 1748 Visitation was the 'very strict enquiry and visitation' threatened by Wilson the previous year is uncertain, for the Vicar-Generals contented themselves with passing mentions of schoolhouses at Ballaugh — 'the schoolhouse is in repair' and Douglas 'very good repair', without further comment. Few of the parish churches escaped severe criticism of their state of repair, with broken seats and decaying chancels among the most frequent faults mentioned. The weekly visit to the schools urged in 1747 gave way in 1749 and 1751 to appeals to the clergy to perform the very basic quarterly visit enjoined by law. 'His Lordship likewise pressingly enjoins his clergy to visit the petty schools of their respective parishes according to the constitutions of 1703'.[55] A last Visitation under Wilson in 1754 commented as its predecessors upon the state of fabric in each parish, Ballaugh slipping to 'tolerable good repair' and contrasting with St. John's in 'very good order', but again omitting any reference to regularity and diligence in teaching and inspecting of schools. Rather surprisingly, the rectories for Bride and Andreas were in total ruin. If this were the fate of the official residences for the best paid clergy in the Island apart from the Bishop, it is less surprising that places of worship and schoolhouses were not the subject of great care. The Glebe House Act of 1734 had attempted to deal with the problem of ruinous parsonages, or in some cases total absence of any house at all, but with limited success.

CONCLUSION

Of the saintly life of Thomas Wilson, there can be no doubt. Weedon Butter, the biographer of Bishop Hildesley, Wilson's successor, wrote 'He . . . established schools . . . and founded parochial libraries . . . His virtues were, in short, so numerous, so amply displayed that he approved himself in every sense an inestimable blessing to the Isle of Mann, and an ornament to human nature. Venerable in his aspect, meek in all his deportment, his face illuminated with true Christian mildness, and his heart glowing with godlike philanthropy, he went about, like his Divine Master, doing good.' Ever since 1693 he had given away a fifth of all income 'for pious uses and particularly for ye poor', and by the end of his episcopate had increased this to over a half. In his writings and by example as well as exhortation he had displayed his true concern for the elementary education of the Manx children. He alone of all Manx bishops had sought to use the full machinery of church and secular law to make compulsory education a reality. Yet despite all his fine qualities, he unintentionally blighted Manx basic education for well over a hundred years. Barrow's clear intention had been for the clergy to give to the petty schools the benefits of their own learning obtained at university or Academic School by undertaking the teaching themselves, receiving in return the fruits of the Impropriate Fund and King's Bounty. Breaking this link openly and officially in the 1704 Constitutions, Wilson had put the petty schools into the charge of lay masters and mistresses, without being able to ensure remuneration adequate to attract any person of reasonable education to undertake the positions. Even had there been no failure in receiving the fruits of the Impropriate Fund, the schoolteachers would still have received only a pittance, while the clergy enjoyed a steadily rising income as the leases expired. Even after 1736 they were cushioned in a way that the schoolteachers were not, and when the dispute was eventually settled, continued to accept the fruits of the Fund largely free of any corresponding duties. Churlish though it may appear to criticise such a saintly man, Wilson's long term influence on Manx education in the petty schools was for worse rather than for better.

THE AGE OF WILSON
ELEMENTARY EDUCATION — THE SAVIOUR SOWS THE SEEDS OF DECAY

1. Derby MS 1719/4. Sacheverell to Derby.
2. C. Cruttwell. *Life of the Right Reverend Father in God. Thomas Wilson*, Bath 1782. 31.
3. Licence dated Sept. 23 1698.
4. Liber Placitorum. Oct. 23 1699.
5. Ibid.
6. Ibid.
7. Liber Causarum 1702.
8. Liber Placitorum. May 7 1698.
9. Ibid. Oct. 23 1699.
10. Ian R. Findley. *Education in Scotland.* David and Charles, Newton Abbot 1973. 12-13.
11. ed Wilbur Smith. *Theories of Education in Early America*, 1655-1819. Bobbs Merrill, Connecticut and New York, 1973. XXV.
12. Presentments 1704.
13. MS 802c. Convocation Book.
14. Statutes of the Isle of Man Vol. I 158.
15. George Waldron. *A Description of the Isle of Man*, 1731 Manx Society, Vol. XI.
16. MS 802c. Convocation Book, June 9 1720.
17. BC 76.
18. Bishop Wilson's *Memoranda Book*. April 22 1708.
19. Liber Causarum June 24 1714.
20. BC 76.
21. MS 802c. Convocation Book, June 6 1734.
22. MS 2169a Feb. 17 1717.
23. Liber Causarum Mar. 8 1722.
24. John Keble. *Life of the Right Reverend Father in God. Thomas Wilson*, DD Vol. 2. 868.
25. Liber Causarum June 4 1715.
26. BC 83.
27. Ibid 87.
28. *Educational Endowments* 1887.
29. Loose paper in St Matthew's File Sodor and Man Diocesan Office.
30. A. W. Moore. *Diocesan Histories; Sodor and Man* 192-207.
31. Wilson to Woods Feb. 15 1730.
32. BC II.
33. Wilson to Murray Aug. 4 1736.
34. Convocation Book May 1738.
35. Petition of May 27 1741.
36. C. E. Medhurst. *The Life of Lady Hastings.* B. Jackson, Leeds 1914. CH VIII.

37 Letter Feb. 6 1730.
38 BC 40.
39 Ibid 41.
40 A. W. Moore. *Op. cit* Vol. II, 511.
41 MS 802c Convocation Book 1740.
42 BC 63.
43 BC 94.
44 William & Constance Radcliffe. *A History of Kirk Maughold. 125.*
45 *John Keble. Op. cit.* Vol. 2 861.
46 BC 72.
47 Ibid.
48 William and Constance Radcliffe *Op. cit* 125.
49 John Keble *Op. cit.* Vol. 2 864.
50 *Peel Endowed Schools Report* 1896.
51 John Keble *Op. cit.* Vol. 2 966.
52 Howell T. Evans. *Modern Wales.* Hughes & Sons Cardiff 1938. 181
53 Convocation Book 1745.
54 Ibid.
55 Ibid 1751.

THE AGE OF WILSON — (2)
THE EXPANSION OF HIGHER EDUCATION FALTERS

THE SCHOOLS AT CASTLETOWN

Wilson's early years also saw energetic efforts to improve the efficiency of the grammar school and to make a reality of the Academic School as originally intended. As noted earlier, he disliked buildings acting as both church and school and almost immediately upon arrival he had made the old St. Mary's Chapel into a permanent school building, moving services to a new church nearby, the foundation stone being laid in 1698. The Liber Causarum includes the contracts whereby a number of dwelling houses were purchased, and articles agreed with Thomas Looney whereby he would put up a new church in their place, partly with materials from the old chapel. The remainder of St. Mary's was to be repaired "to fit it for two convenient schools" with seats for the masters of the grammar and petty schools, a writing desk, and forms for the pupils. Looney eventually received payment of £235.12.10 in 1704.[1] The two schools being under one roof was far from ideal, despite a new wing being added, and in 1708 the petty school went back to its original home, leaving the grammar school in sole possession. The attitude was taken that since the Grammar School benefited the citizens of Castletown, they should pay for improvements, by compulsion if necessary.

> "Whereas the Grammar School House of Castletown was, about two years ago, repair'd, glas'd and made much more commodious with a chimney in it, for the use of the scholars that are or shall hereafter be, educated at the school.
> And forasmuch as the voluntary contributions towards that work have not extended to discharge the expenses of it ... the churchwardens are ordered to collect an assessment from the inhabitants in and bordering the town to clear off the arears due to the several workmen."[2]

The wardens were allowed a shilling for their trouble, and the voluntary contributors justly exempted from the levy.

A. W. Moore wrote of these years that "The academic school at Castletown was now established in the old chapel, the grammar school being carried on in the same building and under the same headmaster".[3] This is precisely what did *not* happen. As had been originally intended, the positions of grammar school master and academic masters were separated. The intended candidate for academic master seems to have been John Kippax, Archdeacon of the Island since 1696.

> 'There is further intended him the Academicke Professor's place of fifty pounds a year (as soon as the sallery thereof can be conveniently settled either there or in England) for his encouragement to reside in the Island.'

However, all these blandishments, with the exemption from the Residence Act as well, failed to have the desired effect, and in 1700 all was resigned in favour of the Vicarage of Ormskirk. In the course of time, two appointments were eventually made. James Makon was appointed to the Grammar School, while William Ross from Musselborough in Scotland became Academic Professor, and he with the Academic Scholars found a home in another place dear to Wilson's heart, his library in Castletown.

An inventory taken at the surrender of Castle Rushen in 1651 to Parliament included 265 Great Books, 54 gilded, and many small books beside.[4] Shortly afterwards in 1657 a further 217 books, mostly religious, many in Latin, were sent over and there exists "a catalogue of the books sent from my Lord Ffayrefax for the library in the Isle of Man".[5] Whether such specialised books were for a public library as Moore assumed as opposed to the Castle Library is not clear. Barrow's will of 1679 made a reference to a library for the clergy he had intended to leave, but instead at the behest of Bridgeman left £100 to purchase a rent charge of five or six pounds, "to buy such books yearly as should be most convenient for the clergy".[6] The Derby family also gave their collection of books to form a combined collection, still housed in the library at Castle Rushen. Wilson wished to see a separate library building, and in 1706 bought a plot for this purpose. According to his biographer Crutwell, Wilson himself provided the greater part of the cost of £83, although the House of Keys found a new home on the lower floor. The upper floor provided the place where Ross and his academic students were able to study, removed from the distractions of the Grammar School. A suitable building had at last been provided under a learned man for Academic Study, but the hopeful "all and every person . . . willing or desirous to study, read, learn . . ." of the 1676 deed had remained for two decades contracted into a handful of ordinands.

Wilson's next effort was to remedy this position. While his library was in course of construction, Wilson sought to increase numbers by gaining help from outside the Island. In 1698 the Society for Promoting Christian Knowledge had been founded, and three years later the Society for the Propogation of the Gospel in Foreign Parts was started as an offshoot, in whose strategy Wilson was very interested. In 1707 he wrote a Memorial to the SPCK asking whether "the Isle of Man would not be the properest place wherein to educate, and out of which to make choice of, the plans for that mission", (the provision of clergy for the American colonies).[7] He pointed to strict discipline on the Island, the frugal condition of the young, so that a clergyman's role in America would satisfy their "utmost ambition", the close eye kept by the bishop, the seafaring tradition, and above all the Island's readiness for such a task.

For already at hand there was an "Academic School founded by the late Bishop Barrow and a Master with a Competeant salary, obliged to teach youths Logic, Moral Philosophy and Ecclesiastical History. These are educated for the service of the Church of Man." Wilson's plan was that a choice could be made from the Island's schools of youths "such as those who would in all likelihood be most serviceable to the Church", and they would grow up expecting to be sent abroad. Fifty pounds would be sufficient to encourage the Academic Master to teach four persons to prosecute their studies for ten pounds a year.

Wilson put forward the notion of a trial period, and the idea was in fact accepted by the SPG in 1711. However, the "lowness of the Society's funds" led to a decision being deferred about putting the scheme into practice.[8] A further reference was made the following year to "the offer of the Bishop of Man for setting on foot a sort of perpetual Seminary for Catechists and Missionaries within that Island", but nothing came of it. John Keble later wrote that had Wilson been dealing with men as far sighted as himself, "St. Augustine's at Canterbury and our recent Theological Colleges might have been happily anticipated in the Isle of Man a century and a half ago."[9]

In practice, the Bishop's own palace at Bishopscourt on the west coast, near Kirk Michael, fulfilled informally the wider role Wilson had intended for the Academic School. Although theology was studied by all, Wilson attracted as students a circle of young men, not all of whom were to be clergymen. The non-juror, Henry Dodwell, sent his son from Shottisbrook near Reading to live in with Wilson for example, although the Bishop, having tutored his own son until the age of seventeen, sent him to Redcar to a new foundation at Kirk Leatham of Sir William Turner.

As might be expected, Wilson took a keen interest in the Academic Students, whether at Castletown with Ross, or afterwards with himself at Bishopscourt. His *"Instruction to Academic Youth"* explained the general framework he expected, although he made it clear he had no intention of interfering with the day to day work of the Academic master.[10] Wilson wanted Theology supplemented not only by 'Logick, Metaphysicks and Ethicks', but also Mathematics, Geography, Astronomy and Natural Philosophy, following the path which John Locke in particular had indicated in *Thoughts on Education* of 1690 would be preferable to the narrower traditions of the past. Although Wilson left the choice of reading to Ross, he did recommend especially Law's *Of Christian Perfection,* the *Whole Duty of Man and the Life of God in the Soul of Man.* He also wanted the Greek New Testament read daily, with a chapter at least translated each afternoon and two sermons to be read and abridged each week, warning that "A habit of trifling, not resisted, will insensibly grow upon you."

Yet despite this concern for the Academical School, Wilson stopped short of attempting anything on the lines of Bridgeman's plans for Rushen Abbey, although resources at last were available. By 1705 through the offices of Willaim Quayle of Dublin, the money belonging to the Master's Fund, which had caused so much trouble, was at last gathered in, the total sum being £1,225.18.10. Not learning by past experience at all, the Trustees put out £650 once more in Ireland, a step which later years were to show as most imprudent. Governor and Bishops were asked to appoint fit persons to settle the claims of Holt, Locay (sic) and Shaw (now deceased) for past arrears. Ross, too, was to have back pay. ". . . the present Academick Master shall receive sixty pounds for his own use for the time past, as soon as he shall be legally admitted by the Bishop into the employment, and the proffitts of the six hundred and fifty pounds aforesaid ever after yearly."[11]

Allowing for incidental charges, there still remained a sum of £250 to be put towards premises for the Academic School. Governor Sacheverell had been a keen supporter of the fully fledged scheme as intended by Barrow, including lodging accommodation for the Students, whom Denton stated had lodgings in the Castle.

> "For as the finishing of the designs of Dr Barrow, late Bishop of St Asaph, would be of the great use, not only in building a library (towards which there are two hundred pounds in the hands of his executors) but some convenient lodgings for the academic youths who are forced to diet in public houses in the town which is very inconvenient."[12]

Sacheverell thought one thousand pounds was needed to be raised to complete the project, and later expressed his hope in a letter to Wilson in 1702 that "you may be the happy instrumernt of completing so necessary a work."[13] Wilson shrank from such a lavish scheme, choosing to use the £250 surplus to broaden the second tier of education by establishing a grammar school at Douglas, to be considered in detail later, rather than expend the money on the Academic School. This diversion, nominally by the trustees, now Peter Legh of Lyme and Frederick Cholmondeley of Vale Royal, but almost certainly under Wilson's direction, was an act which marked the abandonment of the fully fledged Academic School, and displayed a cavalier attitude towards the fund, clearly for the Academic School, and none other. It is hard to escape the conclusion that a gross breach of trust had taken place.

At Wilson's door may be laid the blame for failure to fulfil Barrow's dream of an Academic School with its own premises. Yet on past performance Wilson might justly wonder if the Island had the human resources to justify and support such an institution. His own modified scheme of library and master was as much as the Island demanded, and for over a century a handful of Academic Scholars alone constituted the third tier of education within the Island.

The trustees of the Student's Fund also contined to exercise a certain freedom. According to the testimony of George Waldron, an acerbic commentator on the Manx, Ross did not oversee all the training for those intended to be clergy. Waldron hinted strongly that all Barrow's efforts were a waste of time, diagnosing "innate ignorance" among the Manx people, proved to his own satisfaction by

> "... the little progress made in learning by those who have had the happy advantage of finishing their education in a Scotch or Irish college, which is commonly the case of such as are designed for Holy Orders."[14]

Wilson also sought to ensure that his clergy kept up their reading after they had left Bishopscourt on attaining a cure of souls. Dr. Thomas Bray, later Bishop of Maryland, had been a prime move in England in starting parochial libraries, a work taken over later by the SPCK, and Wilson communicated with him about similar provision for the Island. Only in Castletown and Douglas were there public libraries; in the parishes the books were for the clergy themselves, not for lending, after Bray's example in Maryland. (Parishioners were provided with Bibles, Prayer Books, and Wilson's own works.) By 1725 each parish library had thirty four books, while the minister's own books were, of course, in addition.[15] Even in the late Seventeenth Century, John Crellin of Arbory had possessed seventy one books, and Waldron's censures were probably far less deserved than when Barrow had arrived.[16] Henry Lowcay at Ballaugh, former master of the Grammar School, was remembered as "The Reverend pious and eminently learned Henry Lowcay MA", while even Waldron admitted the learning of his successor, William Walker, who had become rector in 1705. Although it is generally agreed there was a serious falling in the standard of clergy after the early years of the Eighteenth Century, Wilson's successor, Hildesley, pronounced himself well satisfied with his clergy on his arrival.

Of the two Castletown masters, Makon held also the post of Government Chaplain; indeed Ross was not ordained as deacon until 1708. Of their teaching little seems known, but their churchmanship led to charges of popery. When Makon was summoned by Wilson to the Cathedral to explain Roman views on absolution, Ross, who accompanied him, made a robust defence in which he stated that in some matters the doctrine of the two churches overlapped. Wilson agreed, declaring in his judgement of October 1718 there was "no reason to us appearing or known, to charge them with Popery or even being Popishly affected."[17]

The Academic School was also entangled in the dispute of Church and State which flared up after 1720. Ross, Makon and two Academic Students appeared at a court at St. John's in defence of a man called Thomas Harley, who had objected to Archdeacon Horrobin's theology. When Horrobin was eventually suspended for his views on the sufficiency of works, and for his actions over a case of slander, by Convocation in 1722, an ecclesiastical matter suddenly developed into something more serious. For Horrobin made his appeal, not to the Archbishop of York, but to the Governor, claiming that as his Chaplain, he was exempt from normal ecclesiastical jurisdiction. Soon Church and State were very deeply divided, principally over the Church's extensive spiritual discipline, which hitherto had caused no problems, but which could be thought of as interfering with secular rights and powers. In the course of the acrimonious dispute, Earl James sent *"The Independent Whig"* to Castletown Library, a publication which scoffed at holy orders and claimed that religion served only ecclesiastics. Ross refused to accept it, stating he would sooner take poison.[18] In turn Wilson ordered Ross to officiate in Castletown during the Archdeacon's suspension, a move countered by the Governor closing the Chapel and fining Wilson and the Vicar-Generals, casting them into Castle Rushen as prisoners when they would not pay. Although the Privy Council found for Wilson, the Spiritual Courts lost their former efficacy in the long run.

It is against this background that official interest in the Academic School should be weighed. Queries of Lord Derby in 1719 asking who were the trustees lay alongside those asking who appointed the bishop and vicar-generals. Wilson's answer was perhaps deliberately casual "As to the Academic School, I do suppose, (not having a copy of the Trust by me) that Mr. Cholmondeley of Vale Royal and Mr. Legh of Lime are the present Trustees."[19] Again when Wilson wrote that the Governor "sent for me to Castletown to meet him and the other trustees about the academic salary",[20] it is likely that Governor Horne was not acting from the highest of motives. He had given church livings to known profligates because they opposed Wilson, and was described by the Bishop as "most prejudiced against the Church, Churchmen in general, and in particular the laws and discipline of the Church."[21] The controversy spread to direction of the Academic School, Wilson taking a firm stand on the matter.

"Mr Taubman acquainted me that the Governor and Comptroller had sent for books from England for the academic youths and designed to pay for them out of the academic moneys. I told him I would not consent they should be paid for out of the moneys, and that they should read such books only as I or the Academic master should direct them."[22]

Although Wilson had refused to establish the Academic School in its glory, the year 1736 witnessed a marked withdrawal for the position he had established, whereby the Grammar and Academic Schools had different masters. While Ross was not certain that Makon had resigned, he had been asked in a petition from Castletown parents to take over as master of the Grammar School. Ross declared he would indeed "undertake the drudgery" with the aid of "three very good lads that are willing to assist me . . . I shall not take the labour of the Accademy youths for nothing, they shall have a part of what I receive which will be some small help."[23] It was thus only in the latter part of Wilson's episcopate that Moore's remarks about the two schools having the same headmaster came true.

FINANCIAL PROBLEMS

As well as for the petty schools, the provision of higher education was threatened by the financial difficulties when the death of James, Earl of Derby, without male heir meant that the Lordship of Man passed to James, Duke of Atholl, who, as has been seen, exercised his legal right to claim the tithes which formed the Impropriate Fund. Wilson wrote to Governor Murray about the plight not only of his clergy but also of the "free school in Castletown and thirteen petty schools in several parishes: which schools must be utterly laid down, there be no other provision for them."[24] Only the willingness of the Duke of Athol to allow the tithes to be paid as of old — at interest — until the legal case was concluded prevented ruination of the grammar school too. Wilson also feared that the loss of the tithes stopped parents from educating their children for the Church, and was forced in 1751 to obtain permission to ordain deacons at twenty one.[25] Even before the so-called 'Eviction', Wilson was not happy with the quality of ordinands. In 1728 he confessed himself awarding an Academic Scholar's place to a boy "very backward both in Greek and Latin" with great reluctance.

It was not until 1751 that Lord Chancellor Hardwick found for the Bishop and Archdeacon representing the clergy and schoolmasters, and ordered the Earl of Derby to pay from the rents of the Lancashire estates the value of the tithes and Rectories from which the clergy had been evicted. The report which followed this order took until 1757, and only in 1758 were the back claims paid up, and the sum of £219.7.10½ (in Manx money nearly £260) assured each year to the Bishop and Archdeacon.

During this same period there was equally grave doubt about the safety of the Academic Master's Fund. The laying out of the money which had caused such problems earlier continued to be a cause of worry. Legh and Cholmondeley did not watch the fund closely; the remark of Wilson that he supposed them to be the trustees did not indicate his awareness of zeal on their part. The £650 had been invested in blocks of £400, £200 and £50 under the care of one John Walker, but a letter of 1736 admitted there was "trouble in so many divisions".[26] When Vicar-General Wilks was sent over to Ireland to sort things out and reported he found Walker elusive, needing to threaten his arrest to recover the £250 which had caused special concern.[27] The £400 share was on a long life with twenty years to run, but the £250 was in Walker's hands without security. For the success of his threats, Wilks was given £5 by Wilson in 1746, but a few years later the major portion of the fund was suffering from the same lack of security. A long lease of 45 years made in March 1722 to Jonathan Murgitrode was approaching its end and now quite inadequate security for the £400 lent to him. There was a danger that his widow Jane would not be able to repay the principal, and Wilk's friend in Dublin, Councillor Kean, had to agree to an immediate payment of £100 and the remainder at £100 a year. Wilks trusted Kean, but was worried about Kean's declining health. By the time Nicholas Harris took over Kean's task, Mrs. Murgitrode's offer of fifty pounds with interest was considered of doubtful value. Wilks thought her "intentions are good, but question her ability".[28] The other £250 was lent to Samuel Batter on the security of another lease. For his part, Batter was equally cautious and refused an attorney's receipt, insisting that Legh's own signature be attained.

Coupled together, the 'eviction' by the Duke of Athol and the precarious state of the Academic Master's Fund meant that Ross, in theory enjoying two reliable sources of income, in fact had none, needing to rely on the Duke's grace while the suit against Derby went on, and on the efforts of Wilks in Ireland.

Financial problems were compounded by personal ones, as Ross grew older amd more infirm, a process probably hastened by his mode of life. As early as 1731 Wilson had written to him sharply about "drinking to an unbecoming excess", and a dozen years later the

Bishop was concerned about the fabric and master alike. The failure to provide from the outset for repairs and pensions now began to show its effects, although the financial situation was such that had such provision been made, the effect would have been very slight, as funds would not have been available. "... the public school house of Castletown is falling into ruins to the gt concern of all such as have any regard to learning." Wilson felt a moderate sum could effect repairs and recommended recourse to voluntary contributions from parents of past and present scholars. The local vicar, Quayle of Malew, was told to call a vestry meeting and work out a method of repair, "that a school may be kept regularly in it." If the licensed master were too old or infirm, a proper and well qualified usher, with salary, should be appointed.[29] It is clear from later references that little if anything at all was done in response to this letter of 1744. The clergy themselves were asked at Convocation to contribute to the cost of repairs in 1744, and a sum of £4.18.5 was raised and paid to Ross — unable after 1741 to attend Convocation in person — John Quayle of Malew and Paul Crebbin of Santon, so that they might undertake 'firm, decent and substantial' repairs. The following year the clergy contributions were classed as 'having fallen short', and a further levy made to attempt to expedite the incomplete task. No clergyman's contribution, however, exceeded five shillings. The conflict of efficiency and compassion came to a head in 1751, with a new Governor, Basil Cochrane, showing much sympathy with Ross.

> "Mr. Wood's of Ramsey I find is Indeavouring to Turn out old Mr. Ross from being Schoolmaster here. The Bishop I am told is Inclined to it which I think a cruile and barbarous Case as the poor man is in all probability fair dropping into his grave and as he has Lived with a fair and good character it is hard to disturb him."[30]

Cochrane offered to ride to the Bishop to prevent anything being done. "Old Ross knows nothing what is doing against him and I hope he will never be disturbed." The promise of Wilson that Ross would not be disturbed was gained, as Cochrane wrote in triumph to the Duke of Athol.[31] It is likely, however, that Wilson insisted that care be taken of the School in some way, for Ross' daughter wrote how "for three years before his death (he) grew very Feeble and Helpless and was obliged to pay an usher for taking care of the School."[32] Before having to make this payment, debts had mounted, "The small living that he had as Academick Professor being scarse sufficient for that purpose", and certainly there were no funds available for repair of the schoolhouse. The death of Ross on October 9th 1754 marked the nadir of the Castletown School in the Eighteenth Century.

A DIVERSION TO DOUGLAS

Bishop Wilson himself passed to his rest in 1755, aged 92, and in his last years, which co-incided with the dotage of Ross, the Bishop had the consolation of knowing that his own place of higher education was in a happier state.

Although Castletown was the capital of the Island, the excellence of the harbour at Douglas had led it to be, in the words of Denton, the "place of the greatest resort in the whole Island, because the haven is commodious" and Wilson acknowledged it "much the richest, the best market and most populous of any in the whole island."[33] The 1726 census put its population at 810 to Castletown's 785. As part of his wide-ranging church building on the Island, Wilson desired to provide a new chapel for Douglas, and began to build on the quayside St. Matthew's Chapel. (The Parish Church of Douglas was two miles away at Braddan.) The chaplain for Douglas was also the schoolmaster, and Wilson diverted in 1705 for his maintenance £250 (Irish) from the accumulated funds of the Academic Master's Fund.

> "Know ye, that whereas in the late vacancy of the Academic School, within this Isle, the interest of the money laid out in Ireland for that end did amount to a considerable sum, and the Trustees and Feofees in trust appointed for the same having thought fit to assign the sum of two hundred and fifty pounds of the said interest which with the exchange of the money from Ireland makes up to the sum of two hundred and seventy pounds, for and towards the maintenance of a person to officiate as Chaplain and Schoolmaster in the said town of Douglas; Therefore, I, Thomas, Lord Bishop of the said Isle, do hereby nominate and appoint John Stephenson of Balladoole Gent, Ewan Christian of Lezayre, Gent, Mr. John Murray and Phil Moore of Douglas, Merchants, with the Vicar of Braddan for the time being, and the Chaplain or Schoolmaster of the said town of Douglas, to be Trustees for the well securing and laying out to interest the said sum of two hundred and seventy pounds for the use and purpose aforesaid."[34]

The Trustees were given power to appoint fresh trustees when their number decreased, but Wilson was most careful to put the appointment of the Chaplain/Schoolmaster in his own hands.

> "... reserving nevertheless to myself and successors Bishops of this Isle, the right of election and nomination of the said Chaplain and Schoolmaster, unto whom the interest of the said sum ... will become due and payable."[35]

(This unambiguous statement of the Bishop's right to appoint was unfortunately not followed by one of the trustees, the merchant Philip Moore, when he made provision for a further Grammar School at Peel, as will be seen.) Allowing the Douglas Chaplain, the cestui qui trust, to be one of the trustees meant at least one trustee had a vested interest in seeing the trust dutifully administered.

In the Deed of 1706 the status of the school was not mentioned, but the earlier deed of 1705 which authorised the use of the Academic master's Fund was quite specific.

> "Secondly, That two hundred and fifty pounds bee put out to interest upon the like good security, for the use of Grammar Schoole in the town of Douglas."[36]

However, it seems likely that the Grammar School was grafted on to the petty school already in existence and was not a new separate foundation. Douglas had been selected in 1675 as one of the places to recieve the Royal Bounty for its petty school,[37] and this payment after the establishment of St. Matthew's was made to the Grammar School master. Though Wilson very much stressed the grammar aspect, the Book of Charities in 1827 still listed the Royal Bounty money for the petty school as part of the £52 stipend of the Chaplain/Master which strongly suggests the integration of the two levels. As entry in Ballaugh parish Register shows that before the events of 1705-06

William Walker was in Douglas as Chaplain and Schoolmaster. Although George Waldron denigrated the Manx clergy, he admitted there was one clergyman who was indeed a man of letters, invariably taken to be Walker, and in Douglas he may well have introduced an element of higher learning. However there seems no ground for A. W. Moore's statement that Wilson in 1700 appointed him to "the mastership of Douglas Grammar School."[38]

In Wilson's order of priority, the petty school element came low down, even to be dispensed with in certain circumstances.

"... all the youths in the highest class viz such as read Greek shall duly pay two shillings and sixpence a quarter to the said Master and that all such as read the classics in Latin shall pay two shillings a quarter and that all other pay eighteen pence the quarter, except such as learn English, which shall be obliged to pay only twelve pence a quarter, as long as he shall think fit to teach them but if his grammar school shall increase to such a number as that it will be inconvenient for him to attend both, it shall be his own choice whether he will teach English or not."[39]

The words "for and towards" in the 1706 Deed implied the hope that others would come forward and make a contribution, for at 6% interest, there would be only £16 to support the Chaplain/Schoolmaster. Archdeacon Kippax gave thirty pounds and according to an early entry in St. Matthew's Register an investment in cattle proved successful, yielding £300 English, which was worth in Ireland, where it was invested, £330. Phil Moore, one of the Trustees, one of the Island's leading patrons of education and "a considerable benefactor to the School and Chapel",[40] made a generous donation of £100 Irish, and two smaller legacies from the Murray family added a further £40.11.6. Another Trustee, John Murray, , made the sum up to a round £500 Irish by giving £29.8.6, the new round sum being let on mortgage in Ireland by Phil Moore at 6%, and thus producing the reasonable amount of £30 a year by 1734[41] Moore, while duly assigning the mortgage to the Trustees, reserved a power to apply the interest from his £100 as he should direct. The Chaplain would receive only half, the other half going to a petty schoolmaster obliged to teach eight poor scholars nominated by Moore or an appointed Trustee.[42] This provision was less the case of a grammar school bringing in its own new preparatory department than a measure which enabled a dual function in danger of being lost to be effectively maintained.

Having seen the new church safely built, Wilson turned to providing a suitable separate place for the school, and found help from a Dublin alderman, a Manx native, who provided a house in exchange for the perpetuation of his name for posterity.

"I, Wm Dickson, of the city of Dublin, Alderman, at the instance of the Right Rev. Father in God, Thomas, Lord Bishop of Sodor and Mann, do, out of the good inclination I have to promote any charitable and public good within the Isle of Man, and especially in the Town of Douglas, the place of my nativity, have given ... unto the said Rt Rev Thomas, Lord Bishop of Sodor and Man, and to such undertakers or trustees as his Lordship and I shall hereafter nominate and appoint, a certain dwelling-house and garden,situate, lying, and being in the town of Douglas aforesaid, commonly called Dickson's House, of the yearly chief or lord's rent of 14d, with all ways ... for the convenience of a School-house, to be called Dickson's School-house, and an appartmt. for a Schoolmaster, to be built and erected there."[43]

Although the wording of this gift of 1714 is slightly ambiguous, it appears that a new school was erected on the site, the building costs being largely defrayed by William Murrey, merchant; he appeared to be in no hurry to receive full payment. When Alderman William Quayle, who had done such yeoman service for the Academic Master's Fund at the start of the century, left £50 in his will to "Mr John Murrey, of the Isle of Man. Mercht., in Douglas . . . for the use of the School of Douglas, as the Lord Bishop of Mann and said Murrey shall think fit," the money was used for improving the schoolhouse rather than paying off more of the debt. A memorandum in the Episcopal Registry recorded that

> "The Bequesyt of £50, (being Irish currency, the advance of about £3 5s 2d upon the exchange of the money,) is to be applied to the use of the School-house, in plastering and finishing the same, as shall be found necessary this 25 day of June 1736."[44]

This was the type of bequest so desperately needed by the Island's endowed schools, and indeed by those of the mainland to a great extent. In none of the Island foundations was there any systematic approach to the problem of repairs, which was bound to arise in the course of time. Both the original founder's money and later bequests were nearly always applied to funding the master's salary, and unless specifically bound by the terms of a bequest, masters were not likely to undertake repairs even of a modest nature, and certainly could not afford those on a major scale. In Douglas, William Murrey, not having been paid in his lifetime for his school building, generously wrote off the debt in his will of 1756.

> "And whereas there is an arrear of money due to me on the building and finishing of the School-house and vault in the said town of Douglas, amounting to one hundred and fifty pounds; I do therefore altogether acquit and discharge the said arrear, and do order that the said vault now in possession be given up into the hands of the Rev Phil Moore, Chaplain of the said town, and his successors, for the uses and purposes mentioned in the original Deed of Gift."[45]

The list of Chaplain/Schoolmasters associated with St. Matthew's started with Samuel Robinson in 1708 and Peter Lancaster in 1711, but the first lengthy tenure came in theory with Anthony Halsall in 1717. He was nominally in charge until 1732, but spent more and more time in Liverpool, and became master of a grammar school in Crosby. His successor, Philip Moore, wrote of him in St. Matthew's Register as having "many unhappy disputes both of a public and private nature on his hands and was often abroad."[46]

After the short period of Thomas Birkett (1732-1736) the long rule of Philip Moore himself began. Born in 1705, he was himself a product of Douglas Grammar School under first Lancaster, then Halsall. Wilson recorded on November 10th 1726 "I examined Philip Moore in order to an Academic Scholar's place against the next election and found him fit". After two years at Castletown under Ross and some months at Bishopscourt with Wilson, he was made deacon in 1729, but not priested until 1739. Although Wilson apointed him to the plum living of the Rectory of Ballaugh in 1751, Moore stayed in Douglas, using a curate for his northern living. As masters went, Moore would be very comfortably off indeed.

For the school itself, Wilson made it clear as early as 1716 that Douglas should look after the school through its own efforts. By appointing Lancaster, a man "in every way qualified", Wilson felt he had done all that should be expected of him, and suggested that two collectors appointed by the ordinary should secure voluntary contributions from the townsfolk of Douglas who had no children at the school.[47] Again in 1745 he advised Moore to raise fifty pounds to effect a perpetual security on his income, but he himself would offer nothing for the school when he had so many demands, although his generosity was exceptional and over half his income went to charitable purposes.[48] "I cannot do much for one particular school especially when so many rich people and their posterity are likely to reap a perpetual reward."[49]

While Douglas Grammar School received no further major bequests in the lifetime of Wilson, at least it was blessed with a competent master who enjoyed his own independent salary, the Royal Bounty being but a small fraction, and as such was in a far happier state than the Grammar School at Castletown. Although hardly proper in legal terms, Wilson's diversion of some of the Academic Master's funds had been justified in practice by keeping alive the grammar school tradition on the Island.

THE PROPOSED CENTRAL SCHOOL

Yet by the time of Wilson's death, there should have been in existence already another well endowed school, founded through individual generosity, for the purpose of higher education. In the will of the patron of St. Matthew's, the wealthy Douglas merchant Philip Moore, dated August 3rd 1746, he bequeathed

> "... unto the Right Rev. the Lord Bishop and 24 Keyes of this Isle for the time being, Five Hundred Pounds British ... in trust for the use hereafter mentioned, viz., considering what great use and benefit a proper Schoole for the educating of youth in some convenient place, as near the centre of this Island as may be thought most proper, the Interest of which said sum of five hundred pounds to be paid after my decease, unto a proper Schoolemaster, qualified to teach Latin, and such other learning as may fit youth for the service of the country in Church or State ... hoping that their (the Trustees) due care and interest, and by the good and charitable donation of other well disposed persons at some time hereafter, such a foundation may be made as to encourage a Master of Arts, or some other well qualified man of learning, to reside and keep a Free Schoole with this Island for the purposes before mentioned.[50]

Although as with Douglas Grammar Schoole there was hope of help from future patrons of education, the whole of the interest of this endowment too went to the master. The only allowance for costs otherwise was before the master was appointed. His son, Philip Moore junior, was by the terms of the will to pay interest at 5% to the trustees until the capital sum was handed over, and

> "... until a proper Schoolemaster may be found and fixed in the said Schoole, the interest of the said five hundred pounds may be applyed to the building of a Schoole-house or other conveniences, as the said Trustees or a majority of them, shall think most necessary."

Although the will was proved as early as November 1746, the loose wording about the central convenient place led to delays which greatly irritated the Moore family. The reason for the wording was explained in a pamphlet that Philip Moore junior had printed in 1758. His father had indeed "used all means in his power to purchase a small Farm or Estate in Kirk Marown known by the name of Collingil and planned to build an House and othe Conveniences fitting for a School and Schoolmaster", but his attempt had proved fruitless, and he had turned his attention to Peel.[51] His choice fell on houses belonging to a relative, James Cowl, and to avoid any family awkwardness employed the Rev James Wilks, as a third party, "an indifferent person" to do the bargaining. When there was still a five pound gap between the asking price and the predetermined offer, Wilks sought Moore's agreement to the additional sum. Unfortunately within four days Philip Moore died and the deal was not concluded.

Others, however, were not prepared to accept Peel as the obvious choice for the endowment. Bishop Wilson himself thought Kirk Michael was "the best place in the whole Island for the school", offering to add £50 if it were sited there to the endowment.[52] This offer of 1748 did not find much favour with his fellow trustees, the Keys, some of whom thought the endowment a God-send for the troubled school at Castletown. George Moore, another son of the donor, strongly resisted this move, denying that his father, fully knowing the Castletown school, had any intention of increasing "the emolument of any school in Castletown." He compared the Keys' notion with someone leaving money for a bridge at Ballesally (Ballasalla) finding it built at Kirk St Ann (Santan). He further denied the right of the Keys to select a site. "No majority of them seems implied... sufficient or necessary for the appointment of the Scite of the School."[53] He besought Bishop and Keys that their Condescension might support, their Pity relieve and their Kindness indulge his filial efforts to show the "Place at Peeltown should be made choice of, preferable to any other spot in this Isle." But by this time Wilson was already dead, without having had the pleasure of witnessing the generosity of Moore translated into practical terms in the shape of an established grammar school for Peel.

PROBLEMS AT RAMSEY

In the most northerly of the four towns, Ramsey, the age of Wilson saw more problems than progress for its embryonic Grammar School, concerning in particular its endowment, masters and housing.

From the start, the endowment of ten pounds which gave the major share of income to the master was precarious; as early as 1710 Bishop Wilson feared that was totally lost. A visit to Cholmondeley at Warrington "about the £10 he is to pay to Ramsea School" achieved no lasting result, with continued evasion leading to another complaint from Wilson in 1713.[54] Yet a note in *Episcopalia* in 1721 revealed the Bishop's most awkward position. It was one thing for Thomas Cholmondeley himself to tell Wilson that £200 had been put into his hand either by Barrow or Bridgeman by Barrow's direction, but it was another matter to prove this legally. "I cannot find where the bond is after all my search." At the same time the other source of income for the school, the Royal Bounty, could not be claimed to be a reliable and regular emolument. Indeed the master of Ramsey seems to have the worst of both worlds on occasions, with the existence of the Cholmondeley ten pounds being made a reason for Ramsey School being put at the back of the queue when the Royal Bounty was finally received. At the 1749 Convocation for instance, the Vicars-General reported that all masters had been paid — with the exception of no less than eleven quarters due to the petty school at Ramsey. At the specified rate of three pounds a year, this sum owed totalled the not inconsiderable amount of £8.5.0.[55]

For most of Wilson's reign, there was at least a welcome continuity in teaching, with the Knipe family giving nearly forty years of unbroken service. Instead of an ordained chaplain, who would depart after a couple of years to take a living when one fell vacant, the Parish of Maughold relied for most of its services at Ballure Chapel on a Reader, who could take the morning and evening prayer services, providing regular worship for the town of Ramsey. As in other parishes the post of Clerk and that of Schoolmaster could be easily combined, so the offices of Reader and Schoolmaster were also a natural combination. James Knipe, the elder, seems to have served satisfactorily from the turn of the century until his death in 1738. The advanced standard of education offered at Ramsey is almost certainly demonstrated by the books listed in his inventory of goods, with thirty eight books in English outnumbered by fifty three in Latin and Greek.[56] The description of the latter as "Dictionaries" is puzzling, unless some of them were Latin primers. James Knipe the younger, succeeded his father, and his licence from Wilson referred explicitly to his teaching "a Latin and English school". As the school still functioned as a petty school, the term "English school" almost certainly applied to this lower level rather than indicating a conscious attempt at a wider curriculum at the higher level. Unfortunately the cause of education was severely hindered by the derangement of the new master, which caused the Vicar of Maughold to declare that his school was useless. Wilson, while mindful of "the great inconvenience the town labours under", thought it only just to give his licensed master a personal hearing. A sad history of neglect and unseemly behaviour was revealed, forcing Wilson to conclude that Knipe was indeed much disordered in his intellect and incapable of instructing children. The parents of Ramsey had already withdrawn their children; they "do absolutely refuse to commit them to the tuition of a person who is guilty of very silly and extravagant actions." Accordingly in July 1740 Wilson formally pronounced Knipe as being incapable of acting as schoolmaster any longer: "We therefore declare his licence void and the school vacant." With the speedy appointment of Henry Callister "to teach school in Ramsey", this sad episode appeared to be over.[57]

Wilson, however, had not allowed for the perversity of the local clergy and people. Callister wrote to Wilson complaining that Knipe was continuing to teach in the Chapel of Ballure, and neither the Vicar of Maughold or his wardens appeared to care. Wilson marvelled at their indifference after creating such a fuss earlier, commenting "And if they shall want (lack) a regular school, they may thank themselves." Nevertheless he launched the full weight of his episcopal authority against Knipe; "Mr. Knipe has nothing to do to go into the chapel nor to teach school, nor to keep any book belonging to it." The disillusioned Callister, however, moved first to Douglas, and then across the Atlantic to Maryland.[58] To fill the vacancy, Wilson looked to Castletown, and appointed Thomas Woods, the son of the John Woods who himself had been an Academic Youth before becoming master at Peel and then for a brief spell the acting Academic Master in the Sixteen Nineties. His licence of 1743 made clear the dual role of the school.

"These are to authorise you, Mr. Thomas Woods, one of the Academic Youths of the Isle, to teach a Grammar School in the town of Ramsey, as also to instruct the children committeed to your care in learning the English tongue and in good pious manners."[59]

The reference to having to learn English tongue is a reminder that over two thirds of the population spoke Manx as their tongue. The neglect of so many petty schools at this period, about which Wilson complained at the Convocation of 1747, was bound to make the task of the schools offering more advanced education far more difficult. Whether pupils were drawn from other schools of the north of the Island to receive the benefits of Wood's classical learning is not known. Woods was ordained deacon in 1745, and remained as Chaplain and Master until his preferment to the living of Maughold in 1754. After his departure, Daniel Gelling and Daniel Nelson followed in quick succession.

Although the advanced education at Castletown and Douglas had been given at first in the town chapels, the provision of a new church for Castletown and of Dickson's House in Douglas had given Wilson the satisfaction of seeing the dual purpose arrangement come to an end early in his episcopate. Yet despite Wilson's well known dislike of school being taught in a church, Ramsey did not receive a proper school building in his lifetime. Nor could it be said that Ballure Chapel itself was an adequate place for a school for much of the time. When Wilson arrived on the Island, fines at Chapter Courts were being put towards repairs, and a full assessment was needed in 1706 to pay for major works on the church. Yet only six years later James Knipe was pressing for an assessment to maintain the chapel, and also to pay his stipend as Reader.[60] The townspeople of Ramsey may have considered Knipe's schoolmaster's salary sufficient to excuse them from their own obligations. By the Seventy Forties, a petition to Wilson declared the "Chappell is in a most ruinous condition" and even claimed it was too far from the town. After Wilson forbade the use of the chapel in 1742, an appeal was successfully launched for rebuilding, invoking the aid of mainland as well as insular subscribers. In the spring of 1745 Wilson wrote to William Murrey that with the help of Lewhellin (sic), a Ramsey merchant, a new chapel was being built, and that a list of subscribers had been sent to Anthony Halsall in Liverpool in the hope that the former master of Douglas Grammar School would raise money there. Regulations were drawn up putting responsibility for upkeep of the church on those who were allocated seats.[61] As in the case of Patrick Church, the keeping of the school in the restored building was strictly forbidden. Despite the repairs being so extensive that there was a fresh consecration, the floor was described in 1757 as "not in repair". Two years later an attempt to raise an assessment ran into difficulties, and a patching job was undertaken "so Chapel had best be secured from water flowing in".[62] Where Woods taught after his arrival when the old church was still "ruinous" or whether the injunction not to use the church as a school was observed is unknown. It needed the arrival of John Crellin as Chaplain in 1761 to herald a new start in the history of Ramsey School.

CONCLUSION

At the time of Wilson's death in March 1755 at the great age of ninety two, the state of higher education in the Island was almost as gloomy as that at elementary level. In Castletown a Grammar School and an Academic School functioning separately with their own master and Academic Professor respectively had been replaced by a situation where a senile master, deprived of income from both of his supposed sources and forced to borrow from the Duke of Atholl, was quite incapable of running a school, whose premises in any case were in a state of ruin. After nine years had elapsed there was no sign of any agreement where the new grammar school endowed under the will of Philip Moore would be established. The grammar school in Ramsey depended upon an endowment which was irregularly paid and was probably still housed in a chapel in as bad a state as the school in Castletown. Only in Wilson's own endowed foundation in Douglas under Philip Moore as master was there any cause for satisfaction. Yet if only the venerable bishop had known, the second half of the century would see the Golden Age of the Island's grammar schools, and indeed see them joined by a fifth institution for advanced learning of a specialised nature.

THE AGE OF WILSON
THE EXPANSION OF HIGHER EDUCATION
REFERENCES

1. Liber Causa 1704.
2. Ibid Nov 4 1714.
3. A. W. Moore, A History of the Isle of Man, Vol. I, 511.
4. William Cubbon, Island Heritage, 259.
5. A. W. Moore, Op. cit. Vol. I, 302.
6. Athol Papers, 136/4.
7. Minutes of APCK, May 12 1707.
8. Ibid, Apr. 12 1711.
9. John Keble, Life of the Right Reverend Father in God Thomas Wilson DD, Vol. I, 250.
10. Thomas Wilson, Instructions to an Academick Youth, Crutwell's Works 1st Edition, Bath 1781, 469.
11. BC 27, Deed of Apr 9 1705.
12. Sacheverell Op. cit. 13.
13. Ibid.
14. George Waldron, A Description of the Isle of Man, 17.
15. J. P. Ferguson, The Parochial Libraries of Bishop Wilson, Shearwater Press, Douglas, 1973.
16. David Craine, Manx Clerical Life 1600-1800 Proc. of IOMNHAS Vol. V, 368.
17. John Keble, Op. cit. Vol. I, 381.
18. Ibid, 472.
19. BH, 4438C.
20. Thomas Wilson, Sacra Privata, Feb 11 1728.
21. A. W. Moore, Op. cit. Vol. I, 499.
22. Keble, Op. cit. Vol. I, 476, Oct 9 1729.
23. Athol Papers X13/26, Letter Aug 25 1736.
24. Wilson to Murray, Aug 4 1736.
25. Keble, Op. cit, 741 f.
26. MD 436, 20/7.
27. Ibid 20/11 May 10 1745.
28. MD 436 20 June 9 1731.
29. Ibid, Mar 9 1744.
30. Athol Papers X13/26, Dec 23 1751.
31. Ibid X7/1.
32. BH 3594, July 17 1759, Petition of Grissel Ross.
33. Thomas Wilson, History of the Isle of Man, 102.
34. BC 12, Jan 20 1706.

35 Ibid.
36 Ibid 27, Apr 9 1705.
37 Ibid 7.
38 A. W. Moore, Manx Worthies, 22.
39 Bishop Wilson's Register 1716.
40 Sodor and Man Diocesan Office, St. Matthew's Register, 173.
41 Ibid 172.
42 BC 113, Deed of Apr 9 1714.
43 St. Matthew's File, Deed of Apr 9 1714.
44 Ibid, June 25 1736.
45 St. Matthew's Register, 196.
46 Ibid, 29.
47 Ibid.
48 A. W. Moore, Diocesan Histories, Sodor and Man, 227.
49 St. Matthew's Register, 196.
50 BC 61, Will of Aug 3 1746.
51 Athol Papers X/46/5, Mar 4 1758.
52 June Ist 1748.
53 Athol Papers X/46/5.
54 Thomas Wilson Memoranda quoted Keble Op. cit. Vol. 2, 864.
55 MS 802C Convocation Book 1749.
56 Constance Radcliffe, Ramsey 1600-1800, 94.
57 July 10 1740.
50 John Keble, Op. cit. 865.
59 MD 436 2/16 Licence to John Woods.
60 Liber Causarum, June 6 1713.

THE LATE EIGHTEENTH CENTURY — THE PETTY SCHOOLS

It was hardly surprising that in the last years of Wilson his early drive and vigour had considerably abated, yet the Island was indeed fortunate in the choice of his successor, who brought those same qualities to all his work, and especially to the sphere of education in the Isle of Man. Mark Hildesley, a graduate of Trinity College, Cambridge, had served as domestic chaplain in turn to Lord Cobham and Lord Bolinbroke, before being presented to the livings of Hitchin and Holwell, where he had proved an industrious priest well aware of the importance of education. Installed in St. Germans Cathedral in August 1755, he quickly insisted that his clergy dressed soberly and appeared outdoors only with their wigs, but showed himself well aware of their problems, soon providing them with further financial security by the simple expedient of making the local incumbents the proctors to collect the bishop's own tithes, and thereby earning a small percentage for themselves. He further endeared himself to both clergy and schoolmasters not only by "expediting the payment of the Royal Bounty beyond what has hitherto been experienced", as a grateful letter of thanks put it, but also by zealously pursuing the long-standing lawsuit concerning the payment by the Earl of Derby of the collateral for the Impropriate Fund, bringing "our tedious suit to a happy and speedy conclusion."[1]

Although Lord Chancellor Hardwick had found in favour of the Manx Clergy in 1751 in the Court of Chancery, it was not until July 1757 that Master Eld finally made his long awaited report, ruling that in addition to the £1,442 paid already by the Earl of Derby in 1750, a further £1,132 should be paid for the period from the eviction up to 1751, making a total of £2,575. From 1751 onwards an annual sum of £217 was reckoned as due up to 1756, with a tiny increase of two pounds more thereafter, to be payable in future each Easter Monday. However, by no stretch of the imagination could it be said that the parochial schoolteachers did well out of these new arrangements. In percentage terms, an increase of 25% seemed generous compared with 1736, but in real terms the increase from two pounds to fifty shillings meant that from an annual distribution of over two hundred pounds, the total allocated to fifteen schools came to a trivial £37.10.0.[2] Even when the Royal Bounty, worth £2.11.0 in English money, for the six more fortunate schools, or the Lady Betty Hastings Charity money of under thirty shillings was added to the Impropriate Fund salary, paid for the first time for over twenty years in 1758, the fact remained that the petty schoolmaster still earned no more than the average farm labourer of the time, unless he was able to attract sufficient pupils whose parents paid quarterage.

THE MANX LANGUAGE FINDS A FRIEND

Even if Hildesley showed little willingness to redress the imbalance between clergy and schoolteachers, or undo the changes that Wilson had approved in his 1704 Constitutions, whereby the clergy were expected only to exercise a supervisory and not an actual teaching role in the schools, he soon showed not only an eagerness to see that the system was operated as it should have been, but also a remarkable sympathy with the Manx language. A visitation of the diocese was ordered in 1747, and although concerned primarily with the fabric of the churches, their contents and fitness for the worship of the Church, and the incumbents' parsonages and glebes, there appeared for the very first time specific questions on educational matters. In July the Vicar-General with the Episcopal Registrar visited the parishes at the rate of two or three a day, doubtlessly communicating to any of the clergy who were uncertain of the mind of the Bishop, his wishes about the second question which formed part of No. 10 of the Articles of Enquiry, whether the master or mistress taught prayers and the Catechism in Manx. Would they be lauded for the use of the native Manx tongue, or upbraided for needless meddling with a barbarous language? The replies made it clear that the Manx clergy knew that the attitude of this new bishop was very far removed from that of Barrow before or John Wesley afterwards. Lonan, Bride and Marown made faithful promises that Manx would be used in the future, although both Arbory and Onchan showed less anxiety to please in their replies of "I can't say they do" and "Not been accustomed" respectively. The question elicited the interesting fact that four of the schools had non-Manx teachers. In Kirk Michael "the Person who teaches our School is an English Gentlewoman who does not understand the manks, and consequently can't teach them in that language", while in the next parish but one, neither school had a Manx teacher: "The Master of the parish school at Lezayre Church and the Master of the School at Sulby are both foreigners and therefore unable to teach then in Manks." At Jurby too, "our man is not able" was the reason given. In fact only three parishes were able to state that such tuition was given in the language of the people, with Ballaugh providing the answer which probably gave most satisfaction to Hildesley: "The Master of our Petty School carefully do's".[3] While it is unlikely that Hildesley had any intention of removing the teaching of English from the petty schools, both pastor and educator in him realised the artificiality and difficulty of approaching reading and writing through the medium of what was to most a foreign language.

If, however, the Manx tongue were the most fitting means for educating the Island's children, there was still the problem of providing tools for the purpose. Wilson had made a start on the translation of the Bible into Manx with St. Matthew's Gospel, published in 1748 long after the work had been completed, but Hildesley was surprised to find little else had been attempted: "What is very remarkable, there is no grammar, or spelling, or any other book in the Manx tongue, excepting the Gospel of St. Matthew, and some few tranlations of the Catechism." Hildesley resolved to make good such deficiencies, and in the 1758 Convocation announced his attention of having the Catechism printed by itself so that the youth of the diocese might receive copies and learn it in their own tongue. He urged the clergy to do their best to improve the use and practice of Manx, and in 1761 declared the use of Manx was only reasonable, even for young clerks "Lately called out from a Town-School education", denouncing the "flagrant absurdity of the reverse."[4] Upon the completion of a translation of selected Psalms into Manx, Hildesley forbade the use of more than one English psalm in the Manx-speaking areas. This approving attitude towards the native language received the full support of Archbishop Drummond of York, who commended the idea of the more experienced clergy proceeding to translate the rest of the Scriptures and Liturgy. By March 1764 the Gospels in Manx were produced, closely followed by the rest of the New Testament. Books of the Old Testament were allotted to the clergy in 1767, and the whole project was completed just before Hildesley's death in 1772. Printing the Liturgy, Scriptures, and other books of devotion such as *Ferrence Chreestee* or *The Christian Monitor'* was an expensive business, made possible only by generous donations to the SPCK, with Hildesley himself giving over five hundred pounds.[5]

With this provision for the very first time of tools for learning in Manx and the all-important support of the Bishop, it was not surprising that the answers to the same second part of Article 10 in Hildesley's second visitation of 1766 showed marked differences from those elicited in 1757. Instead a mere three, no less than thirteen schools replied in the affirmative to "Do those Masters or Mistresses (who are able) teach Prayers and Catechism in Manx?. The promises of Lonan, Bride and Marown made in 1757 had all been kept. Bride for instance replied that "The Clerk, who was is the present Master, teaches his Scholars their Catechism in Manx." In Rushen, the Rev. Nicholas Christian, relieved of his teaching duties, reported that his master taught in Manx most carefully, while there was almost an apologetic air about the reply from Braddan, by now the sole parish to have a teacher unable to speak the language, with its stress on the "particular care of the children, who are taught to say their Prayers and Catechism".[6] The tide appeared to be flowing strongly in favour of the Manx language, and the language of the home for the first time stood a chance of becoming the medium of instruction.

Yet far too much depended on Hildesley's own zeal and authority. Once his influence was removed, the old tongue had few friends in places that mattered, and his own successors, Richmond (1773-80), Mason (1780-83) and Crigan (1783-1813) displayed no enthusiasm for his educational ideas. Bishop Mason used Hildesley's questions for a visitation in 1782, and the returns revealed a very different state of affairs. Only five schools retained the use of Manx as the norm for Catechism and prayers, namely Lonan, Malew, German, Patrick and Jurby. Three other parishes used both languages, according as the children understood best, although all three, Rushen, Ballaugh and Maughold, were very much rural parishes. Elsewhere English ruled the roost once more, despite the fact that only in two parishes was this necessitated by lack of knowledge on the part of the master of the Manx language. In Braddan the Vicar explained that the "Present Master not being so well qualified in that Way, his Scholars are carefully taught to say their Prayers and Catechism in the English tongue", while at Lezayre the master was once more "not a native". Only Onchan bothered to hold out a note of promise, with "No Manks as yet by the present schoolmaster", the remainder giving replies such as "they do not, the Children are contantly instructed in English" (Kirk Michael); "more frequently instructed in English" (Bride); "I believe they do not" (Marown); or a categorical "only in English" (Arbory). The reply from Andreas noted the change in status with "In Bishop Hildesley's time they did, But for some years past, the Children are more frequently instructed in English". Four years later the visitation under Bishop Crigan in 1786 showed how Manx had lost more ground. Of the five parishes which used it as their norm in 1782, Lonan, Malew and Jurby had swung over to English. With no return for Patrick surviving in the records, only German retained Manx. Of the three bilingual parishes, Ballaugh and Rushen had become English only, leaving Maughold as the sole survivor. Bride blamed lack of suitable teachers; "the wardens complain that there is no Master or Mistress capable of teaching the Manx tongue" while the two parishes of Santan and Marown which on the face of it had swung over to Manx gave replies of such uncertainty with "I Believe they all do" and "I apprehend the master does teach them" that it would be unwise to place too much reliance on them. Even the information about German was secondhand—"I am told Philip Quirk our lycensed Master does".

The truth of the matter was that Hildesley's efforts came too late to rehabilitate the native tongue, for English was too firmly established as the language of social and mercantile advancement. Douglas in particular regarded the Bishop's efforts as reactionary, and he wrote with pain of the cool reception and "actual disapprobriation" which met his plans for a Manx Bible. "This, I believe, is the only country in the world that is ashamed of, and even inclined to extirpate, if it could, its own native tongue." Philip Moore had reported in 1766 that in the Douglas petty schools "they all speak English and know it best", and those who sent their children to school fully expected that an English education would be far more profitable in every way. The Vicar of Onchan in the 1786 Visitation answers went to the heart of the matter when he reported that "the schoolmaster does not teach the children Manx, but as much English as he can, agreable to the request of their parents".[8] In educational terms, Hildesley's plans had made sense, but not to parents eager for their children to "get on". A promising development was thus fading away fast, and apart from one brief flicker early in the next century, Manx as a medium for teaching was destined to be utterly ignored. While the call of John Wesley for the Manx language to be extirpated was an extreme example of prejuduce, the matter of language would no more be a live issue in education, and the total supremacy of English was established beyond doubt.

THE SYSTEM SHOWS THE SIGNS OF NEGLECT

While the preferred answer about the better language for teaching the Catechism might vary from bishop to bishop, there could be no doubt about the correct response to the other question in the tenth article of enquiry about "How often do you visit yr parish school?", as the law by the Act of 1704 enjoined at least a quarterly visit, but the vagueness displayed about the language used in schools indicated that many incumbents were far from well acquainted with what went on in their parish schools. It might not be unduly cynical to employ a rule of thumb that the minimum number of visits claimed amounted in fact to the highest number of visits made. John Christian, Vicar of Marown in 1757, cunningly extended Question 9 so that he wrote "10" in his answer as well, and totally avoided any mention of school visits. It is highly doubtful if the omission was accidental. The Vicar of Jurby made the curt reply "several times", without stating if this were each quarter, each year, or during his entire incumbency. Most claimed the legal quarterly visit with hints that this was a minimum. Ballaugh's reply was typical of such answers: "Once or twice a Quarter, sometimes oftener." James Wilks at Kirk Michael drew a distinction between a mere visit and an examination: "I frequently visit the school, and examine the Scolars at least once every Quarter". Lezayre claimed twice a quarter, Lonan "more than quarterly", but pride of place went to Onchan and Rushen. In the former case, the school was so near to the vicarage that a daily visit was made, while at Rushen Nicholas Christian obsrved, perhaps with a hint of smugness, "As the Vicar is Master himself, this business is particularly observed". This was the sole example of an incumbent fulfilling the original conditions for receipt of the Impropriate Fund payments.

The most informative reply came from John Gill, the Curate of Andreas for Archdeacon Kippax. He probably revealed the reality of the situation in most parishes, although older heads than the inexperienced curate would have stopped after his first four words. "I frequently visit them, but find that few children duly attend the school except in winter and springtime — There hath been public notice frequently given as well by the Curate as Schoolmaster to send their children to School and some few Children come now to be instructed." It is clear that even where conscientious attempts were made to fulfil the law's demands, they now met with a very limited response. Where there were no such attempts, the situation was likely to be even worse.

It is rather strange that in a short paragraph on education contained in an article on this 1757 Visitation it was claimed that Braddan was the only parish where the school was still held in the church, as John Gill stated that in Andreas, "no Schoolhouse belongs to this parish, but the School is kept in the Church". The remark that in Braddan the "Parish School is in church at present" was to be true for decades to come. The Wilson dislike of the use of places of worship as schools had not led to the abandonment in practice of the use of church as school too, and parishes with no separate building still existed. However the extensive list of repairs to the parish churches demanded by Hildesley after the Visitation report showed the unsatisfactory state of the buildings. To take two examples the church at Andreas needed repairs to the roof and doors, the insertion of panes of glass, and cleaning and white-washing of the chancel, while at Lezayre there were large stones loose in both chancel and nave. The continued usage of the parish church did not guarantee room free from wind and rain. Nevertheless, by 1760, certificates of repair had been received from every parish mentioned, and tolerable conditions were provided to this degree for the schools which still met in churches, at least for the moment.

The Visitation revealed the wide variation between the various parochial schools; nearly all were staffed by lay teachers, but Rushen was taught by its vicar; some were using Manx, but the majority not; there was a sprinkling of non-Manx teachers among the Manx majority, with a minority of females as teachers; and some schools were still held in the actual parish churches. The general framework of the system clearly continued in existence, but the concept of universal compulsory education had been abandoned without serious attempt to enforce it. Hildesley was content instead to confine his efforts to exhorting his clergy to fulfil their own legal obligations. At Convocation on June 7 1759 he referred to the 1704 obligations, urging the clergy to "Visit frequently the schools of their respective parishes", checking the fidelity of the masters.[10] Already in 1756 he had issued from the Episcopal Registry a set express form for the masters' certificates, to avoid vagueness, and further requirements of May 1761 made it clear beyond doubt that the supervision by the Church of all education was not going to be surrendered. The clergy were to send to the Bishop

> "the name of all, both men and women, as they know or believe to exercise or undertake the office of teaching schools of any kind in any part of the Diocese, in order that their Character and Qualification may be inquired into and that they may be warned against teaching anything, but what is agreeable and not contrary to the Doctrine and Worship of the Church of England as by law established".[11]

Such a direction would still not meet on the Island any opposition on purely religious grounds. On his arrival Hildesley had pronounced his satisfaction that all the natives were to a man members of the Established Church. Dissenters were unknown on the Island as organised worshipping bodies, as were Roman Catholics, while Methodism had yet to reach the Island's shores. The same regulations still felt confident enough to order the churchwardens to include in their official presentments those whose children were not sent to be catechised on Sunday. But what was striking and significant was the failure to make any mention of presentation of those who failed to send their children to school, while other traditional offences were still included, such as fornication and witchcraft. The only specific mention of schools came in Regulation 14, ordering presentments "if your school be not diligently kept". The practice of presentments for moral offences was fading away in practice and the attempts to retain the old discipline in Hildesley's regulations were very much a rearguard action.[12] The complete omission of even a token reference to compulsory education indicated the realisation on the part of the authorities that this was one matter on which it was hopeless to insist, although it had the full backing of statute law. Like the famous dog who did *not* bark, the silence was most telling.

Hildesley returned in June 1761 to the subject of regularising licences for teachers, laying down that it was "Unlawful for any person or persons whatever to engage in the Business of Employment of Instructing Youth, without the Approbation and Licence of the Ordinary of each respective Diocese". If any were thinking of or were engaged "on the Province of the Instructor", they could get a licence on producing a certificate in set form from the minister and wardens of their parish, stating they were a "Person of Sober Life and good Behaviour and qualified for what (He or She) undertakes", together with a promise to teach only Church of England doctrines, and a formal recommendation. Any who taught without securing a licence were warned that they would be proceeded against.[13] The Bishop's letter was to be read at Morning Prayer and Certificates sent in to the Episcopal Registry. (The normal method of distribution was for the letter to be sent to one minister, who would make a copy and pass it on, until all had received it, endorsing the original. In this case only three signatures from the northern parishes of Andreas, Jurby and Ballaugh appeared on the back, instead of the normal score of names.) The next year, any who remained unlicensed were summoned to the next Chapter Court to show just cause why they should not be proceeded against for "Presuming to teach without authority".[14] The Archbishop of York wrote to Hildesley, alarmed at the possibility of Roman Catholic schools being established. "I hope the Incessant working of the Papists have not produced any of their Schools amongst your people" — He warned of the "utmost ill consequences" which could arise sometimes from parents too readily employing foreigners to act as trustees.[15]

There were no grounds for fears on this score in the Isle of Man, but there were grounds for disquiet for more mundane reasons. The basic system of schools was showing signs of cracking. Some clearly found that one way to supplement their meagre incomes was to follow the example of the clergy a hundred years before and keep ale-houses. Barrow in the Sixteen Sixties had helped to quash such activities not only by denunciation, but also by increased stipends. Hildesley failed to follow this example, threatening instead to remove what little income schoolmasters had, without relieving the economic necessity which drove teachers to such actions. His 1763 Regulations included the command the "No schoolmaster to receive the Annuities, who after notice given, continues to keep a publick house".[16] Already Jurby had been for a year without a teacher to claim a share of the Elizabeth Hastings money, soon to be joined in 1763 by Patrick, their share being awarded instead to the masters who had discharged their duties most faithfully. The Parish of Bride was in the same situation, although being one of the Royal Bounty parishes, the Lady Elizabeth Hastings charity did not extend to it. In 1769 the masters were reminded that without a certificate from the incumbency, no payments would be made, and the clergy themselves the following year had the 1703/4 requirements concerning their visiting duties read out. Hildesley realised that the situation called for some positive action, and gained the agreement of the 1770 Convocation to spending money on the three schools — £16 for the new schoolhouse at Jurby, £4.2.0. for repairs to Patrick and £3.0.0. for forms and tables for Bride. Yet nothing was done to remedy the basic cause which left school bereft of masters and the buildings consequently to deteriorate. The Bishop himself referred to "the total want of a schoolhouse in some parishes and the bad state and condition of them in others".[17] Even if the 1703/4 legal requirement were met, a quarterly visit could not be considered adequate supervision, but at least half the clergy in their visitation answers seemed content with this. Crebbin of Jurby in 1766 visited his school "Four times a year at least when there is one". — a significant qualification. Only Maughold, Marown "Twice a week", and Ballaugh, "monthly" clearly did more than the legal minimum. (Arbory in 1766 had replaced Rushen as the sole parish where the incumbent was himself the parochial schoolmaster.) The vagueness of some replies as to whether Manx was taught probably was a better indicator of attendance than claims to quarterly visits. By 1772 Bride was still reported as having no schoolmaster for some years. The suggestion was made that a woman who taught private families might prove doubly useful to the village if she taught not only reading, but sewing and knitting too, and should be given "such stipend as formerly allowed for a parish school". In Bishop Mason's time, the Rector of Ballaugh gave an impression of normality with quarterly visits duly reported in 1786, but the very same year, the schoolmaster petitioned for an order for repair to a place in "Utter ruin and desolation" where no fire was possible in a hard winter in a building hazardous to master and pupils alike.

As the century progressed, the parochial school teachers saw their share of the Improriate Fund sink lower and lower. Before the so-called eviction of 1736, they had shared £30 among fifteen schools out of a total of £104. Following the settlement of 1758, they received, as mentioned earlier, a further ten shillings only, despite the fact that the fund had risen to a much higher £255 Manx (£219 British). Some of the extra money had gone to the master of Castletown Grammar School, but the greater part had gone into the pockets of the clergy. In 1788 for example the Vicar of Lezayre alone received twenty pounds a year from the Fund, which had certainly been linked in practice if not in strict law with the actual keeping of a school by an incumbent in each parish[18] while the negligent way in which registers were kept and the suspension of no less than seven clergy at one time make it likely that scant notice was taken even of the legal requirement to visit the schools each quarter. Yet the masters of fifteen petty schools only received £37.10.0 between them all. The sole concession made was in respect of the masters in the rectory parishes of Ballaugh, Bride and Andreas, who being recipients of the Royal Bounty, had not hitherto enjoyed any income from the Impropriate Fund, but were now given £1.13.0. each (Manx). The total sum paid from the fund to education at elementary level, £42.9.0., had fallen from one-third of the total yearly income to just one-sixth, and the original reason for the payment was rapidly fading from sight. Occasionally there was help from local endowments. The master at Rushen benefitted from the legacies of Alice Gawne (1749) Thomas Gawne (1777) William Clucas (1797) and John Cain (1803), worth in all over a pound and an acceptable addition to a master's salary.[19] The only sizeable increase was at Peel, where the Clothworkers' Company raised the salary to £16 in 1765. In 1767 Hildesley wrote of a meeting with the Company at which they promised to make the salary £17.10.0. With "Dr. Wilson's 5 guineas per annum and what pay scholars he can pick up" the Bishop thought the master should manage well. However, the Company would not accept liability for the upkeep of the building, and when repairs became unavoidable in 1798 the Vicar-General granted the wardens an order to levy the owners of land and houses to cover the costs of £26.16.9¾, so that in this respect Peel was no different from any other parish or town.

The absence of any pension provision meant that masters were virtually forced to struggle on in their posts when they were too old to fulfil their duties adequately, just like Professor Ross at Castletown at a higher level of education. Constance Radcliffe has unearthed a petition of 1790 from the official parochial schoolmaster of Maughold asking that his salary be kept up, despite admitting he would like permission to dwell in Douglas until the schoolhouse where he and his wife lived was repaired by the neglectful wardens and parishioners. Whether he was "manifestly not performing his duties" as Mrs. Radcliffe claims, is open to question; only his wife's infirmities are mentioned, and he gives the impression that although aged 88 he is willing to carry on! Brideson had been Parish Clerk too when he was at Ballaugh, but did not hold that office in Maughold. The Clerk there, Edward Corkill, appointed in 1776, did fulfil the dual role as a sale of 1778 mentioned, an exception to possession being "one of the cowhouses which Ed Corkhill holds by lease for a schoolhouse for the parishioners' children". Although the wardens could do nothing to remove Brideson, save totally neglect his dwelling, it appears that they had written him off already as far as being a useful schoolmaster was concerned. The authorities were for their part concerned for the future that the official schoolhouse should be "fit, convenient and durable for the present and future schoolmasters of the Parish", and ordered an assesment to be collected. For his part, Brideson blamed not any infirmity of his own but the "Enthusiastical Methodism" of the wardens and parishioners whom he accused of "having . . . no zeal for the Glory of God, His Name, His Day, His House, His Ordinance, His Ministers, or anything releateing thereto especially a Schoolhouse and that wherein your Petr lives".[20]

NEW BUILDING IN TOWN AND COUNTRY

However, it would be wrong to look upon the latter part of the century as a time of unrelieved depression. Douglas in particular seems to have been the home of a number of schools. When the 1766 standard questionaire was put to the Rev. Philip Moore during the Visitation, he replied that "We have many petty schools", although none fell under the category of parochial school.[21] Few details of these schools have survived, although St. Matthew's file in the Diocesan Registry contains a recommendation for a schoolmaster's licence for one William Corlett in April 1781 from the Ministers and Wardens of Douglas, testifying to his sober life, good behaviour, qualification to be a schoolmaster and membership of the Church of England.

More firmly based were two endowed schools established in Castletown. The one for boys, Taubmann's School, was created by the will of John and Esther Taubmann in 1799. They left to their son, also John, lands called Ballahot in the Parish of Malew in trust to provide an annual income of twenty five pounds British "for the support of a Free School in Castletown, for the education of twenty five poor boys". Twenty pounds was for the master's salary "for teaching and instructing the boys in reading, spelling, writing and arithmetic" — a handsome sum matched at elementary level only by the Clothworkers School at Peel. The remaining five pounds was to be used for the purchase of books, ink and paper for the school. The Taubmann family were to have the nomination of both masters and boys, with the Chaplain and Wardens of Castletown Chapel filling any vacancy if the family failed to act within a month.[22]

Some decades earlier, the will of Catherine Halsall in 1758 appointed the four clergy of Rushen Sheading and their successors to be trustees for the "erecting, building and endowing a Free School . . . for teaching Girls only, to read, sew, knit, and spin, the yearly salary of the mistress not to exceed eight pounds Brit.; and two pounds yearly to be allowed for repairs".[23] The Convocation Book for 1760 noted a meeting of the Vicar-General and the four incumbents on May 29th to discuss how to operate the will. The modest sum set apart for repairs was nevertheless a most useful provision; if the girls of the school learned that a stitch in time saves nine, this was a maxim singularly unheeded normally by the Manx.

This special provision for girls' education was copied by Bishop Hildesley himself in 1764 when he bought a plot of ground in Kirk Michael and built a schoolmaster's house for the parochial master, and also a schoolhouse for a mistress.[24] Catherine Halsall's example was further followed by the Bishop providing a capital sum of thirty pounds the interest of which he directed should be used for repairs. Near the close of the century, a girls' school was provided in the neighbouring parish of Ballaugh. A plot nearer the populace than the parochial school was bought for sixteen pounds in 1797, and subscriptions raised to provide a schoolhouse and mistress. This "Village School" as it was known continued well into the Nineteenth Century.[25] Also in the Parish of Rushen, Miss Jane Qualtrough of Kentraugh set up a girls' school in 1798, which by her will of 1810 was endowed with the interest from a hundred pounds British. An earlier legacy of Thomas Gawne of Ballagawne ". . . to a Schoolmistress in the parish ten shillings by the year . . . and she to teach two poor people's children gratis" dated from 1777, but had not been applied for the object stated. The Vicar and Wardens recovered the arrears once Miss Qualtrough's school was established, and gave the mistress twelve shillings extra from the accumulated eleven pounds. The salaries for these schools, although modest, were at least a marked improvement on their prototype on the Island, Bishop Wilson's school for girls in Peel, which had been endowed with but fifty pounds a year, yielding only fifty shillings for the support of the mistress.

Despite the far from satisfactory working of the parochial school system, little by little parishes inched nearer to the fulfilment of the Wilson hope of every parish having its own schoolhouse, often providing a dwelling for the master at the same time, as in the case of Jurby, which received land in 1766 from John Maloony for both purposes. Two years earlier Hildesley built a house for the schoolmaster of Michael, and when in 1787 the Archdeacon's Parish of Andreas finally had its own school from Philip Radcliffe of Ballaradcliffe on part of his estate called Gatt-na-Nain for the consideration of twenty shillings and the right to nominate a free scholar,[26] his action was followed by that of Emmanuel Moore who bequeathed thirty pounds to the school, the money being used with further subscriptions to provide a master's house. Indeed with the provision of land for a school by James Joughin in Bride in 1775, and the restoration of Ballaugh in the late Seventeen Eighties, the northern parishes in particular had made considerable progress in the closing decades of the century. Although Castletown enjoyed a number of schools, the Parish of Malew seems to have received its first school outside the church as late as 1795, while although the writer has found no date for one at Santan, the parochial school there was considered to be old and in need of replacement in 1849. As Wilson had provided a new church for Lonan during his episcopate, it is highly likely that the same prohibition of it being used for school purposes applied as it did for Patrick earlier. It seems probable that by 1800 only Braddan, which was provided with a school at Ballakinnish by Thomas Cain near the Cooil in 1815, still lacked a purpose-built school for its children, the original of Wilson's time having been allowed to decay early in its life.

The late Eighteenth Century also witnessed a further number of gifts aimed at providing schools in parts of parishes which were too remote from the official parochial school. In the Parish of Braddan in 1764 John Cain and Robert Creer sold lands for the technical consideration of one shilling, "Chiefly on account of having a School in the neighbourhood", for the use of the schoolmaster to the Vicar, the Rev. Joseph Cosnahan and the Wardens of Braddan.[27] These were situated in the hilly part of the parish, East Baldwin, and subscriptions raised to build a schoolhouse together with a residence for the master. The Book of Charities noted that the response was more than sufficient for needs, £44 British remaining after costs were paid. A similar provision was made for Lezayre in the same year by John Kelly of Cooil Inchal in the parish of Marown. ". . . he did leave in trust the sum of Sixty Pounds, and by a codicil to his will the future sum of Eleven Pounds, towards funding a School at the Mountains, in the parish of Lezayre, which is a motive and example to all good Christians to do the like, according to their capacity and ability". Two parishioners of Lezayre, Philip Quayle and William Kelly, were moved by this example to endow lands in Lezayre and Ballaugh respectively to support "the said intended school", known as both the Mountain and Kelly's School.[28] Although the Parish of German was already possessed of two petty schools and two advanced schools, William Cain of the Vraney sought through his affection for the place of his residence to help his neighbours "by being, in some measure, instrumental in the erection and establishment of an English School in that part of the Parish, for the education of the present rising, and future generations . . ." For two pounds in 1781 he sold to the Vicar of German, the Rev. Henry Corlett part of his lands "to the intent and end that a School-house and other conveniences be erected thereon . . ."[29] The most ambitious of these new schools supplementing the old parochial ones was at St. Mark's where it formed part of a church expansion scheme; but this will be dealt with in the next chapter.[30] Another mountain school was provided near the end of the century for the Parish of Maughold through the bequest of John Kermeen "to purchase a place, and build a new School-house at William Cashon's Estate, or thereabouts, the sum of forty pounds, if the said Schoolhouse will be built within the space of a year after my decease . . ." If this condition were not fulfilled the forty pounds would pass to his two brothers. With this money the Vicar of Maughold, Thomas Cubbon, and his wardens purchased for fifteen pounds part of the Rhenabb Quarterland known as the Lhiaggyn by deed dated February 4th 1794, within the specified time, Kermeen having died

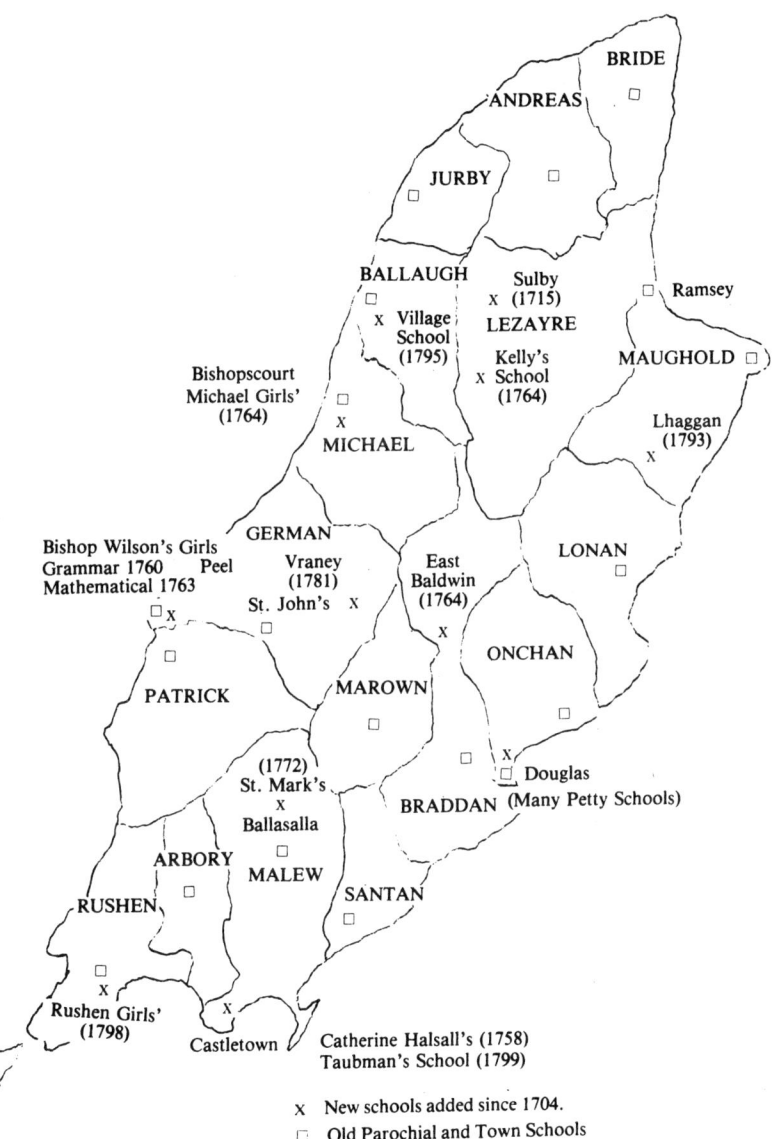

MANX SCHOOLS by 1800

the previous year. Although there was a subscription list opened for the school, which raised an extra £19 by 1796, it appears that no master was appointed until the next century, the funds being allowed to accumulate to provide a better income for the master.[31]

By 1800 then, there had been considerable supplementation of the original pattern of parochial schools and four town schools. A number of parishes now had provision for their remoter parts, which at first sight would seem nothing but gain. However, the wisdom of such moves was to prove a matter of debate in the Nineteenth Century, with different bishops holding differing views. On the one hand children would be more likely to attend a nearby school than walk long distances, especially in the winter, at a time when roads were virtually unknown in the Island. The provision was all the more valuable, if, as was sadly sometimes the case, the parochial school was not in fact functioning through causes of disrepair or lack of master. On the other hand, each district school would be likely to draw away a small number from the parochial school, reducing the master's quarterage, and making it even more difficult to attract suitable masters. None of the new schools themselves would be able to offer an attractive salary either; even the accumulated Lhiaggyn money, £51 in all, produced no more than a miserable two or three pounds — just as poor a salary as that of the parochial schools.

CONCLUSION

Compared with the ambitious plans of Barrow, Levinz and Wilson, the late Eighteenth Century was a disappointing period. The ideal of a sound basic education available and compulsory for every child on the Island, never easy to put into practice at any time, gradually ceased to be taken as the norm. The vigorous enforcement of the first decade through the various systems of presentments faded rapidly as the Church discipline generally ceased to be applied with no secular agency taking on the task in its place. Without any serious attempt at enforcement, the law soon became a dead letter. At the same time, the Impropriate Fund intended to guarantee provision in each parish was now regarded as the automatic right of the incumbents concerned, without any regard being paid to any educational conditions. Certain causes of decay, such as the failure of the Derby to honour their obligations with regard to the collateral security, were outside the control of any on the Island and had done great damage in the middle of the century. Yet without doubt much of the trouble was self-inflicted. The well-intentioned, but disastrous decision of Wilson to remove the clergy from the role of schoolteachers, was a major factor. Although by the standards of polite English society, the Manx clergy were wretchedly poor, by the standards of the Island they were rich enough, and for all their occasional shortcomings, held in high esteem by the natives. The same could not be said of the Island's schoolteachers, starved of a fair share of the Impropriate Fund, unable to exceed for the most part the earnings of a manual labourer, and perforce drawn all too often from the ranks of "the meanest and the worst".

Nevertheless, much remained of the original Seventeenth Century system, and even if ignored to a large extent, the laws demanding universal education remained on the statute book. Although at times the buildings might be neglected, every parish had its own official school, all but one housed by 1800 in buildings built for the purpose, and supplemented not only by extra schools in the towns but by quite a number in the rural parishes too. While assessments to repair the schools were often evaded in practice, the legal right to raise money in this way had not been lost. The bare bones of a remarkable system had survived the vicissitudes of the century. Would the Nineteenth Century breath new life into them, or would the Island have to look elsewhere for its educational inspiration?

REFERENCES

CHAPTER FOUR

1. Convocation Book 1756.
2. BC 13.
3. 1757 Visitation.
4. Convocation Book, Oct 2 1761.
5. BC 51-56.
6. Visitation 1766.
7. Visitation 1782.
8. Visitation 1786.
9. JMM Vol. 6 1958 62, R. E. C. Forster, *The Parochial Visitation of 1757*.
10. Convocation Book June 7 1759.
11. Ibid May 14 1761.
12. This equally true of the mainland too. See Anthony Russell, *The Clerical Profession* SPCK 1980, 149.
13. Convocation Book, June 12 1762.
14. Ibid, Letter of Nov 12 1762.
15. Ibid 1763.
16. Ibid 1770.
17. ed A. W. Moore, *Hildesley's Letters 1755-72*, Mar 6 1772.
18. Convocation Book, Letter of Nov 12 1762.
19. Ibid 1763.
20. Ibid 1770.
21. BC 22.
22. Ibid 132.
23. Constance Radcliffe, *Op. cit.* 127.
24. 1766 Visitation.
25. BC 125.
26. Ibid 43.
27. Ibid 74.
28. *Educational Endowments 1887*.
29. BC 81.
30. Ibid 111.
31. BC 88.
32. BC 69-70.
33. See next chapter.
34. BC 96.

CHAPTER FIVE
THE LATER EIGHTEENTH CENTURY
THE GOLDEN AGE OF THE ENDOWED SCHOOLS

CASTLETOWN IS GIVEN AN EXTRAORDINARY MASTER

Within a couple of years of his arrival as Bishop, Mark Hildesley knew that the vigourous action of the new master as Castletown was bringing order from chaos in the school there, but the man and his methods must surely caused some heart-searching about the suitability of his choice as a permanent successor for Professor Ross. Following the latter's death, a Mr. Wills and then the Rev. John Quayle, Vicar of Malew, filled the gap for short periods, but at least one intended Professor could not be persuaded to take the vacant position. "We were like to lose our intended Academick Master Mr. Whitehouse, who by consent of friends on both sides has laid close seige... with Miss Hutchin."[1] Whether Miss Hutchin was the actual cause of the refusal is not at all clear.

Eventually in January 1758 Peter Legh and Thomas Cholmondeley as Trustees of the Academick Master's Fund elected "The Rev. Thos. Castley, A.M. of the University of Cambridge, to be Academic professor or teacher of philosophy in the Isle of Man." Thus began the tenure of the Castletown school's most renowned master. Yet lauded to the skies as he was by later generations, his early contemporaries saw him in a different light. Statements such as "To eat at Mr. Quillin's would do for a Manxman, but not at all for any Englishman" and a considerable number of others denigrating Manx standards were not the most tactful way of introducing himself to the Islanders, but above all the impression was that of an avaricious man. Governor Cochrane wrote to Bishop Hildesley, "Money I find he will have, nothing will divert him from that which his heart is so much set upon." Yet the avarice so damaging to Castley's soul was extremely beneficial for his school, as he set about repairing the finances, busily concerning himself in a multitude of ways with the funds from which his salary stemmed. This, however, was in the long term, for his concern with the ways in which his salary could be augmented led him quickly into fierce controversy, with the concept of the 'free school' at the heart of the matter.

In England, entrance fees were often charged for boys admitted to Free Schools, for example at Oundle since 1675, although this money was sometimes expended upon repairs. Christopher Wase had approved of those who could afford fees paying them, as long as the free boys were taught with equal diligence. If the income were fixed, it proved difficult to attract a university man with no prospect of fees, and schools would slump rapidly to elementary level. The tradition of accepting freely offered gratuities was a well-established compromise: "... the mixed school was far more common than the totally free one.

... local foundations were hardly ever established for only the poor."[2]

It was this last position that the Rev. James Wilks supported in a Memorial to the Trustees of the Impropriate Fund in 1763. The man who had worked so hard to recover the funds in Ireland found his initial optimism about Castley waning. His letters of 1758 describing how the Bishop with great caution and pains had found a Cambridge man of good morals and learning, and what an ingenious gentleman he was,[3] were replaced by charges that his exorbitant demands had "discouraged and suppressed Learning and Education", and introduced Ignorance and Barbarism. He had not only abused the trust in him reposed, but also "offended gainst the Rights and Priviledges of the People of this Isle." His Memorial defined his conception of the Free School.

> "... and that all Degree of People within this Isle have an unquestionable right to send their persons thereto ... without Fee or Reward to the master thereof for their Education further than that they shall voluntarily think proper to compliment him with."[4]

The charges against Castley were filled out in a Petition of the People of Castletown, which compared the glories of the past with the effects of Castley.

> "... several schools being in a progressive state the lesser to prepare for the greater flourished several years ago and produced several sensible ingenious Schollars who were and are an honour to the Senate Pulpitt Bench and Barr."[5]

Numbers under Makon were put at forty to fifty, almost certainly an exaggeration, and tributes paid to Ross, Wills and Quayle. People had sent their sons from the different parts of the Island to be educated there. (Malew Parish Register records William Christian of Jurby in the far north of the Island "at the Grammar School at Castletown" being confirmed on St. Peter's Day 1761.) On Castley's arrival there was the "highest expectation of an Increase in Learning and the school to be put into the most flourishing state "but instead he discouraged learning by "exacting exorbitant fees as entering money of such Schollars "so that some were withdrawn and others could not start.

Interestingly both Wilks and the Castletown Petition allege that Castley even treated the Academic Students in the same fashion. Wilks stated clearly that there were complaints against him in the capacity of "Academick Lecturer or Publick Reader of Logick, Philosophy and History within this Isle", while the town petition alleged that he refused "to educate youth both in his capacity of Grammar School-Master and Academical Professor, and by that means he has suppressed and stifled the birth and growth of Learning and Education."

Wilks also mentioned harsh and cruel treatment, a charge amplified with graphic detail by the Castletown Petition. In an age when severe physical punishment was the accepted norm, Castley shocked his contempories by his ferocity and cruelty, which made thoughts of his school "odious to his Schollars" and himself "not a fit person to be intrusted with the care of youth." Among his novel punishments was the coiling of a cord in a serpentine manner, called by him a colt, with which he struck the pupil on the temple with such force as to level him to the ground with one stroke, while another consisted of forcing pupils to hold up fingers and thumb, and then strike them on the points of the fingers with a plank. The unfortunate dunce or 'booby' found his hair was pulled out, and then he himself forced to put it on the fire.

Castley's fees and cruelty between them caused a rapid decline in numbers. According to Wilks, the Nursery for Learning and Manners for between fifty and sixty youths was reduced to its lowest state, with not a tenth of those numbers in school. The Petition similarly described the school as 'destitute' with only four or five pupils. The House of Keys appointed a committee of inquiry to look into the matter, but the "Public Nuisance and Grievance" rode out the storm and remained for forty years more.

Castley also fought a long campaign to improve the salary of the master of the Grammar School. The original sum of £30 from the Rushen tithes had remained unchanged. As late as 1749 Ross had a bond for five years for £150,[6] but Castley claimed that he came to the Island on the promise of £100 a year, and was entitled to receive two-thirds of the value of the Rushen tithes. Wilks countered that his total income exceeded his £100 "exclusive of the exorbitant sums by him unjustly demanded and received from his scholars . . . previous to the Admission of such scholars into the said Free School", and that he had no right to two thirds of the tithes for his own use. No master had ever received them, or more than £30.[7]

Castley's own case was strong: the Rushen tithes were now worth double the amount as when they were first applied to the grammar school, and if the proportion of the fund applied to the Free School were to be maintained then the £30 paid from £104 in the last distribution before the eviction should be raised in proportion to at least double the amount from the £219 now fixed by Chancery.

During these exchanges, Castley also showed himself to be concerned with the good of the school as well. In a petition to the Duke of Atholl, he pointed out that after the money owed to Ross was paid at £30 a year, there would still be a surplus of hundreds of pounds, which he requested should be laid out as the Governor and Trustees thought fit "for the good of the foundation".[8] Already some had been applied "to render the schoolhouse lately in a ruinous condition a comfortable and wholesome appartment." Castley supervised this work himself, and wrote complaining to Hildesley that repairs being carried on at Castletown Chapel "check'd our proceedings in the schoolhouse."[9] After asking that the repair accounts should be examined and settled, and he himself discharged, he asked that the surplus money be used to provide a writing master, a "want universally felt and great disadvantage to the school". Castley may have had little confidence in the Petty Schools, in practice by now on the Island left as elsewhere "to the meanest and therefore the worst," as Carlisle put it, and sought to follow mainland examples where the grammar school itself provided basic instruction, although occasionally on the same foundation the English school giving elementary instruction was distinct from the Latin school. On the other hand, the writing master did not necessarily limit himself to elementary level, as his instruction included mercantile writing styles and accounts belonging to more advanced stages of education.[10]

The Trustees of the Impropriate Fund at first heeded Castley's argument and the accounts for 1760 show Castletown Grammar School awarded £60, and the Petty Schools receiving £2/10/0 instead of £2. Only in 1779 did the Trustees return suddenly to paying £30, returning to the arguments already employed with success against the claims of Grissel Ross, daughter of the Professor, whom Castley himself had assumed should have been allowed the bare £30 a year. Miss Ross had claimed £1,393 was owed her father's estate, as he had taken the school in 1736 on the chance of recovering by law the value of the tithes from which the master had been evicted. His estate should therefore be compensated to the value of the tithes as calculated by the Court of Chancery. Wilks had made marginal notes to the effect that the trustees could distribute as they thought fit, only thirty pounds were allowed for the salary, and Ross had entered on a fixed sum of £1/3/4 per pupil. Ross could not have expected to gain more by being evicted than if he had not. (Wilks' figures reveal the gross exaggeration of former numbers he made in his complaint against Castley; otherwise Ross would have been between £59 and £70 per year in his just salary.) The tithe surplus saw to repairs and the Trustees had been generous in paying to the Easter following her father's death. Grissel Ross appealed to the Duke of Atholl, claiming that Governor Cochrane was claiming a debt from her father's bond of £390, which would reduce her to beggary, instead of the true £150.[11] Her claim for the Rushen tithes was now put at £983.

It had been one thing for the Trustees to shrug off Miss Ross, but quite another to cut back Castley after nearly twenty years. The reason was probably the feeling that Castley had sorted out the Academic Master's Fund and therefore was no longer in need of the amount he had so far enjoyed from the Impropriate Fund. Castley promptly took them to court in October 1780. He was aided by John Taubman, Speaker of the House of Keys, who witnessed that before the eviction the master enjoyed the full value of the tithes of Rushen, put into the hands of proctors "for the ease and convenience of the sd schoolmaster": that after the death of Ross the public inconvenience led the Keys to ask Hildesley to find a man from the English Universities, and that they had agreed at a meeting in Castle Rushen that the hundred pounds which Castley demanded would be paid. The tithes would make up £60 and the rest found from the Castletown Chapel salary and the Academic Master's salary. A letter of Bishop Hildesley to this effect, dated October 6th 1757 was produced in support.

The Vicar of Rushen, Nicholas Christian, stated that as Curate of Rushen he became a proctor in 1734, and understood that two-thirds of the tithes were for the maintenance and support of the schoolmaster at Castletown, not for any extraordinary repairs which were the responsibility of the trustees from their general fund. The proctors accounted to the schoolmaster alone, not to bishop or trustees.[12] The Governor, in his capacity of Chancellor of the Court of Chancery on the Island found for Castley, ordering he be paid £120 and costs. The bishop and trustees appealed to the Privy Council, claiming "the said decree is erroneous", but the Lt.-Governor's decree was upheld and a further £100 awarded in costs in April 1783.[13]

Castley displayed equal energy in securing what he could from the Academic Master's Fund. On arrival he asked Hildesley that he might take charge of the money recovered in Ireland by Harris, fearing "a considerable hiatus in the next year's salary", a request which struck the Trustees as 'very bold'.[14] James Wilks for his part was keen to be audited and discharged, having recovered £150, now secured by land in the Island, as he recommends the rest should be, safe under the eye of bishop and governor. Calling in the £500 owed by Batten and Mrs. Murgitrode had been rendered very complicated by Miss Ross, by no means satisfied with a payment of £5/12/5¾, although Wilks maintained she had had her deserts from this fund too, and complained of "abuse and scurrility "in September 1758.[15] The trouble was that Miss Ross and her letters had panicked Mrs. Murgitrode, who refused to pay back any more money. Wilks gladly arranged through Harris that the balance should go to Castley, and was given £10 for his pains — he had coyly informed Legh that he had been educated at Castletown Academy, but would not refuse five pounds.

The clearing-up process was both costly and time-consuming. By 1767 the principal brought to account came to £528, with £400 of it put to two mortgages, but it needed six more years and a lawsuit against one Lindsay to rescue the remainder. The sale of Lindsay's goods did not offset legal costs and expenses, causing a loss of £77. Eventually the clear sum of £124 was recovered, making by 1755 a grand total of £722/19/0¾. After deductions for sundries coming to over a hundred pounds, the principal left was smaller than that set aside in 1705.

> "And whereas, by the great expense of the lawsuit against Lindsay, for recovery of part of the Academic funds in his hands, the sd fund is greatly reduced, we do hereby settle and fix the principal fund hereafter to bear interest for the use and benefit of the Academic Master at the total sum of six hundred and twenty two pounds, eight shillings, and nine-pence farthing Manks currency.[16]

When the money was brought to the Island, Castley laid it out on securities within the Island. A couple of years earlier, Wilks and Philip Moore had corresponded with Thomas Wilson, son of Bishop Wilson, who, generous to the new Ramsey School in its building, was now setting up a fund for clergy widows and children in the Isle of Man.

They wished to combine funds and buy the estate of Ballahutchin for two thousand pounds. Their own fund fell far short, but "the fund appropriated for the support of the Academick master in the Isle of Man, being scattered in different places; it is proposed to be collected and added to the fund..." Wilks was certain that Legh and Cholmondeley would give their consent. Their plans came to nothing, and in the event they bought the tithes of Kirk Michael from the Duke of Atholl for £900, while Castley laid out his money on mortgages at Cooil Injil, Billewin, Ballavarkish, and Creggan Ashlin.[17] As mentioned above, it was at this point the Trustees of the Impropriate Fund felt it fitting to reduce their contribution to the salary of Castley.

Castley had also managed to retain his Cambridge Fellowship at Trinity, threatened if his appointment were for life. Wilks at this early stage had written to Bishop Hildesley expressing sympathy, asking that Castley be able to show his position in Castletown was at the Bishop's pleasure.

In 1764 he had gone to Cambridge to vote for Lord Sandwich as Chancellor, at the request of the Duke of Atholl: "It is very agreeable to me that he comply with Lord Sandwich's request" wrote the Duke to Governor Wood.[18] In 1777 Castley asked for his reward. His counterpart at the Douglas Grammar School, Philip Moore also held the lucrative rectories, first of Ballaugh in 1751 and then of Bride. The death in 1777 of James Wilks, appointed to Ballaugh in 1771, opened up to Castley the prospect of a similar plurality for himself. The Duke regretted that Gelling of Malew had been promised the preferment, and Castley turned his attention to the vacancy arising there, in his local parish. Bishop Richmond, who succeeded Hildesley in 1773 informed the Duke he would please his grace if he could do so with a clear conscience, but pointed out that Castley already held a post "far more lucrative than the vicarage of Malew", and that as Castley spoke no Manx, being apart from the Bishop the only English clergyman on the Island, he was not legally qualified.[19]

Yet despite Castley's undoubted eye for extra income, as the years went by, his merits began to outshine the flaws in his character, and no longer did he write of "contemilous usage" by his fellow clergy. Fitzsimmons, the proud young master of Peel, who later went to Ayr as minister and returned to the Island to become a member of the Keys, displayed shrewd judgement at the time of Castley's early disputes.

"... notwithstanding the evidence he has given and the continued evidence he gives of capacity and science, he has been illiberally treated. The time will come however, in which people will make a better estimate of his worth and of their own misconduct."

The comparisons between Castley and his predecessors ceased to be odious to himself. Waldron in 1726 had been very scathing about standards in his own time at "a small college in Castletown for the education of young gentlemen designed for the pulpit... But how much it deserves the name they give it of a College may be gathered from what I have said concerning the learning of their clergy."[20] Nicholas Christian in his evidence in 1781, spoke as a former pupil of Grammar School and Academy of their repute being as high as ever, but Speaker of the House of Keys, John Taubman, in a generous tribute to Castley claimed that standards were higher than before, owing to his careful attention to his school. Numbers were what they were under Makon in 1731, between twenty and thirty from various parts of the Island, and the school "considered the head school of the Island, both as to Education, and as to number of scholars, and for what the Deponent knows to the contrary is so still", yet

> "... there have been men more learned and abler divines educated by the Complt than under any of the former masters during the dept's time and the Dept steadfastly believes that the Complt is superior in Learning and Abilities to any Master that hath been in the sd School during the Dept's time."[21]

Robert Brown, Vicar of Braddan and father of the Manx poet T. E. Brown, was one such able divine, but occasionally distance of time produced a tinted view. When he wrote in 1835 that the Island had not beheld Castley's equal and "in all probability we will never see the like again", the pupil spoke sincerely, but to add that Castley taught without eyes on earthly riches was enter the realm of hagiography.[22]

Brown's same letter to the *Sun* gave the number of pupils under Castley at the end of the century as between twenty and thirty; in other words there had been no expansion, normally the sign of a successful school. Poor communications were one reason for this. In 1766, John Quayle, Clerk of the Rolls, wrote to Bishop Hildesley that "my little boys could not give daily attendance all weathers to Castletown school. I thought it necessary to engage a collegian from Glasgow to transcribe my papers and instruct my children." The opening of the Peel Schools and the definite upgrading of Ramsey may also have had some effect, as they offered alternatives to long journeys or expensive boarding out. Probably above all it was the fees of Castley which deterred growth. A petition from sometime in the governorship of John Wood (1761-1777) from three pupils, John Clague, John Parr and William Fargher, to be considered for the foundation established "for the Benefit and Encouragement of Students as intended to qualify them for the church "made mention of their years at Castletown being at "considerable expense".[23] One way around restrictive statutes at grammar schools was to charge extra for such things as writing and arithmetic, although whether this was done is uncertain.

At one time, in 1764, a possibility arose that the Academic School might increase its intake, similar to the way that Wilson had suggested fifty years before, but this time the initiative came from the mainland, from no less than Archbishop Secker of Canterbury.

> "Pray doth your lordship educate young people for orders or how are you supplied with ministers. I suppose it is cheap living in your island; will you give us leave to send you over a number of lads, to be taught their business at moderate expense: and then to return to serve small cures? It would really mend the clerical race amongst us very much.[24]

Nothing seems to have come of this suggestion, nor was there any attempt to draw upon a wider circle within the Island, although the concept flickered on. Wilks in 1757 could still refer to the "Academick Master or Teacher of Philosophy within the Isle of Man, whose immediate province is to teach and instruct all youths intended for the service of the church."[25] Although in practice this 'immediate province' became the one and only, Castley gave a broad education. He certainly did not neglect the Classics; Joseph Stowell, an Academic Student from 1786 related how his knowledge of Greek and Latin received at Douglas Grammar School greatly increased under Castley, but it was of mathematics that he wrote to his brother Hugh. "I am plunged over head and ears in mathematical studies — I sup upon cones and circles, angles and triangles."[26] Col. Wilks, who achieved wider fame as Governor of St. Helena when Napoleon was brought there, made special mention of Castley's teaching of natural philosophy in particular: he had never met a superior lecturer. When a Dr. Walker of Moffatt, Scotland, also enquired how the Island educated its ministry, the Rev. Philip Moore replied that Barrow in the reign of Charles II had established an academy for the education of young men to serve the church, who received their education from an academical professor who was a Master of Arts.

> "There is a competent salary for the teacher and a handsome exhibition for the three or four youths on the establishment ... we have the blessing and comfort of a competent share of classical, theological and other learning in the arts *and sciences* to qualify us for the ministry;"[27] (Author's italics).

Castley's broadness of curriculum was not likely to be restricted to his Academic Students only, and it is likely that Castletown was among those schools which sought to break free of Samuel Johnson's description of a Grammar School as one where the "learned languages are taught gramatically". Although R. S. Tompson has challenged the view of Vincent that the broad outlook was very rare, stressing that innovations in this direction "accelerated markedly during the 18th Century", with only four pure grammar foundations contrasting with twenty nine 'mixed', he admits that the teaching of mathematics was very rare in grammar schools before 1800, although finding outlets elsewhere.[28] Castley, described by Joseph Stowell as a man of profound erudition and various attainments, appears very advanced for his time.

The foundation was now very secure financially, chiefly by reason of the flourishing state of the Academic Students' Fund. By Castley's time, the original £20 a year had condsiderably increased. The unfortunate Lace family were bought off for £161 in 1728, and in 1769 John Taubman took a lease of the two farms for thirty one years at an annual rent of £100. In 1771 the Trustees increased the allowance to the Academic Scholars to twelve pounds in money and three pounds in books, while a third Scholar was allowed to pursue his studies at Cambridge, Oxford, or Dublin, with an annual grant of thirty five pounds. Julius Cosnahan was the first student to benefit from this provision, proceeding to Trinity College, Cambridge.[29] Hildesley was asked at the same meeting "to purchase books and mathematical instruments for the use of the sd Academic School, so that the same do not exceed in value the sum of fifty pounds." Castley too was rewarded with £5 for "extraordinary trouble and lecture", while the fund also covered repairs to the school and library.[30] (Almost needless to say, Castley desired to see the terms of the endowment, "being of a local nature", but was informed it could not be found in the Rolls Chapel.[31])

The actual distribution of the Fund however got out of control towards the end of the century. In 1775 it was ruled that three Academic Students should receive £25 a year, but one would continue on the foundation although ordained, "to serve the Church as occasion may require and have the additional sum of ten pounds allowed for his ordination."[32] The use of the fund for supernumeraries, who were based on Castletown until a cure was found for them, meant however that those most recently admitted as scholars sometimes had to wait for years until a backlog was cleared before they received their money. John Allen was examined by Bishop Crigan in July 1796 and found fit to be a scholar, but his petition of 1800 stated that to stay any longer at Castletown would be very burdensome to his family owing to the price of board.[33] He was given £15 for the three years past, but advised to seek a post in the West Indies. Thomas Stephen, elected in 1796 waited until 1803 for payment. Despite the fact the lands were relet to bring in £341 in 1800, putting a son through to ordination was very costly.

Wilson's successor, Bishop Hildesley, preserved the general oversight of the Academic Students under Castley as his great predecessor with Ross. He insisted they, as well as all clergy, wore wigs and also their 'decent apparel'. The Vicar of Maughold, Thomas Cubbon, related how once a month the Scholars were summoned to Bishopscourt "where he personally examined them in the Classicks, the Greek Testament and the Thirty Nine Articles: then had them to read over distinctly some portion of the Holy Scriptures, in order to qualify them for reading in publick:"[34]

Towards the end of Castley's long rule at Castletown, Bishop Crigan wrote to the Duke that the Academic Students' Fund Trustees would not meet without the Duke, nor saw any necessity to meet.

> "... the fund is in as good a state and the education of the youth as well attended to now, as at any other period and the Master and Scholars enjoy even higher than the usual established salaries."[35]

By 1781 the Impropriate Tithes were worth £415 compared with the £219 agreed in 1758, and if the clergy petition for due augmentation were heeded in Castley's time, the Grammar School would have its fair proportion. The Students' Fund was thriving and the Master's Fund in the Island. Even if numbers were still small, the schools enjoyed a high reputation, although the separate Academy hoped for by Barrow and partly realised by Wilson had been abandoned. (The Library books were now with the Grammar School, and the building in disrepair.) The will of Catherine Halsall in 1758 left properties for the building of a house for the Grammar School Master, and the weakness in the first tier of education had been overcome by the provision within the school itself. The breadth of the curriculum lends support to Tompson's plea to view the grammar schools as more adaptable institutions than is often admitted.[36] The Castletown was certainly no example of a decaying school, and all things considered Barrow may well have been reasonably content.

DOUGLAS GRAMMAR SCHOOL

At Douglas, the long and faithful service given by Philip Moore bridged the periods of Wilson and Hildesley. To the latter he was almost a brother, acting as his chaplain and receiving in 1760 the rectory of Bride to replace that of Ballaugh. The Bishop hailed him as "Rector of country parish — minister of a large town — chaplain to a regiment... and archididanalus of a numerous seminary."[37] On occasions the episcopal authority was wielded. Wilson in 1735 had rebuked him for levity, but Hildesley was concerned about academic standards in Latin and the need to keep the young men in their place. Having viewed a specimen from one of Moore's ushers, which Moore had not checked first, the Bishop commended more frequent latin composition and more vigilant inspection. Even if oversights, the errors should have been corrected.

"If they were more exercised in Latin (the language they are to give an account of their faith in, when they come for orders) your eldest scholar would hardly have delivered me a composition in that tongue as a specimen of his Latininty where he made fruor a passive verb and prodere to signify profitting... I recommend to you to let your scholars, especially the head ones, be more versed in making Latin prose than English poetry."[38]

Although it would be tempting in the reference to English poetry to see Moore's broader and liberal curriculum, it is likely to be nothing more than translation of the Latin poets, an easier task than translating English into Latin.

Hildesley warned Moore against "too much tenderness as too much asperity". Judging by other accounts, this was preaching to the converted. According to Hugh Stowell, his talented brother Joseph, who delighted Moore by his quickness and aptitude, was the exception to the rule of rod and ferrule for the majority. The form of 'loiking the booby' under Moore was for the boy who answered correctly to slap the dunce's face: Joseph Stowell was so advanced he could scarcely reach the face of the boy he was intended to smack.[39]

A curious note-book used by Moore gives some insight into the life of the school. It was used partly by a pupil, Jonathan Tiffin, a relation of Moore, and partly by Moore himself. The number of pupils in the years 1749-1760 averaged around eighteen, the "Moore Charity boys" tending to be sons of widows. The boys enter throughout the year and pay the fee of one pound in odd sums at irregular times. In 1751 the school made £21/7/0 from fees. The usher received the five pounds laid down by Phil. Moore the merchant, yet Thomas Corlett, later Vicar of German, received only four in 1760. The ushers tended to last around two years before receiving a curacy, occasionally doing service at Bride — Thomas Cubbon received £20 for this in 1763.[40]

Butler referred to Moore as "eminently distinguished as the divine, the gentleman and the scholar",[41] One visit to Dublin resulted in £12 being spent on books, and in the wider field of Manx history, Moore was above all recalled as the man who superintended the translation of the Bible into Manx, encouraged by Hildesley.

A significant landmark in the history of the school came in 1756, again in the will of William Murrey, not long after the death of Ross and while Castletown was still in ruins. Murrey saw the developmemt of a tertiary stage of learning as a safeguard for the see.

> "And whereas there is a very great decay in the education of youth, for qualifying them to serve in the ministry and service of the church within the Island, I will and bequeath unto the Right Rev. the present Lord Bishop of this diocese, and to his successors the sum of twenty four pounds, Manx value, to be applied unto a Teacher, and to one, two, or three Scholars, as the Lord Bishop, or his successors shall think most useful, for the purpose that the same is intended. And that the said Scholars ... I would wish to have their education at Douglas, while a good school is continued there."[42]

The reference to "while a good school" was almost certainly with one eye on what had happened at Castletown, but Murrey very fairly left his wishes concerning Douglas subject to the Bishop's overruling power if the intended purpose could be achieved better elsewhere. A codicil to the will attached the donation more formally to Douglas, with the two St. Matthew's wardens and the chaplain choosing (with the Bishop and the will's executor) the youths, now expressly limited to two, to be on the foundation, the wardens also acting as trustees with the Bishop and executor, William Teare. Murrey also secured the annuity by having it charged upon his own estates, well aware from the Castletown monies' history that "many unforeseen accidents do happen", as he himself had written in the will. Of the annual twenty four pounds, the Chaplain was to receive twelve, and the two scholars six each. Bishop and Trustees were still empowered to alter the terms if they thought expedient.

The provision of this third tier meant that the Island was no longer totally reliant on Castletown for the supply of native clergy.

In his own will, Moore claimed only to have "been instrumental in the education of several ingenious sensible and pious young men for the service of the church and other publick stations in life" but Butler went further.

> "All the clergy of the Isle of Man, at the time of his death, except four only, were educated by Mr. Moore; and by them he was always distinguished with peculiar respect and affection.[43]

Although taken at face value by David Craine as applying to Douglas Grammar School, it must include the contacts at Bishopscourt, as a greater proportion went through Castletown than Douglas. One Douglas pupil, John Gell had an unusual career. He began with Moore at the age of seven, stayed the long period of seven years, went away to study navigation for two years, was captured at sea by the French, and then returned to the Grammar School, by then under Robert Quayle, eventually being ordained by Bishop Crigan on his arrival.

Douglas had been singled out by Wilson as deserving a Public Library like that of Castletown, as distinct from the Parish Libraries for the clergy only. St. Matthew's Register contains lists from 1725 onwards, while Wilson made his own list in 1740. When the third tier of education, about which Moore was able to write to Moffatt to Dr. Walker in 1766 in his reply about provision of education for the ministry, was set up in Douglas, Bishop Hildesley was most generous in his benefactions — a list of 1775 recorded 233 from this source. When Moore gave way to Quayle in 1783, the incoming chaplain listed the books by size and arrived at a total of 1691, though his columns add up to 332. Whatever the figures, from the point of view of literary resources, Douglas was well equipped to aid its two men proceeding to holy orders. Quayle himself received preferment to the mother church at Braddan in 1792, and after a very short spell under Nicholas Christian who applied incessantly for every vacant living, the school passed to Hugh Stowell, later Rector of Ballaugh, under whom it reached a new peak in numbers.

. His diary kept in his Douglas years cannot now be traced, although in existence this century, but his *Notes for Autobiography* survive. A native of Douglas, he received his education in his early years at Ramsey, and then went to Castley at the age of thirteen in 1782. Soon he looked after three or four boys himself, and was awarded an Academic Scholarship in 1786. He turned to divinity rather than classics, and with fees attained an income of £25. While serving at Arbory as a supplementary clergyman, a memorial from Douglas led to his appointment at the Grammar School there in 1792. He found eighteen pupils at that time, but by 1800 he could record in his diary "My school consists of 50 scholars." His health was not good, and after being confined by a 'putrid fever' to bed for seven weeks, followed by the death of his brother Joseph in 1801, he requested a country parish, moving to Lonan. His future educational work lay in leading the Sunday School movement in the Island from 1808, and later raising money for Bishop Ward for churches and a college.[44]

By 1800 the alternative school established by Wilson was thus flourishing, serving the growing town of Douglas at grammar school level, and making its own contribution to the third tier of education.

THE ENDOWED SCHOOLS FOR HIGHER LEARNING IN PEEL

Despite further dithering over the site of Philip Moore's Grammar School, the same period saw the West of the Island benefit from the establishment in the end of not one but two schools for advanced learning, both in the town of Peel, and thereby giving Peel a total of three endowed schools. The long-suffering Moore brothers knew full well that it had been their father's intention to build at Peel, and they offered witnesses who would testify to the donor's own thoughts. Bishop Hildesley was quite willing as Trustee for the case to be heard in London, but had to retract when his co-Trustees, the House of Keys still doggedly insisted on 'rebuilding or repairing an ancient School-House at Castletown'. The Moores, finding that their Memorandum of January 1758 was not even returned to them, and that they were slandered in 'a most unchristian like manner' before the Bishop, resolved to publish their own side of the matter.

The years passed, and the matter remained unresolved. Another son of Philip Moore, the Rev. James Moore of Dublin, urged that in honour some respect should be given to his father's wishes, and referred 'to most authentic Proofs of my father's intention to purchase nigh unto Peel'.[45] By 1762 the notion of aiding Castletown Grammar School had been laid aside, as that matter had already been solved with the settlement of the Impropriate Fund and the vigilance of Castley, yet the Keys began to consider once more a plot at Coolingen, the site in the Parish of Marown considered more than any place to be the literal centre of the Isle of Man. As an inducement to make the Keys build at Peel instead, James Moore let it be known that he was disposed in that case to give a further four hundred pounds himself.

It soon transpired that James' chosen path was to use his four hundred pounds to finance a separate scheme of his own. He brought from his brother George part of a plot of land purchased from James Cowill 'whereon to build a School House and Office for a Mathematical Teacher which I shall further endow with £20 a year for ever for the perpetual instruction of the boys gratis.'[46] He requested a plan and description of the ground, and hoped it would be complete by May 1763. The "small neat House" and the buildings attached were to be as durable as possible, with solid Manx slate, bricks for the inside from Ballamore, and timber from Norway now the seas were open. In January 1763, James drew up his will, leaving the rents of three houses in Dublin on the Blind Quay, worth twenty pounds a year,

> "In trust for the erection and endowment of a Mathematical School in the Isle of Man, in order to have ten poor scholars taught gratis for ever, in the different branches of that science; the site of the Schoolhouse not to be farther distant from St. John's Chapel than in Peeltown."[47]

This was a new direction in the provision of higher education on the Island. Mathematical Schools were intended to be much more practical and vocational than places of abstract learning without practical application, and navigation and surveying formed important parts of the curriculum. The forerunner in the field, the Mathematical School at Christ's Hospital, where from 1693 forty boys were chosen from the main school to study arithmetic and navigation before being apprenticed to a captain for seven years,[48] was followed at the beginning of the Eighteenth Century not only by Grammar Schools such as Dartmouth where there was one master for Latin and another for English, mathematics and navigation, but also by a number of endowed schools geared to navigation and making no provision for Latin. Most were on the south coast in Kent, Sussex and Hampshire, although Whitby in 1702 was an exception.[49]

In 1701 Lewis Maidwell had urged a national school of navigation be established, and eventually a Naval Academy at Chelsea was started in 1777, but as the century progressed endowments faded, and the private academies became the principal exponents of this specialised training in technical subjects. Those explicitly called Mathematical Schools tended to be one day and evening schools only, normally without boarders, but in the broader based Academies too, there was nearly always the option to study navigation, even if only a minority ever did.[50] (Academies in general will be considered later under Private Schools.) Nicholas Hans has described the Teacher of Mathematics as typically a layman, lacking university education, but able, efficient, and pioneering modern teaching techniques with a stress on experiments, mostly self-taught or 'autodidacts' in his terminology, and often the actual designer of instruments himself.

James Moore was thus following in well trodden paths when he set up his Mathematical School, although endowment as opposed to private venture made it something of a rarity in the latter half of the century. The school was in no way intended to rival his father's intended establishment, but rather to compliment it: for a town which relied so heavily on the sea as Peel, its utility and value was obvious.

The right to nominate scholars was to be vested in brothers Philip and George, the latter as his executor, and their representatives. They were to appoint a master "sufficiently qualified by ample testemonies", exhibiting him to the Bishop (or Vicar-General if the see were vacant). If they neglected this task the Bishop could himself appoint after twelve months had elapsed. The master would be given legal powers to receive the rents, or recover by distress, as much as James Moore himself was able.

One curious feature of the will was that since the site was quite decided upon, why should there be the strange reference to "no further distant from St. John's Chapel than is Peeltown"? The likely answer is that to some extent it mirrored the wording of his father's bequest, and dropped a heavy hint to the Keys. St. John's, the meeting place of Tynwald, was accepted as the centre of the 'Island, and the limitation to Peeltown would indicate that Peel alone would fit the wording of his father's will about the site of the proposed school. There was an implied rebuke to Douglas, which petitioned that it should have the Grammar School, being near the centre of the Island.[51]

James' letters of 1763 display a growing sense of frustration about delays with the Grammar School. He approved the support he received from Peel — "Peeltown right to exert itself in my scheme[52] — but felt the situation was passive until the House of Keys finally determined the issue. He wished to travel to the Island to expedite "our great scheme", fearing delays if he did not come, but doubtful if his health permitted the journey.[53]

Finally the long family pressure was crowned with success. George Moore's colleagues in the Keys and the Bishop at last unanimously agreed in 1764 that the Grammar School should be "forthwith fixed and settled in or near the town of Peel in that plot or parcel of land called Bowaley Spittle which Mr. George Moore lately purchased from James Cowill", and that a proper schoolhouse should be erected alongside the Mathematical School, their Trustees expressing agreement.[54] In 1770 the Bishop with the support of eleven Keys decided that a house in Peel bought from Philip Moore as a potential Grammar School "be forthwith repaired, altered, amended and made commodious for the reception of the schoolmaster out of the interest money in the hands of Capt. Thomas Moore."[55]

Although a manuscript *History of Peel Grammar School to 1785* states that the Rev. John Parr was the first master of the school in 1772, other evidence indicates clearly that the Grammar School was under a master straight after the decision of 1764, and even before, as though it had been set up officially without the explicit approval of Keys and Bishop. The Rev. Philip Moore of Douglas in his note book made an entry as clearly as February 1760; "Crebbin I recommended to the Lord Bishop for the school at Peel."[56] His usher, Charles Crebbin, clearly took the school, for in 1763 a letter of Bishop Hildesley related that the Rev. Paul Crebbin of Santan wanted his son home, and that Peel School would be vacant at mid-summer.[57] If William Fitzsimmon took it, Moore could have Thomas Cubbon as his assistant in his stead. The terms of Fitzsimmon's licence from the Bishop makes explicit mention of the Latin and English School — it is clearly the advanced school of Moore which is being talked about.[58] John Quayle, writing to Hildesley about getting a private tutor to replace a collegian from Glasgow who had died, remarked that Philip Moore recommended Mr. Fitzsimmon "Master of the Peel Grammar School", and Hildesley writing to Philip Moore mentioned the "young man at the head of the grammar school", the "Peel Poedagogue".[59] Fitzsimmon, a brash and arrogant youth, found the position too much for him, 'his proud plumes being cropped', and Hildesley had to bring him back like the slave Onesimus, to whom the Bishop compared him.

The reference in Fitzsimmon's licence to the Latin and English School is significant, as it rules out a facile contrast between the relevant vocational education to be obtained in the Mathematical School and the hidebound traditional Grammar School of the father's foundation. For the phrase "to teach Latin and such other learning" was different from the time-honoured "Grammar School" which totally dominated foundations before 1600, and had been used in the Island by Barrow and Wilson. The Fitzsimmon mention of English reveals that it would be false to think of "such other learning" in terms of the Greek tongue, which would be one possible interpretation. An awareness by founders of the cramping narrowness of a purely classical education and the need for wider learning had led in the Seventeenth Century to a growing number of foundations specifically allowing other learning, although still only one in three.[60] Moore's wording was thus intended to be in full accord with the Eighteenth Century, when 'grammar only' foundations shrank to a mere ten per cent in England. 'Such other learning' left the curriculum very flexible, but the phrase about fitting youth for the service of the country in church and state did seem to hint strongly at what are now classed as 'non-vocational subjects'.

"In curriculum the grammar school had become a diversified and differentiated institution by the 18th century. No longer a school for classical languages only, it was moving towards a new position in a changing educational scene."[61]

On the Island, therefore, as elsewhere, the criticisms of the narrowness of the curriculum and the way it was taught made by teachers within the schools such as John Clarke, John Holmes and James Barclay, and without by Samuel Butler and Joseph Priestley were already being answered to some degree. In Priestley's view, "the necessity of the thing has already in many instances, forced a change..."[62]

Peel thus found itself in the happy situation of having not only a London company providing its elementary education, but no less than two establishments for higher education, each in its own way representative of modern trends.

Compared with the ponderous movements of the Keys, the Moore family acted swiftly when the Mathematical School came into operation. By February 1763 a Jack Smyth had made a "neat and commodious model" and solved the problem of exterior facing by recommending best Liverpool bricks, "which he says will last as long as stone."[63] The school received its equipment as James Moore had arranged before his death. "I order my books to be sold in exchange for Mathematical books and instruments, for the use of the above Mathematical School.[64] Brother George also took a keen interest in the school, writing to the first master, John Barker, about the books and instruments he would recommend as proper and suitable to answer the donor's intention, and what he himself could do to the extent of twenty pounds. Barker supplemented his income through tuition to private pupils. His receipts show Philip and Joseph Cowls paying a guinea a quarter for tuition in Wilson's Navigation and Logarithms, while Miss Sally Moore paid two guineas a quarter.[65] His salary being paid in Irish money meant that it was worth about nineteen pounds Manx and eighteen British rather than the nominal twenty pounds. In the case of this school at least, the clear stipulation of ten boys to be taught gratis, mentioned on Barker's receipts for payment, avoided disputes about the precise meaning of free.

The Mathematical School was thus spared the wranglings which afflicted the Grammar School at Peel, but Barker did not stay long, announcing in a letter of July 1767 "I have given up the teaching of sd branches and the School at Peeltown."[66], and a letter to George Moore in 1768 told how he rented a Belfast house at £12 a year and had eight pupils. An illustrious successor soon presented himself. Richard Wilson, a schoolmaster from Whitehaven, where he taught English, Mathematics and specialised in Navigation, according to his handbill of 1762, wrote to enquire "what the said school may be worth yearly in a medium way, and the price at which you think scholars should be taken in at."[67] The response was clearly satisfactory as Wilson stayed for over twenty years. He typified the practical nature of mathematical teachers, obtaining a high reputation for his work on the Island as cartographer and surveyor. He complied in 1784 a most valuable list of the pupils he had taught, complete with dates of entering and leaving. The list is presumably complete, and if so, notable for the fact there appear no names other than those educated free on the foundation or through benefactions. The total of ninety five pupils over sixteen years makes an average intake of six a year. Entries occur in every month of the year, but occasionally small clusters of three or four enter within the space of a fortnight. The average school life was less than two years, with one John Quay staying the longest at nearly four full years. Three former pupils were captains of ships and five were chief mates. The majority were at sea, but the school had produced a surveyor and three schoolmasters, including two teachers of mathematics.[68] At the time of compiling his list, Wilson had fifteen boys at the school, though not one had been there two years.

Apart from the ten boys on the foundation, a Manxman living at Walton-on-Thames, John Stevenson, gave £100 to the school in 1775" from his affection to his native country... for the education of two poor scholars for ever," with the Governor and Bishop, appointed as Trustees, to nominate alternatively.[69] Caesar and John Quirk were the first scholars to be nominated, but Caesar lasted only one year. John managed over two years, long enough to see the entrance of John Cottier, the first nomination under the gift of five guineas from Governor Smith, who gained by his annual donation the right to nominate two scholars. Smith was a good friend to the school, whose potential he recognised: "I hope some solid good may arise to the Island".[70] His deputy, Lt.-Governor Dawson, on the other hand, took a very dim view of being asked to forward to Smith a petition from clergy and High Bailiffs asking for British Government assistance to enable Wilson to increase the number of his pupils. The end, of helping Manxmen gain promotion on the seas to which so many were forced to turn to earn a living, was made into a cause deserving of English support. They would become "more serviceable to their King, to their country" as well to themselves. Dawson would not even present the petition to Smith, stating testily

> "... the people who wished to give their children a mathemetical (sic) education ought to pay for it and were well able, that if they found such a school useful to the Island, no better way could be devised to encourage it than to make a subscription among themselves, for as for being an advantage to England that

Manx beggars should be mathematically educated I was sure it was not the Navy of England being in much more want of common sailors than of officers."[71]

The petition did eventually bear fruit. In 1789 William Wyndham Grenville wrote to Smith that His Majesty George III was pleased to authorise from the Island revenue thirty pounds a year for "the support of the Charity School in the town of Peel for the Education of a number of Boys for the Service of the Navy."[72] The Governor was to see this was carried out under the "Inspection and Direction of the Resident Governor." Although there was probably some confusion in London about the school — it was thought to be in Douglas at first — this was in fact an interesting early example of direct state aid for secondary education.

Wilson's reputation stood high within a short space of time. By 1771 his income was augmented by an annual gift from the Academic Students Fund of five pounds: "Mr. Richard Wilson of the Mathematical School, in Peel-town, has by his great care and pains instructed several youths in Mathematical knowledge, who have become great proficients therein..."[73] Archdeacon Mylrea too referred to the "great utility and benefit the inhabitants of this Isle have received... from the Mathematical School" and himself gave a house and gardens for the use of the school in 1776.[75] In his will, the founder's brother, Sir George Moore, left the school in trust to his grandson, George Quayle of Castletown, together with "my house in Peeltown, formerly known by the name of Gibony's House, now occupied by the present Mathematical teacher, Richard Wilson" to be enjoyed by him and his successors

Although the education was free, it was hard to spare boys from poor families, and in 1771 the Academic Students Fund provided five pounds to the family of John Cannell to enable him to stay on at school, an early example of a maintenance grant. In Wilson's 1784 list, Cannel (sic) was at sea in the East Indies.

The course of events did not run as smoothly at the Grammar School where the loose wording of Phil. Moore's will caused his institution to run into yet further difficulties. When John Parr died in April 1777, the question of his successor split the Keys and Bishop, posing the problem of voting powers. Were there in effect two trustees, bishop and Keys, or twenty five, with the Keys easily able to swamp the Bishop. When the opinion of Sir Wadsworth Busk, the Attorney-General, was sought by Bishop Richmond, who favoured a Mr. Callow for the post, he stated he found it hard to accept that the Bishop should be equal only to one insignificant member of "that most insignificant body of men, the House of Keys", although he confessed the will to be vague — "in my opinion totally undecided."[76] He held the report of the Duke of Athol on the rival candidates to be binding on the Keys. Further reflection convinced him there were only two trustees, and if the Bishop gave Callow a licence, he would be "completely in office".[77] The Keys fought back, stressing the temporal nature of the school, and learned references concerning the scope of Canon 77 of the Lateran Council of 1215, of Elizabethan decisions of Convocation and Statutes of James I, were tossed to and fro.

By 1781 the principal inhabitants of Peel, Patrick and German, sent a petition to the House of Keys complaining that the lack of a master frustrated the founder's intent and deprived the youth of the area.[78] For their part the people of Douglas submitted a Petition asking that the Grammar School be moved there, as Douglas was the real centre of the Island, offered greater opportunities, and considered the Peel School "totally annihilated and extinguished".[79] The Trustees resolved in October to postpone consideration of the Douglas petition, and to appoint instead to Peel "with all convenient speed". They would meet again on November 5th, and invited candidates to appear with their certificates. One application was received from David Harrison of St. Mark's Chapel, who declared himself a pupil of Castley, with several years' experience of teaching, and believed that his progress fitted him well for Peel Grammar School. He regretted that he had not had time to secure testimonials. The Keys were more impressed with Mr. Heterick, who did produce good testimonials, and was accordingly in the opinion of a majority the sole candidate. He was duly appointed and the bishop's licence to teach was applied for.[80]

However, the new bishop, George Mason, was no more inclined than his predecessor Richmond to accept that the Keys had such powers. Before the meeting of November 5th, Mason had declared his willingness to assist in changing the site of the school, if that were to be found necessary, but categorically denied the will gave any right to the Keys to make a nomination to the school together with the Bishop; that right "pertains wholly to the Diocesan of this Isle". To avoid inconvenience to the public, he had already appointed John Bridson, the Curate of Santan, as master.[81] Indeed Bridson had on November 2nd informed Henry Corlett, the Vicar of German, of his appointment and requested immediate possession of the school.

While Bridson may have been first off the mark, it was Heterick who emerged as the victor in the struggle, and soon showed himself to be a man of vigour, sending one letter to the House of Keys stating he had successfully entered the school, and had found that the principal could easily yield interest greater than the salary paid to him, and another to William Callow, M.H.K. inviting members of the Keys to inspect the condition of the schoolroom and see what alterations would be desirable.[82] In April 1782 Callow informed the Bishop that he was one of four in a Committee appointed by the House of Keys, and sought a meeting to discuss repairs and alterations. The Bishop in return demanded a clear definition of their powers, refusing to answer the request for a meeting as the Keys proposed. The Keys' messenger Thomas Stowell reported back that the Bishop merely repeated over and over that he would give no answer.[83] The Committee offered the Bishop one last chance, stating that as he had not replied they must proceed, or they would fail their trust, but he was welcome to attend a meeting they had fixed with Deemster Moore, who held the school's funds, at Kirk Michael on May 22nd. If this were not possible another date around that time would be possible.[84] The Keys vigorously upheld their right to have appointed Heterick, refusing to acknowledge the application to them of Canon 77 which said that schoolmasters needed the bishop's permission to teach. This ought not to bind laity, who had no voice in Convocation, and any act to the contrary did not extend to the Isle of Man.

The Keys found difficulties not only with the Bishop, but also with Deemster Thomas Moore, who by an agreement of March 19 1760 had promised to pay interest at 4%, but owed in June 1782 £240 in interest. Since the Keys' Committee could get at least 5%, it was agreed with Moore that he pay both principal and interest on April 19th 1783. However in November of that year, Moore was still offering only promises. Eventually the Keys demanded payment by March 19th 1784, or they would ask for 5%. Moore in return would only offer to pay back £300 and 5% on his own personal security (not land) on the rest. A Petition was sent to Governor Dawson, asking him to deal with Moore to get both principal and interest.[85]

Initial repair to the schoolhouse in 1770 had cost £42, the total rising to £79 by 1778. Heterick's plans however, involved more extensive alterations, involving the raising of the schoolroom one storey higher, and cost £163. A statement of accounts in 1785 showed a reasonably healthy state of affairs. The debt for the repairs was only £38, and trustees awarded a back-dated £5 per annum to Heterick for his 'particular attention to the duties of the said school and of his trouble and superintendence of repairs.', which totalled £16. There was a balance left of nearly £60 which would be added to the principal bringing it up to £560, making it possible to raise the master's salary to £28 a year in the future.[86] Some of the expenses were paid by contributions, George Moore for instance giving ten pounds,[86] but the total absorption of the interest in the master's salary meant that nothing was put by systematically for repairs. Reliance purely on outside contributions for future maintenance boded ill for the future of any school, and the Peel Schools were to be no exceptions to this rule.

For the time being however all seemed well. The claim of Douglas that it had been the site in the mind of Philip Moore had been successfully resisted, as had the earlier attempt to divert the funds to the aid of Castletown in 1758, disputes between bishop and Keys had died down, and the school restored and flourishing, providing a Classical and English education for around two dozen pupils.

In July 1792, when John Stowell, the eldest of fifteen brothers, became master, an early advertisement showed the teaching of Latin was not being neglected.

"J. Stowell, successor of the Rev Mr Christian to the Classical Free School at Peel respectfully informs the public that he intends teaching young ladies English Grammar: to which purpose he means to allot extra hours so as not to interrupt his Latin students."[88]

John Stowell's place in Manx history owes more to his witty poems than his teaching, of which the sole reference in his biography states "his pupils spoke well of him."[89] An example of his writing comes from the Retrospect, a look at 1790, especially the Duke's desire to gain compensation for the loss of his rights.

> "Alas! what language or what poet's quill
> Can tell how Mona dreaded Atholl's *Bill*
> No timid dove so much the eagle feared
> Nor partridge when the gunner's note she heard
> 'Twas confidently whispered by the wise
> He fully meant to peck out Mona's eyes.

Joseph Stowell, who in 1799 succeeded his brother John at the Grammar School and also applied successfully for the mastership of the Mathematical School in the same year, thus bringing the two schools under one master, was the most outstanding of all Manx teachers. The very fact he was elected to two schools with different emphases speaks volumes in itself. The young man who was spared Philip Moore's rod and supped on cones and circles with Castley was a man of wide abilities and advanced ideas. His first venture into teaching was a tutor for Dawson's successor, Lt.-Governor Shaw at Castle Rushen. Shaw had a machine used for treating ailments by electricity which intrigued Stowell, who read up the subject and conducted experiments. In 1795 he opened up his own academy at the Bowling Green, Castletown, very quickly gaining an excellent reputation. Col. Mark Wilks suggested his nephew be sent there even in preference to Castley — "I believe that to be your best seminary." Pupils came from England and Ireland, and Stowell soon required the assistance of an emigré from Nantes, M. Le Reaux, "a good classicist, complete French teacher and powerful co-adjutator."[90] This seems to be the first reference to modern languages being taught on the Island. Stowell's very success with his school brought problems, his brother Hugh recalling how having to switch from boys of seven learning the first rudiments to advanced students studying Euclid or Newton's Principia proved very tiring for Joseph.

His approach to education varied greatly from the ferrule-wielding Moore or the sadistic Castley. He claimed in an advertisement for his private academy "to study the peculiar geniuses and dispositions of his pupils, as well as to cultivate their talent for composition, and their taste in belles lettres," and for once this was not mere platitude. He worked upon systems of reward rather than the usual punishment, and "avoided all harshness in the treatment of his pupils." Good work was recognised by oval ornamented cards or by books: "AB ingenuus et optimae spei puer hoc diligentiae et virtitis testimonium merito consecutus est."[91] He was of course not unique in this view. The Rev. Mr. Fitzsimmons, the proud youth who annoyed Hildesley so much by his arrogance, later in life attacked the usual mode of learning, which broke the spirit and extinguished every spark of native genius by painful plodding, urging a Mr. Oughton to develop a love of reading in his son.[92]

Fitzsimmons too had formulated a scheme of education, "widely different from the public seminaries", but that of Stowell and his friend Dr. Haskins proved too novel when their plan for Peel was sent in a prospectus to Governor Shaw and Bishop Crigan. Stowell was in favour of mixed education, but the Bishop "decidedly condemned" the admission of females into the school, as well as the notion of an annual travelling expedition for pupils. Yet although he deemed it impracticable to execute in this country, the Bishop approved of the notion of a workshop for practical mechanics. Stowell also introduced the idea of annual public examinations, and the Bishop and Governor Shaw set down their names for a guinea to provide books for the most deserving, although Crigan had doubts. "I rather imagine it will be difficult to engage the higher class to concur in carrying out some parts of your plan into execution." Yet he offered to attend the examination, dining with masters and scholars "to give the highest respectability and effect to the plan," and to select the examiners from the most learned of his clergy. Some parts were modified by Stowell in answer to the Bishop's points, to the annoyance of Haskins who protested he had incurred expense in procuring his philosophical (i.e. scientific) apparatus. Some of Crigan's suggestions were improvements on the original, such as books instead of medals, with impressions in the manner of Trinity College, Dublin, and dividing the school into six rather than two for the examinations. He also suggested special subject prizes for Geography, History, Elocution, English Grammar, and two for Mathematics. Governor Shaw was delighted — "it will tend in some degree to give celebrity to your school." Stowell himself was convinced he was on the right road.

> "That the Happiness of Society in a great measure depends upon the education of youth is universally admitted. The adoption of judicious methods in public schools is therefore an object of material importance. In such seminaries, public examinations are intended with most beneficial consequences. They are of course, it is humbly suggested, not beneath the attention of the great."[93]

Sadly Stowell's health did not match his other capacities and his brother recorded that even at Castletown, his pupils refrained from seeking assistance as they perceived the burden was proving too heavily for him. At Peel, despite the help of an assistant from Scotland with methematics, looking after two schools and taking private pupils wore him out, especially when renting a farm to increase income proved to yield no profits, even after his intensive reading in agriculture. On top of failing nerves and digestive difficulties, he caught typhus, and died in 1801, not yet twenty-nine years old. An article in the *Monthly Magazine* of May 1802 by W. H. Watts, entitled "A Sketch of the State of Mann and of the Present Conditions of the Isle of Man", expressed the sorrow felt at the death of Stowell, a man free from pedantry, yet "Languages, mathematics, theology and natural philosophy were all equally familiar to him."[94]

RAMSEY GRAMMAR SCHOOL

Of the places of higher education, Ramsey was the last to cease to use a church building. Castletown and Douglas had by 1760 long been accustomed to have exclusive use of a school, even if in Castletown's case the building was the old mediaeval chapel. The two Peel schools had no connections, as far as is known, with any church building from their foundation. As with the earlier case of Patrick, Bishop Wilson had insisted that the reconsecrated Ballure Chapel of 1747 should not be used as a school, but whether any heed was paid to this episcopal injunction is doubtful. It is more likely that the inflow of water in 1759 concentrated minds on finding a site for a purpose-built school to greater effect. Shortly after the arrival of the Rev. John Crellin as Chaplain of Ramsey, Charles Cowle and wife Jane conveyed to Crellin and his wardens a plot of land called Croit Vess for 'a chapel and schoolroom for the clerk and children of the town of Ramsey and for such other purposes as the Ordinary, the Chaplain and wardens with the captain and six of the principal of the town of Ramsey shall at any time think fit to appropriate to'[95] (The latitude offered by the closing words was fully used at the close of the century by its use as a courthouse). John Feltham, an observant visitor to the Island in the last decade of the Eighteenth Century, stated that the schoolhouse built about thirty years ago measured forty feet by seventeen, somewhat smaller than the chapel at Ballure.[96]

How long the thirty pounds from the Insular Revenue was paid to the Peel Mathematical School is unknown, but the total emoluments for that school alone came to £60 a year in 1789, without including any gratuities from parents. In Ramsey by contrast, John Crellin had to work for far less. As Chaplain too of Ramsey, he had the work of an incumbent, but received only £10 a year, and as he was the only master in higher education not provided with a house or a parsonage, he reckoned his stipend was in reality £4/18/0. He was thus very glad of his teaching quarterage, for when in 1769 he applied for a share in the Impropriate Fund, he pleaded dire poverty "had not your memorialist Recourse to some other method of procuring a Livelyhood."[97] Hugh Stowell wrote in his notes for his autobiography that under Crellin he "made a considerable progress in classical learning", but an ominous sign for the school was the sale in 1766 by Mr. Cholmondeley of the saltworks at Winford, upon which the payment of the ten pounds had been secured. It appears that already the money had been commuted to salt. Although Bishop Hildesley secured a deed in which the Woods family took over the obligation to pay the salt, performance did not match up to the promise. Ramsey was not considered a title in the church to be esteemed, and after Crellin's departure there was another period of rapid turnover of Chaplains. The son of Vicar-General Moore should have succeeded Crellin in the opinion of an indignant letter writer, who thought it was disgraceful that Moore became Chaplain to the Lord Lieutenant of Ireland, and yet was paid a supernumery stipend of £30 still — a "sad prostitution of that fund especially as Ramsey Chapel stands now idle".[98] Daniel Mylrea (1783), John Bridson (1785) and Nicholas Christian (1788) soon came and went and stability only returned with

Henry Maddrell in 1790.[99] Virtually the only reference to Maddrell's time was that of Sir Mark Cubbon, later Commissioner of Mysore in India, who went to Maddrell from the parochial school in Maughold. Yet his brief reference to "I wish he had taken more pains to thrash Latin into me" at least shows that the more advanced learning was being pursued still at Ramsey. Another of Maddrell's pupils was Thomas Howard, later Rector of Ballaugh, but his career suggests that Ramsey was regarded as being at the bottom of the second tier of education. He was sent from Ramsey to Joseph Stowell at Castletown and then to St. Bee's, where he stayed until he joined the Royal Manx Fencibles.[100]

There was at least one other attempt to combine two levels of education in one school, when in 1772 the small hamlet of St. Marks in the Parish of Malew was given its own school and chapel, for which it had appealed on account of distance. The deed referred to the officiating clergyman receiving "for Latin, three shillings and sixpence".[101] There is no evidence to suggest that higher learning took place, yet the ambition for such a small place is interesting, especially being reasonably near to Castletown where Castley was in his prime.

One bare mention of a possible intention to establish a grammar school dates from the same time, in 1767. In one of his letters Bishop Hildesley, mentioned the desire of the Vicar of Marown to have William Clucas as curate. "He has the notion I believe of setting up a Grammar School for I think his strong body cannot want help in the duties of the Church." Although Coolingen was in the parish of Marown, and previously considered as the site of Moore's Grammar School, nothing appears to have gone further.

CONCLUSION

Although not all schemes came to fruition, by the end of the Eighteenth Century the Island's provision for higher education was quite impressive. Each of the four Manx towns was able to boast of at last one school giving a higher level of education. The schools had come into existence in a variety of ways, by quasi-governmental action at Castletown, by private endowment by the Moore family in the two Peel Schools, and the injection of new endowments into originally petty schools in the case of Douglas and Ramsey: yet all flourished in the late Eighteenth Century, and there was little sign of the malaise that afflicted many grammar schools in England and Ireland. The Parliamentary Enquiry into the Royal Schools of Ulster in 1791 for instance found a deplorable state of affairs: a master at Banagher had a residence and 204 acres but no pupils since 1777; the Raphoe master had done no duty for six years; the Carysford master resided elsewhere and had never kept a school at all.[102]

Nor could it be claimed that the education the Manx higher school offered was out of touch with modern demands and developments, a charge levied against many of the English grammar schools. By evolution and practice at Castletown, particularly under Castley, and by the founders' direct intentions at the schools of Peel, the classical straight-jacket had been successfully avoided. Although Ramsey is an unknown quantity, Douglas under Hugh Stowell, pupil of Castley and brother of the brilliant Joseph, is not likely to have lagged behind in making his teaching relevant to the needs of the age, as the increase in his numbers suggests. Although Mark Wilks regretted in 1799 that "Modern Chymistry which (after Mathematics and the science to which it is allied) is worth all the rest of the Sciences . . . had not made much progress in the Island", even this suggests that some had been made. The hopes of Haskins for Peel that boys would have a knowledge of all arts and sciences, with a practical knowledge of manufacturing processes, was indicative of the forward-looking spirit of the Island, also reflected in the new approach to the art of teaching, with motivation of pupils achieved by encouragement rather than by fear, and rewards rather than by punishment. A careful and thorough observer, John Feltham, concluded that the Island "afforded a sufficient share of schools for teaching the classics, theology and the arts and sciences".[103] Even at the third level where training in practice had been whittled down from early hopes to provision of clergymen, the curriculum was broad and comprehensive, with opportunity for the outstanding youth to study at university in England or Ireland. All in all. the rather remote Island could, as far as higher education as well as elementary learning was concerned, make a reasonable claim to be in the vanguard of progress.

REFERENCES

CHAPTER FIVE

1. MD 436 3/33 James Wilks to Hildesley, Aug 12 1756.
2. R. S. Tompson, *Op cit* 27, 84. See also Vincent, *Op cit* 40f.
3. MD 436 20/25 Feb 3 1758 Ibid 20/26.
4. MD 436 20/22 Apr 7 1758, Memorial of James Wilks.
5. MS 4283.
6. Athol Papers 60/26.
7. MD 436 20/22.
8. Ibid 20/24. Undated.
9. Ibid 20/23 May 10 1757.
10. Tompson, Op cit 23.
11. BH 3594.
12. MD 441 172.
13. MS 4834 Apr 30 1783.
14. MD 436 20/23 May 10m1757.
15. Ibid 20/25 Sept 12 1758.
16. Liber Cancell June 20 1775.
17. BC 30.
18. Athol Papers 121/7.
19. Ibid Book 68 July 11 1777; 121/11 and 12.
20. George Waldron, *A Description of the Isle of Man* 62.
21. MD 441 172.
22. Sun Aug 5 1835, Letter of Robert Brown.
23. BH 3598 Petition to Governor Wood (undated).
24. Butler *Hildesley's Memoirs* 505 July 3 1764.
25. MD 436 20/14 Jan 24 1757.
26. Hugh Stowell, *Memoir of the Rev Joseph Stowell* Houlst and Son, Wellington, Salop 1821 Oct 3 1792 45.
27. Butler, *Op cit* 569.
28. Vincent, *Op cit* 99; Tompson *Op cit* 23.
29. BC 37-38.
30. Athol Papers 136/13.
31. MS 4315C.
32. Athol Papers 122 (3rd) 28.
33. Ibid 116 (2nd) 26.
34. Butler, *Op cit* 70.
35. Athol Papers 116 (2nd) 10.
36. Tompson, *Op cit Chapter* 3.
37. Ed. A. W. Moore, *The Letters of Bishop Hildesley 1755-1776*. Dec. 16 1764.

38 Ibid Dec 31 1764.
39 Hugh Stowell, *Op cit* 5.
40 Hildesley's Letter, Jan 27 1763.
41 Butler, *Op cit* 186.
42 BC 114.
43 Butler, *Op cit* 186.
44 Hugh Stowell *Notes for Autobiography*, AMM Ms 221A.
45 MS 2830C Dec 13 1762.
46 Ibid.
47 BH 3316C.
48 Vincent, *Op cit* 99.
49 Tompson, *Op cit* 24.
50 Nicholas Hans, *New Trends in Education in the Eighteenth Century*, Routledge and Kegan Paul, 1951, 66f.
51 Sodor and Man Diocesan Office, St. Matthew's File, Undated.
52 MS 2833C Feb 26 1763.
53 Ibid, April 26 1763.
54 MD 612/50, 34 (Bishopscourt papers).
55 Ibid 35.
56 AWM 177A, Philip Moore's Note Book, pace MS 5285, History of Peel Grammar School to 1785 (based on MD 612/50 papers).
57 Hildesley's Letters, Dec 11 1764.
58 MD 225 49, Licence of William Fitzsimmon.
59 Hildesley's Letters, Dec 11 1764.
60 Tompson, *Op cit* 54.
61 Ibid, 70.
62 Joseph Priestley, *An Essay on a Course of Liberal Education for Civil and Active Life*, 1768.
63 MS 2833 Feb 26 1763.
64 BH 3316C Will of James Moore.
65 BH 3137, Dec 23 1766.
66 MS 4937 July 5 1767.
67 Ibid May 17 1767.
68 Goldie Taubman Papers (Not available for research through fragility, but list reproduced in Ann Harrison *Peel Mathematical School* Journal of Manx Museum Vol. VII 215.
69 BC 62.
70 BH 1513.
71 Goldie Taubman papers per Ann Harrison, *Op cit* 213.
72 MS 1875C Jan 11 1789.
73 MS 943/3C.
74 MS 4284.

75 MS 4937C.
76 MD 612 50 Letter April.
77 Ibid, Letter April 29 1779.
78 Ibid 50/36, Petition July 24 1781.
79 Ibid 50/30, Petition Oct 2 1781.
80 Ibid 50/43.
81 Ibid 50/39 Nov 2 1781.
82 Ibid 50/33 Jan 2 1782.
83 Ibid 50/28, Undated.
84 Ibid May 50/29 May 13 1782.
85 Ibid 50/22, Undated 1784.
86 Ibid 50/20 Mar 19 1785.
87 MS 4937.
88 Manks Mercury May 7 1793.
89 R. J. Moore, Biography of J. Stowell (Manuscript).
90 Hugh Stowell, Op cit 74.
91 Ibid 83.
92 MD 225/58 July 4 1777.
93 H. Stowell, *Op cit* 84.
94 *Op cit* 90.
95 Educational Endowments 1887.
96 John Feltham. *A Tour Through the Isle of Man in 1797 and 1798*. Manx Society, Vol. VI, 1861. Cruttwell, Bath, 1798.
97 MD 225 17/4.
98 Athol Papers 122 (3rd) 28.
99 Whether Daniel Myrea taught the school at all is doubtful, as a Mr. Nugent demanded compensation for resigning to let the Rev. John Bridson act as master on his arrival, as the town inhabitants petitioned. See Constance Radcliffe, Ramsey, 1600-1800, 94.
100 A. W. Moore, Manx Worthies.
101 BC 127.
102 Norman Atkinson, Irish Education — A History of Educational Institutions, 31f.

CHAPTER SIX

THE FAILURE OF THE ENDOWED SCHOOLS

Despite the flourishing state of higher education in 1800, scarecely had the Nineteenth Century reached its third decade than the decline at this level became so obvious that the House of Keys stepped in, addressing a petition to the House of Commons. They explained that while the Island had powers to appoint commissioners to investigate, "in a small society like that of the sd island, there is a great risk that such Commissioners might be influenced in making out their report by the private feelings towards the present trustees."[1] They accordingly suggested that the English Commissioners who investigated educational charities should come to the Isle of Man.

"The said funds if well and duly administered would at the present time produce a very considerable annual revenue which would be sufficient for the endowment of such a number of schools as the present state of the population would require.

That some of the said funds have been mismanaged and diverted from their original intention, the consequences of which have been that the public Institutions for Education in this Island have become quite incompetent to the purpose for which they were originally intended, and that learning which half a century ago had made considerable progress is now repidly declining."[2]

Sadly the Keys were far more interested in the target than in the substance of their complaints, in which matters, as will be seen, they were by no means without blame themselves. The educational matters were just one of a number of convenient issues where ammunition for the political fighting between the Keys, still self-elected, and the Duke of Atholl might be found. The petition was part of this political struggle, and while there were very valid points to be made, motives other than a thirst for reform were uttermost.

The Keys knew well that Henry Brougham had already attempted to investigate educational charities in the Island. The Select Committee of 1816 "to enquire into the education of the lower orders of the Metropolis" had grown, partly through unscrupulous use of the Brentwood "scandal", into a full nationwide enquiry.[3] The scope widened to all schools, and the mandate increased in May 1818 to include Brougham's native Scotland. Ireland had long been the subject of such enquiries, starting with the 1763 Act for the Better Discovery of Charitable Donations and Bequests, which led to a settled body of Commissioners with full powers being established after the Act of Union, to carry on the work of a Committee of 1764 which would otherwise have come to an end. Another separate commission of 1788 also had wide powers, and issued a number of reports after the Union. With Ireland thus catered for, Brougham saw no incongruity in extending his net to cover the Island when he sent letters to all clergy in England, Wales, and Scotland, asking for full details of funds, numbers and salaries.

However, John, Duke of Atholl, and his nephew, Bishop George Murray, saw no need to respond. Although since the Revestment of

1765 the Atholl family were no longer Lords of the Isle, the Duke was His Majesty's Governor, and not answerable to any British Parliament at Westminster. The Bishop informed his uncle that he had forbidden the Manx clergy to reply to the enquiries which they had received from Brougham.[5]

The issue was thus a convenient one in which to discredit the Duke, especially as they accused him in an official statement of the House of Keys of being implicated in mismanagement and even misappropriation.[6] The Duke for his part defended himself with vigour, claiming the Keys, being a self-elected body, kept the people in utter bondage, and regretted their attacks on the highest authorities in Church and State "without the slighest investigation of, or inquiry into the facts".[7] Home Secretary Peel, as the correct channel as far as the Island was concerned, professed himself quite unable to act unless details of the Charities and the misappropriations were given to him.[8] The Keys' target was the wrong one, and yet the sad state of affairs outlined by them was only too true.

The success in the Twentieth Century of a large and well-staffed Comprehensive School depends, it is recognised, to a large extent on the personality and ability of the headmaster. When the teaching of a school was given by one master alone, sometimes with the assistance of an usher, he was to a large extent the school itself. After the excellent masters of the late Eighteenth Century, it was the Island's misfortune to have men in charge of the higher schools who did not match the calibre of their predecessors. Joseph Haskins, the associate of Joseph Stowell at Peel, had recognised the inherent danger, and presented to the Duke of Atholl a scheme whereby the power of the master was reduced to that of a limited monarch only by the supervision of a committee, and thus give a school "a better support than the caprice either of the Master or the Parents".[9] Haskins showed his wisdom by presenting his ideas when all seemed to be going well under Joseph Stowell, whom Haskins thought to be "a very able man", and not when a poor master more obviously revealed the deficiencies of the usual arrangements.

RAMSEY: THE ENDOWMENT VANISHES

Of the higher schools, Ramsey was the first to suffer. Whether indeed Henry Maddrell remained faithful to his teaching duties even to 1800 is open to some doubt. Feltham recorded that the schoolhouse was being converted into a courtroom,[10] but unfortunately a 1799 bill for work done in this respect which might throw light on the subject is not at hand in the Manx Museum.[11] Certainly the reputation of Maddrell in the parish to which he moved, that of Lezayre, was of an idle man who allowed buildings to fall into decay.[12] Once Maddrell departed in 1803, there was another rapid bout of changes, with William Stuart (1803), Robert Craine (1804), Thomas Phillips (1808) leaving in quick succession. The reason for the short duration of each was the fact that the £10 was no longer being paid, either in salt or cash. The *Book of Charities* of 1831 stated that Henry Maddrell had received the last payment in 1802, and the only official income with the position was the Royal Bounty of £3 Manx, (even this was reduced to £2/11/0 when translated to British money.) There were references in the first decade to the stuffed up windows of the school/courthouse, and Thomas Phillips started to teach in his own private school.[13] When he moved to Douglas to a wider market, his successor, Alexander Gelling, stayed a bare year, until Bowyer Harrison (1809-1816) brought some degree of stability.

The population of Ramsey meanwhile rose rapidly from 920 in 1792 to 1,523 in 1821, and their educational needs at elementary level were catered for in theory, after 1812 by the Ramsey Charities School.[14]

Now that provision had been made, however imperfect the working in practice, for the elementary needs of the town, it was felt that the old dual role of the so-called endowed school could give place to an avowedly higher school. In 1822 a new chapel, dedicated to St. Paul, was established in the middle of the town, largely through the gift of £300 from the Church Building Society, supplemented by subscription. The Chaplain's stipend was to be the Royal Bounty and the rent from pews. At the time of the *Book of Charities* only 42 of a possible 68 pews were let, giving a total income of £40/3/0.[16] The Trust Deed of St. Paul's stated that the "chaplain must secure in the town a well conducted Grammar School and if he declines management he is to be a qualified person to be licensed and approved by the bishop." Whether the chaplain at the time, Philip Corlett, heeded this charge is unknown, but unlikely. *Pigot's Directory* of 1824 makes no mention of any grammar school. Peel in 1822 wrote in September to the Bishop, having received no official reply to his letter of May 25th, asking for information. He eventually had a reply in December, and the lost endowment of Ramsey was portrayed as the only failure on the Island of those charities devoted to education. After the *Rising Sun* had given details of the endowment by the Cholmondeley family, the paper had to make it clear that the family were in no way responsible for the failure to pay since 1802, and that Lord Delamere, its head, in particular owed no duty to the school. The whole question of the school surfaced three years later with a letter from Observator to the *Rising Sun* concerning the Free Grammar School, an institution which once had "very beneficial effects", but had been allowed to "moulder into decay". ". . . how then comes it to pass that a once flourishing institution is permitted to fall into ruins?"[18] In the House of Keys' list of abuses, sent to Peel in response to his request for information, there was no mention made of Ramsey and the lost endowment, nor the cessation of the Grammar School there.[19]

Wherever the blame lay, the fact was that the north of the Island which had enjoyed and evolved, with a little help from outside, its own higher education, was instead without a building in repair, an endowment of any kind, or any master. The directive of St. Paul's Trust Deed remained for the time being a pious hope.

PEEL: THE DISASTROUS DUO, GELLING AND DODD

For its part, Peel was almost in as bad a state. Both higher schools were just about still in existence, but their state was deplorable.

Just before the death of Joseph Stowell deprived the town of an outstanding master, his colleague, Joseph Haskins, seemed fully confident that he would take of over the Peel School.[20] The trustees, however, ignored, his message to the Duke that this was so, and, recognising that masters who could run both schools together were few and far between, decided that the two should once again be distinct units. James Gelling, a Supernumary Clergyman in the diocese, sent a Memorial to the Bishop Barrow's Trustees, explaining that he had hoped to succeed Stowell at both schools.

> "Your memorialist has so far been fortunate as to receive an appointment to the Grammar School but finds difficulty in obtaining an appointment to the Mathematical School, as there is a Difference of opinion respecting the good effects of the union of the said Schools.
>
> That under these circumstances your Memorialist cannot undertake the Grammar School and resign his establishment on the Fund as the emoluments of the said Grammar School are inadequate to his maintenance.[21]

Gelling applied for and received permission to reside in Peel and do his supernumerary duties from there instead of the usual base of Castletown. The Barrow Trustees ruled "It is ordered that the Petitioner do continue to receive the stipend already allowed him of Forty Pounds per annum notwithstanding his acceptance of the Grammar School at Peeltown.[22] Gelling thus found the major part of his income unaffected by his school duties, and this was even more so when he became Vicar of German, the parish which included Peel, the stipend there being valued at £95 in 1821.[23] For scarcely had Gelling arrived in Peel than the Vicar, Thomas Corlett, providentially died in November 1801. At one time Gelling did think of paying a master for the *Manx Advertiser* in April 1809 included an advertisement desiring a master for the Grammar School at a salary of £16 a year, offering "a very large dwelling house, a large loft and teaching room put into complete repair".[24] Gelling added that none need apply but "a person of Sobriety and Good Character". Was this a shaft at his colleague at the Mathematical School?

Joseph Dodd's advertisement on arrival in 1801 had promised much:—

> "Mr. Dodds, mathematician, will open the Mathematical School of Peeltown, teaching Arithmetic, Book-Keeping, Mensuration, Surveying, Dialling, Gauging Geography and the use of Globes, Plain and Spherical Trigonometry, Navigation with modern methods of finding Longtitude and Latitude at sea by observation, Theoretical and Practical Geometry, Algerbra, Conic Sections, Method of Infinites, Increments, Flaxions with other modern inventions in the Analytic Art, Philosophy etc."[24]

He boasted that a long practice in teaching, public and private, enabled him "to bring down ideas to almost any capacity, and that he would follow the order of teaching of Edinburgh University, where he had studied, for those who required regular Mathematical Education.

Disillusion followed very shortly. By December 1802 the *Manx Advertiser* informed its readers that

> "A correspondent from a neighbouring town informs us, that one part of the Free Mathematical School house there is at present occupied by a family of a character too well known by the inhabitants of the town. Such conduct of the schoolmaster is both singular and unpleasant and leaves the public to pass their own opinion of such proceedings. It is hoped that the Trustees will make further inquiry in the business."[25]

There was some correspondence between Gelling and Dodd in 1813, with Gelling making enquiries about the Mathematical Schools which Dodd could not answer, save to supply the terms of James Moore's will, and details of the inscriptions on the school walls. The reason for Gelling's interest is not clear.[26] By the time the Keys took a hand in 1822, it was clear that both schools were in a very bad way. Their investigation only dealt with the Mathematical School, and concluded that "of late years the building has been allowed to fall into decay and the School into disrepute". There were references to former pupils who "since distinguished themselves as able Navigators in the Merchant Ships of Liverpool", but as for the trustees, the terms of reference were so vague that there were "doubts in whom the appointment is vested". The Keys were reluctant to venture a reason why the school had declined, but a report to the Duke the following year blamed faulty terms of endowment rather than James Dodd. The cause of the building being in disrepair was very simple.

> "The school have no other funds except those dedicated to the Master's salary — There not being the least provision even for repairs or any other incidental Expenses."[27]

Some extra money had accrued to Dodds through fee-paying pupils, but he stated the trustees had never objected to his own salary being increased this way, as long as the foundationers were not affected.

The high moral tone of the Keys probably abated when it was revealed that the Trustees were John Moore of the Hills, Douglas, and their own Speaker, George Quayle, whose sole positive act in connection with the school had been to ask Dodd for the names of the boys. He had done nothing to avert or reverse the decline, and other writers to the Duke poured scorn upon the hypocrisy of the Keys with their charges of misappropriation, when it was known that Quayle had written to the Duke confirming he was a Trustee. "Are they ignorant that their speaker is the sole trustee?" — that the Mathematical School was "the worst conducted charity school perhaps on the face of the earth — that the master is a worthless drunkard and that he has £40 and free house. He has no scholars because in fact from his habits, he is unable to teach any."[28]

The Duke of Atholl, having been viciously attacked by the Keys over the charities, showed remarkable restraint in the matter of Peel Mathematical School, which with Taubman's School in Castletown he personally investigated, leaving his nephew, Bishop Murray, to deal with the rest. Instead of exposing the negligence of the Trustees, he scorned the revenge that might with justice have been his to enjoy, and eventually replied to Peel in 1825 concerning his two schools, "I have to report that on investigation I do not find any abuse in the management of them."[29] There was indeed no evidence of misappropriation, but a great deal might have been said of a schoolhouse used as an auction room.

Indeed the loud clamour of the Keys for investigation into the Island's educational charities backfired seriously in the case of Peel. In their statement of abuses, drawn up on July 30th 1822, there was no mention of Peel Grammar School. The *Rising Sun* two years later purported to give the reason: the school had sunk so low that there was ridicule at the notion of including it. The Trustees had left all to Gelling, who for twenty years had received his salary without any restriction or surveillance, and preferred *otium cum dignatate* to *labor cum diligentia*. There was but one scholar, the schoolroom had been "very properly converted into a barn", the yard was full of the animals belonging to the Bull family, and the cellars were let to herring traders. If properly regulated, the school, once a place of repute, could have been a blessing to thousands. The present Bishop's excuse that the appointment had been made by a predecessor was rightly dismissed by the *Rising Sun* as being very feeble.[30]

However, the fact the school was a place worthy of ridicule would surely have made its inclusion in the list of abuses more to be expected. The omission is much more likely to have been the Keys' awareness of their own role as official trustees with the bishop, and to have exposed the state of the school would have made their own cries about mismanagement appear a classic case of pot calling kettle black, in view of such palpable neglect on their part.

Nevertheless, in March 1824 the House of Keys appointed a Committee of three, Anthony Dunlop, Thomas Harris and John Quane, who reported back in June what they had found on a visit to Peel in April.[31] The house and school were in a ruinous state, with broken windows and slovenly filth in the garret. The playground was used for a dunghill and haystack, while in the herring season, they were told, it amounted to a public nuisance. Gelling informed the Committee that he leased the yard and vault for £18 a year, and admitted that the main schoolroom itself was used as a barn and slaughterhouse. William Bridson told of threshing and the sight of carcases, while John Crellin recalled the room as being full of sheaves. The Committee, although exceeding the scope of their instructions, went on to visit the other Peel schools. Dodd was eventually discovered hiding under a bed! He refused to let the Committee see the school-room, but it appeared in "much disorder". According to a witness, it was used for sales and auctions, while the house itself had been converted into a ale house. "Filth and disorder seemed to reign throughout", a marked contrast with the Clothworker's School, where good order and systematic arrangement did great credit to the master, Thomas Quine. Dodd, described by a witness as a "dissolute idle man, quite unfit for his situation" had two pupils at the most, but even that was better than Gelling, who had only one pupil, and he was off sick. The Committee recommended that the schools should be united once more. The Grammar School building should be sold, fetching about £400, and the proceeds added to Moore's endowment, giving a sum, which, if properly invested in land, would provide the master's salary. If the Mathematical School trustees, George Quayle and John Moore, would follow suit, then the united salary would attract a good master, and as rents increased, the resources would steadily increase. They felt that the people of Peel should be willing to provide a schoolhouse at their own expense, and would look after repairs better than distant trustees.

The House of Keys, on receiving the report, resolved to keep the Committee in being, in order that it might meet with the Bishop, not only to regulate the interests of the Grammar School, but also to confer about the necessity of appointing a new master.[32]Gelling wrote directly to the Bishop, putting his side of the case. With regard to the state of the buildings, he had found the house in bad repair at his entry in 1801, and had done what he could with a very large house requiring constant attention and large sums of money from his own pocket. No funds for repair had been put at his disposal for twenty three years, nor had he ever received any instructions from the Trustees. Only last year the roofs had been rendered at heavy cost, and should be good for forty years. The schoolroom was, as he had admitted to the Committee, out of repair, but he was intending to proceed, and had indeed purchased the necessary materials. However, complete repair would cost the equivalent of two years pay, and that he would never afford by himself. He had used the room for storing sheaves, but only during the vacation. There was no practice made of this, although in fact this was not his teaching room, which was a warmer and smaller room. Joseph Stowell before him had not used the schoolroom, preferring the Mathematical School premises. The yard had been provided with a ball alley by Joseph Stowell for the use of his boarders, of whom there were many, so the complaint that boys were unable to play fives in the yard was not really to the point. Stowell's widow backed up these assertions in a letter that Gelling presented. Furthermore, it was not fair to compare his buildings with those of the Clothworkers' School. The house of Thomas Quine had been put into a state of complete repair some years ago at public expense, with new forms provided at no cost to the master.

When the Bishop and the Committee met at Douglas Custom House on July 21 1824,[23] the Bishop alluded to Gelling's defence, and to the fact that the depositions of some witness in Peel to the Committee were contradicted when the same people wrote supporting Gelling. For instance, Thomas Carran wrote denying that he had ever told the Committee that all scholars had left on the account of the master's neglect. As Gelling had been given no instructions by the Trustees concerning the running of the school, he should not be removed. There could be no dismissal without the Bishop's authority, and he would not sanction such injustice, for Gelling had expressed his willingness in his defence to obey any directions of the Trustees.

The arguments which had raged in 1782 emerged once more, although the point at issue now was removal of a master rather than his appointment. Dunlop challenged the Bishop's power over lay trustees, but Bishop Murray insisted the powers of the House of Keys were over funds, not the master himself. Even if the Trustees appointed Gelling together, only an Ecclesiastical Court could dismiss him. Vicar-General Roper supported the Bishop's position, citing Irish cases where Trustees had failed to sack a schoolmaster. In point of fact, Gelling had been appointed in 1801 as Master of the Latin School "dependent on the Bishop's pleasure and diligent and satisfactory discharge".[34] As the Bishop stated that he would sack Gelling if duty had been violated, it was agreed that petition from Peel against Gelling should be invited to be brought to the Bishop at an Ecclesiastical Court. A formal resolution was passed to this effect, and the Trustees were also called upon to make rules and regulations for the school. Gelling, called in, "reluctantly acquiesced" in this proposed investigation, where confusing testimony would be sorted out in evidence taken upon oath.

When evidence was heard before the Vicar-General in November 1824 the charges of neglect and misuse of premises were once more brought up. It was alleged that, contrary to Gelling's assertions, the house was in very good condition when Gelling was appointed, and his recent "repairs" amounted to nothing more than a coat of paint. A Mr. Quiggin, supporting the charge of "most slovenly filth in the garrett" made by the Committee of the House of Keys, but denied by Gelling, estimated that rubbish would have filled some carts. Four witnesses testified that threshing was done during term time. Some days the schoolroom was so full of corn that the stairs would be used for lessons. Gelling had denied that the schoolroom was used as a slaughter house, when he wrote to the Bishop (although the Committee had included an admission to this effect in their April evidence) and had suggested that the corroborative evidence of William Bridson was mistaken. But witnesses remembered carcases being cut up, and the offensive smell which pervaded the room.[35]

Even more damning was the evidence given that the boys were used as Gelling's labourers, and their tuition neglected to the point that numbers had faded away to nothing. James Cowin, the father of the only pupil in April 1824, had told the Committee that his son was not taught but given jobs to do. Charles Cannell's son spent his time with Gelling looking after cattle while he was at the school. Gelling admitted that two or three boys worked for him, but tried to justify this by saying that they received free tuition in English in exchange.

This explanation was totally unacceptable to the complainants, who firmly believed that in a Free School the tuition ought to be free. Gelling on the other hand made a distinction between Latin, which he claimed he taught for nothing, and other subjects, for which he felt justified in charging quarterage. There was no ground for this distinction in the wording of Philip Moore's will, or in past custom. Gelling had informed the Committee on their visit of April 22nd that the school was free for Latin only, and had it been otherwise he would not have undertaken the school, especially if there would be no limitation of numbers. He pleaded that he was only following the precedent of John and Joseph Stowell, and in this had the agreement of Mr. Cowle, the Captain of the parish of German. However, the Clerk of the Rolls had been taught English without paying anything by Joseph Stowell, while John Gawne and others testified before the Vicar-General that Mr. Christian and John Stowell similarly made no charge. Older men like Thomas Carran claimed that there had been no quarterage under Heterick, whereas Gelling made him pay half a guinea for his own son. A number of witnesses told of paying 7/6d quarterage, 5/- entrance and 2/6d for fire. The Bishop in his conference with the House of Keys Committee in July admitted that Gelling's views rested on no solid foundation, but felt that as he had received no instructions, his mistaken belief that the school was for Latin only should not be a cause for dismissal.[36]

Furthermore, the complainants hotly denied that even Latin was taught free, whatever Gelling claimed. Thomas Costain told the Keys' Committee that he was charged 7/- per quarter for his sons to learn the Classics, being informed by Gelling that there were only three or four on the foundation. Thomas Taubman told of a further charge of 2/- per quarter if Latin were taught, in addition to a charge of 7/6d for English and Arithmetic. John Gawne alleged that even those who were supposed to study only Latin were charged a quarterage of 7/6d. Doubts were cast as to whether those who were admitted for nothing learned anything at all apart from how to look after cows and clean corn.

What was beyond doubt was the decline in the fortunes of the school. Numbers under Heterick had not been high — 24 in 1782, with an average of 18 in succeeding years — and Joseph Stowell's numbers had been swollen not only by his dual mastership, but also by a large number of boarding pupils. Yet Gelling's own evidence told of a decline from a peak of 40-50 in earlier days to a single pupil. His reasons were not consistent. In speaking to the Committee in April 1824 he blamed being undercut in fees, but his letter to the Bishop stated he had raised his English fees to make his school more select, while remaining cheaper than other masters in the Isle of Man. He was, however, able to produce testimonials from persons of repute. La Mothe, a surgeon of Ramsey, stated his son had made great progress in 1819 under Gelling "one of the best teachers in the Island",[37] while Hugh Stowell, the revered Rector of Ballaugh, thought the "progress of pupils in classical learning, highly creditable to their master". He was "fully satisfied with the education of his own son", while another Gelling pupil was "highly esteemed" at Queen's College, Oxford. Other parents too felt they "had every reason to be satisfied".[38]

Yet the fact remained that in the last five years there had only been one or two pupils each year, including Gelling's own daughter, and most of the parents were not at all satisfied. Joseph Quayle felt his son had learned no Latin Grammar in two years, while Mrs. Catherine Frizell could see no improvement in her son, and sent him off to Scotland instead. As has been mentioned, the father of the only pupil on April 1824 complained that his son was given jobs, and not taught. The Commmittee had warned Gelling he must take all applicants, and by July he had ten pupils once more. Yet as far as the House of Keys was concerned, it was too late to restore his reputation. It was reckoned that with a house worth £20, a salary of £30, and the letting of vault and yard bringing in a further £18, Gelling was receiving £68 in addition to his clergymen's stipend. Over twenty three years, taking an average of £65 per annum, Gelling had received £1,496, and the Committee obviously felt that value for money was not being given. A formal resolution was passed by the House of Keys on December 10th 1824 that while Gelling's moral and religious character was satisfactory yet, in the light of the Petition from Peel natives, it was inexpedient that he be in charge of the Grammar School. The Committee should seek the Bishop's advice so that all the Trustees might consider that matter. In the meantime, Trust funds should be diverted to the Committee so that the interest could cover the cost of repairs, and talks be held with George Quayle and John Moore about unifying the two schools, the Committee to report back if such a union ws practicable.[39] The Resolution was duly passed on to Bishop Murray, who professed that he did not know what specific charges the House were bringing to merit "so severe a sentence", which demanded serious consideration at a meeting. A February date was suggested, but the House of Keys were not moved, appointing advocates to apply to the Chancellor of the Isle of Man to remove Gelling from Peel Grammar School[40] and by May seeking a progress report from Messrs. Kelly and Kinley.[41]

A strange war broke out in the press. The *Manx Patriot* and the *Rising Sun* attacked Gelling, but the *Manx Advertiser* sprang to Gelling's defence in an amazing manner, referring to "wanton attacks", "undeserved opprobrium", malignant allegations of a disappointed tradesman or two, who neither knew what learning is or appreciate those who do".[42] This defence of Gelling argued in editorials and the letter of "Peter Fairplay" seems woefully weak. The cause of the fuss, it was claimed, was Gelling's care for the poor, and the lack of respectable families for a Latin School. There was nothing to forbid the letting of schoolroom, yard, or vault; the room used — nine feet by eleven — was sunnier and healthier for scholars; Joseph Stowell had not used the official room either, and after all, a schoolroom was but where the master taught. According to the *Advertiser*, Gelling could well claim that Bishop Cregan had appointed him without naming it a free school as his opponents used the term, that he had spent money to make house, yard and vaults fit enough to be let, that he taught Latin freely ex gratia, and also Greek, Hebrew and Navigation for nothing save a salary of £30, when at his appointment the Keys had led him to expect something in the region of £80.[43]

In the face of the facts, the eulogy of Gelling verged on the ridiculous. A better testimonial concerning study and diligence could not be asked for: "If an academical professor were requisite, could he come more strongly recommended, unless as a graduate?" Peter Fairplay concluded that all the noise had shown Gelling to be a well-qualified master, as numbers were now reasonable, ignoring dark reports that Gelling had lured from another school to make his numbers appear adequate.[44] Where his defenders were on stronger ground lay in pointing out the vagueness concerning the school, even compared with the Mathematical School, in the original will. Peter Fairplay likened it to a city without walls. Gelling had kept the premises in a state of repair far better than they were at his arrival. It was even denied that the school hoped for in Philip Moore's will had ever been truly founded, as the "good and charitable donation of other well disposed persons" mentioned in it had not materialised.

Whether the whole affair was blown up through pique against Gelling, or whether Peter Fairplay was merely a "poor sneaking hypocritical canting sychophant" as the *Rising Sun* alleged, the harsh fact remained that as the years progressed the fabrics of the schools would decay, Liverpool bricks or not, and there were no settled funds to deal with this situation. It was thus only part of the truth when the *Rising Sun* alleged that was "great culpability and neglect" in a situation where, although the Clothworkers' School was well attended, the Classical School was very moderately so, and the Mathematical School "is represented as a sinecure and the schoolroom like the school itself is in a dreadful state of decay."[45] The *Rising Sun* was right to demand an investigation, but quite wrong to assert that there were three schols "well provided with funds."

One old legal argument was at least settled as a result of the fuss. The Keys attempted to sack Gelling, ordering him to vacate the school by May 12th 1826: the Bishop ordered Gelling to stay put. Could the Keys outvote the Bishop, or were there but two trustees? The dispute caused the *Manx Advertiser* to resurrect the learned opinion of Sir Wadsworth Busk in 1779, and regarded the Key's move with "a degree of astonishment little short of in credulity."[46] Yet when the matter came to be judged after the presentation of a petition by the Keys to the Lt.-Governor, it was held that each member of the Keys was a trustee, and that there were fully twenty five trustees, not just two. The Keys therefore were free to institute proceedings against Gelling.[47] However, Gelling remained as Master as well as Vicar right up to 1839. When the material for McHutchin and Quirk's Book of Charities was being collected, Gelling was described as having sixteen scholars "who generally pay quarterage for being taught to read and write English."[48] The accolade of being the 'Classical School' was clearly unfitting, although R. S. Tompson has warned that such charges might at times be evidence of life and relevance rather than signs of decay, a response to demand rather than degregation.[49]

At least Gelling had some pupils, and buildings fit to be let. The Mathematical School under Dodd, who likewise remained another decade as nominal master until he was at last dismissed, had gone from bad to worse. In 1821 the building had been good enough to host the inaugural meeting of the local branch of the British and Foreign Bible Society, held in the schoolhouse.[50] By the end of 1827 things were far worse.

> "No provision has been made for the repairs of this school or the house and building bequeathed by Sir George Moore. The Schoolhouse is partly unroofed. The books and mathematical instruments are in a very bad condition: and the whole establishment is in a state of rapid decay. There are at present only two scholars, and those not on the foundation."[51]

Two documents with more than a touch of irony date from this troubled time. Caesar Corrin, a merchant of Peel, left by his will of 1826 £100 to the Mathematical School, the interest to be paid to the master for teaching two of his kindred if such might be found or as his brother and heirs might nominate "all sorts of useful and Mathematical learning in the said School, according to the most approved method thereof, without any charge."[52] The second was a letter to the *Manx Advertiser* in 1825, where the writer, completely ignoring the collapse of higher education in Peel, favoured that town as the centre of a small university to be established in the Island. "The site of the Cathedral at Peel would be an antique and venerable situation for the founding of a small College or University." Hopes were pinned as patron and promoter on "our political mediator; our intercessor and benefactor" the Duke of Atholl.[53]

At the elementary level, Christian's School was fulfilling its function. McHutchin found seventy scholars under Thomas Quine, with voluntary subscriptions keeping house and school in repair. Yet at the higher level, a maximum of eighteen pupils were in theory receiving advanced education; in reality the total was more likely to be nil. The deadly combination of inadequate endowment for repairs and the sloth of individual masters meant that to all intents and purposes the hopes and dreams of the Moore family for their two schools were, if not dead, fast dying.

CASTLETOWN: INCOMPETENCE, NEGLECT AND GREED

At Castletown Castley eventually resigned his position, not hanging on to the bitter end as Ross had done. He saw that the mortgages held in his name were duly assigned to Bishop Crigan and Archdeacon Mylrea on behalf of the Trustees of the "Free Grammar

School or Academic School". So long had the two schools, nominally distinct, been together that their titles were considered alternatives. In strictly legal terms, the correct Trustees of the money were the successors of Legh and Cholmondeley as Trustees of the Academic Master's Fund, but they were now ignored, and the monies merged with those of the Academic Students' Fund: "Since Mr. Castley assigned over the above mentioned Mortgages to the Bishop and Archdeacon, no account of this fund has been kept distinct from the Academic Students' Fund".[54] With the lands of Hango Hill and Ballagilley alone bringing in £341 after the new leases of 1800, the financial problems of Ramsey and Peel were not paralleled at Castletown.

Unfortunately the human element intruded at Castletown as it had done at Peel. The Trustees of the Students' Fund did their best to ensure a smooth takeover. Bishop Crigan wrote in November 1806 to the Duke of Atholl, since 1793 Governor of the Island under the crown, informing him that Lt.-Governor Smelt, who arrived the previous year, was urging him to make a speedy appointment and fix a salary at a meeting of the Trustees. Did the Duke wish to be present?[55]

Castley's successor was the Rev. Joseph Bown, like Dodd from Scotland, equally appealing on paper, but equally disastrous in practice. He came highly commended by William Routledge of the Episcopal Chapel, Glasgow, who had two sons under Brown's care and hoped he was "sufficiently qualified for this important trust."[56] For his part, Brown expressed himself as being well qualified "to take direction of the Academy at Castletown." The title flowed naturally from his pen, for he had been educated at Perth Academy in Scotland. The term there and in England indicated usually a wider curriculum than the traditional grammar school, with a stress often on mathematics and vocational subjects.[57] Thus at Perth, Brown studied not only the ancient languages, but also French, Geography, Arithmetic and Practical Mathematics. His advanced education had been at St. Andrew's and Glasgow College, gaining his Master of Arts degree and adding a diploma. He had experience of teaching with "many genteel families in Glasgow", and at Castletown he would offer Latin, Greek, English and Rhetoric, Theology, Church History, Geography, Astronomy, Moral Philosophy and Logic, with Hebrew if required. (Castley had taught Hebrew to his most promising pupils.) Brown also claimed knowledge enough to teach Arithmetic, Mensuration, Practical Geometry, Bookkeeping and French.[58] For his part he wished to know what was taught at Castletown, the number of assistants and pupils, fees charged, and what accommodation and salary was offered: also whether a curacy would be available in addition.

The Trustees awarded Brown a salary of £60 from the Impropriate Fund and a further £100 from the Academic Fund, and the Castletown foundation appeared to be entering a long period of stability.[59]

Unfortunately Brown proved a flop: perhaps Manx youths proved harder to control than the "genteel families in Glasgow". This was despite the help of his namesake, Robert Brown, later Master of Douglas Grammar School, who was with him from 1809 until 1816, receiving for his last term three years the high sum of £60 from the Academic Fund. The arrival of George Murray, the Duke's nephew, as Bishop, soon lead to pressure on Brown to move. Murray shifted his clergy about to "lead to removal of Mr. Brown the Academical Master from Castletown, an object very desirable if it can be obtained for the School is nearly ruined."[60] The timely death of the Vicar of Kirk Michael created "an eligible situation for Brown" and Murray persuaded the Duke to appoint him: "he is not calculated for a school."[61] The Bishop looked for a successor, quickly found one in the Rev. Thomas Thimbleby, and arranged a handsome remuneration. The hapless Brown received at the very same meeting an award for £10 for repairs, and an order he repay £120 through the Coroner. More importantly the Trustees broke up the link between the post of Academic Master and the Grammar School premises.

> "Resolved that it is expedient that the Academic Master may provide himself with a residence, and hold or keep the Academy in the town of Castletown, or within a mile thereof, and that a sum of two hundred and twenty pounds Brit. be allowed out of the Academic Funds to the Academic Professor annually."[62]

Although this new freedom for the Academic School was in the spirit of Barrow's original intention, the result was totally disastrous for the Grammar School. As the post of Government Chaplain added to that of Academic Professor yielded nearly £300 a year, there was little incentive to bother with the Grammar School at £60 a year, to which Thimbleby had also been appointed, and the building was simply closed.

The actual separation of the schools had been strongly urged by a pamphleteer of the time, possibly Hugh Stowell, former head of Douglas Grammar School, and now Rector of Ballaugh.

> "As the School and the Academy do not appear to be necessarily connected, it might be better to separate them intirely so leaving the Academic Professor to give a complete finish to the education of the academic scholars and such other *limited number* of young men as he might be disposed to take under his tuition upon any such terms that might be agreed upon by the parties."

The writer pointed out that the combination of the two posts in 1736 had been the result of financial crisis when there was danger of the master's money in Ireland being lost through neglect, and funds were very inadequate. When now the Scholars' fund was very rich through the increased rents for Hango Hill and Ballagilley, with far more than needed for four ordinands, it was consistent "with the true spirit of the Foundation to apply a part of the overflowings of the said fund to make upon for the inadequacy of the Academic Master's Fund."[63] (A mention of the £220 salary award settles the date of the pamphlet at 1818.) The Professor could then confine himself to four for the church and those who would pay for an academic education. The Castletown School would remain as a Free Grammar School for the general public, becoming "a handsome establishment as a nursery for the future clergy preparatory to the Academic Exhibition" with a salary of £100 from the Impropriate Fund, augmented by gratuities from the scholars and house rents.

If implemented fully, these excellent suggestions would at last have brought about Barrow's desire for three distinct levels of education, which had been fulfilled to some degree in Wilson's early years. The failure of the Trustees of the Impropriate Fund to appoint a separate master completely wrecked the scheme. Thimbleby did not even confine himself to the Academic level: he proceeded to set up an expensive boarding school, increasing his income yet more, and further reducing any need or desire to have anything to do with the Castletown Grammar School. A ten year old day boy was charged ten guineas with two and a half guineas entrance, while a sixteen year old boarder was charged no less than sixty pounds with five guineas entrance. Even the Academic Scholars were charged thirty guineas for board and two and a half guineas entrance.[64] The Academic Students did not thus have the benefit of full-time attention as was intended, and the Grammar School boys had absolutely nothing.

The Keys were outraged, and in their Statement of Charities presented to Peel the protests about the state of affairs in Castletown were fully justified. However, they widened their target to include the whole administration of the Impropriate Fund. Correctly citing the aims of the Fund as the establishment of a free Grammar School, English schools in each parish, and the augmentation of poor livings, the Keys sought to link the augmentation wth teaching, relying on the 1670 Jurby paper statement that "every Minister is obliged to teach an English School in his parish by the increase of his stipend", which was not in the original deed. The Keys thought it wrong that funds were "appropriated almost exclusively to the clergy who no longer perform the function for which they scruple not to receive the salary."[65] The Keys wanted the clergy to benefit only if they performed functions they had long ceased to undertake.

This was uncertain ground, but the treatment of the Grammar School was undoubtedly inequitable. In Robert Curphey's valuable paper for the Manx Antiquarian Society he stated that "from 1757 there was insufficient income to maintain the purpose for which the (Impropriate) Fund had been established . . . the Master's salary could only be increased from another source."[66] Yet the whole strength of the Keys' case was that there was ample money in the Fund, indefensibly diverted from the proper recipients.

In the case of the Grammar School, its devaluation had been obscured by the high total salary that Brown had received. In 1782 the clergy had put their case for a revision of the amount of £219 agreed in 1757, as the Impropriate Tithes were now worth far more. Eventually in 1809 Bishop Crigan filed a Bill of Revivor against the Earl of Derby, the upshot being that in February 1811 Derby paid £16,000 to buy off any future claims on Bispham and Methop. An Act of Parliament confirmed the agreement, with monies to be laid out in the Isle of Man, and terms of leases not to exceed twenty one years. (The Keys also criticised the laying out of the money as poorly done, but land prices were artificially high on the Island as elsewhere during the Napoleonic Wars.) The sum produced in rents from the purchased lands in 1819 amounted to £534/6/6 compared with the value of the original tithe lands of £898/8/6 gross (after reserved rents, collection fees, etc., £663/8/0 net) which made the deal appear a poor one. The sum distributed by the Fund in 1821, £495, was nevertheless more than double the £219 of 1757. Castletown Grammar School, awarded a third of the Fund under Barrow, still received only £60. Seen from another angle of comparison, at the outset of the fund under Barrow, the master received thirty pounds at the Grammar School, while the average incumbent received seventeen pounds; at Castley's time, he received sixty pounds and the average incumbent forty two: in 1822 the master received sixty pounds still, but the average incumbent had ninety five pounds. The vicars had done well from the Fund, while the Grammar School master's share had decreased markedly. The church officials had received eight pounds to the master's thirty at the outset: now their grants exceeded the master's salary.

Even the small proportion of the master's salary from the fund could hardly be classed as spent on education, since he "has thought it proper to shut it up altogether." The Duke's dark influence was detected, as after the advowsons had passed to the Atholl's, "popular education appears not to have received encouragement." Instead there was the galling sight of the paid master setting up a lucrative boarding school under the patronage of the Bishop.

Although Thimbleby was to some degree fulfilling his duties as Academic Master, the Keys were no more enthusiastic about the way the Academic Fund monies were disposed. Ignoring the wording of Barrow's will as opposed to the deed, they felt that after three students were provided for, the surplus should go to charity, not to support supplementary clergy. Certainly the greatest part of income from Hango Hill and Ballagilley ought not to go to the Professor merely for taking three students and running a boarding school.[68]

The Bishop insisted that the Impropriate Fund was shared fairly, and the richer clergy excluded.[69] Robert Peel, who seems content to have acted merely as a go-between, passed the Keys' complaints to the Bishop, concluding the Trust was "admirably conducted".[70] Thimbleby was ordered by the Trustees of the Academic Fund to "make inquiries and obtain all documents relative to this fund from the original grant to Bishop Barrow, to this present time."[71] The Professor was, however, shamed into resigning the Grammar School, although his successor, the Rev. George Parsons, was still only given a salary of sixty pounds.[72] The Grammar School remained starved of proper funds. A Mr. Brine was called in during 1822 to repair the dilapidated roof, but reported in 1829 the school was "in as bad a state as before."

Parsons did manage to revive the school as an Academic Fund Resolution of 1825 revealed. The occasion was the bottleneck in the Academic Fund, when the four places on the Foundation were all occupied by those already ordained.

"... Academic Students not having any Ecclesiastical Preferment and still being on the Fund, thereby preventing other youth from being placed thereon ... it is deemed expedient to select four from the Grammar School to be under the Care and Tuition of the Academic Master."[73]

Further repairs to the fabric were ordered in 1829, when all timbers were renewed, and new desks, tables, and floors put in. The work was completed by July 1829 and inspected, yet this did not indicate a fresh concern or fairer allocation of the Impropriate Fund, being 'financed' by the simple expedient of not paying Mr. Brine's bill of £110. Ten years later he was still owed £116, the excuse being that "funds were very low".[74]

Barrow's system of three tiers of education in Castletown had not been completely extinguished, despite the temporary closure of the Grammar School building. But by this time the Keys and Governo Smelt were prepared to write off the Grammar School as a lost cause, and laid plans to exact their revenge for what they regarded as scandalous mismanagement.

DOUGLAS: INNOVATION AND DECAY

At Douglas Grammar School the first two decades of the Nineteenth Century were noticeable, not for sudden decline as at Peel and Castletown, but for an entirely new approach by the Chaplains of St. Matthew's. Hitherto they had run the school with the aid of an assistant or usher, usually a young man proceeding to orders in the church. Shortly after the arrival of the Rev. John Kewley, himself a product of the school and a holder of the William Murrey foundation from 1788,[75] as Chaplain to succeed Hugh Stowell, he engaged the Rev. J. Colquhoun, an established schoolmaster of Douglas, and an advertisement of 1804 made it clear that something new at the Grammar School was intended. The Revs. J. Kewley and J. Colquhoun "intend to open an Academy in the Grammar School House belonging to St. Matthew's Chapel".[76] A grand and impressive list of subjects to be taught was given, and even for ladies in the summer months Colquhoun offered geography, domestic accounts and astronomy, thereby supplementing his income.[77] Unfortunately Colquhoun was found drowned in May 1807 and Kewley employed first Mr. Muir and then Mr. McMeekin as assistants. This was not reverting to the former type of assistant, for Muir from Edinburgh was a married man whose wife had a school of her own. In 1809 Kewley again linked up with already established masters, the partnership of Laurence and Imeson, who had come together themselves earlier that year at Muckle Gate, running a ladies' section and evening classes in addition to their boys' school. In June it was announced that "the Rev. Kewley with Messrs. Laurence and Imeson will open an Academy in the Grammar School of Douglas for Young Ladies and Gentlemen, the Grammar School being recently fitted up for this purpose... Young Gentlemen intended for the Church or the Bar may be taught the Manx language grammatically."[78] What happened to the poorer boys to be taught free in these years of private collaboration is not known, and Kewley's advertisements contined to use the word 'Academy' with its connotations of choice and relevance, discussed more fully in the next chapter, which deals with the contribution of the private sector.

The advent of the Rev. Joseph Qualtrough brought rapid changes. Laurence quickly departed to team up with Mr. Conolly, newly arrived from Dublin, in their own Thomas Street Academy, while Qualtrough's first advertisement made it clear who was in charge. He was "Master of the Academic School of Mr. Murrey's Establishment" and Imeson was merely his assistant.

A most interesting advertisement of July 1813 gave a list of all students and subjects studied, giving a rare glimpse into the working of the school. Although Qualtrough promised pupils would be "carefully instructed in English, Latin, Greek and Manx Languages, Writing, Arithmetic, Book-keeping, Mathematics and Geography", this did not mean a pupil would tackle all subjects. The number of students was sixty, ranging from five year old John Fell, who learned just English, to nineteen year old J. Kay, studying Latin and Greek, Scriptural History, and Manx. Two other senior boys, Jurby Caine and Blake studied English, Writing and Arithmetic, and Geometry, Logarithms, Trigonometry and Navigation respectively. Although only one other boy studied Navigation, a number did book-keeping. A varied curriculum according to choice and ability was thus offered. Of the sixty boys, forty one were ten or over, and twenty two above the age of thirteen. Two years later Qualtrough's prize list had winners in Latin, History, Geography, English, and mathematics, but no sign of Greek. According to the examiners "Young gentlemen construed, parsed, and applied the rules of Syntax both in Latin and English and read with a degree of judgement and taste hardly to be expected from boys at school."[79]

(Since the title 'Grammar School' had been dropped, the way was open for private enterprise to borrow it for a while. The Grand Divertisement given by the Young Gentlemen of Douglas Grammar School at the Assembly Rooms had no connection with St. Matthew's at all, only with Mr. J. Barton's school. When he changed his own title to Heywood House Academy, another enterprising young teacher borrowed the title, announcing he would open Douglas Grammar School in Duke Street in 1814. When, however, Qualtrough was made Vicar of Rushen, and Robert Brown became Chaplain, life returned to normal.)

Qualtrough sought at Rushen to continue an Academy in a room annexed to the vicarage, offering room for two boarders, and Imeson moved to Fort Street, becoming one of Douglas' best known schoolmasters. Robert Brown was, like John Kewley, whom he succeeded as a William Murrey Scholar in 1803, a product of Douglas Grammar School, and again like Kewley, had to wait a long time for a cure in the church. As many others did in his position, he helped to support himself by teaching. One of his early pupils was William Hendry Stowell, nephew of Hugh, who later achieved prominence as a Congregationalist minister, and a Doctor of Divinity of Glasgow. He referred to having "a most profound esteem of Robert Brown from whom he acquired those severe canons of taste never afterwards neglected."[80] As this branch of the Stowell family left for Liverpool in 1810, the connection with Brown was well before his St. Matthew's days as master. Brown's financial position was eased in 1809 in theory when appointed to the first vacancy in the Academic Students' Fund, but this did not occur until 1813.[81] During these years, as mentioned earlier, he acted as assistant to Joseph Brown at Castletown.

An insight into life under Brown at Douglas Grammar School is given in one of Hugh Stowell's short books, the *Memorial of Mr. F. D. P. Geneste,* which incorporates parts of the young man's diary. The Geneste family, of Huguenot origin , had long links with the Grammar School — Philip Moore in 1749 had noted the entry of a member into his school. Geneste was very gifted at languages, even starting Hebrew in 1815 at the age of eleven with the aid of his elder brother. He had learned the elements of Latin and shorthand at the school of the Rev. Samuel Haining, before arriving at the Douglas Grammar School. He wrote of his rapid progress in the Classics under Brown. His diary for April 3rd 1818 recorded rising at four thirty, reading three chapters of Hebrew, and then going to school where he read twenty four lines of Virgil. At eleven o'clock the scholars went to church, as they did each Wednesday and Friday. In the afternoon the main task was to construe thirty lines of Virgil. Having found it very easy to keep up in the Hebrew with the lessons at St. Matthew's, Geneste turned his attention to cognate tongues. "Began also ... to translate a Syriac grammar from Latin into English. At night got off the Syriac alphabet in about twenty minutes."[82] He drew up lists of words in Syriac which had no resemblance to Hebrew words, and soon followed the example of Edward VI and his Greek, by writing his diary in Syriac characters. His interests extended to deciphering runic inscriptions and then to studying mathematics. It is significant that he did not do this with Brown, who seems to have kept closely to the traditional study of the classics. Except for the brief Academy period, Douglas Grammar School was by no means as venturesome in curriculum as Castletown. The tradition of its own old boys becoming masters prevented the wider influence of Castley being felt. Geneste turned to *Mr. G n* from Scotland newly arrived, almost certainly Andrew Gunn of Edinburgh who opened a school in February 1818 and announced a class aimed at preparing pupils for university in April that year.[83] Whether Geneste actually left Brown to attend Gunn's school is not clear. Certainly his classical studies continued: the Aeneid of Virgil, Cicero's Orationes, Livy and Horace were digested, and at least some connection with the Grammar School was retained when he attended a course in logic and studied Homer with James Crail of Lisburn, whom Brown had brought to the Island, having informed the public of Douglas that he would employ an assistant if numbers increased.[84]

Geneste himself studied to be a lawyer, indentured to his brother, but carried on with his Hebrew both as student and teacher. "My Hebrew pupils persevere with great ardour in their studies "he wrote to his brother in 1824.[85] A year after being admitted to the Manx Bar in 1825, he died, his short life showing the breadth of learning which Douglas could produce, and his diary revealing the existence of very advanced, but informal, learning, which would not be likely to be documented.

Geneste's brother went on to Queen's College, Oxford, and corresponded regularly with Hugh Stowell, the former master of the Douglas Grammar School. His letters were sent in the same envelope as those of Hugh's nephew, John Stowell, who found the high standards of Oxford, especially in Greek, a hardship "at least for those of us who have not had the advantage of previous Academic Education, regular and uninterrupted."[86] Nevertheless, although little time was left at Oxford for theology after classical studies, boys from Douglas Grammar School were sufficiently well grounded to cope with university standards, albeit with difficulty in some cases. The education offered by Brown may well have been considered rather old-fashioned compared with that offered by the numerous competing Academies, to be considered in the next chapter. The surprising fact revealed in McHutchin's survey of current provision in 1827, the Book of Charities, is that Brown had only eight scholars, a great fall since Hugh Stowell in 1800 with his fifty, and Qualtrough's Academy days with sixty.

In Douglas church life, the leading development in the late Eighteenth Century had been the founding of St. George's Chapel, whose extremely high pew rents marked it as the place of worship for the upper classes. Thomas Howard, Vicar of Braddan, in whose parish all Douglas lay, decided in 1832 he would take over St. George's himself, and Robert Brown moved out to Braddan, succeeding to the living in 1834. His place at St. Matthew's was taken by John La Mothe Stowell, who informed the Douglas public through the pages of the *Advertiser* that he was to reopen "St. Matthew's School, the original Grammar School of Douglas." If any weight is to be given to the testimony of Hugh Stowell Brown, son of Robert Brown and named after his father's friend, the intellectual standard of the Grammar School collapsed. "I should think that few clergymen's sons have had a worse schooling than that which fell to our lot."[87] The assistant was a former ship's painter, William Stowell, who had lost a leg and turned to schooling — "that profession was in those days the refuge of the destitute" — and is credited by Brown with a moderate knowledge of the three Rs. John Stowell had no Greek and "was supposed to teach Latin . . . the united teaching power of both being hardly equal to that of any National or Board School of the present day." In Latin, John Stowell found the easiest and most discreet course to announce translations were correct, while William carefully compared spelling with Walker's Dictionary. Neither understood Euclid or used the cane with any regard to justice or mercy. Brown recalled the books used as Murray's English Grammar, Rudimann's Rudiments of the Latin Tongue, Caesar, Cornelius Lepos, Virgil and the New Testament in Latin.

How far this picture should be taken seriously is open to doubt. A. W. Moore in his outline of H. S. Brown in *Manx Worthies* swallowed it hook, line and sinker. "He went to the Grammar School there which was then kept by the Rev. Thomas (sic.) Stowell. His education at that institution was of the most elementary education."[88] Yet even accepting every word of H. S. Brown, it is hard to equate the study of Virgil and Caesar with very elementary education. Although John Stowell's letters from Oxford indicated he found his degree course difficult, he was the only graduate master that the Grammar School had in its history. After leaving Oxford he had run schools in Castletown and Douglas, where his reputation would have been known to the church authorities, and later was given the post of staff member and bursar of the new College at Castletown, dealt with in Chapter Seven. Almost certainly, H. S. Brown's sneers fail to do Stowell justice.

On Stowell's departure for the new College in 1833, H. S. Brown was not removed from the Grammar School as Moore states, but confined his attendance to the mornings, picking up his classical learning by reading to his father, whose eyesight was failing, such authors as Cicero, Horace and Ovid, as well as the works of Paley, Hume, Gibbon and Hooker. Eventually he was elected to a Murrey Scholarship, for which the formula of appointment made reference to "a youth of whose morals and competency in Learning for his age we are well satisfied." The scholar was entitled to receive "all the Emoluments, Benefits and Advantages belonging thereto", but Brown found that of the £5/2/6 British put into the care of his father, he saw the 2/6d but no more!

H. S. Brown was even less complimentary about Stowell's successor;— "Of all men who undertook to keep a school . . . the greatest duffer." According to William Harrison's list of the Chaplains of St. Matthew's, this was John Cannell, as two months only are allotted to the immediate successor, Samuel Gelling.[89] However, the actual registers of St. Matthew's present a confusing picture, with services taken by Gelling and Cannell until 1835, when Cannell became official Chaplain. The 'duffer', probably Gelling, made no effort to run the school, according to H. S. Brown. The morning was spent reading two chapters of the Bible 'verse about', while the afternoons saw the boys left to their own devices, while the master read for his own pleasure. It was for this reason that Brown ceased to attend in the afternoons. A picture is painted of 'the downright savage', As Brown labelled the master, literally fighting to keep control, and expelling a boy for pulling a knife on him.

One thing is certain, that John Cannell proved to be the last master of the Douglas Grammar School. He came from a long line of Manx clergy, and his father before him had been a Murrey Scholar before becoming Vicar of Onchan in 1798.[90] He appeared when aged ten in Qualtrough's list of 1811, and himself became a Murrey's Scholar, mentioned as such in the Book of Charities.[91] With only the Murrey six pounds to support him, he may well have been the Mr. Cannell who opened a school in February 1825.[92] It would be difficult to dismiss Cannell as poorly educated without raising a large question mark about the efficiency of the teaching of Robert Brown himself. His appointment to the level of official Supplementary Clergyman on the Castletown Fund in 1832 at thirty pounds a year doubtless helped his finances before taking over as St. Matthew's Chaplain.[93] Certainly he took services at St. Matthew's during this time and possibly Gelling let him take the school. The very long waiting period before he received a cure of souls was no reflection on Cannell. The man he replaced as supernumerary had found a clerical title only by moving to the mainland.

In 1830 the *Sun* expressed a sense of injustice that the Chaplain of St. Matthew's, with a large populace and a school, should receive only sixty pounds, while incumbents in rural areas receiving nearly a hundred. Yet this was double the supplementary salary. As there was no way that the income of St. Matthew's could be separated into elements of chaplain and schoolmaster, and the numbers at the school had not increased considerably, Cannell may well have considered the school an unequal struggle it was wise to avoid. Already the clergy had ceased to teach the catechism on Saturday mornings, preferring to write their sermons. It was as a result of this being left to 'Peg-leg' Stowell, who carefully omitted certain parts, that H. S. Stowell later became a Congregationalist. By 1837 the school was closed, and the Register of St. Matthew's which recorded on June 24th 1835 Cannell's official appointment has the words "and Schoolmaster" very carefully and neatly crossed out. After a hundred and thirty years, Wilson's provision of higher education for Douglas had come to a halt.

All that survived was the financial provision for the third level of education. In the year the school was closed, Cannell's own son replaced Thomas Cain. given St. Luke's, Baldwin.[94] He held the position until 1846 and was then succeeded by his younger brother, who resigned immediately. Edward Kissack, appointed in March 1846, held the Scholarship until 1862, when he became Curate of Andreas. The Murrey Foundation was now probably devoid of educational content.

The town of Douglas thus ceased to provide a general education at grammar school level at its church school, and the higher education of its own clergy. This has usually been accepted as the end of what might be labelled for convenience as secondary education until the later Nineteenth Century, but as the next chapter will demonstrate, nothing could be further from the truth.

CONCLUSION

The Isle of Man, which at the close of the Eighteenth Century appeared set fair for a prosperous future as far as its endowed schools were concerned, in marked contrast to many parts of England and Ireland, within decades suffered from the same malaise. There was no special Island factor to account for this, but rather varying combinations of well known and widespread causes of decline.

It is difficult to overestimate the role of individual masters. The replacement of man of the calibre of Joseph Stowell, Hugh Stowell, and Castley by the indolent, such as Dodd and Gelling at Peel, or the incapable, such as Joseph Brown at Castletown and Gelling (or Cannell?) at Douglas, was probably the single greatest factor. With such people, the potential weakness of pluralism, where the master already had a guaranteed income from the cure of souls, became very evident: what A. F. Leach labelled "the pernicious practice of employing parsons as schoolmasters."[95] (The worst case of all, however, was Dodd at Peel, who did not come into this category.)

Yet even within the Island, marked differences were detectable. In Ramsey the small endowment disappeared altogether. "It may well be that poverty was the most important factor contributing to the decade of many grammar schools." In Peel the haziness of the original benefactors concerning responsibility for repair let buildings deteriorate, while in Castletown the artificial shortage of funds for repairs was caused by the failure to apply a good endowment in an equitable manner. Douglas Grammar School had the whiff of competition from other schools offering a more relevant education.

In no case did Trustees emerge with much credit, although the harshest words of Carlise that "... ample endowments have fallen to decay by the negligence or cupidity of ignorant or unprincipled Trustees who ... suffered the furtive alienation of the very lands which they were called upon so solemnly to defend", did not really apply to the Island.[96] Ramsey was never an ample endowment: Castletown did not decay exactly, the money being not applied to the school. Yet in Peel particularly it was true that "in a worsening situation school governors did little or nothing to prevent or delay the decline of schools. It is reasonable to surmise that apathy and discouragement were . . . aggravated by indifference and irresponsibility on the part of their governors."[97] The dual appointment of Thimbleby was an act of pure folly, when the realisation of Barrow's hopes lay within grasp and a separate appointment with judicious allowance for repair could have clinched it.

The facts made sober reading. Douglas had closed its doors for ever: Ramsey had a grammar school on paper only: Peel schools were both in a dreadful state: Castletown had been shut up, and was struggling on, yet its friends were looking for its demise and had given it up. The promising higher education given by the endowed schools had failed, but even as traditional institutions had run out of steam, new and vigorous forces in education were making themselves felt — the forces of the market place.

REFERENCES
CHAPTER SIX

1. *Journal of the House of Keys*, March 28 1822.
2. *Ibid*.
3. R. S. Tompson, *The Charity Commission and the Age of Reform*, Routledge and Kegan Paul 1979 98.
4. *Ibid*, 82-83.
5. *Athol papers*, 117 (3rd) 3. MD 441/173 April 13 1818.
6. *Journal of the House of Keys*, July 30 1822.
7. *Athol Papers* BK 99 49.
8. PRO HO 99 17 Letter May 25 1822.
9. Athol Papers 104/1.
10. Feltham, *Op cit* 163.
11. *Diocesan Records* 154.
12. R. D. Kermode, *The Annals of Kirk Christ Lezayre*, Norris Modern Press, Douglas, 1954.
13. See Chapter Three.
14. *Manks Advertiser*, April 4 1812.
15. *Ibid*, April 13 1818.
16. *BC* 96.
17. *Rising Sun*, Oct 5 1822.
18. *Ibid*, May 21 1825.
19. *Athol Papers*, 99 House of Keys Statement July 30 1822.
20. *Ibid*, 104-1.
21. *BBT*, July 21 1801.
22. *Ibid*.
23. *BC*, 23.
24. *Manks Advertiser*, Oct 3 1801.
25. *Ibid*, Dec 18 1802.
26. *Athol Papers*, 107-7.
27. *Ibid* x/41 (2) Feb 4 1823.
28. *Ibid*, 124 (2nd) 27, James Crone to Duke of Athol.
29. *Ibid*, 66 (3rd) 15.
30. *Rising Sun*, Sept 7 1824.
31. *Manks Advertiser*, Jan 13 1825.
32. *Ibid*, Feb 3 1825.
33. MD 612 50/16 Mar 15 1824; 50/17 June 24 1824.
34. Ibid 50/15 Resolution of House of Keys June 10 1824.
35. Ibid 50/19.
36. Ibid 50/18 June 20 1801.
37. Ibid 50/8.
38. Ibid 50 /19.
39. Ibid 50/31 Nov 23 1824.
40. Ibid 50/3 Feb 22 1825.

41. Ibid 50/50.
42. Ibid 50/3 Feb 22 1825.
43. Ibid 50/4 may 6 1825.
44. Manx Advertiser, Jan 13 1825 (Editorial).
45. Ibid.
46. Ibid Feb 3 1828.
47. *Rising Sun*, June 25 1828.
48. *Manks Advertiser*, Feb 16 1828.
49. BC 61 (MD 612 50/16 The Keys wanted a united school).
50. *Ibid* 69.
51. R. S. Tompson, *Classics or Charity* 126.
52. Edmund Goodwin, *Manx Annals of Eighty Years Ago 1815-1825* MS 2165A 78.
53. *BC* 69.
54. *Ibid* 63.
55. *Manks Advertiser*, Jan 27 1825.
56. *BC* 31.
57. *Athol Papers* 116 (2nd) 38 Nov 25 1806.
58. *Ibid*, 105/40.
59. Hans, *Op cit ch 3. (See Chapter Three)*.
60. *Athol Papers* 105/32.
61. *BC* 38.
62. *Athol Papers* 116 (2nd) 38.
63. *Ibid* 117 (2nd) 18.
64. *BBT* Aug 25 1818.
65. MD 441/166.
66. Ibid 441/169.
67. *Athol Papers* 99 5.
68. R. Curphey, *Bishop Barrow's Trusts* 5.
69. *Athol Papers* 99 37.
70. *Ibid* 99 9.
71. *Ibid* Bk 53.
72. *Ibid* 117 (3rd) 28 Aug 8 1822.
73. *BBT* Oct 21 1822.
74. *BC* 39.
75. *BBT* Feb 23 1825.
76. MD 511 6718.
77. *St. Matthew's Register*, 266, Sept 29 1788.
78. *Manks Advertiser*, May 12 1804.
79. *Ibid*, June 6 1804.
80. *Ibid*, June 10 1809.
81. See Appendix 2 for full list of boys and subjects.
82. William Stowell, *A Memoir of the Life and Labours of the Rev. William Hendry Stowell, DD*, Judd and Glass, London 1859 9.

83 *BBT*, Jan 12 1813; July 22 1809.
84 Hugh Stowell, *A Memoir of Mr. F. D. P. Geneste*, Marples and Son, Liverpool 1822. Diary entry April 24 1818.
85 *Manks Advertiser*, April 16 1818.
86 *Ibid*, Dec 30 1819.
87 Hugh Stowell, *Op cit*, Oct 9 1824.
88 AWM MS 233B Letter May 13 1822.
89 Fd William Caine, MP, *Hugh Stowell Brown, His Autobiography, His Commonplace Book and Extracts from his Sermons and Addresses*, Routledge, London 1887, 9.
90 A. W. Moore, *Manx Worthies*, 53.
91 William Harrison, *An Account of the Diocese of Sodor and Man and St. German's Cathedral*, Manx Society Vol. XXIX, 1879. 115 The close links between Gelling and Cannell are partly explained by the fact they were brothers-in-law.
92 *St. Matthew's Register* 267, April 7 1798.
93 *BC* 115.
94 *Rising Sun*, Feb. 19 1825.
95 *BBT*, July 20 1832.
96 *St. Matthew's Register* 270.
97 A. F. Leach, *Victoria Country History: Sussex*, ii 401.
98 N. Carlisle, *A Concise Description of the Endowed Grammar Schools of England and Wales*, London 1818, Vol. i XXXV.
90 Vincent, *Op cit* 190.

CHAPTER SEVEN

THE EXPLOSION IN EDUCATION
THE ROLE OF THE PRIVATE SECTOR

The sad decline in the vitality of higher education offered under the foundation or nominal oversight of the authorities in church and state was only part of the picture in the early Nineteenth Century. The tendency to concentrate solely upon endowed schools and 'official' establishments results in a view of education which would be quite alien to those who actually lived at the time.

On the mainland of Britain, the Eighteenth Century had seen a great growth in private academies, following the establishment of the first in Soho Square, London, at the end of the preceding century. At the highest level, the dissenting academies moved from being training places for ministers to being centres of a wider curriculum, such as Warrington Academy, where preparation for careers in law, commerce and medicine was offered.[1] At a lower level, the widespread discontent with the classical diet that still often dominated the grammar schools, despite the attempts to be more relevant, led to an abundance of academies offering an education more in touch with the actual needs of society. As might be expected, London itself was the main centre of activity, accounting for two-thirds of the two hundred academies in existence between 1780 and 1800.[2] In the largest academies there was a very wide choice of subjects, and they prided themselves on fitting a pupil's individual needs and strengths; Nicholas Hans likens them to the modern comprehensive schools in this respect. Others catered for the upper middle classes, with mainly literary and scientific subjects, with some vocational ones, while others still specialised in technical and vocational subjects. The titles often gave some indication of what was offered, or perhaps more correctly, what was claimed was on offer. One area hitherto neglected was preparation for commercial life. Malachy Postlethwayt asserted in 1750 that England lacked any seminary for trade, and proposed a commercial academy with a full two year course. Soon "Classical and Commercial Academies" abounded, together with Commercial and Mathematical Schools such as the one opened in Salford in 1765. North of the border, writing or commercial schools were founded as at Stirling in 1747, while Perth Academy was the first of its kind giving a wide range of subjects, opened in 1761.[3] Wherever the location, the term "Academy" promised above all a relevance to life that many of the old grammar schools failed to deliver; the world of education too was to be opened fully to the laws of supply and demand.

In the Isle of Man, at the same time as the endowed schools were at their nadir, the greatest upsurge in Manx educational provision was taking place in Douglas through the private sector, yet this movement was totally ignored by E. W. Corlett in his survey of Manx education.[4]

Part of the reason for the upsurge being in Douglas lay in the growing distinction between society in Douglas and the rest of the Island. It has been noted already that Bishop Hildesley found Douglas society hostile to the Manx tongue, and John Stowell's poems at the end of the Eighteenth Century teased those aspiring to enter high society

"*Daphne would fain disown from whence she sprung
Although the herring scales are her tongue*".[5]

The advent of the Duke of Atholl as Governor, residing in Douglas, created its own little court, and the ending of the Napoleonic Wars led to an influx of half-pay officers who found living costs on the Island very cheap. Douglas in the Eighteen Twenties has been described as "making up in some respects in quality for what it lacked in quantity".[6]

"Then was the fair island town the haunt and home of many of the younger scions of noble families, of the gentlemen of good old lineage but impoverished fortune, of numerous retired military and naval officers, and of the dilettante in search of literary and artistic quiet ... Wealth was at a discount, and society so exclusive, that anyone ever so remotely connected with trade aspired in vain to gain an entry into the privileged sets"[7]

Even the clergy, highly regarded elsewhere in the Island, were, with the exception of the bishop and archdeacon, quite excluded from the dinners given by the Duke at Casle Mona on Douglas Bay, "wholly debarred by poverty from intercourse with the wealthier part of the community", with their wives in particular out of their social depth, "incapable of being part of better society".[8] Here was a stratum of society which could afford and expected to have private education of a standard beyond elementary.

Leading families of the Island had indeed sent their children across to the mainland. Receipts survive of the Moore family which show their children educated partly by the local clergy such as Vicar-General Evan Christian, but chiefly in England, the girls at Liverpool and Whitehaven, and young James with the Rev. Thomas Murray in London.[9] William Watson Christian (1799-1893) a noted Manx Lawyer born in Ramsey was educated in Whitehaven.[10] There was in particular a strong link with St. Bee's School conveniently near to Whitehaven, the closest mainland port, and Kirk Maughold boys were given an education there to compensate for the tithes once given to the Priory of St. Bee's. A manuscript list of St. Bee's pupils from the Isle of Man includes the names of Edward Moore Gawne of Kentraugh, later Speaker of the House of Keys, and the Rev. Thomas Howard, Rector of Braddan when Robert Brown was in Douglas.[11] Some aspired to the great public schools, not always through wealth. Thus while John Christian Curwen of Miltown, a notable house in the North of the Isle of Man, attended Eton before going on to Cambridge,[12] the Rev. James Wilks wrote to Hildesley in 1771 to ask if there "any prospects of getting on the Charterhouse foundation" for his son Mark, later reported as having "received a highly classical education ... at one of the Publck Schools in London".[13]

Yet some of the earliest private schools in Douglas were strictly functional, and gave the town something equivalent to the Peel Mathematical School. Certainly the absence of endowed schools for the purpose did not mean Douglas was deprived of this vital subject for a sea-faring town. (As was noted in Chapter Five, the majority of Mathematical Schools were in the private sector, the early endowed ones yielding place to new private schools such as those of Thomas Haseldon at Wapping (1721) and George Donn at Bideford (1720)). The Rev. John Gell in his curious career left Douglas Grammar School to go to Peter Fannin's school, "by whom I was perfectly instructed in navigation".[14] Fannin, who had been with Captain Cook in the South Pacific set up his school in 1775: his 1789 map of the Island was praised for its notation of anchorages. A little earlier a Mr. Brown of Marown wrote books on navigation and mathematics for the aid of schoolmasters, but whether for a particular school is unknown[15] C. Radcliffe in 1803 specialised in navigation and surveying,[16] while a little later Broadfoot's Academy did the same in 1812.[17] One of the more interesting teachers of navigation was Robert Corteen whose announcement that his "delicate health precluded him from following his usual occupation" might mislead the reader into thinking he was one who turned to teaching because he was unfit for anything else. In the case of Corteen this was quite untrue. He had started gasworks in Douglas, surveying the town for that purpose and also the first iron foundry. After his schoolmastering in Douglas was over, he surveyed for the Lancashire and Yorkshire Railway, returning to the Island to manage the Douglas Gas Company. He wrote the first compendious work on British lighthouses, and like others of the period, taught himself Greek and Hebrew. "Many of our most skilful navigators... were taught by him".[18]

Some of the earliest schools probably made no claim to offer anything more than elementary education. Mr. Hargreaves offered in his Academy writing, arithmetic and elocution,[19] while Mr. Simpson similarly offered grammar, writing and arithmetic in a room adjoining the Assembly Room,[20] but even here Tompson's comment about the secondary nature of some of this teaching needs to be taken into account.

CLERGY SCHOOLS

Many of the early schools were run by clergymen, and on the Island too offered a source of income for some while they waited for a vacant living. Of the 260 private English classical schools listed by Hans, 240 were run by clergy. When parents had little idea of the veracity of claims by schoolmasters, the clergyman was felt to be likely "to have been well educated himself and a man of decent life".[21] Before the turn of the century, the Rev. J. Colquoun, whose link with Douglas Grammar School was considered in the last chapter, was offering advanced tuition in navigation, astronomy and geography, to young ladies as well as young gentlemen.[22] In 1803 the Academic

Student, the Rev. Thomas Harrison announced his intention to set up a school near the Quay, soon moving to Muckle's Gate, and later forming a partnership with the Rev. P. Peters[23,24] whose own room was taken by Mr. Muir, himself shortly to join the Rev. J. Kewley at the Grammar School.[25] The list of subjects and fees of Harrison and Peters made the advanced nature of the education quite clear. Obviously demand was growing, and another cleric, Philips, the Chaplain of Ramsey, who had informed the inhabitants of that town of his intention to open a Classical Academy[26] announced his removal to Thomas Street, Douglas to Mr. Rimmer's house.[27] Philips was proud of his Trinity College Dublin degree: he presumed "not on experience but the advantages of a regular university Education" and invited those going to university to read part of the undergraduate course with him to facilitate progress. His fees were shortly raised from £1.11.6 to two guineas a quarter except for present pupils.

Philips was one of the first in the Isle of Man to exploit the potential of the press. An open letter from the people of Ramsey extending good wishes,[26] lists of prizewinners, the hiring of "able and experienced assistants", and letters from pupils such as Samuel White Talbot expressing thanks for care and attention received, all found their way into the pages of the *Advertiser*.[27] By 1815 the house in Thomas Street was up to be let. Perhap's Philips' second marriage in 1813 to a Rear Admiral's daughter was not unconnected with his fading from the scene.[28]

Although the link on the mainland between Dissent and the Academies emphasised by Irene Parker[29] was not really to the fore on the Island, it was true that not all reverend schoolmasters belonged to the Established Church, and the private sector alone offered exceptions to the complete domination of education by the church authorities. The Rev. Samuel Haining, a Congregationalist who arrived in 1804 and was a prime mover in establishing a Manx branch of the British and Foreign Bible Society, held a school in the Club Room for several decades, using eventually his son as assistant.[29] (It has already been mentioned how Haining taught the Geneste family their early Latin). A Presbyterian influence was also making itself felt. In 1811 the Rev. James McGhee kept three boarders in his small school for ten boys, and in 1816 he was joined in Douglas by the Rev. Robert Steven, who used his school in Athol Street as a preaching house on Sundays. The statement by Bishop Hildesley on his arrival in 1756 that all the Island belonged to the Church of England was now clearly out of date. Yet surprisingly there was little concerted effort by Methodists to enter the field of education, although after the visits of Wesley to the Island there were very substantial numbers of adherents, to the great alarm of many Anglicans.

The only exception in the early Nineteenth Century came with the efforts of the Rev. Robert Aitken, by no means a typical Methodist. He had appeared first on the Island as an Anglican, acting as honorary curate to the Rev. Benjamin Philpott at St. George's, Douglas, but his Calvinistic theology led him to abandon the Church of England. (The suggestion by E. V. Chapman[30] that Philpott suffered for this link by being banished to a country parish is quite wrong: it was in fact the Rectory of Andreas, the parish of the Archdeacons, and the highest promotion the Island could offer.) Aitken bought the estate of Eyreton between Peel and Marown in 1831 and aimed to build a full scale college on the lines of Kingswood and Woodhouse Grove. Two hours of Bible study and prayer were part of the daily regimen envisaged in the syllabus. Fees were to be £22-£30 per annum, and the governors and visitors were to include the Superintendent of the Douglas Wesleyan Circuit.[31] Despite the imposing facade and the arrangements to link with Liverpool steamers, it was a nine day wonder. Aitken was not welcomed by the Methodists, and was turned down as a minister by Conference in 1834 and 1835, merely allowed to be a lay preacher. When he moved to Lancashire he was charged with subversion by the Methodist authorities. One Thomas Moffatt was left in charge of the teaching at Eyreton, but without official Methodist support the grandiose scheme was doomed. Chapman states that by 1847 Moffat is referred to as being the agent, rather than the schoolmaster, of Aitken, but *Pigot's Directory* for 1837 already gave the occupier of Eyreton as Geoffrey Palfreyman under the heading "Gentry", with no mention of a school[32.] Moffat's daughter seems to have tried her hand at a school in 1846[33] but six years later the heading for Eyreton is under gentry again, with David Moffat.

FEMALE EDUCATION

Although the endowed schools of the Island had totally neglected any provision of education for females this was not at all true of the private sector. Even on the mainland the start had been late: Nicholas Hans traced only one school in the Seventeenth Century, run by a Mrs. Frankland for daughters of Dissenters in Manchester,[34] and throughout the Eighteenth Century home tuition was still predominant, given more often by family than by private tutor. Yet by 1800 there was a recognised market for female education, even if there was little response in practice to the pleas of such writers as Erasmus Darwin, Marie Edgeworth, and Mary Godwin-Wollstonecroft for a scientific education. Hans found only two schools which taught mathematics and science. "The only thing which society required of women of the upper classes was the "accomplishments and a smattering of foreign languages".[35] The Rev. J. Colqouun's lectures to young ladies in astronomy were quite advanced for the time, revealing that the Island should not be dismissed entirely as a backwater.

Sometimes the classes for young ladies were run by a wife as an adjunct to the husband's efforts. Thus Mrs. Philips started to teach girls up to the age of eighteen, her advertisements making it clear that her pupils would not be in contact with those of her husband. Yet many schools sprang up expressly for girls, some going on to include boys later. L. W. Wenham set up in Douglas as a music master, but in 1804 joined a Mr. Cropper in the old Printing Office in teaching young ladies only — it would be "highly improper to receive young gentlemen".[36] After this declaration of principle it is surprising to find the school was advertised the following year as being for young gentlemen also.

Probably the type of education experienced by Sophia Leece was typical. Born in 1798, she had early lessons with the Rev. Charles Crebbin, living with his family, and from 1809 went to what her biographer, the Rev. Hugh Stowell, described as a "competent teacher", learning English, geography, and French, spoken with "correctness and elegance".[37]

Since the private tutor had until recently been thought the best way of educating the young, early private schools often stressed the 'domestic' nature of their establishments.[38] Thus Conolly's school, which started in 1809 with Mr. Conolly teaching girls only, and later took both sexes when Conolly joined with Laurence (recently ousted from Douglas Grammar School by the Rev. John Qualtrough) found it prudent in 1811 to stress the young ladies were in the care of Mrs. Conolly.[39.]

The Smythe family illustrate not only the family nature of many private schools, but also a marked feature of the private sector, the frequent changing of premises. The school which lasted a decade in the same spot was a rarity. The Smythes came from "the Carlisle Academy" in 1821, settling in Duke Street, Douglas, with husband and wife having their own schools,[40] Mr. Smythe's specialism lay in writing by Carstair's and Rapier's new method, and he crossed into his wife's domain to teach calligraphy to the young ladies. An evening school was added in Athol Street by November 1821, removed to Wellington Buildings, Duke Street in 1823, when a Miss Shaw appeared on the scene as one of the staff.[41] The main boarding school was removed to Drumgold Street a matter of months later to offer more comfortable lodging to a "limited number of boarders"[42] The 'second branch' was also widely used by the more ambitious establishments, and the idea of having been partly tried out with the evening school, the Smythes opened a school in Onchan under another daughter. This seems to have been shortlived, the Misses Symthe reuniting when the family moved yet again to Shaw's Brow at No. 12, with Mr. Smythe informing the public he would resume full-time teaching having almost completed his map of the Isle of Man.[43] The Smythes also put into practice the public examination recommended by Joseph Stowell, a way for the private school to display its prowess in a highly competitive situation. It was announced that these examinations would be held before all holidays.[44]

Of some schools virtually nothing is known beyond the fact of their existence. Miss Allen opened a ladies' school in 1810, but for how long it lasted is unknown.[45] The same is true of Miss Christian and her niece, Miss Clucas, at Ballaquinnen House, although at least her fees are known and her hope to have twelve young ladies.[46] The magnet pull of Douglas is instanced in a number of cases, as when G. Davis left Castletown to open in King Street, Douglas, in 1818, and within Douglas, the prestigious address of Athol Street attracted a great number of schools.

The rate of turnover was high as some left and others failed. Mrs. Cover and Miss Barlace left no trace after one solitary advertisement,[47] and often only notices of premises to let, without the flourishing of an advertised move to better premises, indicate the end of a school. Mrs. St. George survived at least eight years, including a move from Heywood House to Shaw's Brow, but by March 1818 her rooms were to let.[48]

The reason for frequent changes of premises was not only that of prestige. As the cheapness of the cost of living in the Isle of Man was sufficient to attract large numbers of half-pay officers, so the keeping of boarding pupils was even more profitable than usual. The more roomy the premises, the greater the potential profits. Thus the Misses Barrow in Cambrian Place had financial incentives to move to a "commodious and airy residence at the west end of Athol Street" beyond the repute of the street.[49] Mrs. Digby of 3 Wellington Buildings cautiously announced her intent to open a school, and to take boarders when a suitable house presented itself, as it did the next year on the south side of the river.[50] Of course the moves were not all in one direction; as in Snakes and Ladders, there were both climbs and falls. The Misses Pring exemplify moving about to the point of being worthy of one of the satires of John Stowell. Having opened in Athol Street in 1826, they moved down to the Parade in 1828, to Fort Street in 1829, to Moore's Court in 1830, and on in the same year to Gt. Nelson Street, proclaiming the advantage of two gardens, and then back to Moore's Court in 1831. Their ventures came to an end in 1832 with the announcement of sale of their furniture and effects on leaving the Island.[51] Mrs. Holiday was another example of dreams unfulfilled. In 1818 she advertised for a few boarders in 2 Church Street, and moved on to Thomas Street. In the spring of 1822 she declared that she was breaking up her present establishment, intending to "commence on an entirely new plan and render her seminary select by advancing her terms".[52] The "entirely new plan" apparently misfired, for the next news of Mrs. Holiday was that her furniture was to be sold as she was leaving the Island, and Mr. Prince would be teaching dancing in her rooms. Other advertisements of the time show this to have been in Society Lane, King Street. (Within two years the room was again a school, but the Academy of Mr. M. Smith was another failure, despite or maybe because of his low fees.[53] He moved away to Ramsey, and tried his luck at "Peter Cannel's near Deemster Moore's".[54]).

The educational world in Douglas was thus an ever-changing kaleidoscope: an attempt to pinpoint schools and teachers would be hopelessly out of date in respect of both personnel and sites within a matter of two or three years. The laws of supply and demand operated without any mitigation, and the less successful went to the wall. This intense competition was a source of both weakness and strength. The failures were weeded out quickly, but only the most successful could offer any degree of continuity, and even with these personal circumstances could change very quickly.

Whatever the standards might have been, there is no doubt that in sheer numbers, the private schools of Douglas catered for young ladies very well, giving them parity with males in thinking that education was important, even if the content consisted of "accomplishments" for the young lady in society. While few followed the example of the Rev. Colquoun in offering navigation and astronomy, the majority offered at least one foreign language to their clientele, who would expect more than a polite version of elementary education (especially after the Lancastrian School moved in 1812 to fine new premises in Athol Street[55]). If the children of the poor received a sound, basic education, those who paid would expect something extra, such as the French and Italian taught by Madame Benderac at the Athol Street school of Miss Jayne Rigg.[56]

Most of the features which marked the development of female education were naturally mirrored in that for males. There was the same coming and going of a large number of teachers, the same rapid changing of premises, the public examinations and the displays of work, which Mr. Markett at the Hills, Douglas, was the first to introduce in 1804. (The sale of his furnishings the following year was due to health rather than public disapproval, for he died at Castletown in September 1805).[57]

There were, however, differences. There were few father and son relationships to match frequent mother and daughter establishments. The Miss Rigg, mentioned above, had started in 1822 in Thomas Street with her mother, for example, and even when there was discord, such as when Miss Meudell informed the Douglas public that there was no connection between her school and her mother's, the link was there despite the acrimony.[58] Although this might have been expected to provide greater continuity, there is little evidence for this. Only two schools for girls achieved a period of continuity lasting a number of decades, and it was among the men that a greater number of schools established themselves successfully, with stronger threads linking the multitude of names, splits and takeovers proving more effective than family blood ties. Leinster-Mackay rightly argues that when these are taken into account the charge of ephemerality usually levied at the private schools is not borne out to quite the degree imagined by those dismissive of the contribution of the private schools.[59]

For instance, Angus Gunn, who arrived from Edinburgh in 1817, started his class preparatory to university in 1818,[60] and then expanded to run courses for young ladies which included astronomy as well as the more usual French. In order to be able to receive more pupils, he employed George Lowe as assistant.[61] When Gunn left the Island in 1820, Lowe took over the school, with the help of a partner, T. M. White.[62] The partnership was shortlived. White — not the T. M. Whyte who assisted the Rev. Philips and opened his own grammar school in 1814, borrowing the title of Douglas Grammar School — was a classicist from Dublin, and opened in 1821 his English and Classical School, advertising as being late of "White and Lowe": Lowe for his part joined forces with Garvin, who had opened the Duke Street Academy in 1820,[63] to form the Athol Street Academy and Grammar School.[64] There was thus a thread between Gunn and Garvin which covered nearly two decades in all, not apparent at first sight. Occasionally among the ladies there were flashes of continuity. Mrs. Busby, opening her school on the quay in 1811, informed Douglas parents she was the successor to Mrs. Connolly, whose illness the previous year had caused Mr. Connolly to give up his day scholars.[65] With ladies too, a new married name could mask the continuance of an existing school; Mrs. Quilleash at King Street turned out to be none other than the Miss Meudell who quarrelled with her mother.[66] Although there was never on the Island anything to equal the continuity of Cheam or Soho Square, or the long association of the Newcombe family with Hackney Academy, what degree of continuity there was prevailed chiefly in the boys' schools rather than the girls'.

THE COUNTRY HOUSE SCHOOL

More schools for boys too succeeded in realising the ambition of the private schoolteacher to move away from premises in a town street into the more imposing setting of a country house not too far from Douglas, but with limited success.

The first to achieve this seems to have been William Rimmer, who arrived in Douglas from Chester in 1808, taking "a large and airy room" in King Street for a maximum of twenty pupils.[67] The following year he had forty pupils in a room behind the Parade, paying especial attention to French and geography.[68] Later in the Autumn came the move out to Ballabrooie on the Peel Road, and a boarding school set up, with an assistant for English. His wife continued her supportive role in Douglas, with her own young ladies. This early venture seems to have quickly come to grief, for Rimmer's last advertisement was offering a reward for tracing the person responsible for making injurious remarks!

J. Barton felt his way more cautiously, taking a number of years to build up his clientele, and started modestly with private lessons in Classics at Mr. Allen's House, Queen Street.[69] After the inspiration of borrowing the title Douglas Grammar School, noted in the last chapter, he moved to King Street, making space for his wife to have twelve pupils herself.[70] After a change of address to Thomas Street and of title to "The Military Naval Classical and Commercial Academy", he moved once more to Heywood House, "the most salubrious and eligible in all Douglas", and called his school Heywood House Academy, judging that a prestigious address had greater appeal than all-inclusive title. Not all the building was taken at once — a Mrs. Maddocks had opened a school in 1809 there — but by 1814 the remaining wing was taken and Mr. and Mrs. Barton ran two separate establishments for day and boarding pupils.[71] After pains were taken to demonstrate the advantages of education at Heywood House, the elocutionary methods, the Professor of Dancing, and plans for the future, Barton surprisingly left his part of the house to his wife and went to Athol Street.[72] His last press announcement was of the end of vacation in 1821, and, as Barton made great use of the press, the silence would indicate his school ceased to exist. There is no mention of him in *Pigot and Co's Directory* of 1824 in the list of schools, although this was by no means proof of non-existence.

For another master omitted from Pigot's list, but very much in existence was John Anson Garvin, of Garvin and Lowe. Lowe soon faded from the scene, but Garvin expanded into larger premises, still in Athol Street, in 1826. At thirty guineas for boarders and eight guineas for day boys, his fees were not cheap. A ladies class started in 1821, dropped in 1822, but revived by 1827,[73] flourished to the point that a Miss Forster was hired as an assistant, although care was taken to preserve the family image of education "with his own daughters".[74] However, the *Sun* announced the sale of the ladies' seminary furniture, and Garvin left Douglas for Oakhill, two miles to the south. The annoymous Stranger who wrote his *Six Day Tour* was very impressed. "Oak Hill, one of those sweet seclusions you meet with in every country . . . latterly taken over by Mr. Garvin for an academy for young gentlemen: a finer situation for an academical eatablishment of this nature could not be picked out".[75] Garvin aimed to prepare pupils for the Higher Public Schools or directly for University and Public Office, but this essay in the country house school came to an end in 1840, an advertisement announcing furniture for sale as Garvin had left the Island.[76]

A mile to the south of Oakhill was the country house called Hampton Court, for a short time the home of the school of Edward May. He had started off in Fort Street, Douglas, succeeding where two predecessors, John Richardson and a Mr. Norris had failed, both selling off their furniture. May stayed there a short time only: the phrase "select and limited number of respectable young gentlemen" could usually be accurately translated as meaning room for very few. (Norris had found room for six boarders compared with Richardson's three![77] The rapid changes of premises followed: *Pigot's Directory* located May at the "Classical and Mathematical Academy, Bath Cottage, the Parade,[78] but he soon returned to Fort Street, gaining the assistance of the Rev Samuel Haining and successful enough to advertise for a large, airy schoolroom, moving on first to Bond Street and then to Wellington Square.[79] In April 1828 he made the ambitious move to Hampton Court, charging twenty guineas for tuition in Latin French, Mathematics, English, Navigation, Mapping and Land Measuring. "The Commercial Department is directed pursuant to the actual practice of life in a merchant's counting house".[80]

In 1830 May sought to keep one foot in the day-boy market by opening the Collegiate School in Thomas Street, under the supervision of John May of London and Wilson of Dublin. This was clearly a parallel establishment, not a feeder for Hampton Court, and was for pupils of advanced years to finish their education and prepare them for Naval and Military Colleges and university.[81] Echoes of new developments across the water were now heard in the Island with the announcement that London University courses were to be followed. In January 1832 Wilson was running the school by himself, and by July it was under his name, Wilson stressing his own Trinity College education and preparation for university although calling the academy "Classical Commercial". When he left the Island in 1837, Wilson put up the school for sale as "an old established school"[82]

Perhaps May regretted the loss of his Douglas interest, for he failed to establish himself at Hampton Court; the *Sun* announced in 1832 that May was resuming at Peel.[83] By 1833 he was back in Fort Street, reduced to "a large room", but after quick moves to Moore's Place and St. Barnabas, he faded from the educational scene, with silence after May 1834.[84]

Thus not one of the masters who had attempted to run a country house type school had successfully operated his establishment for more than a handful of years. By contrast, two girls' schools which entered this area stood the test of time with far greater success.

The Misses Dutton came to the Island from Tranmere in 1822, leaving some of their family behind, so that in early years there were references to the Duttons of Tranmere and Douglas.[85] The school was opened in Athol Street, with the usual subjects including French at two guineas extra, but a further branch was started in Ramsey in 1827 by Miss M. Dutton. This faded from the scene by 1832, but two years later the major step was taken of moving to the Villa Marina on the seafront of Douglas Bay, away from the town at that time.[86] An excellent reputation was very quickly built up and soon the Duttons felt able to dispense with day pupils at the Villa and render their school more exclusive by having boarders only. The reason given for this change, the distance involved for day girls from Douglas, seemed rather transparent in view of the short distance involved. Advertisements stressed the lofty bedrooms, the good library and the gymnasium complete with "apparatus of Kalesthenic Exercises", while the setting received many compliments. Laughton's Guide of 1842 stated

> "The Villa Marina was built by the late Colonel Stewart and at his decease was purchased for a Boarding School by the Misses Dutton, a purpose to which its seclusion and airy situation admirably adapt it."[87]

Slater's Commercial Directory of 1846 listed the Villa among the "superior seminaries", the only female school to gain a mention, with a note about the acres of enclosed grounds with their protecting walls setting off the elegant mansion. The Stranger for his part had his thoughts fixed on the Villa as a place "where with every grace and accomplishment, valuable and fascinating in life, these lovely creatures are but too irresistibly qualified for expert fishers of men". Kerruish's Guide of 1855 went so far as to claim that "the establishment of the Villa Marina conducted by the Misses Dutton has no superior in the British Isles".[88]

The Dutton ladies did not give up taking day pupils altogether. Miss Eliza returned to Athol Street to run a new Athol Street branch, doubtlessly not to the joy of the Miss Hodson who had taken over their original premises.[89] In 1840 Eliza crossed the street to more roomy premises and proceeded to take in boarders herself, offering places for six young ladies. This Athol Street branch offered a wider curriculum than usual. Teachers were not only employed for the normal specialist subjects of French and music, but also for chemistry, a subject normally regarded as outside the field of suitable female education.[90]

Miss Eliza is absent from the *Pigot and Slater Directory* for 1843, only the Villa being mentioned, but in the later directories of 1846 and 1852 Miss Jane Dutton emerges with schools at the Esplanade and Victoria Road respectively. By 1857, Miss Frances at the Villa gave way to Miss Lydia, but the only school singled out for praise in that year in *Slater's Directory* belonged to the other long established sisters, the Misses Stowell.

Although not listed in Pigot's Directory of 1824, Ellen Stowell was advertising in 1825 as reopening in 6 Shaw's Brow. After a spell in St. George's Walk with John Lamothe Stowell, running separate seminaries, she moved to Athol Street in 1827. Mrs. Stowell appeared on the scene from 1830, but after her death in 1833, Ellen was joined by sister Bellanne. Their modest boarding establishment being overshadowed for many years by the Villa Marina, the sisters eventually took the plunge and leased Rushen Abbey for a country boarding school. Ellen's letters stated her conviction the country was preferable for education, and that extra pupils were attracted by the "healthy residence".[91]

The year 1852 almost brought disaster when the sisters were at the point of being forced to move. The house was considered the best site for a lunatic asylum being urged upon the Island by the Home Ofice. The sisters were told that if they rejected an offer of £100 for the lease, the lunatic asylum would be sited in nearby cottages. Ellen protested to the Vicar of Malew "we could not attempt to keep on our school a single day". Governor Hope was told ". . . the injury inflicted on our establishment by the bare idea of having a Lunatic Asylum within the very grounds of a Young Ladies Boarding School is surely to be depreciated.'"[92] Money had been laid out; to move would cost £20, and premises of the quality of Rushen Abbey would cost £70 per annum, with more repairs to pay for in addition. The sisters held out for £200, which they reckoned was "scarcely enough". Bishop Auckland, who had suggested the Stowells be bought out, considered that this was fair enough, as did the vendor of the property. Fate, however, intervened; the failure of Holmes Bank in 1853 meant the loss of the £1,500 collected towards the building of the asylum. No asylum was built until 1868, and then outside Douglas, not at the Rushen Abbey site.[93] The Misses Stowell were free to develop their school to appeal to the top end of the educational market. *Slater's Directory* for 1857 noted that "Adjoining the ruins is the Rushen Abbey boarding school, a superior establishment for young ladies conducted by the Misses Stowell." Their aim was "the attainment of excellence in all feminine accomplishments and the forming of solid and useful character", but this was to be achieved at quite a cost. It was made clear that if the young ladies had the full range of activities thought desirable by the Misses Stowell — the music, languages, horse-riding, singing, drawing, etc. — the total charge would not be "much less than £60."[94]

Where the Duttons led, others beside the Stowells aspired to follow. Merely to follow into a school of repute, or even a high class former occupant, such as Mrs. Vinell's announcement that her Athol Street school was lately occupied by the Hon. N. Wyndam, was no longer enough.[95] The villa or country house was now the fashion for the ladies. At the same time, to throw over day pupils was a risky business. Mrs. George decided to move from the new prestigious address of Strathallan Crescent to Glenlyon Terrace "for the convenience of day pupils", strangely at the same time the Duttons were announcing that the Villa Marina, which was actually nearer to Douglas, was too far for day pupils.[96] Mrs. George later called her school Castle Mona Lawn, perhaps hoping that some of the Duke of Athol's Douglas home connotations would assist the well-being of her school through subconscious associations. By 1840 her hopes were realised, and complete with French governess, she moved to Elsinor, "a commodious and elegant Marine Villa".[97] Madame St. Laurent, who followed her at Castle Mona Lawn had no such luck, for by the end of the same year she was at Mrs. Barker's on the South Quay, teaching French and English from ten till one o'clock.[98] Mrs. George herself does not seem to have lasted long; she is absent from Slater's list of 1843.

BOYS' SCHOOLS IN DOUGLAS — QUANTITY AND QUALITY

The masters who came fresh to the Island in the Eighteen Thirties were content to remain in or near the town, although some of them too succeeded in building up schools of boarders only. The influx of newcomers may have been of considerable effect in foiling the hopes of May and Garvin, with their out-of-town residences. The growth in numbers of schools providing a higher education is hard to measures with exactitude, but certainly every year saw additions to the names of teachers. Bullock in 1816, commenting on the effect of the Lancasterian School started in 1810, felt "the blessings of education which not many years since were unobtainable even by the higher ranks in society in the Island will now be extended to the lowest."[99] As has been seen, of the four schools mentioned in the newspapers of the Seventeen Nineties, only one was unambiguously offering higher education. The first decade of the Nineteenth Century brought in thirteen new names: the second saw the start of twenty two new schools, with half a dozen from the first decade still in existence. The Eighteen Twenties witnessed twenty six new schools, and the following decade a further nineteen, the total number in existence increasing steadily. The commercial directories with their lists of schools, although very informative, give a false impression by suggesting that the real growth in schools came a decade later than it actually did. Pigot in 1824 listed only six schools apart from Cretney at the Lancastrian School and Robert Brown at the Grammar School, when the real total was far higher, as indeed the preface hinted; "private seminaries for the education of young ladies and gentlemen are numerous: the oldest of these is conducted by Mr. Christopher Imeson".[100] Although there had been real growth in numbers, the leap to twenty nine by 1837 in the list reflected better information rather than a meteoric rise. The glaring omissions such as that of Garvin from the 1824 list are avoided. Yet since a number of schools did not use the press apart from announcing their start, it is difficult to know whether A. G. Henderson's Commercial and Mathematical Academy opened in Fort Street in 1833, James Kelly (1834), Miss Lane (1835), C. Thompson of Queen's College Cambridge (1833), Miss Watterson (1836) and W. J. Lewis (1835), had been overlooked or had all faded out. On the other hand even omitting four out of town private schools at Baldwin and the Strang, Pigot's list of 1837 included seven schools, Francis Armstrong in Market Place, William Bewley of Bigwell Street, Charlotte Coastain of Athol Court, Catherine Cowan of Queen Street, William Cubbon of Post Office Place and an unknown Cubbon in Society Lane, and Margaret Thompson in Athol Street, whose services were never offered through the press. The figure of about twenty private schools being in existence at one given time is probably a fair reflection of the state of events.

Pigot's 1837 total of twenty nine schools for the Douglas area fell slightly to twenty six by 1843, but rose to thirty five by 1846. Quiggin in 1840 provided a list of twenty two private schools, while Joseph Train described the schools of Douglas as "of every variety and grade, amounting to nearly thirty in number".[100] Slater gave a total in the 1852 directory as thirty five, and a surge to forty two by 1857 is partly accounted for by an increase in provision of schooling for infants.

The quantity of higher education offered was adequate, but what of the quality? Bullock in his *History of the Isle of Man* written in 1816 had serious reservations about the education of both sexes.

"In the course of education pursued by the young ladies all that is commonly called accomplishment is attained with such difficulty or expence that the attempt is generally relinquished: for although in Douglas there are two female schools of tolerable celebrity, yet their plans are too superficial for essential good, and their efforts entirely crippled by the want of masters to assist in those branches of knowledge usually conducted by the other sex."[102]

He felt that "The foundation of scholastic learning is yet to be laid", for there was no incentive "to advance nearer the goal", and the Island required one or two schoolmasters of real learning.

"I trust the attempt will be made, but to the success of such an undertaking moderation of terms are essential at the outset, the value of education not being sufficiently appreciated to command profuse returns."[103]

However, these words were penned when newcomers to the Island were usually assumed to be escaping their creditors, taking advantage of Manx laws only amended in 1804,[104] and it was not until about 1820 that the influx of half-pay officers mentioned at the start of this chapter became significant. A. W. Moore stated that they expended around £100,000 on the Island each year. It is noticeable that after 1820, the standard of education offered received nothing but praise. For instance the "Stranger" has been identified with an architect chiefly on the grounds of the praise given to his buildings, but he was equally complimentary about the schools of Douglas. "Young people may be as well educated here as in any part of the Empire at the various seminaries... by masters equally talented with those of the surrounding shores."[105] The sole deficiency in his opinion was the lack of a good dancing master!

Prominent among the new masters who came to the Island in the Eighteen Thirties was Alexander Steele. An early advertisement explained that he had resigned the position of Rector of Moffat Academy, Scotland, where the systems of Wood and Pestalozzi had been employed, in order to open in the Isle of Man. The academy was near the sea, beyond the Villa Marina.[106] With what degree of prompting is unknown, but the following year parents signed a letter of appreciation, which was sent to the local press, stating they "esteem it a benefit conferred upon the public to draw to their attention an Institution so ably and admirably conducted as the Crescent Academy."[107] In a field of intense competition, Steele's very survival up to 1882 was a considerable witness to him. A report book of the era shows how parents were asked to inspect the book daily and sign it weekly. Comments of the masters covered not only academic work, but also attendance, preparation, behaviour and personal appearance.[108] Steele called his academy Classical, Mathematical and Commercial, but it is interesting to see in the annual report for 1840 that chemistry, taught by a Mr. Henderson, included in the list of subjects for prizes. The reporter at the annual public examination was, however, more impressed by other things; "The prowess in the mental arithmetic demonstration excited particular admiration astonishing the audience by sheer rapidity."[109]

The premises of the Crescent Academy in Bay View Road were enlarged, and a spacious school room added, a rarity for the private sector. "The Crescent Academy conducted by Mr. Anthony Steele was erected at that gentleman's own expense, due regard being paid to the requirements of such an institution — its situation is remarkably pleasant and salubrious". The tribute from *Slater's Directory* of 1857 was but one of many. However, other schools set up in the Eighteen Thirties provided Steele with ample competition, and as the years passed the directories of Pigot and later Slater were less loathe to pass judgement on the merits of respective schools. Pigot in 1824 had noted the seniority of Imeson's Classical Commercial and mathematical Academy, while the 1837 Directory had made a general commendation of efficiency of the schools. However, in *Pigot's and Slater's Directory* of 1843 an individual school was singled out, apart from the general favourable comments. "The educational institutions of Douglas are most efficient, particularly the boarding classical and commercial seminary of Walter Forrester in Athol Street."[110] Forrester had actually opened in Douglas before Steele in 1831, starting off in Shaw's Brow.[111] It was he who taught chemistry for the Duttons in Athol Street, but by 1837 his school was flourishing enough to have an assistant, Mr. Pearson, who was allowed to hold his own evening classes in Forrester's schoolroom.[112] A move to Athol Street in the early Eighteen Forties led to new levels of success, and he was able to do without day boys altogether, moving to the Crescent on Douglas Bay, near Steele. The etching of the school premises which accompanied his advertisements certainly looked impressive, and an advertisement of 1852 looked back with pride on the "high reputation of upward of twenty years". In the last eighteen years, there had been an average attendance of forty boys. Local parents had included Archdeacon Philpott, Thomas Howard, the Rector of Ballaugh, and a long list of army officers, but in addition to Island boys, the list for 1825 showed boys from places as diverse as Hatfield (Herts.), Liverpool, St. Andrew's and Dublin. The claim of the school — "Young gentlemen are prepared for entry to the Universities, for Woolwich and other Military Schools or for mercantile pursuits" — had been achieved by numerous entries, of which inspection was invited. The complete course of study embraced "English, Greek, Latin and Antiquities, Mythology, History, Chronology, Geography with use of Globes, Writing and Book-keeping; the various branches of Pure and Applied Mathematics, Natural Philosophy, Chemistry, etc."

Accommodation was good, with seventeen of the twenty three bedrooms having extensive sea views, and every boy had his own bed. The fees ranged from £32 a year for the under twelves to £40 for the over fifteens, with French and Drawing charged as extras.[113] On the mainland fees were felt to be a classification of the private schools, with those charging £50 being in the first rank, and under £20 being in the third.[114] It is not clear whether these criteria should be applied directly to the Island, or whether some consideration should be given to the widely acknowledged cheapness of living on the Island, and thus make a £40 Manx school the equivalent of one charging £50 on the mainland. Certainly on the Island the reputation of Forrester was such as to lead the Clucas family in the far south to send their son, John Thomas, later Treasurer of the Isle of Man, to his school rather than to the new King William's College, the subject of the next chapter.[115]

By 1846 Forrester was bracketed with Steele and a newcomer in being singled out for praise from the mass of boys school. "... the superior seminaries of Walter Forrester AM in Athol Street; Mr. H. De Ruvignes, Mona Terrace; A Steele, The Crescent; Miss Dutton, Marina Terrace..."[116] The De Ruvignes were a husband and wife team with their own separate schools, although Georgina failed to gain a mention, and their dual school system continued until 1857 when Henri De Ruvignes moved to Derby Square to enable him to accommodate more boarders, and Georgina then looked after the five to ten year old boys.[117] De Ruvignes had dropped back slightly in the 1852 *Slater's Directory*, just Forester and Steele hailed as the "superior seminaries", with "Mr. Sutherland Mt. Pleasant and Mr. H. De Ruvignes are also respectable and well conducted boarding schools". Patrick Sutherland, like Forrester and Steele, a Master of Arts, had set up his school in the Oddfellows Hall, calling it the English, Classical and Mathematical Academy for Young Gentlemen, but offering some specialised commercial extras on top of a wide-ranging syllabus.

> "The course of instruction embraces the English, Latin and Greek languages with the Collateral Branches of Analysis and Composition, History and Chronology, Ancient and Modern Geography, Arithmetic including Mental Calculation, Mathematics, Theoretical and Practical Algebra, Elementary Science, Chemistry, ... Penmanship in a variety of styles, Book-keeping by Single and Double Entry etc. Phonographic Shorthand and Phonotypic Reading taught if required."[118]

Kerruish's Guide of 1855 listed some of the factors "which have induced preceptors of distinguished eminence and talent to originate establishments on a very superior scale" — the mildness of the climate, the cheapness of living, the roomy and substantial houses, moderate rentals and excellent facilities for intellectual and physical recreation.[119] This Island publication might be accused of local bias, but the 1857 *Slater's Directory* concurred; "The educational establishments of Douglas are most efficient", with costs estimated to be a third cheaper for Island schoolmasters. Both these publications put Steele first in their rankings. "Amongst those of Douglas, that of Mr. Steele ranks very high and is particularly celebrated for its high class character and its many excellencies" stated the Kerruish publication.[120] Yet the decade witnessed other new ventures which quickly gained high reputations, and four new schools received a mention by name, with Forrester reduced to being almost an also-ran.

> "All the above seminaries together with one conducted by Mr. W. Forrester, M.A., prepare scholars either for the universities, the army, military colleges or for commercial pursuits".[121]

Two of the new-comers were members of the College of Preceptors, founded, in 1848, to promote the teaching profession, at first by the examination of teachers and schools, awarding three grades, Associate, Licentiate and Fellow. The theory of the practice of education was an obligatory subject, and even the Associate grade was counted as higher than the First Class Certified Teacher. A rather cynical book of 1892 by "An Assistant" described those who merely used the letters MCP as "semi-educated". Nevertheless, Henry Kellett impressed the Kerruish Guide, which placed him second only to Steele.

> "Stanley House Academy is conducted by Mr. Henry Kellett MCP whose systematic tuition and attention to the intellectual and physical advancement of his pupils have deservedly gained for him a distinguished reputation of considerable eminence".[112]

Kellett offered the usual range of subjects, from classics to "Merchants' Accounts" with boarding fees of thirty guineas for the over-tens. The eye on the mainland can be seen in the mention that his school was thirteen minutes from the pier as well as five from the shore. George Saunders, who ran his Woodburn Academy from an imposing villa on the edge of Douglas keeping twelve boarders, was also highly praised. It is not possible to be dogmatic about the motives of proprietors. Possibly the interest in the College of Preceptors witnessed a genuine desire to keep abreast of educational matters: possibly the flourishing of letters might impress the citizens of Douglas who might not distinguish between membership only and the grades won by dint of examination.

ASSISTANT MASTERS

Another feature of the Fifties was the growing emphasis upon plurality of masters, due largely to the movement towards competitive examinations just beginning, soon to be the specialism of the private sector. 1847 saw an entry examination for the army introduced, and general examination of pupils began with the College of Preceptors (1854), with the Royal Society of Arts (1856) and the University Local Examinations (1858) following closely. "The effect of the newly introduced examination system was to raise the assistant from being a poorly paid usher to a more pedagogic role assisting preparations for the examinations."[123] When *Slater's Directory* for 1857 mentioned the Douglas Collegiate School established under J. McMullen in 1853, and already by 1855 "fast rising in repute and importance" according to Kerruish's New Illustrated Guide,[124] it referred significantly to the "efficient superintendence" of McMullan and drew attention to his assistance by competent masters, giving the names of the three main assistants and also of those who taught languages, thereby recognising that in this establishment the man in charge was the head of a team in a way quite different from being the master who was aided by ushers. Another school praised by Slater as "a well-regulated establishment", Mona House under William Adams, also stressed in its advertisements the "well qualified masters" who were on the staff. The Misses Kayle of Derby Square found it necessary to assure their readers that they would avail themselves "of the most talented and accomplished masters."

The employment of specialist assistants gave an extra reason to seek more extensive accommodation in addition to the prestige of large premises and the promise of an increase in the number of pupils. The Mona's Herald in 1857 carried McMullen's boast of another house added to his establishment now with five classrooms and a frontage of over a hundred feet.[125] The former main school-room was now a thirty foot dining and evening room for the boarders, and McMullen looked forward to having a hundred pupils. (Shortly after his arrival, he had taken twenty one boys away from Steele and a vicious war in the newspapers resulted about the credit for the successes of pupils concerned).[126] For his part, McMullen decided he was entitled to claim sixteen university honours and military commissions in three years which were not open to challenge.[127] With both Steele and Adams writing of "great additional space" from recent improvements to their premises, De Ruvignes moving from the Hills to Derby Square to take on more boarders, and the Misses Kayle moving from "the too limited Derby Square" to the fine house Woodbourne, the upward spiral in the provision of higher education in Douglas seemed certain to continue. Even John Green aiming at "various branches of education useful to tradesmen" was offering lessons in shorthand.[128]

OUTSIDE THE DOUGLAS AREA

Although Douglas was outstanding in the degree of the activity which took place in the first half of the Nineteenth Century, the educational surge reached other parts of the Island. While the clergy for many years had supplemented stipends by taking in a few boarders, the start of the century saw recourse to the press to advertise for pupils rather than rely solely upon traditional contacts. The Rev. John Christian of Arbory offered board and lodge for four children at twenty guineas a year in 1804,[129] while a little later, as has been seen, in the next parish of Rushen, the former Chaplain of St. Matthew's Douglas, the Rev. John Qualtrough use an annexe as a schoolroom, and offered two places to boarders.[130] The Rev. J. T. Clark, of St. Mark's, saw a market for boarders even if he did not teach them all. In addition to tuition and board at his new Glebe House at £16 per annum, he offered accommodation to three or four who preferred the new college at Castletown, promising to take them in a "closed vehicle".[131] The local clergy sometimes prepared boys for the more advanced schools of Douglas, as did the Rev. William Corrin of Rushen for J. T. Clucas, before he went to Forrester's School and on to the Manx Bar.[132]

As in Douglas, so in the country, running a school was one way in which unbeneficed clergy could support themselves without having to rely entirely on the pay of a curate or supernumerary. William Gill, later a noted Vicar of Malew, kept boarders at the house Rockmont when Curate of St. John's, and when he moved to Ballaugh in 1824 launched the Ballaugh Glen Academy, moving into the house of a

Capt. Kelly to fit in a few more pupils.[133] Interestingly his pupils were from the mainland, and prepared for university in that remote spot.[134]

In the northern parish of Andreas, the school at the rectory was run by a layman. Archdeacon Philpot had decided that the rectory, enormous to modern eyes, was too confined to be his own residence while he kept under his roof the supernumary clergy, known locally as the Minor Prophets, and let the rectory to a D. S. Smith, who rather ambitiously attempted to set up a boarding school in the isloated north charging fees for the over-twelves of forty guineas a year, equal to any in Douglas, in 1832.[135] By the summer, the give away phrase of the "few vacancies" which so often concealed the actual many vacancies, appeared in the press, and by October 1833 it was announced that Smith's furniture and effects were to be sold. His neighbour, the Rev. G. J. Freeman, at Bride, who offered to take in pupils to be educated with his own son at Thurot's Cottage around the same time, showed greater caution, but seems to have fared little better.[136]

One country gentleman, north of Castletown, decided that his house had potential as a school for boarders. The public through the *Advertiser* were informed that Joseph Faulds of Ronaldsway had engaged a well-known and qualified master from England for his proposed school, and would take day-boys until his number of twenty boarders was reached.[137] The tutor, Mr. Docker, stayed long enough to subscribe 12/6 to the Lancastrian School at Douglas in 1812, but was soon succeeded by Mr. Todhunter. What success Faulds achieved with his entrepreurial scheme is unknown; it would be naive to read into an announcement of two or three vacancies an actual roll of seventeen or eighteen pupils.[138] The last mention of the school is made in 1815, when a Mr. Douglas was tutor, but thereafter the school fades from the scene.

THE OTHER TOWNS

It was in the towns that the real potential for growth lay, but the others lacked the population of Douglas, and especially the large privileged stratum of society. Castletown indeed had a tradition of learning, and the Rev. Joseph Stowell, as has been seen, had successfully run his academy even when Castley held sway at the Grammar School. The disastrous period under Brown offered opportunities, but the only recorder advertisment was for the school of A. Miller, a Glaswegian, informing the public of a move from his current house to John Kneale's, where separate rooms for young ladies and gentlemen would be provided.[139] A little later, by 1822, the Classical and Commercial Directory of the Rev. James Bateman was undoubtedly offering higher education as his list of subjects showed,[140] while it is highly likely that the Mr. Stowell who left to go to Douglas in 1826 was the Rev J. L. Stowell, later master of the Douglas Grammar School.[141] As for young ladies before 1830, the only

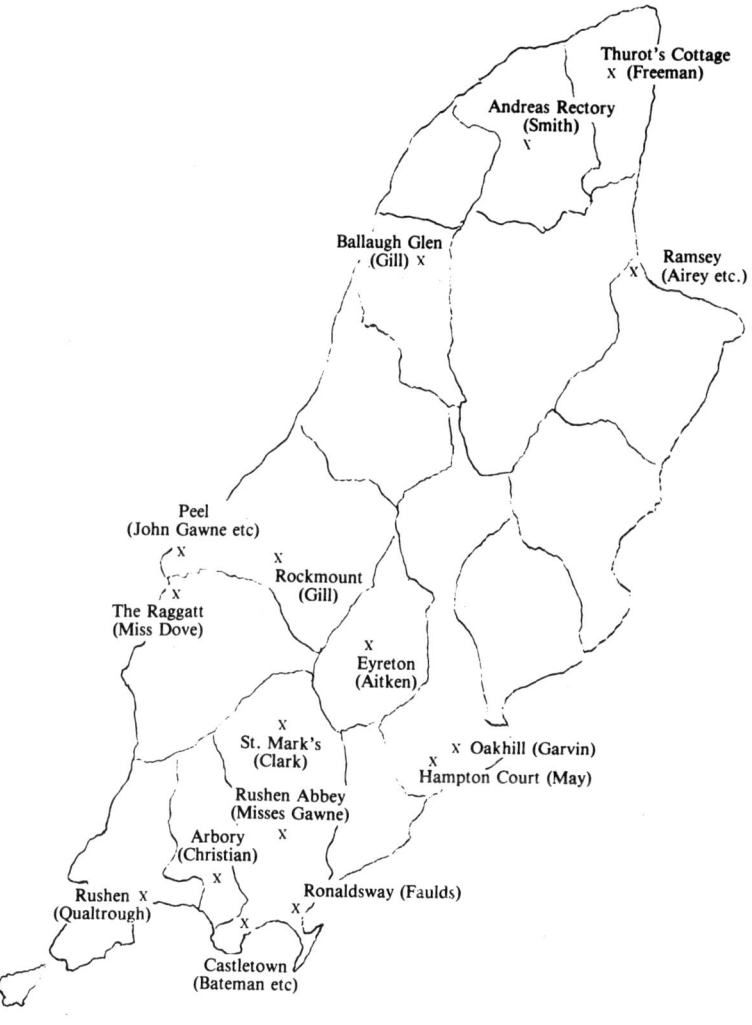

SOME PRIVATE SCHOOLS OFFERING SECONDARY EDUCATION OUTSIDE DOUGLAS 1800-1860

mentions are of Miss Vernon in 1805,[142] Mesdames Cotteen in *Pigot's Directory* of 1824, and Miss Hill in 1825.

By 1837 the number of schools in Pigot had risen from five to sixteen, with the private element going from two to nine, including the school at St. Mark's under the Rev. John James Clark. One of the two boarding schools for girls, that of Mrs. Gray at the Green, had an assistant despite having only six boarders,[143] and a surviving pamphlet reveals French, History and Geography among the subjects taught.[144] The standard of the other private schools is unknown, but certain facts peculiar to Castletown make it unlikely that the schools would not offer something a little higher than an elementary diet. For Castletown was very well provided with schools, and furthermore offered a high proportion of free places. Apart from the Petty School, which had only 16 scholars at the time of the Book of Charities, Taubman's School (for boys) established under his will of 1799 had 45 scholars, 25 taught reading, writing and arithmetic by the terms of the will:[145] Catherine Halsall's School had 40, all girls, with 20 having free places by the will of 1758:[146] and the National Schools had 106 boys and 90 girls in their registers. For people like Mary Ann Ray, who appeared remarkably promptly in *Pigot's Directory* for 1837 although she only announced an intention to move from Rockmount, St. John's to Castletown in the spring of that year,[147] the obvious niche to fill was that of supplying a little French and some "accomplishments" such as music to parents desiring a superior education for their daughters. To offer only the elementary curriculum would not make sense if it could possibly be avoided. Miss Ray, later Mrs. Lloyd, lasted at least from 1837 to 1846, as did Mary Oldridge, her premises making the short move from Arbory Street to Malew Street.

Schools for boys had a harder task, for not only was there an usually good elementary choice — and even here by 1850 Taubman's School was offering navigation to the boys — but also in attempting to offer anything higher they were likely to be caught between the revived Grammar School and the imposing King William's College, the subject of the next chapter. Although listed under Castletown, the Rev. John James of St. Marks was a number of miles away, and did not rely on his teaching as the sole means of income, as the Chaplaincy of St. Marks had a modest stipend. The Gick family lasted for a while in the town, but there was nothing in Castletown to match the vitality of the private sector in Douglas.

Although Peel seemed to offer more opportunities to private adventure schools, because the endowed schools were in such a deplorable state, there is little evidence of any marked support of higher education. Apart from Joseph Stowell's classes for young ladies,[147] the earliest advertisement is that of James Kinnon who announced that he had started teaching in Peel in 1817,[148] but who is absent from the Pigot list of 1824, which names Jas. Cain, John Clark and William Quail. The number was still only three in the 1837 *Pigot's Directory* and the sole user of the press was a Mrs. Hancock who offered boarding for three or four young ladies in addition to her day pupils.[149] By 1843 the only private schools in Peel were those of Margaret Kneale and Thomas Gawne, if *Pigot and Slater's Directory* is accurate, and an increase in the total number of schools in 1846 was accounted for simply by a new National School in the village of Cronkyvoddy. John Gawne ran the only school of note in the Eighteen Fifties, establishing a reputation for excellent tuition in navigation, although Margaret Kneale in Mill Street lasted at least until 1857.[150] Half a mile out of Peel, Miss Hester Dove opened up at the Raggatt, a large country house, and gained the accolade in *Slater's Directory* for 1857 of a mention as "a superior establishment with well laid out gardens and playgrounds". Miss Dove claimed to have taught in the best English families, and offered English, Modern Languages, Music, Singing and Dancing for a basic fee of £35 with the Music £4 extra and French and Italian £2 each. The domestic image was carefully projected still. "The establishment, conducted by Miss Dove, was opened for the purpose of imparting to Young Ladies a sound and accomplished Education as well as securing for them all the advantages of a home."[151] While doubtlessly adding "tone" to the neighbourhood of Peel, Miss Dove was more in line with the country house boarding school establishment typified by the Misses Stowell of Rushen Abbey than anything to do with the town of Peel, and the fishing town showed no signs of any explosion in education.

Rather more progress was made in Ramsey where demand grew with the passing of the years. The commercial directories taken alone would exaggerate the rate of change, for the only schoolteacher mentioned in *Pigot's Directory* of 1824 was Thomas Henderson, described as "shopkeeper and schoolmaster". Yet, as has been noted earlier in this chapter, the Rev. Phillips had opened his Classical Academy in Ramsey before moving to Douglas.[152] A Mrs. Hull had included French among the subjects for her young ladies in 1814,[153] and Mr. Corlett in 1820 announced he was opening on a more extensive plan than before — whether he had failed already or was merely omitted by *Pigot's Directory* is unknown.[154] The schools of Joseph Hetherington (1824) and Miss Baker (1825) followed quickly,[155] and in 1828, Mr. M. Smith went against the usual trend, leaving Douglas to set up in Ramsey.[156] Miss M. Dutton set up the Ramsey branch the preceeding year, and William King established his College Street Academy in 1830. By 1837 nine schools were listed under Ramsey by Pigot, including a boarding school run by Anne Atkinson, and one under Richard Mark. (As with John Gawne in Peel, the successful private teacher was persuaded to take on the endowed school, and Mark sought to instill new life into Ramsey Grammar School).

In boys' education there arose only one school to rival in stature the better establishments of Douglas. The Rev. Robert Airey had, according to *Slater's Directory* of 1857, "an excellent classical and commercial academy".[157] "Belgrave House, the superior seminary of the Rev. Robert Airey, is situated on rising ground near the shore; in it scholars are prepared for the universities, military schools and commercial pursuits". The curriculum consisted of Greek, Latin, Algebra, Geometry, Land Surveying, Arithmetic, Book-keeping, History and Geography, with French charged as usual as an extra on top of the normal fees, in this case £35 for the over tens. Joseph Coates of Dartmouth House, the only other boarding school for boys, received no special mention at all.

Although none was singled out for praise, the real growth area in Ramsey lay with girls' boarding schools, and by 1857 there were half a dozen in the total number of sixteen schools. The older established schools of Mrs. and Miss Dodds in Solway Terrace, and Frances Somerville, who improved her position with a move from Albion Terrace to Lezayre Mount, were joined by those of newcomers such as Sarah Ann Mercer and Sarah Henry.

While, therefore, there was nothing quite as dramatic as the startling developments in Douglas, the town of Ramsey, unlike Peel or Castletown, did present a picture of steady improvement in the provision of higher education by the private sector.

The days of the notoriously unreliable packet from Whitehaven being the only link with the Island were long gone, and the regular scheduled steamship sailings from Liverpool attracted a steady stream of boarders to the Island, with the cheapness of living a notable inducement. Yet the traffic was not in one direction only, nor was the use of mainland schools confined only to the upper classes continuing to send their sons to Eton, as did the Goldie-Taubmans of the Nunnery, Douglas, or the Gawnes of Kentraugh in the south of the Island. Schools near to the Island, or on the sailing routes, in Cumberland and near Liverpool, thought it well worthwhile to insert advertisements in the Manx papers. Occasionally the name of the proprietor betrays a Manx connection, as with Thomas Karran offering places in "a respectable boarding school near Manchester".[158] yet more often the likes of Dickenson of Workington, Galway Gibson and Turton of Liverpool, and Macaulay of Stranraer, do not appear to have Manx personal connections. Sometimes English schools were used to polish a Manx beginning, as with the Forbes brothers, who both ended up geologists of note, Edward as Professor of Geology at Edinburgh in 1854, and David as foreign secretary to the Iron and Steel Institute in 1866, having been elected a Fellow of the Royal Society in 1856. Although both went to Edinburgh University, Edward was at first thought to have artistic gifts and went from Forrester's Athol Academy to an art school in London, while David went from Douglas to Brentwood, Essex, to continue his education. Chapter Twelve will show how McMullen's pupils often left him for English schools for the final years of schooling. The Callister family of Bride sent their son, William (1808-72), a noted M.H.K., across to the Liverpool Institute, and then to a private school at Daresborough, Cheshire.[159] There was thus considerable movement between the

Island and the mainland, in which the private adventure schools played a large part.

CONCLUSION

Although apart from occasional forays into the countryside and some growth at Ramsey, Douglas was very much the centre of the educational explosion in private schooling, the size and scale of it was indeed impressive. The general belief that, because the Grammar Schools had decayed or ceased, higher education was consequently in a very bad state, and redeemed only by the foundation of King William's College (to be considered in the next chapter) is totally untrue. While for the poor there was little scope beyond elementary level, for those who could pay a modest amount, there was a growing number of establishments seeking their patronage. For those who could afford high fees, the variety of provision was very wide, and pupils were attracted from the mainland as well as from the Island itself. The notable concern with female education had no parallel whatever in any 'official' or endowed schools. With fierce market competition, proprietors could not possibly afford to indulge in the widespread complacency that characterised so many endowed schools, for even to stand still was to fall behind while rival newcomers improved curricula, accommodation and staffing. Only those who passed the crucial test of satisfying their patrons that they provided a good education for the fees charged were able to survive. 'No charlatan could get away for very long with an inadequate curriculum'.[160] Yet this period of rapid growth in private schools, a veritable explosion in education, is treated as an educational equivalent, especially where Douglas is concerned, of the Dark Ages, merely because the Grammar School had closed. In general, the eventual demise of such schools ought not to lead to a hasty dismissal of the very important role played by them in the history of education in Britain. In particular, with respect to the Isle of Man, to look through Twentieth Century spectacles and concentrate only on 'official' schools and their like, would lead to a highly distorted view of the early Nineteenth Century, and turn into a time of decay what was in reality a period of tremendous expansion and advance.

REFERENCES

CHAPTER SEVEN

1. Brian Simon, *The Two Nations and the Educational Structure 1780-1870.* Lawrence and Wishart 1974. 29. 30.
2. Nicholas Hans, *New Trends in Education in the Eighteenth Century.* Routledge and Kegan Paul 1951. Chapter Three.
3. J. Strong, *History of Secondary Education in Scotland.* CUP 1909. 160f. Rosemary O'Day, *Scotland Education and Society,* Longmans 1982. 133f.
4. E. W. Corlett, *Education in the Isle of Man.* MEd Thesis, Manchester 1931.
5. John Stowell, *The Sallad.* Quoted in A. W. Moore, *Manx Worthies.* Broadbent and Co., Douglas 1901. 98.
6. Katherine A. Forrest, *Manx Recollections.* James Nesbet, London 1894. 10.
7. *Ibid.*
8. Lord Teignmouth, *Sketches of the Coast and Islands of Scotland and the Isle of Man.* Vol. 11. 278.
9. BH 4937c. BH 3097c.
10. A. W. Moore, *Op. cit.* 67.
11. MS 5369c.
12. A. W. Moore, *Op. cit.* 73.
13. MD 436 Folio. 24/3.
14. Rev. John Gell, *Journal of the Rev. John Gell.* 1789. Manx Society 1880. Vol. 11, *Manx Miscellany.*
15. MMMS 34a, 35a.
16. *Manks Mercury,* Sept. 24 1803.
17. *Manks Advertiser,* Oct. 3 1812.
18. A. W. Moore, *Op. cit.* 122.
19. *Manks Mercury,* July 19 1794.
20. *Ibid,* July 2 1793.
21. Leinster-Mackay, *Private Schools in England 1830-1914.* PhD. Thesis, Durham 1979. 132.
22. *Manks Mercury,* April 30 1793.
23. *Manks Advertiser,* April 9 1803.
24. *Ibid,* Nov. 18 1806.
25. *Ibid,* March 25 1807.
26. *Ibid,* June 24 1809.
27. *Ibid,* Aug. 8 1812.
28. *Ibid,* Jan. 27 1813.
29. *Ibid,* Jan. 8 1828.
30. E. V. Chapman, *Robert Aitken,* Manx Methodist Historical Society 1977.
31. Prospectus, MD 515 6723.
32. *Pigot's Directory,* 1837.

33 *Pigot and Slater's Directory*, 1846.
34 N. Hans, *Op. cit.* 196.
35 *Ibid.* 207.
36 *Manks Advertiser*, Jan. 14 1804.
37 Hugh Stowell, *Narrative of the Life of Miss Sophia Leece*. D. Marples, Liverpool 1828.
38 D. Leinster-Mackay, *Op. cit.* 72.
39 *Manks Advertiser*, Jan. 5 1811.
40 *Rising Sun*, June 28 1821.
41 *Manks Advertiser*, Feb. 1 1823.
42 *Rising Sun*, May 13 1823.
43 *Manks Advertiser*, July 7 1825.
44 *Ibid*, July 1 1823.
45 *Ibid*, Nov. 21 1810.
46 *Ibid*, April 8 1816.
47 *Ibid*, March 18 1824.
48 *Ibid*, March 26 1818.
49 *Ibid*, June 19 1823.
50 *Rising Sun*, Dec. 12 1821. Jan. 19 1822.
51 *Manks Advertiser*, April 3 1823.
52 *Ibid*, March 21 1822.
53 *Rising Sun*, Oct. 21 1826.
54 *Ibid*, April 29 1827.
55 BC 118.
56 *Rising Sun*, July 22 1826.
57 *Manks Advertiser*, Jan. 7 1804.
58 *Ibid*, May 14 1808.
59 D. Leinster-Mackay, *Op. cit.* 50.
60 *Manks Advertiser*, April 16 1818.
61 *Ibid*, Oct. 21 1819.
62 *Ibid*, Jan. 26 1820.
63 *Ibid*, Aug. 17 1820.
64 *Ibid*, April 5 1821.
65 *Ibid*, June 2 1810.
66 *Ibid*, Feb. 1 1812.
67 *Ibid*, Jan. 9 1808.
68 *Ibid*, Sept. 17 1808.
69 *Gazette*, Oct. 1 1812.
70 *Manks Advertiser*, Feb. 20 1813.
71 *Gazette*, July 28 1814.
72 *Ibid*, Jan. 26 1815.
73 *Rising Sun*, July 24 1827.
74 *Ibid*, June 26 1835.

75 A Stranger, *A Six Day Tour Through the Isle of Man.* William Dillon, Douglas, 1836. 84.
76 *Sun,* Sept. 18 1840.
77 *Manks Advertiser,* Jan. 1 1822.
78 *Pigot's Directory,* 1824. 196.
79 *Rising Sun,* July 13 1826.
80 *Manks Advertiser,* Sept. 25 1828.
81 *Rising Sun,* July 13 1830.
82 *Ibid,* Feb 15 1837.
83 *Ibid,* June 19 1832.
84 *Ibid,* March 28 1834.
85 *Manks Advertiser,* Dec. 29 1825.
86 *Rising Sun,* Jan 10 1834.
87 *Laughton's Guide,* 1842. 18.
88 *Kerruish's New Illustrated Guide,* 1855. 121.
89 *Rising Sun,* July 3, 1835.
90 *Sun,* Jan. 4 1839.
91 BH 4146. May 16 1852.
92 *Ibid,* May 26 1852.
93 A. W. Moore, *History of the Isle of Man.* T. Fisher Unwin, London 1900. Vol. 11. 578.
94 *Slater's Directory,* 1857. 270.
95 *Gazette,* July 13 1815.
96 *Manks Advertiser,* March 3 1837.
97 *Sun,* June 5 1840.
98 *Ibid,* Dec. 25 1840.
99 H. A. Bullock, *History of the Isle of Man.* Longman Hunt, 1816. 186.
100 *Pigot's Directory,* 1824. 196.
101 J. Train, *A Historical and Statistical Account of the Isle of Man.* Quiggan Douglas. Vol. 11. 371.
102 H. A. Bullock, *Op. cit.* 186.
103 *Ibid.*
104 George Woods, *An Account of the Past and Present State of the Isle of Man.*
105 A Stranger, *Op. cit.* 105
106 *Sun,* Aug. 26 1836.
107 *Ibid,* July 14 1837.
108 MS. 5161A.
109 *Sun,* June 5 1840.
110 *Slater and Pigot's Dirtectory,* 1843.
111 *Manks Advertiser,* Feb. 22 1831.
112 *Ibid,* Aug. 11 1837.
113 *Slater's Directory,* 1852.
114 D. Leinster-Mackay, *Op. cit.*69.

115 A. W. Moore, *Manx Worthies.* 81.
116 *Slater's Directory,* 1846.
117 *Mona's Herald,* Jan. 21 1857.
118 *Slater's Directory,* 1852.
119 *Kerruish's New Illustrated Guide,* 1855. 120.
120 *Ibid.*
121 *Pigot's Directory,* 1837.
122 *Kerruish's New Illustrated Guide,* Ibid.
123 D. Leinster-Mackay, *Op. cit.* 105.
124 *Kerruish's New Illustrated Guide,* Ibid.
125 *Mona's Herald,* Jan. 21 1857.
126 *Ibid,* Jan. 19 1856.
127 *Ibid,* Jan. 19 1856.
128 *Ibid,* Jan. 21 1857.
129 *Manks Advertiser,* Feb. 15 1804.
130 *Ibid,* Nov.13 1817.
131 For King William's College, see Chapter Four.
132 A. W. Moore, *Op. cit.* 80.
133 *Manks Advertiser,* Sept. 1 1825.
134 T. E. Brown, *Ramsey Church Magazine,* 1896. 170.
135 *Rising Sun,* Dec. 25 1832.
136 *Ibid,* Nov 11 1832.
137 *Manks Advertiser,* march 28 1812.
138 *Ibid,* July 7 1813.
139 *Ibid,* March 18 1815.
140 *Ibid,* June 30 1822.
142 *Ibid,* April 6 1805.
143 *Ibid,* Jan 1 1833.
144 Mrs. Gray's Terms. D 426 (31).
145 BC 125.
146 *Ibid.* 215.
147 *Manks Mercury,* April 30 1793.
148 *Manks Advertiser,* Aug. 18 1817.
149 *Ibid,* Nov. 30 1839.
150 *Slater's Directory,* 1857. 28.
151 *Ibid,* Advertisement. 268.
152 *Gazette,* July 29 1808.
153 *Ibid,* Nov. 12 1814.
154 *Manks Advertiser,* Oct. 12 1820.
155 *Ibid,* Jan. 8 1824. *Rising Sun,* June 11 1825.
156 *Ibid,* April 29 1828.
157 *Slater's Directory,* 1857. 29.
158 *Sun,* Jan. 4 1839.
159 A. W. Moore, *Op. cit.* 76.
160 D. Leinster-Mackay, *Op. cit.* 92.

CHAPTER EIGHT

KING WILLIAM'S COLLEGE — FULFILMENT OR BETRAYAL?

The advent of a new bishop in 1827 to the Island led to another attempt to realise the dreams of Bishop Barrow. William Ward had been born in Ireland in 1726, taken his degree at Caius College, and served in the dioceses of London and Salisbury before being appointed Bishop of Sodor and Man through the influence of the Prime Minister, Viscount Goderich, to whom he had been tutor in 1790 when his lordship, soon in 1833 to be the Earl of Ripon, had been the Rt. Hon. F. J. Robinson.[1] Ward was genuinely interested in education, a real enthusiast for the National Society and the British and Foreign Bible Society, and already in contact with Bishop Philander Chase of Ohio, who came to England to raise money for his theological college, Kenyon College.[2] In the Diocese of Salisbury, his bishop was Thomas Burgess, formerly of St. David's, who had opened his own theological college at Lampeter in Cardiganshire in 1827, and Ward, allowed through the poverty of Sodor and Man to retain his Salisbury living, drew inspiration from Burgess' achievement. Indeed, at his first meeting with his fellow trustees of the Academic Fund, in addition to one student being allowed £100 as a sizar at Cambridge, another was awarded £50 a year to attend St. David's College, Lampter.[3]

> "The Bishop does not despair of executing another project — the foundation of a College for the Manks clergy. The success of a similar plan of the Bishop of St. David's affords him such encouragement and hopes that Mona may become once more, as in ancient times, the fountain of honest learning and erudition."[4]

The time was indeed ripe. Academic Professor Thimbleby's health was failing fast. In 1826 he resigned the position of agent to collect the rents. (The Duke of Atholl in his defence against the Keys claimed his appointment of Thimbleby to this post had saved £20 a year, and constituted his sole act of interference with the Trusts).[5] The following year Thimbleby was incapable of teaching, and Benjamin Philpott, a clergyman invited to take St. George's, Douglas, by Bishop Murray to improve the social tone of the Manx clergy, was awarded fifty pounds from the Master's salary for instructing the Academic Students.[6] According to his family, Philpott generously did not touch this money but let it accumulate for the bishop's new college fund.[7] The death of Thimbleby in 1828 enabled the Academic Fund Trustees to make the large grants to students for Cambridge and Lampter, and fine gifts of fifty pounds each were made to two clergy, John Clark and Robert Brown, for past services. Owing to increased rents, Hango Hill and Ballagilley now yielded £489 a year, while interest of £26 on loans equalled the outgoings, chiefly the new agent's salary of £20. For teaching the four students previously selected from the Grammar School, small payments were made to the Rev. W. Gill, the Bishop's secretary, Mr. Chatsfield, and the Rev. George Parsons of the Grammar School. Philpott's promotion to the Archdeacon's parish of

Andreas in the north put him out of reach, although the supernumeraries already ordained lived with him there, and became known to the neighbourhood as the "Minor Prophets". There was still left a handsome yearly sum for the future. How should it be employed?

THE TWO PROTAGONISTS : SMELT AND WARD

Two contrasting views emerged. Lt.-Governor Cornelius Smelt and the Keys, thwarted by clerical voting power from doing anything to amend what they considered the scandalously small portion of the Impropriate Fund allocated to the Castletown Grammar School, instead sought to take full advantage of their numerical ascendancy on the board of the Bishop Barrow Trustees. A resolution of 1826 had determined that, in addition to the Governor, the other three "Chief Temporal Officers" laid down by the Barrow Deed should consist of the Receiver-General, the Clerk of the Rolls, and the Water Bailiff. Yet a fresh resolution stated in October 1828 that "before any future appropriation of the Trust Fund takes place, that the whole of the principal temporal officers viz the Govr. or Lt.-Gov., the Atty.-General, the Deemsters, Revr. General, Clerk of the Rolls and Water Bailiff be summoned to attend that meeting."[8] In other words, the Bishop and Archdeacon would be hopelessly out-numbered. Smelt made his own desires quite clear. "Since the death of Mr. Castley ... learning has rapidly declined and the greatest anxiety is now felt throughout the Island to restore the Free Grammar School to its former usefulness and celebrity."[10] Smelt wanted a good grammar school and nothing more. There was no room in his mind for any Academic School, whose very existence he firmly denied; "The Academical School mentioned in Bishop Barrow's will has never been established." The condition of the will had not been fulfilled, and while he favoured a "liberal and sound education to young men intended for Holy Orders", their advanced education should be off the Island at university. In this sense he could concur that the money should be applied "as *originally* designed for the express purpose of improving the education of the clergy." Ward considered this was the essential point and believed it was gained at the meeting of February 1829.[11] Yet the statement meant vastly different things to the Governor and Bishop. For Smelt, it meant obeying the deed of 1668, with the will apparently making very little difference because the Academical School had not come into being.

Ward on the other hand had a much more ambitious scheme in mind. When Robert Curphey states, "the officials and the Keys wanted a school: the Bishop wanted a theological college",[12] this underestimates the breadth of the Bishop's plans. The contrast was less that of two parties each wanting his own type of school, the Governor a grammar school, and the Bishop an Academical School for the clergy, than of the Lt.-Governor's narrow view and the Bishop's comprehensive plan embracing a wide range under one roof. Indeed even the elementary tier was not forgotten. Lord Teignmouth referred to "the comprehensive plan originally proposed, of reviving the parochial schools which are for the most part, lamentably neglected."[13] Ward sought to reassure Smelt that the plan he had in mind would show "Bishop Ward has the public good of the Island at heart, as well as the particular good of the clergy." Like Barrow before him, he appreciated that education for the clergy must begin at humbler levels, which would also provide for the general good.

Confronted with the narrowness of Smelt's aims, Ward sought refuge in legal problems. The wording in Barrow's deed, that he appointed as trustees "The Right Rev. the Lord Bishop the Archdeacon, or in their absence, the Vicars Genll. and the Official, and four more of the Chief Temporal Officers of this Isle" was hard to reconcile with the resolution of October 1828 inviting all the temporal officers to be party to decisions. Col. Steuart of the Villa Marina in Douglas wrote to Ward in February 1829 expressing his belief that the Resolution was illegal. In neither the Deed or Will was any number greater than four Trustees countenanced, but the Resolution had increased the number to seven. The Bishop, although intended as the head of the fund as the first named, would be swamped by the whole of the Council of the Island. The Colonel suggested that the Home Secretary should rule on the matter.[14] Ward took the advice, and wrote to Robert Peel, complaining that an ecclesiastical fund was in danger. If the Council could suddenly become the Trustees — "which is the thing now aimed at" — the Bishop would be reduced to a "subordinate and ordinary member of the Council" and the intended benefit to the church would be lost. He craved Peel's attention to stop this "attempt to get ye power out of my hands". Col. Steuart continued to stress the role of the Crown, urging in October 1830 that Peel should appoint the Lay Trustees, and the following year in April that the Crown, exercising the rights of the Lord of Man and representing the founder who had no surviving heirs, should use its authority in the matter.

Ward was loathe to recognise the letter of the Deed, for that would only serve to confirm the lay majority among the Trustees, preferring to believe that Barrow's will had altered the composition of the Trustees, substituting for the four temporal officers, the Governor or his deputy and the two senior clergy on the Island, thereby giving a clerical majority on the Trustees. Even more important was the fact that the legal basis for traditional maintenance of clergy from the Academic Fund rested on the part of the Will which stated that monies returned by those who failed to serve in the Church on the Island and should be "Employed for the benefit of the Church". When the revenues exceeded the needs of a handful of students, this clause was invoked to justify the wider application of funds for such purposes as the payment of the supplementary ministers. Smelt on the other hand, claimed that as the Academical School had never been founded, the Deed should still be followed, by which after the supply of clergy was sufficient, the monies returned would be applied "to what other publicke work or charity shall be by my trustees be thought most profitable for the Island". In his eyes the use of funds for the replacement of the Grammar School fulfilled admirably the definition of a "publicke work or charity". As the Keys had pointed out to Robert Peel in 1828, the Bishop Barrow Trust lands produced an income "much more than sufficient for the Maintenance of three Scholars at the Academical School", while since the same master had run the Grammar School and acted as Academic Master for most of the time since Barrow, there seemed little point to the Lay Trustees in preserving a fine legal distinction between the Academic and Impropriate Funds. The point made by Col. Steuart that the Academic Fund was solely for educating and supplying ministers was either ignored or considered unreasonable. A typical lay view was expressed in a Memorial of November 1829 presented to Smelt.[15] Castletown Grammar School, it declared, was for the youth of the Isle to be brought up in the learned professions, not just for those intending Holy Orders, and regretted the school was suffered to languish "for want of the ample funds being appropriate". The petition favoured the enlargement of the Grammar School, or a move to Hango Hill if this were needed, and did not approve of a rumoured move to Sulby Glen in the north of the Island. Although the memorialists were willing to contribute, they understood that there was a thousand pounds already in hand. Smelt was thus following public opinion in believing that the long connection of Grammar and Academic Schools justified his regarding both funds as a common pool, a view to which reliance upon the Deed gave a plausible legal foundation.

Smelt ignored the part of the deed which expressly reserved "a liberty, during my life, of disposing of the sd yearly rent of twenty pounds, to any other use in the Island". In the will the benefit of the church had clearly replaced the public work or charity. The failure of the Academic School, if indeed it had failed, made no difference whatsoever. The wording about returning immediately to the Island on the call of the Bishop to "take Holy Orders, and supply the vacant living", far better fitted youths at one of the universities, kept there if the Academical School was not established. Whereas by the deed, the trustees, normally accepted as the Bishop, Archdeacon, and four temporal officers, had discretion to apply the monies returned, in the will this was a matter for the Bishop, Archdeacon, Governor, and two senior clergymen of the diocese. In other words, if the will were followed, the clerical voices outnumbered the lay by four to one. However, Ward did not pursue a legal ruling on this precise matter. Success would have enabled him to prevent all the Academic Funds being devoured by the proposed College, and dictate how much was to be reserved for the general use of the clergy.

Perhaps the Bishop was a little bemused by the legal advice that he did receive. The fullest opinion came from a certain Mr. Bluett who examined the issues meticulously. Only in the Will was there a clear conveyance of the whole of the estates of Ballagilley and Hango Hill as oposed to a mere twenty pounds in the Deed. Bishop Barrow did have

5 King William's College, the original design

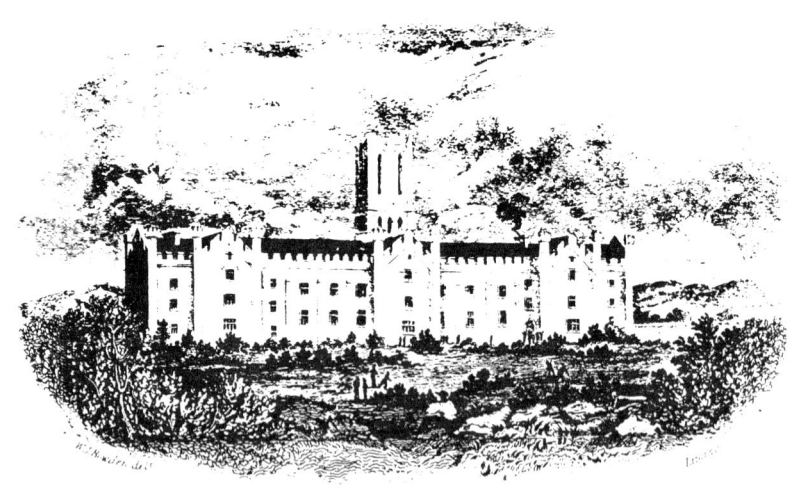

6 King William's College, two early views

St. Stephen's Sulby 1838

St. James' Dalby 1839

7   Two of Ward's 'Mountain Schools'

Thomas St. Weslyan

8   The Day-school keeping Churches of Douglas 1840

St. Mathew's

St. Georges

 St. Barnabas

the right to alter his Deed, and his opinion should be conclusive against all others. The argument that the Will had never been acted upon fell flat; in practice it had been "abundantly recognised and acted upon". In particular the sending in 1686 "of Academic Students to Gilbert Holt in Castletown was conclusive proof", being "palpably opposite to the letter of the deed", while the mixture of education at home and abroad approved in 1771 was "utterly at variance with the direction of the Deed".[16] This was indeed comforting to Ward, but Mr. Bluett also pointed out that the same meeting had made grants to Peel Mathematical School and that the Trustees had referred to "the powers vested in us by the deed of Trust or Feoffments", thereby lending support to those who wished to rely on the "other public work or charity" clause of the Deed. Instead of the definite legal answer that Ward was hoping to receive, Mr. Bluett left a list of no less than twenty five legal points which needed to be decided. A second opinion which claimed that "the Will was always considered as abrogating the Deed, save in one or two instances," (a qualification which rather blunted the writer's confident "invariably employed with strict accordance with his Will")[17] was balanced by Attorney General Clarke coming down firmly on the side of the Deed. Instead there were appeals to London for a government ruling that fell on deaf ears. Home Secretary, Peel, enquired of Bishop, Governor and Attorney-General what the fuss was about.[18] He protested to Smelt that references to "government views" meant nothing to him, and the King in Council was the body to deal with this.[19] When Melbourne took over as Home Secretary, he merely passed on the Bishop's letters to the Manx Attorney-General and vice-versa. Treated as a court of appeal, he settled for the less demanding role of the post-box.[20]

THE BISHOP OUT-MANOEUVRED

For two reasons, Ward was reluctant to countenance prompt action in the erection of the proposed College. If implemented fully, his own scheme would be expensive and require a long period of time to accumulate sufficient funds, and he feared, quite rightly, that a hasty start would lead to a more limited result. Equally he feared that premature commitment would absorb the total resources of the Academic Fund, leaving no surplus to maintain the supernumerary clergy as in the past. Smelt's party realised, on the other hand, that vigorous action might see the grammar school established, and the Academic School part of Ward's plan left as only a possibility for the future. In December 1829 Philpot, then Vicar-General, and John McHutchin, the influential Clerk of the Rolls, were asked to report to the Trustees on the "most eligible site in their opinion for building a Seminary or College on the lands of Hango Hill and also that they cause an estimate to be made of the expense which may attend such Building with a plan of the same."[21] In just over a month, a report drawn up by the two men was accepted, and they were empowered to procure estimates and plans, and "immediately to commence and prepare the lands adjoining the site for planting."[22.]

A prospectus was called for at the same meeting, and issued in April 1830. It announced that the Trustees had resolved a College should be immediately established for general education "in which — while the various branches of Literature and Science are to be made the subject of instruction, the minds of youth will be imbued with a knowledge of religious truths and moral duties." As George IV had given a thousand pounds to St. David's College, Lampeter, there was hope the royal generosity would continue; "that his royal and paternal solicitude for the same objects will be extended to this Island ... admits of at least reasonable expectation." The Principal and masters would be members of the Church of England, the masters for classics and mathematics being from Oxford or Cambridge, and the public examinations would include evidence of natural and revealed religion, and of the doctrines and duties of Christianity.[23]

However, despite the stress on Christian teaching, it was clear that the grammar school was to be a reality, but the Academic School end merely a possibility for the future. Professors of Divinity, Law, Physics and Surgery would "if means exist, be appointed" for those who might be "unable elsewhere to complete their studies" as the institution progressed. This apparently reasonable statement marked the death of Ward's dream of the comprehensive college, for the Trustees went on to announce a fund for education at university "of youths of the most pregnant parts for the supply of the Manx Church, according to the directions of Bishop Barrow's gift." With this provision made for them, it was impossible for Manx ordinands to claim they could not complete their studies elsewhere. The hopes of the *Sun* newspaper that the higher instruction for the learned professions would encourage strangers "to select this tranquil isle for their residence" would clearly not be realised.[24]

There was some debate about the right level of fees. The *Sun* wished fees to range between one and four pounds annually, arguing that, the greater number admitted, the greater the benefits conferred, and that all classes were indeed to provide three or four hundred boys; the rich alone could not fill the places. There was also a warning to look at Peel, where the same subjects were offered, "yet the school buildings are dilapidated and without scholars."[25] The Trustees proposed three to seven pounds a year as reasonable fees, and the *Sun* eventually concurred.

Where the *Sun* was proved more accurate was in the question of costs. McHutchin and Philpot in their Circular thought £3,000 would be needed, and a contract for this amount was signed with John Fitzsimmons in July 1830.[26] Even allowing for the fact that the Church would pay for the College Chapel, which was also to serve the people of Derbyhaven, the *Sun* thought £4,000 would be needed. (The Church money would come from the funds collected in England by the Rev. Hugh Stowell for building Manx churches, a sum of nearly £10,000.)

The *Sun* hoped that the wealthy of the Island, the general populace, and the Crown — following the Lampeter precedent — would each contribute a thousand pounds, to be added to the savings of the Academic Fund.[27]

An anonymous writer made some percipient "Remarks on the Report of the Intended new college at Castletown", warning that even £4,000 would not prove sufficient, and that if the work were tackled properly with masters' houses and room for fifty boarders each, then only a small part of the funds would be left. The scale of the buildings was too big for the Island, more suited in fact to Manchester or Liverpool. He recommended that such features as a public dining hall should be dispensed with to reduce costs, but that there should be generous salaries offered, much higher than those being proposed, even if they absorbed nearly all the annual income, for otherwise there would be no incentive for masters to come to the Island. The sum of £200 was suggested as suitable for the Headmaster.

He believed the College should concentrate on quality of pupils rather than quantity. If there were to be nearly four hundred boys, four masters could not suffice and three of four assistants would be needed. How were they to be paid? A certain "tone" was desirable, and this entailed doubling the proposed fees if the institution were to be for gentlemen, and not a mere common free school. If the paltry sum of three pounds were charged, "the lowest Mechanic may send his son to the College". What gentlemen would send their son to mix with "sons of the most common tavern keepers in Castletown", and pick up their bad language?

The College should be governed by a Committee of twelve, with nine as a quorum, with the headmaster an ex-officio member carrying a double vote when internal matters were discussed.[28]

The Lay Trustees were prepared to settle such problems as and when they arose, and were determined to translate their plans for a new grammar school into action as speedily as possible.

In April 1830 Ward was astonished to find himself informed of a date for laying the foundation stone of the College, and also that he was expected to lay the Chapel foundation stone on the same day. Smelt's letter told him the public and Robert Peel were already aware that April 23rd was the fixed date, which "cannot now be altered".[29] He had not expected any building until costs were covered, but praised the generosity of Castletown as evidenced by the list of subscriptions sent by Smelt, and promised to do everything in his power to help. Yet he reserved the "sacred trust money" for completion of the project: it would not be touched until he saw a fair prospect of success.[30]

The *Manx Advertiser*, reporting the opening ceremony, estimated a crowd of five thousand witnessed Smelt and Ward performing their respective duties. The mist dutifully cleared as the College stone was laid: "the sun burst forth in all its splendour, casting its brilliant rays on all around."³¹ The *Sun* for its part, thought the spirit of Bishop Barrow appeared to preside.

Outwardly all proceeded smoothly, despite criticism in the press about the folly of employing an English architect, who would increase costs, and about the absence of Navigation from the list of subjects to be studied.³² A further telling point was that only Castletown and Douglas could use the College for day-boys, so that elsewhere on the Island it would be only the wealthy, who could afford board and lodge, who would benefit.³³ Nevertheless the building began to rise quickly, and by the end of the year the assent of the new sovereign, William IV, to the use of his name was secured.³⁴ Even the disputes about the trustees was smoothed over to all intents and appearance when Ward said the matter would make no difference in his day, although it was well the Lord Chancellor should put the matter on safe legal ground.³⁵ When the Treasurer stated that some subscriptions had been withheld because of the wrangle, the trustees in November 1830 agreed to revert to the Bishop, Archdeacon and only four chief temporal officers, to put an end to future misgivings.³⁶ Peel, however, was astounded to have a letter from Ward stating the Bishop would "part with his right hand rather than agree to what he had signed", and frostily informed Ward that only his official consent would be heeded.³⁷

Ward was by now seriously worried whether the scheme he had produced with such high hopes would, even in its present truncated form, devour the whole of the Barrow Fund, leaving nothing for the Church. He expressed his concern over arrears from rents which amounted to nearly £800, and urged a proper land agent be appointed.³⁸ In May 1831 he suggested a formal division of the trust estate between the College and the Church in equal shares, but the Trustees refused to countenance the idea. They passed a resolution to the effect that, as they could not ascertain what funds might be needed to support the College, they could not say what sums might be set aside for the supernumerary clergy.³⁹ A further attempt by the Bishop directly to the Trustees as a body met with no more success.

> "Resolved that his Lordship's proposition would have the certain effect of preventing the completion of the College and thereby disappointing the wishes of the contributors... who have given their support to the intended establishment upon the faith that the funds would in first instance be made available to its support."⁴⁰

The election of supernumerary clergy did continue, although the vacancies arose only through acceptance of curacies in England, there still being a surfeit of Manx clergy; the Trustees were merely unwilling to set aside a specific portion of their funds.

Despite his fears about future support for his clergy, the dispute about the composition of the Trustees, and the remoteness of having his full plans realised, which caused occasional acts of pique such as refusing to attend the August 1832 meeting of the Trustees, the Bishop did not cease to work with pride and enthusiasm for the

College itself. In his letters he referred often to "My College", and noted its rise with satisfaction. By January 1831 the College was up to its first floor level, and he wrote to Bishop Chase, now of Illinois, in May that "You will see my college towering high the next time you approach our shores."[41] He was especially proud of his dual-purpose chapel and schoolroom, sliding doors being used to shut off the sanctuary, "a plan of my own devising which wd suit admirably to be planted up and down in your new diocese."[42] His general attitude was "I trust the Lord will spare me until I see it completed."[43]

For escalating costs began to worry Ward, who feared that "without foreign aid the rising generation must continue to be educated and reared in the Methodist meeting houses."[44] £4,000 had been raised but still another £1,000 was needed, despite the efforts of the Manx people who "aid me most zealously". The Trustees at their meeting of June 1832 agreed that Ward should try to use his inheritance with Lord Brougham, the Lord Chancellor, to procure a living in England for the Rev. Temple Chevallier "as an inducement to that Gentleman to accept of the situation of principal of King William's College and as the only means which the Trustees can at present hold out of obtaining an able talented and learned man for so desirable an object."[45] Obviously Temple Chevallier was not induced to accept the post, for within two months William Blamise, M.P., was sent all the information on the College, not only showing how means to remunerate a principal were so "very inadequate for the first few years of the establishment", but also asking that Brougham grant some preferment to a clergyman "of Talents and high professional character" nominated by his Lordship.[46]

Appeals to the National Society, founded in 1811 for the education of the poor, and really concerned with elementary education, proved fruitless. The use of the royal name instead of 'King's College' as originally intended, brought no response from William IV. It was this hope that possibly caused the name of Bishop Barrow to be overlooked. The Stranger in his *Six Day Tour of the Isle of Man* commented shrewdly that the Trustees were "fishing in shallow streams."[47]

Not long after his arrival on the Island, Ward had an interview with Peel, in which he expressed the hope that the tithes in Crown hands might be given to the use of the clergy, especially for their education. Peel had asked for this to be left, but now Ward pursued the matter afresh, hoping for a "college endowment within ourselves, independent of the world."[48] This regular sum of the order of £800 a year would in fact be far more advantageous than the thousand pounds that George IV had given Lampeter. The tithes proved to be tantalizingly elusive. At one time it seemed that Brougham was so close to securing them for the College that Edward Wilson, a native of Wakefield, and Sizar and afterwards Fellow of St. John's College, Cambridge, before moving to Bath, accepted the post of Principal fully believing the tithes would be given. Ward wrote that "the certainty of this endowment would be a great inducement to that excellent man, Mr. Wilson to accept the principalship."[49]

The Trustees formally apointed Wilson on April 1st 1833 at a salary of £200 a year and a third of quarterage, with £20 extra as Dean of Chapel, with pew rents. After £300 was set aside for paying the Principal and Vice-Principal, the rest of the estates' rents would be "appropriated for the payment of the supernumerary clergymen and other Ecclesiastical purposes", while future improvements in rents would be divided equally between the College and the Church.[50] With the full expectation of receiving the tithes, the Trustees virtually conceded Ward's earlier requests which they had rejected before. Smelt's successor, Lt.-Governor Ready, received a letter from Melbourne telling him the king himself wished to be informed about the aims of King William's College, as the Bishop was requesting the Crown tithes.[51]

It appears that William IV agreed in principle with Ward's request and had even gone as far as to order Sir Herbert Taylor to lay Ward's Memorial before his ministers. However, when Grey and Melbourne went into the matter, it became clear that the Crown Tithes were not in fact in the absolute gift of the Crown. Instead they were caught up in the Consolidated Fund, and to grant them to King William's College would involve not the simple acquiescence of the sovereign, but a full Act of Parliament. Who would be willing to give time to act as a patron of the Island and College, helping to circulate back among the people the money raised through tithes on the Manx soil? Unfortunately the same month which saw the appointment of Wilson, (and of Robert Dixon of St. Catherine Hall, Cambridge, as Vice-Principal at £80 a year, with a quarter of the remaining two-thirds quarterage) saw also the removal of Goderich, now Earl of Ripon, away from being Secretary for War and the Colonies, with duties linked with the Island, to the post of Lord Privy Seal. This was a great blow, for his successor Spring Rice proved a very slippery customer. Ward had stressed his need of "an active and influential friend, who will take a warm interest in the prosperity of King William College . . . or I cannot hope to succeed."[52] Althorp, the Chancellor, was well disposed, but too busy to bother unless a bill were drafted for him. Thus Ward hoped that Spring Rice would be happy in "establishing and giving permanency to this Seminary of Learning which must infallibly flourish once possessed of this endowment." After waiting in rain for two hours five days later, Ward commented bitterly that "It is almost as difficult to catch these Ministers as to catch wild duck that duck under the water the moment you approach them."[53]

In the midst of the hunt for the tithes, the College was completed, at least to the point where pupils could be admitted. An advertisement in the *Sun* in June 1833 offered "economical education of the Youth of the Island." The fees were a pound a quarter for boys aged seven to ten, rising to two pounds for those aged thirteen to eighteen. Boarders paid £25 to £30 extra, with higher terms for the Principal's private pupils.⁵⁴ Compared with the laying of the foundation stone, the opening was very subdued. Ward was present, but there was no ceremony. The *Sun* had heard of three hundred applications, but reported only "a considerable number of youth" as entering the College as the first intake.⁵⁵

As the securing of the tithes eluded Ward, the Island's own efforts at fund-raising continued. The parochial clergy did their best both personally and in organising parish collections, which varied in success from German's solitary £1 to the £42/7/0 collected by St. Matthew's and St. George's in Douglas.⁵⁶ Hugh Stowell, so successful on the mainland in raising money for new churches, proved far less successful in his own parish: a new bell had exhausted the charitable instincts of Ballaugh — "Most of them made this an apology for refusing to contribute towards the College."⁵⁷ Although very impressed with Principal Wilson — "he will be a real acquisition to the Institution" — Stowell was forced to rely on 'Bountiful Providence' to supply sufficient funds for the College. According to the *Manks College Account Book* the total raised by donations amounted to £2,692/1/5. When the Academic Fund savings of £2,071 were added, Ward was entitled to claim he had raised £5,000 for the new college.⁵⁸ Stowell wrote at the Trustees' request a general appeal to the Manx public in July 1833, and he was also asked to go to Liverpool and Manchester to raise more funds by preaching in aid of the College, and the Trustees hoped his namesake, the Dissenting minister of Manchester, would do the same. As it was, Vice-Principal Dixon paid for items such as the Steam Kitchen and the painting of the College buildings from his own pocket, the Trustees promising to repay in instalments from the pupils' quarterage.⁵⁹

Lord Teignmouth, in a footnote to his 1829 comments on the proposed College, written about this time, informed his readers how the estimated cost of £3,000 had actually doubled.

> "The trustees have consequently been much in debt and difficulty, from which they hoped to be rescued by the aid of government, the expectation of such aid being held out of them. They recommended the appropriation of a portion of the crown tithes of the Island which are worth 700l or 800l per annum, to the purpose and this suggestion has been favourably received. But as yet nothing has been done.⁶⁰

Hopes of securing the tithes were now fading fast, and Ward, perhaps suspicious of his fellow trustees, very foolishly abandoned the compromise concerning allocation of funds, to which he had signed his name in April 1833. He wrote of his desire to have "a clear definite and unalterable settlement of Bishop Barrow's Estate for the exclusive benefit of the Church as was originally intended by the donor and invariably applied from his day to commencement of his Lordship's Episcopate."⁶¹

In his 'Observations' on the Resolutions of April 1st, he protested that he thought it extraordinary that no provision at all was made for the Academic Scholars, and even more extraordinary that £300 could be promised in salaries without even mentioning their existence. He wanted the money set aside for the Vice-Principal to be used for their maintenance, and two or three rooms in the College put aside for their lodgings. Raising a mortgage to satisfy the 'clamorous creditors' was now becoming more and more a necessity for the trustees. Ward wished that any other means might be found if possible, but if it came to the worst, enough should be borrowed to pay all debts. This course of action, however, very significantly altered the compromise agreed in April 1833, that College and Church should receive half the improved rents. Ward pointed out that if a mortgage had to be repaid from the rents, then the Church would receive less from the *whole* of the remainder than from the half as things stood in April 1833. For this reason he would consent very unwillingly to give still to the College half the improved rents as originally agreed, and demanded that the Church be paid interest on all rents spent on the College buildings and premises.[62] The Trustees resolved on March 11 1834 that the Church should indeed enjoy all the rents, *if* the Bishop successfully obtained the Crown tithes for the College. Ward wanted to know what the situation would be if he successfully obtained just a portion of the tithes.

Ward found himself engaged in a struggle not only to prevent the College from absorbing all the Trust funds, but even to preserve a vestige of official recognition that the College was the successor of the Academic School. He believed that the contemplated mortgage offered an opportunity for him to dig in his heels, and brought out his "Resolutions to be passed by the Trustees before the Bishop consents to the proposed act of Tynwald."[63] The first of his points was that the handsome salary promised to the Principal must be recognised as given to him in his capacity as Academic Master for the Education of Divinity Scholars on Bishop Barrow's Foundation". The three scholars should be "prepared by him for the service of the ministry in the same manner as former Academic Masters had educated and prepared Bishop Barrow's Scholars for Holy Orders". But as for the scholars themselves, Ward recognised that he had already been overtaken by events, and that "Heavy expense actually prevents the due and accustomed administration of the funds to the primary object of the Founder". He could only repeat his hope that the Vice-Principal would indeed help to educate and maintain the Scholars for the present, and that when the current Vice-Principal left his post, the funds would be directly applied for the Scholars. In the meantime he accepted the offer of the Principal and Vice-Principal to perform in practice what they were not bound to do yet in theory, namely to educate and board three Academic Scholars, whom he insisted must always be from King William's College. With regard to the Trust finances he was agreeable to applying the Crown Tithes, if obtained, to paying off the mortgages as a first step, but afterwards they should bring in an income at 5%. As for the rents, any improvement should similarly pay off the mortgage debt, but thereafter be for the use of the Church.

The Trustees, for their part, declared cautiously, "it does not appear competent for the trustees to enter into any such arrangement as that proposed by his Lordship, so as not to become binding on their successors." They professed a wish that the clergy would apply for the tithes on their own behalf, and they, the trustees, would rejoice if the clergy were successful. If on the other hand the Bishop did obtain the tithes for the College, the Trustees would meet the urgent necessities of the Church. They challenged Ward to state how rents had been applied contrary to Barrow's intention: any abuse found would be immediately corrected.[64] Although Ward did not attend this meeting, Archdeacon Philpot was there, and signed with the other Trustees: he seems to have given Ward considerably less than total support.

November 1835 brought some encouragement from Judge Lancelot Shadwell, who wrote to the Bishop that the surplus after educating three boys should be applied first to educating further ordinands and then for the benefit of the Church. He stressed that this was a private opinion, and that the case could be heard by him formally, only if there were an appeal from the Isle of Man Chancery to the Privy Council. Yet a month later in the Manx courts it was held that with reg ard to trustees the Deed ruled over the Will.[65] There was no use appealing to the King directly, and any further proceedings must go through the channels of the Manx Chancery and finally the Committee of the Privy Council. Ward wrote wearily to Archdeacon Philpot about quibbles contrary to custom and common understanding that the Vicar-Generals were not Trustees of Bishop Barrow's Charity, and feared that if the threatened disappearances of the Dioceses occurred and it became part of Carlisle, that would leave the Archdeacon alone as a clerical Trustee. They must make a stand for the Church; "a contest may end in blowing up the Institution" at Castletown.[66]

Ward did indeed return to his original aim of procuring the tithes for the clergy, as the Trustees suggested. He still had hopes, and Melbourne assured him in 1836 that "Ld John Russell will not fail to heed the report held out re Govt Aid."[67] In a letter to his clergy in November 1837, he recalled the repeated promises of the tithes for the College, and continued, "those promises having been, happily perhaps, never fulfilled, I have reverted to my original desire."[68] By then Ward knew that he had lost the legal battle over the composition of the Trustees, which had eventually gone to the Privy Council by agreement of all the parties concerned,[69] and clearly did not trust what the majority might do with the Academic Funds, even if the College secured the tithes, despite the assurances given to him that the Church would be looked after.

THE STATUS OF THE COLLEGE

In spite of the arguments, Ward was very proud of what had been achieved in respect of the College, and there seems little evidence to support the contention of Robert Curphey that Ward "continued to try to keep the College on course to become an ecclesiastical seminary."[70] He wrote in 1834,

> "I have built a noble college for the accommodation of 300 boys with a Chapel annexed... College opened and increasing rapidly in number, having a Principal and Vice-Principal and four other Masters, all Men of the first reputation — three of them graduates of Cambridge, Scholars and Divines of the first celebrity."[71]

This was in January, before his abortive trip to London "to obtain an endowment and a Charter from the Crown for my new College.", so that his journey was made in full awareness of the nature of the institution, catering overwhelmingly for an age-group below that of the Academic Students. The original hope, noted by Teignmouth, had been that cheapness would attract students "from Ireland and adjacent parts of England who could otherwise afford the expenses of a residence at college."[72] The hope had soon been realised. By April 1834 Ward reported the College was filling fast with students and pupils, "not only of the Island, but from the surrounding shore of England, Scotland and Ireland!" By June, Ward was rejoicing that the original forty had grown to "already nearly 100 pupils not only of the Island, but from the three kingdoms and all since last August."[73]

Indeed the charge at the time was that Ward, far from opposing the influx of boys as a betrayal, wished to take all the credit. The Stranger gave chief credit to the work of John McHutchin, Clerk of the Rolls, "though the present Lord Bishop of the Isle would very willingly monopolize the honourable reputation of *Founder.*"[74] Ward also exaggerated the decay of the endowed schools to highlight his achievements. When he wrote that, "for the last half century and more, religion and learning have been suffered to languish and retrograde and fall into wreck and ruin",[75] he was careless of the fact that just over thirty years before had been the golden age of Hugh and Joseph Stowell, and Thomas Castley. Even in his statement that "I found the only school of learning for Clergy and Laity had been for some years vacant", he was not strictly accurate.

Indeed to the annoyance of those Trustees who saw the College as nothing more than a replacement of the Grammar School at Castletown, the Rev. George Parsons continued to conduct the Grammar School after the College was opened. The lay Trustees hoped to fit in Parsons into the New College, but the Home Office refused to concern itself with such matters. Melbourne informed Lt.-Governor Ready that his department did *not* link the College and the School.[76] In January 1834, the Archdeacon was asked to write to Ward "stating the importance to the welfare of the College that the Free Grammar School should be incorporated forthwith by Act of Tynwald with the College."[77] It was further requested that Ward use his influence to find a small North Country living for Parsons.

Ward did not comply, for his comprehensive plan for the role of the College included "putting the grammar schools into connexion with the college", and his friend, Lord Teignmouth, thought that exhibitions from the grammar schools to the College" would prove a most salutary species of endowment."[78] To close Castletown Grammar School would disturb the symmetry of Ward's grand design, and rob the College of the superiority in status which Ward sought to establish. Although he did not use the term 'grades', the Bishop clearly thought in terms of different levels of 'secondary' education, in the way that became increasingly common in the Victorian era, and received the stamp of official approval in the Taunton Report of 1868.[79] Movement from one level to another was a feature of such ideas, with scholarships or exhibitions enabling boys of merit to rise into a more advanced and socially superior school.

However, keen contempories refused to allow the higher status of the College. Although, according to R. S. Tompson, in the Eighteenth Century the term 'public school' "in practice appears to have been completely interchangeable with 'grammar school',"[80] already there were in the Nineteenth Century connotations attached to the term giving it a higher status, and especially linking it with schools serving national rather than local areas, the nine great schools.[81] Later in the century their numbers would be swollen by some of the proprietory boarding schools which sprung up to provide a useful education for the middle classes after the example of Cheltenham (1841), and also by other grammar schools aspiring to greater social distinction, such as Repton and Oundle, in the closing decades. King William's College would be included among them, but in the more restricted application of the term around 1830, the College was not accorded such an accolade, despite the far flung nature of its catchment.

Even Lord Teignmouth made a sharp distinction between the College and public school:—

> "The building is painfully inadequate to the requirements of a college and a large school . . . the object of the college, or rather school, is to give them . . . an education much the same as they would receive at the Superior grammar schools of England. The system resembles rather the grammar than the public schools of England."[82]

To make matters worse, Teignmouth lavished more praise on the Grammar School at Castletown.

> "This is the seminary in which all the Manks clergy are educated, and acquired considerable reputation from the superintendence of the late master, Mr. Cazeles (sic.), who attained the honours of senior wrangler and second medallist at the University of Cambridge and conducted it during half a century."[83]

The first Principal, Edward Wilson, concurred with such views, telling Ward that his College was indeed a grammar school and not a public school. His first sight of the College caused his heart to sink — not a bush, scarcely a building within a mile — and he later advised his son about his life's story, "Better leave out the King William's College part, it is too horrible."[84]

In the light of the state of learning in the public schools revealed by the Clarendon Commission a generation later, when the majority of boys were described as "almost incredibly ignorant" of English, Modern Languages, Natural History and Modern History, and even as extremely weak in the Classics to which so many years had been devoted,[85] the placing of King William's College in the grammar school stratum was, at least in educational terms, to its credit rather than otherwise. For while the famous Leeds Grammar School case of 1805 — or at least its widespread interpretation, for Eldon's judgment was not as restrictive as commonly supposed — retarded adaptation of the traditional curriculum, R. S. Tompson has shown how the strict approach was "out-dated and largely ignored."[86] Most foundations of the Eighteenth Century were more liberally worded regarding the curriculum, and more recent developments such as the Birmingham Grammar School Act of 1831 had enabled radical changes to be made, including the teaching of science. The College's own curriculum built upon the liberal approach which Castley had developed at Castletown, and included English, Mathematics, Geography, History and Writing, although the *Sun* had lamented the absence of Navigation.

A basic difference between the Manx College and the public schools lay in the social ranking of the clientéle. Even Shrewsbury, scarcely truly a national school, drew its pupils from the nobility and gentry over a wide area of the border counties. The raison d'être of the College was to provide for boys of the Island. Yet although the *Sun* was gratified to see in 1834 how many boys were native or at least inhabitants of the Island, according to Lord Teignmouth's breakdown the Manx element was very much in a minority. He gave numbers as seventy English, fifty Irish, thirty Manx, ten Scotch and a few missionaries' children from India. The cheap fees had indeed attracted pupils beyond the seas, but as with many other schools later to become famous, at this period there was little social cachet in attending King William's College. "The boys were drawn from homes which were themselves rough and uncultivated."[87] Although the College passed the criterion of width of catchment area, contemporaries wanted something higher in social appeal before it would be classed as a new public school.

WARD'S FAILURE HIGHLIGHTED

However, for the Island the niceties of nomenclature paled into insignifcance compared with the deadly attack on the College made by the Vicar of Braddan, the Rev. Robert Brown, the former Master of the Douglas Grammar School, and one of the most respected clergymen on the Island. The College had offered in 1836 eight volumes of Bingham's *Antiquities of the Catholic Church* as a prize for the best essay on "The right use of primitive tradition verified as Catholic by the rule quod semper, quod ubique, quod ab omnibus", awarded in the event to W. G. Wilson, the Principal's nephew. Brown in a letter to the *Sun* suggested a better topic rather nearer home than the Vincentian Canon; ". . . a correct account of the nature of the Institution which Bishop Barrow intended to establish: and in the second place with a faithful statement of the nature of the existing institution."[88] The implication was clear: King William's College, Ward's beloved child, was not the fulfilment of Barrow's dream, but a perversion. Barrow's

Academy had intended to offer gratuitous maintenance as well as instruction free from expense, and only after the candidates for the ministry had been taken care of, should any surplus go to "any object of public utility". (It is interesting that Brown here followed the deed, and not the will, unless employing an ad hominem line of reasoning.) Yet the College allotted no portion of its £590 a year income to maintaining theological students, fees being demanded from all. The master spent his time, not in the 'science of theology', but in a class with youths whose parents were neither natives or inhabitants of the Island. As for the expensive edifice erected at such cost, how did it aid the Manx Church? It was "Certainly one with which the divinity students could very well dispense."

Brown's letter had the same effect as the little boy's remark about the emperor's clothes in the Hans Christian Anderson story. The *Sun* which had rejoiced in the "high proportion of natives at the College" in 1834, suddenly discovered the places were "almost entirely" occupied by boys from England and Ireland to the "almost total exclusion of the children of the inhabitants", and suggested once more lower charges to encourage greater numbers. (Ward's figure of three hundred was still taken at face value.) The chief object of "providing pastors for the Manx church is quite passed over." The parochial clergy could not afford thirty pounds for boarding charges, although they were given free tuition for any vocation. Why were three not selected as by the will to receive maintenance while they studied for holy orders? The life and soul of the Bishop's intention was quite lost sight of. As it was, scholars who went to England did not return, finding curacies there, and being able to say that vacancies, especially the more lucrative, were filled by strangers, despite their lack of the Manx tongue.[89]

Brown's case was formidable. An enormous sum of money had been expended, but only thirty Manx boys were receiving education at the College, and two were receiving instruction for the ministry. The situation was in fact identical with that prevailing under Castley, except the ordinands' freedom from charges had been lost. The final bill for the College had amounted to £6,572/16/4½, and to bridge the gap between the aggregate of savings and contributions (£4,766/12/2¾) and the cost incurred, an Act of Tynwald was needed to allow the mortgaging of College lands, thereby diminishing drastically future income. Ward's dream had turned into a nightmare, and ample excess revenue into a desparate fight against poverty.

Brown followed up his attack by challenging how Governor Ready found his statement incorrect, as he had been heard to say. The Governor deftly referred the matter to the House of Keys, who drew up questions for the Trustees to answer.

The first question concerning the Academic Students was fended off without too much difficulty on grounds of supply and demand. When the College was opened, places on the foundation were already filled by men at Cambridge and St. David's College, Lampeter, and those already in orders. After vacant livings and the chaplaincy at Baldwin had been filled, Messrs. Talley, Creer, Gelling, Nelson and Caley were still without places for them. This was the reason that no student was maintained gratuitously, and in point of fact since the College was opened, "no candidate has applied to the Trustees to be admitted on the foundation." Edward Qualtrough had been prepared for ordination at the College but not upon the foundation. (Mary Ward, the Bishop's daughter, wrote of her brother's ordination with five others, "amongst whom was one, the first Papa has ordained of those prepared for the ministry in his New College.")[90] In the Trustees' view, the College "has been fully answering the design contemplated by Bishop Barrow", whose primary object was a well-educated ministry, achieved more effectively since the opening of the College.

The query, "Could this be possible without an edifice so extensive as King William's College?" was less convincingly answered. The chance to take boarders encouraged good masters, and financial inducement to attract them in the first place was possibly only with a greater number of boys than the Island could supply. The College thus provided "as it were at the expense of strangers, a good Education for the natives of the town and neighbourhood." (The number of boarders, given as twenty five natives and thirty others, contrasted greatly with Teignmouth's figures of eighty to ninety in College, thirty with a master, and others in approved lodgings.)

One other question received a lame answer. The heart of the Academical School had been the Lecturer in Philosophy and Logic. Was there one at the College? Taking refuge in legal technicalities, the Trustees responded that the Trustees of Bishop Barrow's fund were not the Trustees for the Lectureship founded by Barrow.

Brown rejected the arguments. He conceded that five boys might have nominal fees of only 2/6, four of them from Castletown Grammar School, but this was not giving free education and maintenance to theological students. Some had indeed been sponsored by the Bishop, Archdeacon, and Clerk of the Rolls, but this only went to prove that their education was not gratuitous. Qualtrough had proceeded to his ordination only by the help of an English patron. Brown knew of young men whose parents could not afford the "exceedingly burdensome" high fees, nor could he accept that the existence of five young men in England meant the Manx Church had a surplus of clergy, for if they chose the option of returning the money spent on their education, the Trustees had no right to make them return to the Island.[91]

The argument about better masters was scorned by Brown, giving his tribute to Castley, whose equal the Island had not beheld. In a small building with twenty to thirty others, he argued, the Academic Professor has far more time to give to his Academic Students than a Principal with large numbers to look after. The Academic Fund now had an income of £616 every year, which would comfortably sustain all the young men mentioned, but all the theological instruction they received was a lecture on the Greek New Testament on Saturday mornings. The only possible conclusion was that the College was "positively injurious" to those whom Barrow had most intended to help.

Although the Keys accepted the Trustees' explanation of the use of the Academic Fund, the clergy vehemently took up Brown's arguments, protesting about the robbery of the Church's assets. Ward was now failing fast, his last campaign to prevent the absorption of his diocese into that of Carlisle having exhausted him; yet the backlash from his clergy against his creation must have wounded him greatly.

In reality, Ward, displaying an admirable broadness of mind regarding education, had been outsmarted, and the laity had exacted their revenge for what they considered the abuse of the Impropriate Fund. Just as the officials and the Keys had intended, the splendid all-embracing plan of the Bishop had been truncated to the degree that the vision of Barrow, Stowell and Ward of Academic Scholars pursuing their studies with other young men preparing for the learned professions was unlikely ever to be realised.

Set against a wider background, the whole affair of the College was, in practice, an unusually elaborate example of the transformation of schools from those which served a local area and provided free places into those which sought boarders from a wide area and effectively suppressed the poor free scholars. The Clarendon Commission which led to the Public School Act of 1868 helped to consolidate a process which in some cases was a century old. As early as 1785 it had been noted by a minority of rebel governors that at Harrow, set in a parish of two thousand, "not one boy belonging to the parish is on the said foundation."[92] The long drift in the grammar schools towards fee-paying and boarders was likewise consolidated by the recommendations of the Taunton Commission and the work of the Endowed School Commissioners.[93] As has been seen, the case of the College was far more complex, with the use of completely different funds from those of the original endowment, the erection of a supposedly quite independent college, and even, although by accident, the survival of the institution which was the intended objec' of change. Yet fundamentally the position was the same: ancient funds intended for free education were subsidising the education of fee-paying boarders, with the usual sops of concessions to a handful of boys.

The local press, especially the *Mona's Herald,* continued to support Brown, complaining of the Trust purpose not being followed, and "all for the object of building an edifice called a College whereat the rich may, at great expense, get their sons exclusively educated." Those on the Island who patronised the College were christened "The Exclusives", who guaranteed to themselves all the best appointments.

(Richness, of course, was a matter of degree: by English standards the education offered at the College was cheap.) Bishop Short (1841-1847) expressed serious episcopal doubts about what his predecessor had done, albeit with the highest of intentions.

"Looking at the whole of the transaction of building the College, I cannot but think that the original intention of Bishop Barrow has been a great deal perverted. He meant all the money to be spent in eduating the Manx clergy."[94]

EARLY YEARS OF THE COLLEGE

While the arguments raged, as they did for most of the century, the massive new building dominated the countryside in the south of the Island. Whether rightly or wrongly, the College had been built and was an established fact. Lord Teignmouth considered it would be an ornament to Oxford architecturally, as the local grey limestone appeared to advantage, and then unplastered stones "gave an appearance of neatness and regularity to the external part of the edifice,"[95] How different it appeared indeed to the humble residences of the parochial schoolmasters on the Island, of whose plight J. T. Cregeen was writing in the *Manx Sun* in 1838.

"There are no suitable residences in the Island for parochial teachers. Most of the present dwellings are wretched hovels — in some cases not habitable."[96]

The case of Ballaugh was mentioned, where the walls shook in every high wind, and candles were extinguished by winds coming through the wall. Yet Wilson lamented that two to three gallons of water could be collected in his own drawing-room on a wet evening, as the rain seeped through the unplastered walls of the College, which "both look and are cold and repulsive to ye eye of boys and parents who must and do behold them."[97]

The desparate card of mortgaging the estates of Hango Hill and Ballagilley had already been played, and £2,500 raised by this means.[98] Robert Brown sent a Memorial of protest against the mortgage, but it arrived after the Royal Assent to the Tynwald Bill had already been given on September 20 1836.[99] The mortgage had paid for the completion of the structure, and helped to secure well-qualified masters, but repayments at £130 each year made serious inroads into the College's annual income.

The Trustees were caught in a classic dilemma: if fees were to be raised substantially, the attraction to overseas parents would be lost, yet by themselves, as Wilson pointed out, "The inhabitants of the Island could not furnish a sufficient number of boys to provide that remuneration", (to the masters). If the money could not come from fees, neither could it come from greater numbers. Although Ward had boasted of room for three hundred, Wilson wrote with despair of seventy to eighty boarders dining in a classroom, and a further increase would only exacerbate problems of space. There was dire need of an endowment of £5,000. "The College wants better endowment. Indeed it can hardly be said to have any endowment at all. Endowment is equally wanting for masters and scholars." If there were none forthcoming, the "King William's College will be a poor and starveling remembrance of ye august Sovereign whose royal name it bears."'[100] His only faint hope was Queen Adelaide, "the illustrious consort of its royal founder... portion of her bounty would not unworthily or unappositely be bestowed on King William's College." Wilson by this time was disillusioned with the whole affair, and having reminded Ward that only Brougham's promise of the tithes had brought him to the Island, he felt justified in accepting a living in Weston-Super-Mare on the grounds of his wife's health. He was greatly relieved that Ward's death had prevented hurt to the "friendly bishop to whose good offices I was chiefly indebted for my appointment."[101] Governor Ready said words could not express his regret, while Dixon, the Vice-Principal, claimed that "No institution so circumstanced has advanced so much in so short a space of time."[102] The words "so circumstanced" held a depth of meaning.

The new Principal, Alfred Phillips, soon sought to provide a more flexible curriculum, with a modern class giving up Greek and Latin at thirteen "if their destination in life were such as to render a practical *modern* education more likely to be beneficial to them."[103] This realism was a feature of the Academies with their range of choices, soon to be followed by the proprietary schools, and a marked contrast to the traditional beliefs, as expressed for instance by Dr. Arnold of Rugby, who saw "The study of language ... given for the very purpose of forming the human mind in youth; and the Greek and Latin languages ... seem the very instruments, by which this is to be effected."[104] Philip's short rule also saw the first academic success, when W. G. Wilson, who had carried off all the College prizes, was awarded the Bell Scholarship at Cambridge in 1839, going on to become 16th Wrangler in the Mathematical Tripos and 8th First Class in the Classical Tripos three years later, finally becoming Fellow of St. John's College in 1844.

More immediately dramatic was the spectacular and devastating fire of January 14th, 1844 which in the early hours gutted four of the five sections of the College, with only the Vice-Principal's house escaping. The interior of the Principal's house, the chapel, school and dormitories, and the central tower were consumed. Oustanding among the losses was that of the Library, which contained books given by local gentry and Bishop Short, but above all those of the old Castletown Library. The cause was never proved, although the evidence of Vice-Principal Cumming pinpointed the place of origin as the dining hall, as flames from there alone were seen at 3.30 a.m. Boys had been seen in the evening fooling with lighted pieces of paper, and a servant who looked in at 11.15 had smelled burning wood, although all was dark.[105] The nearest fire engine was nine miles away in Douglas and took hours to arrive. A strong wind made the conflagration almost impossible to check.

The Trustees responded quickly, arranging timber from Sweden to be shipped to Derbyhaven, and utilised the expertise of Mr.

Timperley, a civil engineer who was residing in Castletown, to look after men and materials. An appeal was launched, and a Circular issued, which contained rather a defensive statement as to aims of the College.

> "... the object of those who took a share in the erection was that, as the majority of the theological students could not hope to attain the advantage of an English University, the Trustees, by establishing a place of general education in the Island, to which strangers might be admitted, would furnish a more liberal education than that which was likely to be obtained in an institution where the members consisted of only a small number of young men, who were preparing themselves for the Manx Church. These objects have, to a certain degree, been accomplished."[105]

The evidence for this last claim was the hundred strangers on the College books, including twenty sons of missionaries with the Church Missionary Society, and the free education given to twelve Islanders, chiefly clergy sons. The Circular made it clear that this was not on the foundation, as the mortgage repayments had caused "the inability of the Trustees to assist the sons of those who have the greatest claim to enjoys the charity..." Principal Wilson's fund for this purpose being exhausted, the clergy sons were taught free only at the expense of, and by the generosity of the masters.

The papers reported that the College was insured for £2,000, but the Trustees' own meeting mentioned the sum of £4,000.[107] Whatever the reason for the discrepancy, the lower sum may have spurred on a more generous response to the Bishop's Circular, aided, too, by widespread coverage such as in the *Illustrated London News*. Bishop Short gave £300, the Archbishop of York £100, Dixon, who succeeded Philips in 1841, £50, as did Governor Ready and Queen Adelaide, at last mindful of her husband's link with the College. Among the lesser contributions were those of the Bishop of St. Asaph (£30), King's College, London (£24.10.0), King's College School (£20.14.0) and the Rev. George Parsons of Castletown Grammar School (£5).[108] In the event, the response was good, raising £1,843.14.0, and the College continued to function in houses nearby. The large schoolroom was once more available for the annual prizegiving in June 1844, and the remainder of the school open by August. The chapel itself did not reopen until the following May. While many library books were not replaceable, friends of the College did what they could to mitigate the losses. The Circular made a special mention of the need for books, and December 1845 the Trustees recorded their thanks to Oxford University for "their munificent grant of books" and the binding of the same by three friends.[109]

The standard of the education given by the College has been fiercely disputed. James Wilson, the son of the first Principal, was a severe critic. "I doubt whether any school could have been worse... teaching I imagine almost as bad as it could be... The plain fact is that no-one on the staff was a scholar and no-one even a tolerable mathematician." He claimed that Dixon, the Principal, copied out his (Wilson's) solutions to quadratic equations in case any pupil might achieve great heights in the future.[110] Wilson, with his brother, entered the College in 1848, and claimed too that in his last two years, he educated himself in his study in the great tower; "We were shamefully neglected in every way."

Reliance upon the list of honours in the school is apt to be misleading in certain cases. James Wilson was awarded a Scholarship at St. John's Cambridge in 1855, and would thus appear to weaken his own case. In fact he was removed in 1853 to Sedburgh, where the brothers found themselves "backward and fragmentary in our attainments", barely fit for the bottom of the First Class of twelve.[111] The credit for the scholarship and the Bell University Scholarship awarded to him in 1856 would thus seem to belong to Sedburgh and Evans rather than to King William's and Dixon. Nor was this removal to another school prior to university entrance an isolated case. Robert Weatherall, son of a recent newcomer to Douglas from Salford, was sent from the College to a school in Chester before entering St. Edmund Hall, Oxford, in 1855.[112]

Yet the three most famous old boys of the College went to university directly from King William's. F. W. Farrar, who left in 1847, was Head of School, Scholar and Fellow of Trinity College, Cambridge, after a period under Maurice at King's College, London. He was headmaster at Marlborough from 1871 to 1876, and finished his days as Dean of Canterbury. Thomas Fowler was born in Castletown, and attended the College as a day-boy. A Postmaster of Merton College, Oxford, he was a double first in Classics and Mathematics, and after being elected a Fellow of Lincoln College, moved in 1881 to be President of Corpus Christi. T. E. Brown, sent to the College despite father Robert's continued battery of letters to the press about the misuse of the Barrow Funds, received free education as a clergyman's son by the generosity of the masters. Ignoring the advice of Archdeacon Moore to read for a Trinity College, Dublin, degree externally, he became a servitor at Christ Church with the aid of a Barrow Exhibition. After gaining a double first in Greats and then in Law and History in 1853, he was prevented by the snobbery of Christ Church from being elected a Fellow ('Student'). Oriel proved less fastidious and gave Brown a fellowship. "The tutors themselves have said that I occupy the same place relatively to the new system that Sir Robert Peel did to the old."[113] How much credit should go to King William's is not clear. James Wilson claimed "Brown must have taught himself for two years at least", and that Farrar and Fowler were also independent of any master. Obviously Robert Brown helped enormously with his son's education, but he had died in 1846, three years before Brown entered Oxford, and probably to the great relief of the Barrow Trustees. Brown himself stated in later life "I can honestly say that from a schoolmaster I never learned anything."[114]

A more objective assessment of the College came from Professor O'Brien of King's College, London. As was common at the time, the Trustees in March 1848 desired an external report on progress, and asked the Bishop to invite O'Brien.[115] After terms were arranged, the inspection was duly carried out and the report presented in June 1848. O'Brien had examined the first class of each department viva voce and the whole school in papers in Theology, Classics, Mathematics and English, finding the answers "generally good". The Theology was very satisfactory, with very fair answers to the Hebrew paper: the Greek test well answered by a considerable number of boys; as for the Classical composition, as much as could be expected was done; in translation the boys did well, especially the first class in Thuycydides, Theocritus, and Tacitus. While History and Geography were generally good, the lower Fifth did "remarkably well for their standing". In Mathematics "the answering was above the average", especially with regard to Euclid, which the boys understood well. A fair proportion were acquainted with conic sections and trigonometry. In English "answering was excellent", written well and neatly by the whole school. The general conclusion was that "The College appears to be in a high state of efficiency, the subjects of study judicially selected, and the whole system of instruction well arranged." There seems nothing here to support the picture of semi-chaos painted by Wilson.[116]

F. W. Farrar's pious *Eric* or *Little by Little* with its picture of a savage institution, based on King William's College, aroused mixed reactions after its publication in 1858. Wilson thought it quite accurate, and no caricature of the school at all. He himself remembered merciless discipline — "I received eight cuts every Monday morning from Mr. Hollis" — and wrote of much cruelty and bullying. "It was a lawless, dirty, degraded life and few survived it without real damage."[117] T. E. Brown on the other hand questioned if any boy who attended the College would recognise the Farrar portrait of it. The likelihood is that the College was indeed a rough and frightening establishment, but little different in this respect from other public schools of the time. As Stanley in his *Life of Dr. Arnold* put it, the general feeling was that "the great end of a public school, in short, was to flog their vices out of bad boys."[118]

The same period also saw the revival at the College of the Academic Students. In 1841 Dixon arranged that £30 a year should be set aside to accumulate "if wants of Manx Church do not render it necessary to place any young man at the College as an Academic Student." Yet in 1849 the Trustees found nothing had been done, and took over the practice themselves. Earlier that year, William Kelly, Samuel Adams and T. E. Brown were elected Academic Students, to continue their studies at Dublin, Oxford or Cambridge, with the usual bonds to serve in the Manx Church still being required.[119] William Kelly, however, found he was unable to go to Dublin, and asked permission to be an Academic Student at the College. His request was granted and Hugh Gill was also accepted as a resident Student. The Principal was asked to submit an annual report on their progress.[120] The following year they were joined by William

Llewellyn, and Dixon was asked for detailed accounts of their studies, especially the theological parts.

Although until then the Trustees had preferred to send men away for training to university, there had been at least one instance before of the College giving training to one not on the Academic Students' Foundation. Hugh Stowell Brown, T. E. Brown's elder brother led a strange life after the rigours of Douglas Grammar School. Having become a land surveyor in Liverpool, he acceded to his mother's wish he train to be a priest, and picked up his studies again at the College at the age of twenty one. Being the son of a clergyman, he was given free education. The generous custom of the masters was soon to be considered as a right by the clergy. Brown wrote of studying Greek with Dixon, Latin with Vice-Principal Cumming, and dabbling in Hebrew. Ironically it was the views of old peg-leg William Stowell of Douglas Grammar School, so mocked by Hugh Stowell Brown, that prevailed over those of his learned tutors. Brown left the College in 1846 without being ordained to the Anglican ministry, and ended up a well known Baptist minister in Liverpool.[121]

Although the final result was not always that which was intended or expected, the tradition of the provision of the third tier in education on the Island itself, concurrent with the sending to overseas universities, was maintained. It was certainly not what Ward had hoped in its fulness, and really differed little from what Castley had done, but at least it was better than the total abandonment which had been feared at one point.

The staff, especially Dixon, showed a giving spirit to both boys and the College. The provision of free education to clergy sons has already been mentioned, and until 1841 the apparatus for lectures, the maps and blackboards, had been Dixon's own property. As Vice-Principal form 1833 to 1841 he had been entitled to £20 a year for services in the chapel, but had given them free, for the chapel ran at a loss. Pew rents came to only £23 (although this was enough to arouse the anger of the Vicar of Malew) while for example a new stove in 1840 cost £45.[122]

In 1839 the College Chest was started, wherby half-a-crown was asked of each boys every quarter.[123] The following year the Trustees decided that income would be increased if the College lands were leased in lots. Yet the great fire and general conditions in the 'Hungry Forties' made life very difficult. The appeal after the fire was aware it came "at a moment when many of the inhabitants are labouring under great pecuniary difficulties". Numbers of pupils were hard to keep up; the Irish intake in particular would be hard hit. The College Chest had to be put to use to replace Dixon's equipment lost in the fire. In the absence of any extra endowment, there could be no guarantee that the College, already mortgaged in respect of its lands, would carry on.

Death came to the College's rescue. In the first flush of enthusiasm for the College in 1831, Mrs. Margaret Quilliam (née Stevenson) of Ballakeighan had left in her will the estate of Orrisdale to the College. She herself died in 1844, and after the death of Mrs. Charlotte Guntan in 1847, the lands of Orrisdale passed into the hands of the Trustees of the Academic Fund. In 1849 Thomas Clague, the sitting tenant of Orrisdale, offered a rent of £170 a year for renewal, and his offer was eventually accepted. This meant that the great drain of £130 each year on the mortgage was more than covered.

The Trustees continued to exercise careful control. Dixon was warned that he must not engage extra staff without permission of the Trustees.[124] Robert Caley suddenly found himself required to pay back on his bond £40 from 1831, the Trustees not settling for anything less than two-thirds of this amount.[125] Yet by 1850 the situation was not as black as five years earlier, and the Trustees felt they were now in a position to counter some of their critics and "carry out more effectively the charitable intentions of Bishop Barrow." Twenty Manx boys would be Scholars receiving free education, and masters would no longer be expected to teach clergy sons for nothing, except for those already on the roll or those who were Scholars. The Principal, when required, would still prepare young men for the Manx Church. Interest from a cash sum of £300, also bequeathed in the Quilliam will, would pay the bulk of the salary of a Navigation master, together with £10 from the Orrisdale rent and quarterage. Adjustments were made to the quarterage. One-sixth would go to the Vice-Principal and Third Master each, one-sixth to the Trustees, two-sixths to the Principal, and the remaining sixth be divided between the three masters.

Dixon, Cumming and Harvey consented to these proposals, which also fixed their salaries at £150, £120 and £100 respectively. Regulations for the choice of Foundation Scholars were drawn up. They would be awarded to Manx boys, or boys with a Manx father, aged between thirteen and fifteen. Unless idle or disobedient they would hold their position until the age of eighteen, and from them would be selected the Barrow Exhibitioners for the Manx Church, after the traditional examination by Bishop and Archdeacon. The material for examing the Foundation Scholars would be the Gospel of Matthew in Greek, Vergil's Eclogues, the first twenty propositions of Euclid, Arithmetic, History and Geography.

A further meeting of December 11th, 1850, confirmed these regulations, and resolved that the thirteen boys then receiving free education should be placed on the list as Foundation Scholars, leaving seven vacancies to be filled. Advertisements announcing these were to be placed in the newspapers. While the salaries appeared at first sight to be less than before, the augmentation from the Orrisdale rents, which suddenly jumped to £341 a year, was considerable, giving Dixon a total salary of £300, Cumming £205, and Harvey £164.

CONCLUSION

By mid-century then, the College was surviving. The financial position had eased a little, despite the disaster of the great fire. Thirteen scholarships had been won by old pupils at Oxford and Cambridge, and the academic standards declared satisfactory. The provision of Foundation Scholarships went some to answering this who had claimed the College was only for the rich on the Island, and once again Academic Students training for the ministry were receiving their third level of education on the Island itself.

Yet certainly the often-made claim that King William's College fulfilled the intention of Barrow regarding his intended Academical School is completely without any foundation in fact. Whatever grandiose intentions had been in Ward's mind, what actually came into being was a superior replacement for Castletown Grammar School pure and simple, just as Smelt and his supporters intended it should be all along. Ward's Academic School, existing side by side with the younger classes benefitting from what would now be called 'secondary education', had been quite deliberately strangled before it was ever born. The Academic School was much more of a reality in the cramped building of Castletown Grammar School in the Eighteenth Century than it ever was in King William's College in the Nineteenth, despite the latter's majestic buildings. The education that the College was offering was for all except a tiny handful an education at the second level, not the third which was equivalent in Barrow's eyes to that provided by a university. The development of different levels of education within the second tier, exemplified on the Island later by scholarships from the grammar schools to the College, must not be allowed to obscure the fact that for the vast majority of its pupils the College simply did not provide an education which could be considered an alternative to a university course.

It is indeed instructive to contrast the nature of King William's College with that of its inspiration, St. David's College, Lampeter. Instead of a tiny handful of students for the ministry being attached incongruosly to a boys' school, St. David's offered what Ward had hoped originally to provide, a residential college with a full corporate life, providing a curriculum which blended general culteral subjects with Christian theology and offering "on very moderate terms an Education *not inferior* (italics in original) to that which is to be obtained at the Universities."[126] Rather like the original terms of the Academic Readership on the Island, the aim was "to receive and educate any person whatsoever, whether destined for Holy Orders or not." (In practice virtually all students did study for the ministry). By 1849 462 students had entered the Lampter College, and its library, built on the foundation of Bishop Burgess' own collection, just as that of King William's was based on the Castletown Library books, grew into the biggest library in Wales. 1835 saw the appointment of a Professor of Science, an example of the very broadness of education which Ward had hoped would be a feature of his own college. Around the same time, St. David's gained the right to confer its own degrees of Bachelor of Divinity and Bachelor of Arts. Although naturally Sodor and Man could not hope to attract the sort of numbers of young men of university age as St. David's Diocese could by itself alone, here in West Wales was an institution which successfully exemplified the *true* fulfilment of the Barrow Academical School.

The real significance of King William's College was not apparent for some time. At the time of its foundation it was the private academies and the day proprietary schools which seemed to embody the latest educational advances, and the foundation of a predominantly boarding school set by the seaside was a comparatively minor event. Yet it was to this type of school that the future would belong. King William's College might only "Make a modest name for itself in the north", as Archdeacon Philpot's grandson stated rather patronizingly, but in historical terms, even if fortuitously, the Island was once more in the van of progress. If not knowingly or consciously, the pattern of King William's College would be imitated as the decades passed until by the end of the century such schools became the only possible choice for the education of the sons of English gentlemen. Even if contempories refused to the College the title, Ward's stunted child turned out to be possibly the very first of the Nineteenth Century public schools.

REFERENCES

CHAPTER EIGHT

1. Edith Caroline Wilson. *An Island Bishop William Ward, DD.* 1762-1838. SPCK 19831.
2. MS 2079B. *Ward Letters* 1824-1836.
3. BBT Oct 27 1828.
4. Lord Teignmouth. *Sketches of the Coast and Islands of Scotland and the Isle of Man.* Vol II. 251.
5. *Athol Papers* bk 99. 74.
6. BBT Aug 15 1827.
7. A. G. Bradley. *Our Centenarian Grandfather.* John Bale, London 1925. 160.
8. BBT Nov 14 1826.
9. *Ibid.* Oct 27 1826.
10. GO 4/30 Smelt to Peel. April 29 1829.
11. BBT. Feb 12 1829; Oct 28 1829.
12. R. Curphey. *Bishop Barrow's Trusts* MS.
13. Lord Teignmouth. *Op. cit.* Vol II. 251
14. MD 612 10/47 Feb 14 1829.
15. *Ibid.* 10/70.
16. *Ibid.* 10/38.
17. *Ibid.* 10/31.
18. PRO HO 99. 18. Oct 5 1830; Oct 12 1830.
19. *Ibid.* Nov 12 1830.
20. *Ibid.* Dec 10 1830.
21. BBT Dec 10 1829.
22. *Ibid.* Jan 14 1830.
23. GO 33/12. Circular April 6 1830.
24. *Rising Sun* Jan 12 1830.
25. *Ibid.* April 20 1830.
26. BBT July 5 1830.
27. *Rising Sun* Jan 5 1830.
28. MD 612. 10/49.
29. GO 33/13. April 19 1830.
30. *Ibid.* April 20 1830.
31. *Manx Advertiser.* April 24 1830.
32. *Rising Sun.* April 27 1830.
33. *Manx Advertiser.* June 19 1830.
34. *Rising Sun.* Dec 1 1830.
35. GO/33. 19 Nov 10 1830.
36. BBT Nov 7 1830.
37. PRO HO 99. 18. Nov 19 1830.
38. GO/33. 43. April 8 1831.
39. BBT May 14 1831.

40 *Ibid* Aug 5 1831.
41 Philander Chase. *Bishop Chase — Reminiscences and Autobiography.* James Dew Boston 2nd Edition 1848. Letter May 5 1832.
42 *Ibid.* Feb 8 1836.
43 MS 2079B. *Ward Letters 1824-1836.* Dec 27 1830.
44 Edward Churton.*Memorial of Joshua Watson.*
45 BBT June 2 1832.
46 *Ibid.* Aug 11 1832.
47 A. Stranger. *A Six Day Tour in the Isle of Man.*
48 GO/33 42. *Ward to Lt.-Governor.* Jan 8 1833.
49 *Ibid.*
50 BBT April 1 1833.
51 PRO HO 99. 18.
52 E. C. Wilson. *Op. cit. 141.* Letter Feb 1 1834.
53 *Ibid.* Feb 7 1834.
54 *Rising Sun.* June 11 1834.
55 *Ibid.* Aug 9 1833.
56 *KWC Manks College Account Book.* 184.
57 *Ibid. Loose leaf letter.* April 2 1833.
58 MS 2079B. *Ward Letters.* Sept 11 1833.
59 BBT. Sept 12 1834.
60 Lord Teignmouth. *Op. cit.* Vol II. 251. Note.
61 BBT. July 7 1834.
62 MD 612 10/91.
63 *Ibid.* 10/90.
64 BBT July 7 1834.
65 MD 612 10/76. Dec 7 1835.
66 *Ibid* 10/80.
67 PRO HO 99 May 10 1836.
68 E 205 6 (l) William Ward. *A letter Addressed to the Clergy of the Isle of Mann.*
69 BBT April 30 1835.
70 R. Curphey. *Bishop Barrow's Trusts.* 15.
71 MS 2079B. Jan 3 1834.
72 Lord Teignmouth. *Op. cit.* Vol II 251.
73 MS 2079B April 3 1834; June 111834.
74 A. Stranger. *Op cit.*
75 MS 2079B. Dec 27 1830.
76 PRO HO 99. 18. Nov 5 1833.
77 BBT Jan 8 1834.
78 Lord Teignmouth. *Op. cit. Ibid.*
79 *Taunton Report.* Vol I 16.
80 R. S. Tompson. *Classics or Charity.* 127.

81 Brian Simon. *The Two Nations and the Educational Structures 1780-1870.* 300.
82 Lord Teignmouth. *Op cit. Ibid.*
83 *Ibid.*
84 James M. Wilson. *James M. Wilson. An Autobiography.* Sidwick and Jackson, London, 1932. 6.
85 *Clarendon Commission.* Vol II. 49.
86 R. S. Tompson. *Op cit.* 125.
87 James M. Wilson. *Op cit.* 12.
88 *Sun.* July 11 1836.
89 *Ibid.* July 8 1836.
90 MS 2079B. Mar 1 1836.
91 *Sun.* Aug 5 1836.
92 D. T. W. Price. *Bishop Burgess and Lampter College.* University of Wales 1987. 67.
93 R. S. Tomson. *Op cit* 90.
94 Brian Simon. *Op cit* 318-336.
95 E 205/2/3. *(Reproduced Ramsey Church Magazine. July 1896).*
96 *Pictorial Times.* Jan 1844.
97 *Manx Sun* 1838.
98 James Wilson. *Op cit* 5.
99 *Statutes of the Isle of Man.* Vol II 1823-1859. 103.
100 PRO HO 99 19. Nov 20 1836.
101 E. C. Ward. *Op cit* 210. Jan 29 1838.
102 *Ibid* 211. Mar 2 1838.
103 *Sun.* June 29 1838.
104 *Ibid.* Nov 2 1838.
105 Arthur Penrhyn Stanley. *Life of Dr. Arnold. John Murray 1887 (14th Edition).* Vol I 118.
106 BBT Jan 15; Jan 22; Feb 5 1844.
107 D 426 Ix. Circular 1844.
108 BBT Feb 6 1844.
109 KWC. *Manks College Account Book 200.*
110 BBT. Dec 18 1845.
111 James M. Wilson. *Op cit* 12.
112 T. E. Brown. *A Memorial Volume 1830-1930.* CUP 1930. 76.
113 Kathleeen A. Forrest. *Manx Recollections.* 30.
114 A. W. Moore. *Manx Worthies.* 110. Letter of May 1853.
115 Samuel Norris. *Two Men of Manxland.* Norris Modern Press. 89. *Burns Night Speech 1895.*
116 BBT Mar 8 1848.
117 *Ibid.* June 2 1848.
118 James M. Wilson. *Op cit* 12.
119 Arthur Penrhyn Stanley.6 Op cit. Vol. I. 109.
120 BBT April 20 1849.

121 *Ibid.* Nov 20 1849.
122 Hugh Stowell Brown. *Hugh Stowell Brown. An Autobiography.* Routledge, London, 1887.
123 BBT. May 29 1850.
124 *Ibid.* June 16 1839.
125 *Ibid.* May 29 1848.
126 *Ibid.5 Oct 24 1849.*
127 D. T. W. Price, *Bishop Burgess and Lampter College.* University of Wales 1987. 67.

CHAPTER 9

ELEMENTARY EDUCATION — 1800-1847 INFLUENCES FROM THE MAINLAND

The Isle of Man, as has been seen, was by no means immune from the influences of new ideas in education, but it was in the elementary sphere in the Nineteenth Century that more direct links were forged with the mainland of Britain, and the influence of the British Government brought to bear in ways unknown in previous centuries. There were signs of this in the early decades of the century, when the new organisations for education in England often had the same impact upon the Isle of Man as they did on the Mainland.

SUNDAY SCHOOLS

The first of these was the Sunday School movement, associated particularly with Robert Raikes, a prosperous newspaper owner in Gloucester, who started a school on Sundays for children who toiled in local pin factories. In 1785 the Society for Establishment and Support of Sunday Schools in the different Counties of England, was founded. The movement spread very rapidly. Scholars numbered 250,000 in all Great Britain by 1787, but at the start of the century in 1801 there were 156,490 in London alone. By 1833 it was estimated that one and a half million children attended Sunday Schools in Great Britain.[1] The local committees were formed from both Church and Dissent, a contrast with the bitterness later found, and particularly in industrial areas gave an education to many thousands who had no other chance of learning, even if the emphasis was very much confined to reading, the rules of the Society stating that 'Neither writing nor arithmetic is to be taught on Sundays'. Unfortunately to some degree their existence actually hindered progress in education, as they flourished at the expense of day schools. Robert Southey, writing to Lord Ashley, pointed out they had been made 'Subservient to the merciless love of gain. The manufacturers know that a cry would be raised against them if their little white slaves received no instruction; and so they have converted Sunday into a Schoolday'.[2] Despite the rules many learned to write and do arithmetic through the Sunday Schools. (Sometimes the instruction was quite unlike what the founders of the movement had intended, as in the case of the secular Lancashire Sunday Schools, whose members spent their Sabbath studying such writers as Tom Paine and Francis Place, and regarded the Church as the main obstacle to enlightenment and reform.) Three out of ten children in 1833 were found to have their only source of education in the Sunday Schools, much to the disgust of the reformers who wished them to be superseded by a system of day schools. 'The necessity that exists for Sunday Schools at all, is a strong condemnation of all our fiscal, political and social arrangements.'[3]

While the movement did not gain a proper footing on the Island until the Nineteenth Century, there was one attempt in Douglas in 1786 at a room in Mucclesgate, with fifty children attending and supported by £33 in subscriptions. The children had schooling from eight o'clock to eleven, when they went to church. They resumed at two, attended evening prayers and had further teaching until eight. The school lasted sixteen months, and was unlike the host that followed by reason of the fact that the teachers received payment for their labours. This early burst of enthusiam was not imitated until 1802 when the Methodists in Douglas offered 'to educate children gratis in reading to impress on their minds moral and religious principles'.[4] The following year the school was said to be very flourishing with 150 boys and girls[5] and a similar school had been set up by the Castletown Methodists. These schools seem to have faded as quickly as the one of 1786, and it was not until 1808 that the movement really put down firm roots. The Rev. Hugh Stowell, former master of Douglas Grammar School and now Vicar of Lonan, established one in that parish, holding the teaching in the church, with himself, together with his family, as the instructors. "Having heard of the happy consequences attending Sunday Schools in the neighbouring kingdoms . . . on Sunday the 27th March 1808 I opened a Sunday School". With the help of one of the Geneste family, Stowell had printed a special book entitled 'A present for the Scholars who attended the Sunday School in Kirk Lonan'.[6] (This was in one way a more permanent development of the expedient method used by Bishop Wilson in harvest times, when he required those children needed, as he wisely realised, for harvesting, to report to their minister for Sunday tuition in case they began to forget their reading from day school). Two miles away, still within the parish, a second school was opened, and the Manx Advertiser hailed the salutary effect which the two schools had in that area, urging that all through the Island similar schools should be established, with resolution, vigour, and despatch, so that no child would be without the means of instruction. The challenge was quickly taken up in Douglas by the Rev. T. Harrison of St. George's, by the Methodists again, and by the Independent minister, the Rev. Samuel Haining. All three attracted large numbers, and further copies of Stowell's book, now entitled 'A Present for the Scholars who attend Sunday Schools in the Isle of Man' were printed and distributed. According to an article in the Advertiser, it "appeared to give them peculiar pleasure".

This time there was no fading away. On the contrary 1809 saw a number of clergy follow Stowell's example, in the parishes of Marown, Malew, Jurby, Rushen, and the Chapelry of St. Mark's. Two were opened in Lezayre, although these were under the direction of ladies rather than the clergy, and two in Ramsey, one of them at the Independent Chapel, followed by one in Bride. An application was made for help to the Sunday School Society, who responded by sending 160 New Testaments and 300 large spelling books for the use of the fifteen schools. Most important in the Island's educational history were the Day and Sunday Schools established by subscriptions in Douglas and Ramsey, but consideration of these will be deferred for a moment. Although 1815 saw further new schools at Ballaugh, Rushen and Onchan and Peel, the last attracting over 200 children to the Methodist Church each Sunday almost from the start, not all the other schools remained in existence, and by the close of the year there were only eleven Sunday Schools, with a total of 982 children on their books. Nevertheless the trend was strongly in favour of the Sunday Schools, despite the number of failures, and 1817 witnessed eight new starts. Two were under the Methodists at Castletown and Ramsey, and the rest founded by interested individuals — three in Braddan parish, at Oak Hill, Baldwin and Ballaoats, one in Douglas, Sulby, the Howe (Rushen Parish) and Glen Maye. The Sunday School Society supplied a further 240 spelling books, 60 alphabets and five sets of lessons. The total number of Sunday Schools stood at a new record of seventeen, with 1,497 scholars attending, but the following year saw a marked surge, with no less than fifteen new schools being started, with Kirk Michael and Union Mills among the new areas reached.[7]

Of potentially far greater importance in the history of Manx education was the despatch from London, printed by the Sunday School Society on the recommendation of a Mr. Mills, of a further supply of spelling books, but for the very first time, in the *Manx* language. A writer in the Manx Advertiser in July 1821 explained the reasoning

> It seemed most desirable that the Inhabitants should be taught to read their vernacular tongue, which had not been taught to any of the children attending schools, nor for a very long period, (if indeed ever in the schools), a primer or spelling book in Manx, having never before been printed. The rich boon was considered a real acquisition, as hereby many children would become enabled to read the Holy Scriptures to their parents in the only language which they understood.'[8]

As has been seen, the Bible and Prayer Book had been translated into the native tongue under Hildesley, but here was the first attempt to provide the means to bridge the gap between the vernacular tongue, still the language of the majority of the populace, and the reading of the holy books translated a generation or more early. No longer would Manx children have to learn to read only through the difficult medium of a foreign language. The Liverpool Tract Society followed this up by having printed at their own expense four thousand copies each of 'James Covey' and 'Poor Joseph' in Manx, while the Bristol Church of England Tract Society had printed two thousand copies of a tract about preparing for death — a strange choice to Twentieth Century eyes, but sadly relevant to the 1820s. Four hundred children in seventeen of the Sunday Schools began to learn the Manx tongue, and by 1821 this number had risen to 612. A tremendous boost to literary among the Manx-speaking populace had been given, and the exertions of the Eighteenth Century translators of the Scriptures seemed at last to be on the point of receiving the widespread reception which had been their aim. Not all approved, however, of such developments, and the association of the native Celtic tongue with backwardness and moral laxity was still a commonly held view. Although the Manx revered John Wesley, he had desired to extirpate the Manx language, and Bishop Murray, although certainly *not* revered by the Manx, shared his views. More importantly, unlike Wesley, the Bishop wielded power in these matters. The minutes of the Standing Committee of the Society for Promoting Christian Knowledge for July 13 1825 included the entry 'Read a Letter from the Bishop of Sodor and Mann, stating there is no longer any necessity for impressions of the Bible and Book of Common Prayer in the Manks Tongue; but that in the English Tongue they are much wanted, and sought after with great avidity." He further informed the Society that the teaching of the Manx language was prohibited by Act of Parliament, a statement totally without foundation, but probably very effective in persuading the Society to cease its support for the Manx language.

A return in 1818 put the number of Sunday Schools at thirty three, with 187 teachers and 2,390 children. New schools were opened in 1819 at Greeba, Douglas (2), Maughold (2), Laxey, Glen Aulden, Sulby Gill, Lambfell and Arbory. The number given for that year was 3,447, a remarkable increase in one year, but a figure the writer quoted in a long appeal for support of the Sunday Schools in the Manx Advertiser was inclined to doubt. He put the population of the Island at that time at 36,000, with 46 Sunday Schools staffed by 344 teachers in charge of 2,827 scholars. 1,301 of these could read the Testament in English, compared with the 612 in Manx. On the Island the Sunday Schools were above all for children; there were very few signs of active involvement of adults as students, a mere 24, or less than 1% of the total of children, a great contrast with some areas of the mainland. The first official census in 1821 gave the total population of the Island as being 40,081, while a survey of the Island's Sunday Schools in October 1822 gave a total of 3,280 scholars. The largest schools were as to be expected in the towns. Douglas, then with a population of 6,054 had a total of 655 scholars, of whom 341 attended the Sunday and Daily School in Athol Street, with the largest Methodist Sunday School lagging far behind with 150. In Peel the Methodists had 170 and the Independents 100 but there was no record of any Church Sunday School in the town. Castletown followed the Douglas pattern, with the Church Sunday Schools 206 outnumbering the Methodists at 130 quite comfortably. In Ramsey with 205 scholars out of a population of 1,523, the Church, Methodists and Independent Schools were fairly evenly split. Every parish was represented by at least two Sunday Schools, save Santan and Ballaugh which had one each, and Marown, which did not appear at all. Braddan with eleven was the parish with the highest numbers, but as this included Douglas, over three times bigger in numbers than its nearest rival, Castletown with 2,036, it was only to be expected. In all sixty Sunday Schools were listed, but whether this was a complete list is uncertain.[9] A list of Sunday Schools which paraded in Douglas in 1824 to celebrate George IV's coronation anniversary included a number not in the 1822 list, Marown being among them. In view of the difficulties of travelling on the Island, there was a very impressive turn-out of 2,016 scholars and 200 teachers.[10] Douglas Methodists fielded 200, and the Douglas Independents contingents of 180 and 93, and the valley across to Peel was well represented with Union Mills (66), Marown (67), Greeba (42) and St. John's (90) all putting Braddan Parish with only 20 rather in the shade. Apart from Castletown Methodists the South of the Island was poorly represented; indeed Ramsey Methodists (59) and Independents (70) and even remote Andreas (34) had made a better effort.

It was nevertheless in the South, in the Parish of Rushen, that the most notable out-of-town Sunday School was to be found. The Manks Advertiser in an editorial of March 1829 commented on the fact that nearly three hundred in the Sunday School there went to church once a fortnight, and gave the credit for this rare event to a young lady, probable one of the Gawnes of Kentraugh.[11] Yet the parochial schoolmasters received quite a large proportion of his pay for teaching a Sunday School, a notable exception to the general rule of free instruction. Esther Clague, in 1813, had left in her will "three pounds British to a Schoolmaster, for keeping a public Sunday School in the parish of Rushen" to be chosen by the vicar and wardens, while her husband, the Rev. John Clague, the incumbent, left a further sum of money, three pounds Manx, "to a Schoolmaster, for teaching the youth of the parish of Rushen their catechism, and other necessary branches of erudition, as shall be deemed right to the Captain, Vicar and Wardens of the said parish:" The hours of tuition, eight to ten and three to five, were carefully laid down in his will.[12] The parochial master was the obvious choice for the task, which, as will be seen, made him among the best paid parochial schoolmasters in the Island. Rushen was also singled out for mention in another of the rare references to Sunday Schools in the Manx newspapers, when in 1831, the Sun put the strength of the Sunday School there at up to four hundred.[13] Sometimes the impetus in the growth of the movement came from outside the Island. The glaring gap of no Church Sunday School in Peel was filled in 1828 by a lady from Sheffield, Miss Harris, who was spending the summer there on holiday, and the following year provided books for her brainchild.

Normally expenses were covered by an annual charity sermon, although in 1830 the Advertiser suggested that a better option was the building up of a permanent fund, which even at the modest rate of 2d a quarter from wellwishers would not only provide for books, but also help the country children to be provided with something better than their wretched clothing, tattered garments and bare feet.[14] This suggestion, as was the fate of most ideas of a similar nature, fell upon deaf ears. A review of education in the Island published in 1844, to be considered in more detail later, showed that apart from Sunday Schools supported by the Bishop, Archdeacon or private contribution, nearly all the fifty Sunday Schools who responded to the request for statistics still relied on public collection at the charity sermons, ranging from just £1.3.0. at Jurby East to £24 at Castletown Wesleyans.

Contemporary comments were concerned more with the perceived ends of the Sunday Schools than with the educational means employed The Advertiser for instance in 1829 thought that the effect of the recent big increase in the number of Sunday Schools could be discerned in the behaviour of the children. They were now far different from the rude animals they were before the system was introduced, with vacant stare replaced by 'cap off, the gentle inclination of the head, the neat curtsey'.[15] The advocates of the Sunday School as a means of social control inducing deference among the lower classes were undoubtedly pleased by such apparent success. Yet on the Island, as elsewhere, the educational tools employed to this end brought a degree of learning to great numbers who were otherwise beyond the normal reach of schools. The 1844 total of scholars at 3,597 greatly underestimated the true figure as a result of failure to submitt returns — the Douglas Wesleyans and Independent Churches for instance omitted to do so — and there is no doubt that in the first half of the Nineteenth Century the Sunday School movement affected many more children than the day schools. In view of the Manx educational system set up in the time of Barrow and Wilson, it would not be entirely true to claim that the movement initiated, as it did in England, the notion of universal education applied to all ages and free of cost, but it certainly played a notable part in Manx history, and its contribution in purely educational terms must not be overlooked.

THE MONITORIAL SYSTEM

The opening decades of the Nineteenth Century saw profound changes in teaching methods, reflecting to a large degree the factory system. The leading exponents of the new method, Andrew Bell and Joseph Lancaster, both maintained that "the principle in school and manufactories is the same".[16] Schools were to mirror large scale production, and efficiency was the new watchword. Schools had hitherto been conducted to a very large degree by the teacher hearing work from individuals or small groups, with the rest of the pupils doing their 'prep' as they awaited their return. The numbers with which one master could cope were quite limited. The new thinking claimed that matters would be transformed. Bell seems to have been first in the field when, at the Madras Male Orphan Asylum, he found himself short of teachers and utilised the elder children themselves. On his return to England he wrote pamphlets describing his system. At the same time Joseph Lancaster in his school at Borough Road used the elder children or monitors to keep the rest occupied, when he could not afford assistants. Bell's system was the more complicated, with pairs of able and less able children, and a hierarchy of ushers and assistants, while Lancaster used a monitor directly to twenty children. Whole classes would now concentrate together on dictation or around the class reading. It was claimed that by using monitors, one teacher could oversee a thousand children. "Give me twenty four pupils today, and I will give you twenty four teachers tomorrow", claimed Bell. The master was left only to organise the monitors, and to reward or punish — sometimes in bizzare ways such as Lancaster's famous punishment of putting children in a basket on the school roof. The comparisons with factory life were not eschewed. Bell spoke of "this intellectual and moral machine", which, "like the steam engine or spinning machinery, ... diminishes labour and multiple work". Bell's aims in education were extremely limited:—

> "It is not proposed that the children of the poor be educated in an expensive manner, or even taught to write and cypher ... There is a risk of elevating them from the drudgery of daily labour above their condition, and thereby render them discontented and unhappy in their lot. It may suffice to teach the generality, on an economical plan, to read their Bible, and understand the doctrines of our Holy Religion."[17]

The shadow of the French Revolution loomed large still. The debate about education for the poor was largely between those who thought like Hannah Moore, that a little learning would lead the lower orders into better habits of piety and industry, and those who believed that any education would be the start of a slippery slope to revolution. These divisions were clearly seen in a debate in Parliament in 1807, when Samuel Whitbread praised the "plan for the instruction of youth which is now brought to a state of great perfection; happily combining rules, by which the object of learning must be infallibly attained with expedition and cheapness", but Davies Giddy warned of labouring classes who despised their lot: "Instead of teaching them subordination it would render them fractious and refractory."[18] Nevertheless, there was an attraction in a system which taught pupils to work in an orderly manner, at very little cost, and after Lancaster published his 'Improvement in Education' in 1803, Borough Road School achieved great fame. Lancaster's biographer, Corston, related how "Foreign princes, ambassadors, peers, commoner, ladies of distinction, bishops and archbishops, Jews and Turks, all visited it with wonder waiting eyes."[19]

However, in 1805 Mrs Sarah Trimmer created a divide between the two protagonists deeper than that of personalities alone. Apart from accusing Lancaster of taking all his good ideas from Bell, she denounced his undenominational schools as a menace to the Church of England, as no distinct Church teaching was given. Although King George III was himself a subscriber to Borough Road, and the association formally constituted in 1810 was called the Royal Lancasterian Society, it was true particularly in the North of England that dissenters far less orthodox than Presbyterians played prominent parts. The Royal Lancastrian Free School of Manchester, opened in 1809, and having a full thousand children in attendance, was, for instance, under a committee with a Quaker chairman and a Unitarian among its members, who also included John Owens, the future founder of Owens College in 1851, (destined to become Manchester University.)[20] If education were to be under the influence of sects who denied in one case the point of priests and sacraments, and the doctrine of the Trinity in the other, the Church party felt it necessary to organise itself in opposition. The year 1811 saw the foundation of 'The National Society for promoting the Education of the Poor in the Principles of the Established Church throughout England and Wales'. Although conscience clauses allowed the withdrawal of Nonconformist pupils, the official teaching of the schools included instruction in the Liturgy and Catechism of the Church of England.

When the new ideas reached the Isle of Man, the very strong Church influence on the Island made it inevitable that the influence of the National Society's ideas should previal over those of the British and Foreign School Society, as the Lancasterian Society had been renamed in 1814, although no National money grants were made to the Island on account of its being beyond England and Wales. Although the very first school of this type on the Island was known initially as a Lancasterian School, the British and Foreign School Society which (just as the name applies) was not as limited in its geographical area, never succeeded in making any headway in the Island, and the rivalry of National and British School which lasted many decades across the water, was unknown in the Isle of Man.

THE DAY AND SUNDAY SCHOOL OF DOUGLAS

Although in theory the Manx system of parochial schools, now liberally supplemented with other foundations in less accessible areas of the parishes, meant that the new schools were to a large degree not needed, in practice this was not so. Particularly in the growing towns, especially Douglas, the old tutorial methods could not cope with an increasing population, even had the teaching been of a high standard. As has been seen, the private sector to a large degree took care of those who could afford to pay, but this left many of the poor still without schooling in the week. The new ideas percolating from the mainland held out the promise of effective and economical training of the poorer classes in good citizenship and godliness.

As might have been expected, Douglas led the way, and the Manx Advertiser in April 1810 published a list of subscribers to a school, stated in February, and a month later an editorial referred to "two fine new streets being built on the estate of the Hills in the most pleasant part of the town, with several new buildings springing up, among them the Lancasterian School". The school actually began life in

Muckle Gate, and was visited there by the Rev. Hugh Stowell who extolled its merits to the Advertiser's readers.[21] Proficiency was at least ten times greater than in ordinary schools, the pupils "all deeply and seriously engaged in their various occupations", because every individual knew his place and his employment. Stowell suggested that all Douglas should see the school and have any prejudices removed. He feared that the full advantages were not yet sufficiently estimated. In August a selection from Handel's Messiah joined the usual charity sermon as a way of supplementing subscriptions, while the Advertiser lent its own backing, remarking on the benefits to Douglas visible in such a short time. By November things were sufficiently advanced for the Advertiser to announce that "the school for gratuitous instruction of Boys agreeable to Mr. Lancaster's plan" would be open in the New Room, Athol Street in January. The following month saw arrangements made for a girls school to occupy the vacated premises in Muckle Gate.

The official opening of the "Spacious new room" took place on January 19th, 1811, but more ambitious plans were soon in the offing. A February meeting of subscribers elected a committee, who by April announced their wish to have a purpose built school of their own to replace the rented rooms. John Moore of the Hills generously gave a site in Athol Street in return for the nomination of twelve boys to the school, and sold another plot for a ground rent of three guineas.[23] Even before the ground was formally conveyed on May 23rd, tenders for building were requested. The committee already had £200 towards "the erection of a building to belong for ever to the Charity", and with full details of the plans and costs open to public inspection in the present schoolroom, the corner stone of the new school was laid on June 4th. Over two hundred scholars in procession marched to the site, and the ceremony was witnessed by many ladies and gentlemen, despite the severity of the weather, according to the Advertiser.[24] The annual report of February 1812 stated that 51 had been taught to read, 114 to write and 60 to do arithmetic, as well as being "Trained as heirs of immortality". A great improvement in Douglas was noted, there being a general reformation in habits and manners, with the benefits of the school daily evident. The school was hailed as "most flourishing", and already 500 children had been educated in the school in its short existence. A small library of fifty books was given in 1812, and the fine new building, costing a total of £1,118.8.8 was opened on February 10th, 1813, with a public examination of the children taking place. The Advertiser noted the support for the school from all quarters of the Island. The Duke of Atholl himself paid a visit to the school and two medals were made from two pieces of silver he gave. In Hugh Stowell's Charity Sermon of 1813, he noted how the school "Attracted the notice and secured the patronage of the highest authority among us". While again stressing that the schools did not aim to raise children above the state of life to which they were called, but rather to make them "simple, humble and pious", he did allow himself to reflect as to what harm was done if some did rise in society, citing the example of the philanthropist Colston in Bristol. Although the education was free, children paid weekly towards buying a Bible in a scheme run by the Bible Association. To give to the school, he assured his hearers, was both a duty and privilege. Letters of approbation from satisfied employers of children from the school became a feature of the annual inspections. The school certainly reached the poorest classes of Douglas: an editorial in the Advertiser in 1818 remarked on the destitute condition of some of the children attending the Day and Sunday School.[25] In the same year the school was left its first legacy, £100 from Miss Jane Allen, and the money was used to purchase the annual ground rent, with the remainder helping to reduce the loan of £297 left from the expense of the building. A further £100 legacy the following year from Margaret Craine of Douglas enabled the remainder of the loans, on which interest at 6% was paid, to be cleared to a large extent, a surplus from subscriptions finally clearing the outstanding amount. The Committee expressed their great satisfaction with the efforts of the master, John Radcliffe, in June 1818, and again paid tribute to his "zeal and ability" the following year, when he retired.[26] How closely this was linked with his marriage in the spring of 1819 is not clear. An advertisement for a successor offered a salary of between forty and fifty pounds. While, of course, there was no quarterage to be added in a free school, there was a vast gap between this salary and that given to the parochial schoolmasters.

The Douglas School was very much a school of the Established Church, and its early description as a Lancasterian School seems quickly to have become something of an embarrassment, once the National Society emerged as the society for good churchpeople. Although there was no outward act of changing allegiance, the description of 'Lancasterian' was quietly laid aside after 1813, and the safer neutral title of 'Day and Sunday School' used instead.

The annual Charity Sermons were an effective aid to the schools' finances, raising on average between £40 and £50, while each annual report delighted in giving not only the total number of pupils years past, but also the total of those educated since the inception of the school. It was ruled in 1814 that all families on poor relief must send their children to the School, although these seem to have been a small proportion of the children. The same article in the Advertiser stated that 816 children had now been educated through the school, and there were 336 currently on the roll. Numbers fell towards the end of the decade, and stood at 206 at the time of Radcliffe's retirement in 1819, yet soon rose again under William Cain to around 300 in 1823. By 1820 the number of children educated had risen to 2,036, while the following year a rather fuller account than usual gave precise numbers of admissions and departures each year from 1810 onwards, together with an interesting analysis of the fortunes of the original boys intake of 141 in the first year of 1810. A very wide range of trades had been followed, many with a single representative from the school. There were 19 sailors, 17 labourers, 11 shoemakers and 9 joiners, with 8 deceased being the next largest group, a reminder of the uncertainty of life at that time. Also for the current year of 1821 the facts were given that of 119 boys in the school, 72 were destitute of shoes and stockings, although only 8 were from families receiving Poor House relief. (The number of girls stood at 137).

THE RAMSEY CHARITY SCHOOL

The new school had very quickly prompted attempts to promote similar schools in other towns on the Island. At Castletown at this stage there was but a brief flicker of interest. The Gazette in October, 1812, published a list of subscribers to the Daily and Sunday Charity Schools in Castletown, but thereafter came an ominous silence, not broken until 1820. Nothing seems to have been attempted at Peel, while at Ramsey early success was quickly followed by difficulties. On January 1st, 1812, a public meeting was called in Ramsey to consider the introduction of Dr. Bell's system of education, which had been found to be most beneficial. It was agreed to follow the example of the Douglas Day and Sunday School and form a committee, and to ask the Bishop to be the Patron of the Ramsey Charity School. The school would follow the principles of the National Society, and a copy of their resolutions would be sent to National Society headquarters. Ramsey thus from the outset avoided the stigma of being associated with the "wrong side". By April a room had been rented and a master engaged. The young man had been trained at the Douglas school, and the Advertiser reported in September that he kept seventy children in Ramsey in perfect order. The school actually opened in June with fifty boys as the first pupils, but the promising start lost its momentum. The advertisement of April, 1812, had warned that the expense of running such a school was considerable, and in addition to an annual sermon, the schools relied on annual subscriptions. In Douglas the arrangement was that a subscriber was entitled to send two children to the school for each guinea provided yearly, and a Life Member who donated five guineas or more nominated one child for each five guineas. Unfortunately for Ramsey, the novelty of being a subscriber wore off quickly in many cases. By April 1818 the schoolmaster was owed £20 in salary and some subscribers were three or four years in arrears with their payments.[27] An article in December warned that the annual subscriptions were entirely inadequate, the school was in consequence seriously embarrassed, and if there were not further contributions forthcoming, the school would "inevitably drop".[28] The annual sermons failed to generate sufficient support, often raising only in the order of £16-£17. (Among those appealing was the Rev. Joseph Brown, the failure from Castletown Grammar School). Even Bishop Murray himself in 1821 could do no more than raise £16. The venture seems to have ground to a halt, but following a meeting of subscribers in March, 1823, the Sun announced that the Rev. Thomas

Thimbleby would preach a sermon, and a collection would be taken to "re-establish the Daily and Sunday Schools". Although Thimbleby's eloquence drew only £14 from Ramsey pockets, a new committee steered the school to eventual success, despite some unjustified criticism of their management. "Observation", writing to the Sun in May 1825, wondered why a school which once promised the most flattering results was permitted to moulder into decay. If it fell into ruins, there must be a cause. The Bishop should see what money had been received, and how it had been applied.[29] "A Wellwisher" sprang to the defence of the new Committee, challenging anyone to see evidence of misapplication in the accounts, duly printed in the paper. These revealed that from December 1823 until March 1825, total receipts were only £62, from which annual salaries of £20 had to be paid to the master, J. Corlett, and the mistress — considerably lower than those paid in the sister schools at Douglas and Castletown. The Rev. George Parsons' sermon had been the least successful in melting hearts and opening purse-strings, realising only £8.14.6. The Advertiser in May 1826 expressed the desire to see the Ramsey school prospering like the one at Douglas, which enjoyed a munificent subscription list, and was in a flourishing state.

Despite these financial worries, in terms of educational provision the Ramsey National Schools were making a valuable contribution, and numbers rose steadily as years went by. From an estimated 80 in a return of 1822, there were 46 boys and 68 girls in 1827[30] and by 1829 the Advertiser reported 75 boys and 70 girls in attendance. The number of girls dipped in 1823 down to 42 as against 70 boys, but numbers reached new peaks at the end of the decade, with 87 and 85 in 1838 rising to 100 boys and 95 girls in 1839.[31] The school continued to be run economically; 1833 advertisements for a new master and mistress still offered only £20 each per year. (The following year saw the death of the young mistress, Elizabeth Bridson, aged only 18.) The system's promise of cheap and effective education for large numbers of pupils, impossible under the old methods, was certainly being fulfilled in Ramsey.

ANXIOUS TIMES IN DOUGLAS

Despite the reference in the Advertiser to the success and prosperity of the Douglas School, the Eighteen Twenties brought times of anxiety there as well. A survey of 1822 put subscriptions at the very healthy rate of £200 a year, but two years earlier a letter of praise from "A Sojourner" reminded readers of the Advertiser that money was still needed.[32] 1822 saw some notable visitors: in February the Duke of Atholl and his nephew paid a visit to the school, while in July, the Rev. Andrew Bell, D.D., the founder of the Bell system himself, preached the annual Charity Sermon on July 7th. It was perhaps a sign of the times that the great man himself only managed to raise £38.5.0., a significant fall from the average of the previous decade. The total educated rose steadily from 2,036 in 1820, to 2,421 by

1823, and past the three thousand mark at 3,095 by the time the Book of Charities was composed in 1827.[33] Following the unfortunate early death of the master, William Cain, at the age of 29, the advertisements for his successor showed no hint of crisis, promising that the salary would not be less than £50 a year. (The successful applicant, James Cretney, was described by the Advertiser as a printer by trade.) Yet the annual Sermon delivered by the Rev. Robert Aitken in 1826 raised a mere £23.16.9. The Committee attributed this poor showing to an ineffective address by Aitken, and their slight on his sermon brought about a rebuke from the editor of the Advertiser.[34] In his opinion, the sermon, published as usual for all to read and respond to, would stand any scrutiny. The Committee, nevertheless, invited the Rev. Robert Brown of Douglas Grammar School to make up some of the deficiency with a second Charity Sermon. 'Philomath', writing to the Advertiser, saw apathy as the enemy; it now required the utmost exertion of the few to stop the school from a rapid decline and fatal fall. He was, however, sure that the apathy was merely temporary rather than a real lack of generous spirit.[35] The numbers attending the school began to decline from a high point of 160 boys and 150 girls in 1827 to 120 of each in the years 1831-1833. While Margaret Gelling left £100 to the school in 1828, the Committee in the spring of that year held a meeting to consider the expediency of requiring a small weekly payment from the scholars. although it was hoped to lay out this money at the year's end in rewards. (Despite the visit of Bell himself, the early ambiguous position of the school remained: the Gelling legacy was to the 'Lancasterian School', while the Book of Charities stated that "The mode of instruction is formed on a combination of the plans of Dr. Bell and Mr. Lancaster.")[36] A letter from 'A.T.' in March 1829 went so far as to refer to the ruinous state of the free school, which needed sympathy and attention. Comparing the situation with that which prevailed in Scotland 'A.T.' was struck by the "extraordinary apathy", and, like Hugh Stowell before him, urged people to visit the school for themselves. The visit from Manchester of Hugh Stowell the younger as preacher for 1829 yielded £60 in collections, but this was only achieved through several sermons, including one preached in the South of the Island at Malew.[37]

The crisis was averted, and throughout the Eighteen Thirties numbers rose once more towards the three hundred mark. (The five hundred who paraded for the coronation of George IV and the Sunday School Jubilee in September, 1831, must have included past pupils for the Sunday School children were identical with those on the roll of the Daily School.) Generous praise in the Manx newspapers helped to keep the school before the public mind from time to time. The annual examination in 1836 so impressed Vicar-General Hartwell, according to the Sun, that he gave a guinea to buy buns for the children.[38] A Mr. J. Fell eventually joined Cretney as assistant master in the Boys' School, their combined salaries far exceeding the amount spent on any other elementary school in the Island.

A FRESH START AT CASTLETOWN

A decade after the abortive attempt to introduce a monitorial charity school at Castletown in 1810, a fresh approach was made at a meeting of potential subscribers in February 1820 to found a National School. A committee was formed with the Rev. Thomas Thimbleby as its secretary. The motive for the move was quite straightforward; — "The Respectable lament the state of morals of the lowest orders" — and believed the cure lay in religious instruction. A general meeting a month later decided that the school should be for those aged five to thirteen years. Months were spent searching for a suitable building, but two days after a committee meeting of January 3rd, 1821, was told of a suitable site in Malew Street, and a building 60 feet by 19 planned, it was found that the land was not available. Another year passed before other premises were rented for £12 a year.[39] Immediately Thimbleby was asked to advertise for a master and mistress at £40 and £30 a year respectively — not as well paid as the position at Atholl Street, Douglas, but far above the rates offered at Ramsey. The Committee prepared the ground carefully and refused to rush matters. All seven applicants who were considered on April 20th were rejected, and fresh advertisements placed. Of fifteen further applicants, three were interviewed, and the post awarded to Thomas Kewley, who was then dispatched to Douglas to learn the National System, returning with a certificate that he had been diligent and attentive there. A meeting of subcsribers on August 19th, 1822 gave the go-ahead, and a week late, on August 26th, 128 boys and girls met in a warehouse fitted up as a school. A December meeting of subscribers heard that only one boy had left, and that already there was good cause to be pleased with the results, although even better were to be expected as the system became more familiar. Over £35 had been received in subscriptions, and there was a government promise of four guineas for education of the children of the soldiers. Fitting out the warehouse with forms, desks, slates, books and other necessities cost £21, and stress was laid on the need for regular subscriptions.[40] Numbers rose sharply to 170, and by March 23rd, 1823, there were 132 boys and 101 girls receiving education. There was obviously a satisfactory relationship between the master and the mistress, Ann Stowell, as they were married in November, 1824!

As elsewhere promises of subscriptions were not always translated into payment. A hard line was taken against two gentlemen in October, 1822, who flatly refused to pay, and threats of prosecution were uttered. It was doubtlessly embarrassing for the Committee's secretary to have to write at the end of December, 1826, to both the Bishop and the Duke of Atholl that they were in arrears still for 1825! No legacies seem to have been bequeathed to the school, and the annual sermons raised only £20-25. The Committee were forced at their February, 1828 meeting to introduce a fee of ½d a week, payment to be noted in the attendance book, and raised to 1d in September. The Committee evolved their own system of providing rewards for diligent monitors, who were given tickets each week for their efforts. According to the number of tickets each possessed, the monitors shared every six months a pool of money made up of fines of one shilling which the Committee members paid if they missed a meeting without sending a substitute. Absence from Castletown was accepted as a valid excuse, although this was watered down from an original absence from the Island.[41] Attendance by the Committee seems to have been very good, as in December, 1828, the monitors received only 6d and the head monitor a shilling. Each month the school was examined by the Grammar School master, the Rev. George Parsons, who also provided the school with a number of books. At Christmas 1828 the scholars were pronounced as being "pretty proficient in their reading, spelling and catechisms". Despite the financial uncertainties, the school survived, and the Book of Charities noted that it educated 106 boys and 90 girls "on the Lancasterian system", the authors clearly not realising the heresy of using such a description under the heading 'National Schools, Castletown.'[42]

National Schools were now established, albeit somewhat precariously, in three of the Island's four towns, successfully educating greater numbers of children than any other type of school had ever done.

INFANTS' EDUCATION

The education of infants was yet another example of mainland influence being felt on the Isle of Man within a few years of its inception on the mainland. In 1816 as part of his experiment at his factory in New Lanark, near Glasgow, Robert Owen opened the first infant school in Great Britain, taking in children from the age of eighteen months. This was the logical inference from his belief that environment was all important, and therefore the right environment should be provided from the earliest possible time. ". . . by judicious training the infants of any one class in the world may be readily transformed into men of any other class.[43] The Utilitarians, James Mill, Brougham and Zachary Macaulay, brought Owen's ideas to London and founded schools for infants at Westminster and Spitalfields. The master in charge of Spitalfields, Samuel Wilderspin, published in 1823 a treatise 'On the Importance of Educating the Infant Children of the Poor', which led the following year to the founding of the London Infant School Society with the aim of providing schools for children aged two to six. Like Bell before him, Wilderspin travelled extensively, propagating his theories: "The great secret in training children was to descend to their level and become a child".[44] "The error had been to expect in infancy what is only the product of after years." Activity and play were considered most important, and he stressed the vital role of the playground in school life generally and for the development of the indivdual, calling it "the uncovered schoolroom".[45]

These new ideas spread very quickly to the Island, and a practical start was made under the Rev. Louis Genests as early as 1824, the same year as the founding of the London Infant School Society. The Advertiser reported the hiring of a room at Callow Slip for Douglas Infant School, which had 25 scholars up to the age of eight.[46] The school was under the auspices of St. George's Church and supported by the usual charity sermons, although the collections were distinctly more modest than those for the Athol Street Schools. Hugh Stowell, of Ballaugh, was the preacher in 1825, followed the next year by his son and namesake, Hugh Stowell, of Manchester. Numbers rose steadily from 60 in 1825 to 100 in 1829. The collection remained low at £6.4.0 in that year, but the Chaplain of St. George's, Benjamin Philpott, managed a more respectable £14 the following year. The only impact the school had on the papers of the time was through bad reporting. An indignant letter about the unjust dismissal of the mistress, Anne Kelly, in May, 1830, was soon followed by a letter from the lady herself, stating there was no truth in such a story and that she had left of her own desire! Her successor was reported to be a Miss Costain, but a later issue stated that Miss Costain in fact ran a different school altogether.[47] The annual reports showed some fluctuations in the age range admitted to the school. It was stated in 1826 that pupils between two and six were taken, but in 1831 the range had widened to between eighteen months and seven years. The increasing interest in education in the Eighteen Thirties saw a rise in numbers to 160, and as a consequence a second mistress was engaged.[48]

THE OLD PAROCHIAL SCHOOLS

With the new methods established in three of the four towns, and the Christian School at Peel receiving high praise from the House of Keys Committee in 1822, it became clear that the major weakness in Manx elementary provision was for the most part precisely where in theory lay its greatest strength, the old parochial school system. The cause of the weakness was to be found in totally inadequate salaries, and although this was pointed out every decade of the first half of the Nineteenth Century, virtually nothing effective was done to remedy the situation. Despite the growth in the funds available to those who handled the Impropriate Fund finances, the fact was that those who taught in the parochial schools around 1800 received a mere pittance for their pay, to which was added a quarterage unchanged since 1703, yielding a total which the manual labourer could easily surpass. 'Friend of Man' writing to the Advertiser in 1808 pleaded for an increase in salaries, and a reform of the parochial school system.[49] He referred to the extreme ignorance of the Manx peasantry, where few could decipher the contents of a book, and one out of a hundred could write. This was not irrelevant to everyday life as some thought, for without such basic skills the Manx would not keep up with developments in agriculture. Sometimes the post of schoolmaster was still combined with that of parish clerk, as in an 1803 advertisement for the Parish of Bride. The "sober and discreet person to act as Parish Schoolmaster and Clerk . . . must read well, write a good hand and be well versed in practical arithmetic . . . His defects as a sweet singer will be dispensed with, provided he has excellence as a schoolmaster to commend him".[50] At least in this case the schoolmaster portion of the dual role received priority. An Act of 1813 did manage to recognise that the quarterage from feepayers of 6d for reading and 9d for writing, "which allowance is found to be altogether inadequate in the Present Day" had to be changed, and the rate was altered to 2s.11d for reading and 3s.6d for writing. Yet nothing was done to raise the basic salaries, although it was well known that the clergy had been allotted money from the Impropriate Fund in consideration of their keeping an English school in each parish. If they no longer did so, should not the parochial schoolmasters be given an equitable portion of the fund? Despite the increased quarterage, 'Friend of Mann' felt obliged to return in 1814 to do battle for the schoolteachers once more.

> "The general condition of the parochial Schoolmasters in the Isle of Mann calls for commiseration. The pittance allotted to their subsistence is insufficient to procure the very necessaries of life. Their privations are numerous and often distressing. It will scarcely gain credit, though literally true, that in the most populous and opulent parish of the Island, the exigencies of the parochial schoolmaster are such that he has been hesitating whether he shall not exchange his office for the more productive employment of a day labourer, in order to procure bread for himself and his family".[51]

It was scarcely to be expected that in the Nineteenth Century a man of unblemished character and "no contemptible literary attainments", should be unable to supply his daily needs. Were parents such Goths and Vandals not to value education? "If we want competent teachers, we must furnish them in a competent subsistence". He pointed out that this was no isolated case. In the majority of parishes the present provision was hopelessly insufficient: quarterage was paid with great reluctance and very often not paid at all. Friend of Mann looked directly to the wealthy. Help must come to the parochial schoolmasters from those of rank and authority, who could unite to secure a sum for their schoolmaster and make the parochial schools respectable. It was obvious that Friend of Mann looked for the extension of the ideas of Bell into the Manx system, for he praised the Doctor as one who wanted light in all quarters.

This eminently sensible letter was quickly followed by one from 'XYZ', whose disdainful tone and arrogance would have done little to arouse the sympathy of the public. He announced that he was literally half-starved, but admitted to getting £25-£30 as a parochial schoolmaster. What clearly irked him was the fact that he could not live in the style of a gentleman, and that others obtained up to £40 a year for tutoring one boy, while he endured the toil of "teaching a hundred for this pittance", although he had been selected out of a dozen candidates, and was a match in learning for the parson himself. His attitude to the Impropriate Fund was lofty — five pounds would not make much difference to him, and he suggested that the schoolmasters were probably dependent "on the charity of the reverend corps" for anything from this source.[52]

Although the reference to a dozen condidates was doubtlessly an exaggeration, the letter does suggest that the posts of schoolmaster were not short of applicants, and that not all could be dismissed as devoid of learning. ('Friend of Mann' too, had paid tribute to the learning of his friend at Braddan).

'A Schoolmaster' replied in words suggesting that XYZ was most comfortable compared with the vast majority of parochial masters who certainly would not sniff at an increase of £5 from the Impropriate Fund, in which they most definitely had rights. XYZ had land to keep a cow and a sheep, whereas he had not sufficient even for a goose. Some sarcastic remarks about XYZ's desire to be an Archdeacon on account of his learning makes it likely that the identity of XYZ was known to the writer, although interestingly XYZ had criticised the parson's rigidity in insisting upon the teaching of the catechism.[53]

A week before 'A Schoolmaster' had his reply published, the Advertiser carried an announcement of potentially great import. The new bishop, George Murray, nephew of the Duke of Atholl, informed the public that "Dr. Bell's improved system of education is to be adopted through the Diocese", and that Marown Parochial School would be the first to adopt the new system. There were two important but distinct elements here: the first was the method of teaching, and the second was the method of supporting the schools by subscriptions, which would in effect give substance to the hopes of the 'Friend of Mann', that local people would support directly their own parish school. This pronouncement which promised so much in fact delivered very little. There was no instant widespread adoption of the monitorial method: over thirty years later the old methods were still being employed in some parochial schools. Also there was no attempt made at all to increase the parochial schoolmasters' salaries through a system of subscriptions as used to provide for the town schools. At the time of Dr. Bell's visit to the Island, the Advertiser published a letter regretting the way the improvements in educational practice had been spurned, and the monitorial methods thought to be merely an excuse for a schoolmaster being indolent. It had been Bishop Wilson's wish that all should have the benefit of learning, and the writer assured the parochial schoolmasters that the new methods would not hurt them.[54]

It may be recalled that the Atholl family were not over-pleased by the attempts of the Brougham enquiry into education, set up in 1818, to extend their researches to include the Isle of Man. The Bishop's reasons for instructing his clergy not to co-operate were published in April, 1822, by the Sun (Sun April, 1822), but by the autumn that paper was able to carry the results of the clergy's enquiries.

These parochial returns, eventually allowed by the Bishop to be given to the Select Committee of the House of Commons on the Education of the Poor, varied greatly from parish to parish in the amount of information given. Salaries, too, varied, with Jurby, Bride, Braddan and Malew having only £5 a year, yet with Lonan, Patrick and Andreas having even less at varying amounts between £4 and £5. Above this level were Ballaugh (£5.12.0), German (£6), Lezayre (£6.12.0), Rushen and Santon (£7.13.6), with Onchan at £9 topping the list. Quarterage was standard at 3s.6d, although at Ballaugh the entry clearly gives the lower figures of 2s.6d. The numbers given for the schools show an equal variation, although in any case they may often be idealised rather than strictly accurate. Lezayre with 172 claimed the highest total, this figure including those at a school for girls whose mistress received £10.16.1. Others over a hundred strong were Andreas (150), Michael (142), Braddan (100), and Marown (110), while at the other end of the scale were Santan and Onchan (40 each). As might have been expected, the most informative reply came from Hugh Stowell, now Rector of Ballaugh. He reported the schools in his parish as being the parochial school with an attendance of 80-90, but varying with the seasons, and a girls school of 40-50, whose mistress received a free house and 2s. quarterage. The master also had a small house and a glebe besides. The old law about free schooling for the poor seems to have died out in the parochial system in practice, as Stowell mentions, apart from the Sunday School, a school which he and his family ran themselves one day a week for poorer families who could not afford to pay for education. 40 to 60 pupils generally attended, and they were taught principally in the Manx language. This impression receives support from the observations of the Vicar of Onchan that the lower classes "have not sufficient means of education and are desirous of possessing them." Stowell's own remarks suggested that there was a shortage of means rather than provision which hindered the spread of education; "The poorer classes have not the means of educating their children within themselves, but the schools afford the necessary accommodations at present." Stowell was almost the only respondent to give his own name and the population of the parish according to the recent 1821 census. The recipients would be able quickly to ascertain that, leaving aside the Sunday School which had a summer attendance of 100-150, and a winter attendance of half those numbers, Ballaugh with a population of 1136 had a maximum total of two hundred children having some form of weekday education, a very respectable proportion indeed. His, too, was the only return which gave any indication of the method of tuition at the parochial schools: "The school is in a great measure conducted on the new system of education." In the towns the mention of the 'national school' speaks for itself, although there is also under German Parish a mention of a 'national school' apart from the Clothworkers' School. Only Ramsey gave a number of pupils at the National School (80), although the Braddan entry does give the total of annual subscriptions as £200 for the one at Douglas. The total number of pupils at 1870 excludes over 300 at the Daily and Sunday Schools at Douglas and Castletown and 850 in the private schools of Douglas (650) and Ramsey (200). No numbers were given, too, for the Clothworkers' School, and scarcely any mention made of the schools which had filled the gaps in the parochial system. With these factors taken into account the total number of pupils would rise to well over three thousand. On the other hand the numbers given by the clergy for the parochial schools are generally inflated to a degree where they would be balanced in their excess by a consideration of schools omitted, and some parishes did indeed still have no other schools other than the parochial school. It seems likely that the number of children in day schools was in total markedly lower than the number attending Sunday Schools, even allowing for some inflation in those numbers too, and that Stowell was perfectly correct in his observation "that education has been for the last ten years rapidly on the advance in the Isle of Mann, principally through the medium of Sunday Schools."[55]

A more sobre and realistic view of the schools is to be found in the Book of Charities, completed by late 1827, although not published until 1831. McHutchin and Quirk in their preface state that if all the charities are not correcty described, "we cannot reproach ourelves with any want of care in the preparation of it, having diligently applied all the time we could spare . . ." Some of the disparities are extremely marked, although in some cases the differences in numbers are to a certain extent narrowed when it is remembered that the 1822 return gave total numbers of pupils, whereas the Book of Charities gave an average number. Nevertheless, the falls in Lezayre from 172 to just 30-40, in Braddan from 100 to 20-30, Castletown from 75 to 16, Andreas from 150 to 50, and in Marown from 110 to 30-40 significantly alters the picture of the number of children receiving education. In Lonan, there was not only a fall from 80 to 40, but also a note to the effect that this was indeed the number on the roll, and the school was in point of fact badly attended. The Vicar of Lonan's neighbour at Maughold had been less prone to exaggeration: both surveys give a figure of 40 pupils. In one case, that of Santan, the 1822 total of 40 actually rose to 50-60.

The strange fluctuations between parishes in the 1822 returns regarding salaries disappear in the Book of Charities, where, apart from clearly recorded local legacies, the payments from the Impropriate Fund had been raised to £5.10.0, to which was added either the King's Bounty (worth, after deductions, £2.11.0 British), or the Lady Elizabeth Hastings Charity money (now worth £2.13.7 British), making totals of £8.1.0 and £8.3.7 respectively. Only Santan, having an extra £5 under the 1805 will of William Leece, and Rushen, with six small legacies (including the two from 1813 worth together £5.11.5 a year for Sunday School duties) totalling from all sources £15.5.11 to any great extent broke the pattern. In addition Bride continued the joint appointment of schoolmaster and parish clerk which brought in an extra two guineas to give £10.5.0. One puzzling feature compared with 1822 is the fall from its top place of Onchan, given in that year an income of £9, and with fees a total of £20 a year. In the Book of Charities only a small legacy bringing in 8s.7d. a year lifts it above the norm to £8.12.2.

By the figures in the Book of Charities, even taking the higher figure in the range of pupils' numbers, there were 772 pupils in the twenty parochial and petty schools which formed the original structure of the Seventeenth Century. Nine other more recent foundations increased this number by 337 (including the Clothworkers' School with 70) and the three charity schools at Douglas, Castletown and Ramsey had between them 590 pupils. No attempt was made to include the private schools, being outside the scope of enquiry into charities, but the total of the schools listed at 1699 undoubtedly reflected more accurately the actual state of Manx education than the 1822 figures. What also seems clear at this stage is that, as in England, there was still a large percentage of children reached by the Sunday School movement who were outside the influence of any type of day schools.

The small rises in salary for the parochial teachers did little to remedy the real problem faced in attracting teachers of ability. Letters to the local press again attempted to draw attention to the crisis in the parochial schools. For as other types of school advanced beyond recognition, the parochial schools scarcely moved. 'Anglo-Manxman' contrasted the improvements in the endowed, private and charity schools, which made these schools the equal to those in England, with the static nature of rural education in the parochial schools. The masters clung on the whole still to the old modes of teaching, were devoid of qualifications of any sort, including physical and moral, and all improvement was thereby retarded: "incompetency on the part of your parochial schoolmasters does to a considerable degree exist" as many testified. He tried to arouse interest by showing the relevance of education to agriculture in particular, pointing out how newcomers managed their lands and made profits where natives of the Island had dismally failed. The essential prerequisite of improvement was "better provision for maintenance of the teacher", for without this "no hope of a thorough reformation of plan can be entertained". He, too, appealed to Manx landowners themselves to give their financial support. If fifty gentlemen from each parish would give a guinea, and the non-subscribers pay an equivalent sum in quarterage, then able instructors of real talent could be obtained, and the return to the Island would soon be apparent.[56] Although there was often a lively press correspondence, the letters of 'Anglo-Manxman' from Liverpool provoked no reply at all. The sole other letter in the Manx newspapers on this topic was written in 1834 by 'An Old Schoolmaster' whose points could in many respects have been written twenty years before, and even more sadly twenty years later as well. On his salary of £8.3.0 and quarterage he could scarcely clothe himself, and often needed "other avocation" to preserve him from debt. His poverty checked him for realising his hopes for the education of his own children, and now even at this level of education, the parochial schools were being hit by competition from the private schools, and income from quarterage accordingly diminished. He trusted that the Governor and the House of Keys would do something to raise "the distressed and rather degraded state" of parochial schoolmasters, and that the Bishop and clergy would follow the lead of the House of Commons, at that moment discussing the pay of Scotch schoolmasters.[57] Apart from a letter to the Manx Sun from J. T. Cregeen about the lack of suitable residences for masters who lived in "wretched hovels", quoted in a previous chapter, citing the example of Ballaugh with wind whistling through unrendered walls, no other demonstration of interest was expressed in the press.

In the course of a squabble about the election of a Parish Clerk for Maughold, petitioners complaining of irregularities also thought the winning candidate was not qualified to be a Parochial Schoolmaster, and added "... should he be permitted to enter into the office of Parish Clerk your Petitioners and the rising generation would be entirely deprived of a good Schoolmaster as is there is not sufficient salary when separated from the Clerkship to induce any person of abilities to enter into the office.". Bishop Murray was asked to ensure that any Clerk elected would be a "competent Schoolmaster" and to examine the successful candidate, Robert Faragher as to his competence. The dispute was rather strange, as the petitioners supported one Robert Corteen, but there was already a serving Parish Schoolmaster, James Fargher, who indeed continued in his work until 1870.[58] It is interesting that no direct attack on Robert Fargher's ability as a Clerk is made, suggesting that something at least a little extra beyond bare literacy was now expected from parochial schoolmasters.

The masters themselves sent their Petition of Parochial Schoolmasters in June 1835 to the Crown officials on the Island, receiving the sympathy of the Agent, James McCrone, who thought them "a most useful Class of Society and equal to and above the parish Clergyman in laying the foundation of good morals ... here at least the remuneration is so small that it is impossible to expect that any well educated person would ever apply to being appointed to fill such a situation." He believed they had a fair claim for their case to be "brought under consideration of His Majesty's Ministers".[59] Yet even this useful support failed to bring about any improvement.

THE WORK OF BISHOP WARD WITH ELEMENTARY EDUCATION

While the plight of the parochial schoolmasters remained unalleviated, the provision of education outside the towns continued to improve. Bishop William Ward in particular helped to keep the Island to some degree abreast of the sheer growth in education which was a feature of the mainland in the early decades of the century. Henry Brougham, speaking to the House of Commons in 1820, stated that before 1803 "England might justly be looked on as the worst educated country of Europe". Only one in twenty one was receiving education before Bell and Lancaster's influence changed the educational scene. By 1820 the proportion was one in sixteen, or one in fourteen if the dame schools were included. The proportion varied from area to area as was only to be expected. A large percentage of children in Manchester and Liverpool had no sort of education at all, and brought the proportion of children in Lancashire as a whole down to one in twenty four, almost as bad as Middlesex, "beyond all doubt the worst educated part of Christendom" according to Brougham. On the other hand, in Westmoreland, a county which could more fairly be compared with the Isle of Man, the proportion was as high as one in seven of the total population — better than Brougham's target of one in eight. The number of children in English schools doubled between 1820 and 1834, according to Sir Llewllyn Woodward,[60] although a rising population meant, of course, that the proportions did not improve in a simple ratio. There was no way which the Isle of Man could match this startling rate of increase, but Ward, a keen supporter of the National Society from its inception, did his best.

Where Ward was very successful in the elementary sphere was when he managed to combine the needs of education and religion. Hugh Stowell had been sent early in his episcopate on a preaching tour to raise funds for new Manx churches, most of which were replacements for dilapidated buildings, but others new foundations. Both Archbishops gave £100, as did Ward himself, while Col. Wilks on the Island led the Islanders own response. Soon £4,000 was raised, and the services of John Welch, the architect of King William College, secured to erect nine new churches. Welch, if indeed the 'Stranger' who wrote the Six Day Tour of the Isle of Man, was rather caustic about his patron: "The secret of such surprising labour consists in keeping the begging bowl constantly on the move." Ward was particularly concerned with what he described as "the mountain districts", and his first venture was in Baldwin, where in November, 1834, he himself selected a site, choosing the place where the stones of old Keill Abban could still be seen protruding through the ground. Although primarily the building was to serve as a church for the seventy-odd families in the area, Ward adopted the interior plan he had utilized at King William College. Only the sanctuary area, easily divisible from the rest of the building by sliding doors, was consecrated, so that the remainder could be used as a school and thus subsidised by Government grants. From an economical point of view, especially in the country districts, this idea had much to commend it. Daughter Mary wrote of her father's glowing countenance following his hitting upon this idea, although this use of church as school was something to which the revered Bishop Wilson had been bitterly opposed, and whether a scheme of sliding doors would have satisfied Wilson's misgivings is open to question. The prototype of Baldwin was followed very closely at Sulby in the Parish of Lezayre and at Dalby in the Parish of Patrick.

In these last two cases, Ward managed to use his influence with his friends in the National Society to good effect, taking advantage of a radically new development in official attitudes towards education in England. Bills providing for elementary education on the rates had been introduced into Parliament by Samule Whitbread in 1807, and by Henry Brougham in 1820, the first of which foundered not only because of widespread suspicion of the effects of education but also because of the misgivings of the Established Church, while the second conceded so much to Church control that fierce opposition was aroused. Masters were to be from the Established Church, appointed by the Parish Vestry, but dismissible by the local clergyman, who indeed could veto the appointment, have unlimited right of entry and decided the curriculum. These abortive attempts was followed by a more thorough-going bill introduced in 1833 by John Arthur Roebuck, who proposed a cabinet minister should head education, run locally by elected school committees, and financed from endowments and taxation. Roebuck pointed out that France, Prussia and Saxony had systems of compulsory popular education, as, of course, the Isle of Man still had in theory. Although the Bill had little hope of being passed, the debate aroused by it led to a resolution "That a sum, not exceeding twenty thousand pounds, be granted to His Majesty, to be issued in aid of Private Subscriptions for the Erection of School Houses, to be issued in aid of Private Subscriptions for the Erection of School Houses, for the Education of the Children of the Poorer Classes in Great Britain . . ." This was the first Government grant towards education since a vote by Parliament in 1649, and in practice the money was paid over to the National Society and the British and Foreign Society, who used the money only where local subscriptions were equivalent to at least half the grant made. There were no regulations about standards for building, inspection or efficiency of instruction, save that the donating Society would undertake the maintenance of the buildings.

It has been seen that at this stage the National Society resolutely maintained that help from them to the Isle of Man lay beyond the scope of their charter. Furthermore preference in the giving of grants was shown to applications from large cities and towns, and for school with at least four hundred pupils. Nevertheless, Bishop Ward managed to obtain treasury grants not only for his new foundations but also for some of the old parochial schools.

The dating of the various grants in the 1887 list of Educational Endowments is not to be taken at face value, despite the official authoritative status awarded to this compilation. The datings for treasury grants contained in List IX under National Society grants and in List VIII under Parliamentary Grants are often contradictory. List IX allots nearly all the grants in Ward's episcopate to 1834, making a total of £727, well over 7% of a £10,000 grant to the National Society — not even Ward's influence went that far. List VIII for its part records a grant of 1832 to building works at Santon Parochial School from the Treasury, which, if correct, would be a historic landmark in the history of British Education, preceding the main grant of 1833 by a year, and giving a notable "first" to the Isle of Man. Scrutiny of the grant elsewhere reveals, however, that the correct date for this award belongs to 1851, nearly twenty years later. Nevertheless, for Ward to obtain £899 for the schools on the Island which he founded, rebuilt or repaired was quite an extraordinary achievement for a bishop whose see lay outside the domain of the British Parliament and the National Society. The highest grant for a new school was that for Dalby with £150, while the other church cum-school which secured a grant was Sulby with £100. In the parish of Rushen, the growing fishing port of Port St. Mary had £75 towards its school, for which an advertisement for a master was placed in the Sun in July 1837.[61] (The new schools did not offer very attractive salaries, but even so, Sulby, for instance, with £15 for both schoolmaster and schoolmistress, offered twice the amount obtainable from most of the ancient parochial schools.) In the Parish of Malew, the inland area of Grenaby had £50 towards its school (the salary there was only £5), in the Parish of Lonan, Laxey Glen £38, and the Dhoon area of the Parish of Maughold £44. No less than seven of the ancient parishes thus had schools provided by Ward for their remoter areas.

This amazing old man, who was already sixty five when he came to the see in 1827, still had energy to spare for improvements of existing schools. Lord Teignmouth once referred to his "comprehensive plan originally proposed, of reviving the parochial schools which are for the most part lamentably neglected."[62] Archdeacon Philpott's Visitation Questions of 1833 to the clergy included not only whether they had Sunday Schools, but also whether they paid attention to the fabric and conduct of the parochial schools. Question 11 asked if the schoolhouse were sufficient, "and is it whitewashed frequently, well ventilated and kept in good order and repair? Do you visit it frequently and take account of the improvement of the children? Does the master discharge his duty faithfully according to the terms of his subscription and appointment?" Although the questions were standard, the answers from the parishes varied greatly in the amount of useful information given. Many clergy provided terse and cautious answers, while Robert Brown, at Braddan, wrote a scrawling hand over many pages. Edward Craine, at Onchan, provided possibly the most cautious answer of all, when he thought the school "may be sufficiently ventilated." Quite a number of the schoolhouses were felt to be too small. At Jurby it was described as "insufficient", the incumbent explaining how they were trying to build a new school on his glebe, "in every respect more convenient". Maughold also was too small, and Onchan "not comfortable". A couple of parishes mention how the situation was eased by other petty schools within the parish. Otherwise wrote the Vicar of Lonan, his school would be "scarcely large enough". Robert Brown too said there would be insufficient room if it were not for a school at the Strang, run by "a very superior master", and "very numerously attended". Brown lays claim to having two Parochial Schools in Braddan, probably including East Baldwin as the second school. Other parishes such as Rushen, Santan and Marown felt accommodation was sufficient, while the Vicar of Patrick wrote with such warmth that he muddled the numbers of the Archdeacon's questions. "The Schoolhouse is more than sufficient for the parish, having been enlarged, which enlargement and the disputes consequent have brought the parish to much needless expense and infringed on the unalienable property of the Vicar." He mentioned four other petty schools, each having as many scholars as the parochial school, Glenmoij, Ballelby, Booinane and Foxdale. The provision at the parochial school was thus adequate for the area it could reasonably serve, a point picked up by William Gill at Malew when he commented upon the parochial school at Ballasalla. "It is sufficient for that part of the Parish for which children can attend."

The odd man out was the Parish of Arbory, where the Rev. A. Gelling reported that "There is in this parish no schoolhouse of the kind mentioned by this query.", the parish school being kept in a normal house.

Most incumbents were reasonably happy with the condition of the buildings, verdicts ranging from "tolerable repair" at Michael, "in good order" at Braddan and "kept in very good order and repair" at Marown. Few mentioned the whitewashing, Gill at Malew proffering "occasionally whitewashed" for the Archdeacon's "frequently", and the ventilation received few specific remarks. The most trenchant remarks on the subject came once more from Mr. Stephens at Patrick. "The school-house is ventilated often too well by an almost perpetual breaking of windows, for which there is no remedy but a better discipline of the children at school, as well as of idle boys in the neighbourhood."

Only the Vicar of Marown answered the question about frequent visiting by the clergy with assurance. His "weekly, or oftener" was replaced by most of his colleagues with a word of extreme vagueness, namely "occasionally". The Vicar of Rushen avoided embarrassment by refusing to distinguish between sufficient accommodation, state of repair and his own activities by making one single "Yes" suffice for all. One very unexpected "occasional" visitor is the Rector of Ballaugh, Hugh Stowell, whose devotion to education was beyond doubt, but who gave the most perfunctory of replies to Philpott's questions. Was there possibly some degree of resentment, quite understandable, at the elevation to the position of Archdeacon of one who had only recently come to the Island? Gill at Malew stated he visited often, although he took no written record of progress. In view of his later genuine interest in education, his word may indeed be accepted, but a large question mark hangs over the claim of the Rector of Bride, John Nelson, that he visited "frequently".

With his report of repairs being undertaken to the schoolhouse, frequent visits and the faithfulness of the master, it would seem that all was well at Bride. Yet in December 1836 it was alleged that Mr. J. Cowle, schoolmaster at Bride for thirteen years, had not attended the school for three or four years, preferring instead to act as overseer of the highways. Ward duly asserted his authority and cancelled Cowle's licence to teach .[63] While the general tenor of replies to the question about the master's discharge of his duties was to the effect that "I think he does", at least two replies indicate the difficulty experienced in procuring suitable teachers. Stephen's comment on lack of discipline at Patrick has already been quoted. He continued with "The master has lately undergone a public trial. I am happy to say that he is more diligent than formerly. He was appointed by the Bishop . . . The scholars are seldom or never taken to church, their parents having no care about them, or authority over them." Stephens also commented on the private schoolmasters of the area, whom he named as William Ellison and John Quirk at Dalby, and John Corris at

Glenmoij. "The masters follow in general no occupations excepting that Mr. Ellison lets tythes and Mr. Quirk breaks stones by the roadside. They are in a general way moral. Their qualifications are sufficient for their situations." At Malew, the parochial master until 1812 had been the Rev. John Gell of sea-faring fame, who had at least received advanced education at Douglas Grammar School until he was twenty[64] but the master at the time of Philpott's visitation was quite unsatisfactory. "He is competent" wrote the Rev. William Gill, "to instruct the children, but not to maintain the active discipline of the school, being disabled in his limbs. The school is not in a flourishing condition, but I think he performs the duties of it as well as he is able. He is said to have been addicted to drink, and there was formerly too much ground for the report, but for upwards of 12 months I have not known any instance, nor do I believe that one has existed, of his being intoxicated." The pupils were taken to church but by the Sunday School teachers — the master could not do so.

Ward took as much care as he could to secure masters of the right calibre. When Malew at last fell vacant in 1835, the successful candidate was William Cowley, later to be the Island's most famous teacher at elementary level. He had been a pupil of Dodds at Peel Mathematical School, and first began teaching at Cronk-y-Voddy, attracting at the start only one pupil, but soon building up a favourable reputation. John Caine of Cronk-y-Voddy furnished a good reference, noting that Cowley did not resort to any harshness or cruelty. In addition, Cowley was carefully examined by Gill in the presence of Hugh Stowell, who gave written testimony concerning Cowley's favourable impression. Gill for his part, commented on Cowley's promise, but due caution was exercised by appointing him initially only for a probationary period of one year.[65]

With regard to the fabric of the parochial schools, there was not sufficient money to attend to the needs of all those felt to be inadquate. The most obvious need was for Arbory to be provided again with a proper schoolhouse like the rest of the parishes. A site was obtained and a modest building measuring thirty feet by eighteen was erected with the help of a treasury grant of £50. Most of the other parochial schools which were too small had to wait for several decades for alteration or replacement. The exception was the Archdeacon's own parish of Andreas, for which no formal return was made in 1833 by Philpott as incumbent to himself as Archdeacon. Here in the north of the Island, the old parochial school was replaced with a new building on the Archdeacon's glebe. The vestry vote of 1832 was not put fully into effect until Tynwald gave its sanction in 1836, and only in August 1836 were the authorities able to place an advertisement in the Sun announcing the sale of the old premises. A treasury grant of £72 was obtained towards the building of the new school.

In the towns new premises were found for the National Schools at Castletown and Ramsey. The Castletown Committee at their neeting of February 4th, 1834, were acquainted with the Parliamentary grant of

£20,000 in a letter from the Bishop, and resolved to take advantage of this, especially as the present building was not sufficiently large. Yet it was well into the following year when James McCrone, the agent for the Crown, sent the Governor minutes of a meeting which had considered a site for the proposed new school, which had Crone's own backing.[66] A month later followed a Petition from the people of Castletown, asking for a plot of land (34 yards by 20), near the bridge for a school. McCrone commented that he could see no possible objection", the land could not be applied to a better purpose. The Crown on January 18th, 1836 consented to the use of the land, with the proviso that if ever there were no school on the site, the land would immediately revert to the Crown. (Strict implementation of this condition would cause considerable embarrassment for the Parish of Castletown who now use the buildings as their parish church and hall). The deed of sale was made out in the name of John Kelly the High Bailiff of Castletown, the old and rather curious name for a piece of land, 'Castletown Lake', indicating its proximity to the inner harbour waters. The new Committee which took over in January 1836 had first to raise five guineas to pay for the title deeds, before they proceeded to issue a subscription list to match the grant of £90 obtained from the Treasury through the National Society.[67] By May, 1837, the Committee were able to place advertisements calling for tenders for the new school in the Manx papers[68] and a year later the coronation of Queen Victoria on June 28th was marked in Castletown by the laying of the foundation stone. Before the school moved to its new premises, there was a certain tightening up in the management of the school. Then neighbouring clergy at King Williams College were asked to be visitors of the school, and an attendance book was to be carefully kept, with the threat of dismissal from the school following on shortly in the case of certain named boys, unless their attendance were better. By the summer of 1839, the Advertiser reported that there were now 270 children at the school.[69] One feature of interest in the Castletown situation was that there alone existed one of the old parochial or petty schools alongside a new National School. In the parishes the old schools eased smoothly into being National Schools as they took advantages of the grants of Parliament given through the Society; in Douglas and Ramsey the old petty schools had long been transformed primarily into grammar schools before falling into decay. But in Castletown the Book of Charities records the petty school there still being carried out in 1827 by Thomas Cubbon with sixteen pupils, some years after the National School was opened. At one stage the pointlessness of running two general elementary schools led to the fading out of the old petty school, and the releasing of its income from the Royal Bounty and the Impropriate Fund to the younger institution. When exactly this place the writer has failed to discover. The National School Log Book rather surprisingly notes only the time when the method of payment was changed, the money now going to the Committee of Mangement whereas before it went directly

9 The National Schools of Douglas and Castletown

10   Episcopal enthusiasts for education
Bishop William Ward

Bishop Yowler Short

11 Ramsey around 1840

12 Douglas around 1840

to the master. Possibly the silence concerning the petty school in Pigot's Directory of 1837 is significant, when Thomas Kewley and Isabella Joyner are listed as being at the National School, but as neither school received a mention in the 1824 Directory when both were in certain existence a certain caution must be exercised.

A similar provision of the permanent building took place in Ramsey for the National School there, the Parliamentary Grant providing the higher amount of £155. A little belatedly, Castletown and Ramsey thus joined Douglas in possessing purpose built schools for elementary education run on the new monitorial lines.

Ward was very concerned to increase the provision of churches for the town of Douglas, where he estimated that four thousand members of the Established Church had no place to accommodate them, and made an attempt to rectify this situation with the building of a new church dedicated to St. Barnabas, not far from St. Matthew's Church, in 1823. The Sun carried an advertisement for a clerk and schoolmaster in its issues for November, 1832, but educationally the new church's chief interest soon lay in its provision of a purpose built infant's school.

The first incumbent of the new church (built with the Irish population of Douglas in mind, according to 'The Stranger') was Dr. Carpenter, a man much like Ward in his drive and energy. Among his other foundations in the parish were the House of Industry and the Widows' House.[70] In 1837 a school at first primarily for infants was opened at a cost of £500 in Cattlemarket Street.[71] The first charity sermon raised the excellent sum of £60. Two years later, the earlier existing infant school associated with St. George's Church also invited tenders for a new building in Barrack Street, but here again it was apparently Dr. Carpenter who was the driving force.[72] The new schoolroom was opened in March the following year with room for over two hundred pupils. The Advertiser reported that many infants had already been admitted.

The Douglas infant schools now looked to Scotland for their inspiration regarding teaching methods. A Glasgow merchant, David Stow, had founded in 1826 the Glasgow Infant School Society, and after contact with Samuel Wilderspin, eventually in 1836 began to train teachers at his Glasgow Normal Seminary. Stress was laid on the teacher's role in stimulating and awakening thought, and one device used was that of giving verbal pictures. The aim was that the child might "Perceive as vividly by the mental eye as he would real objects by the bodily eye." The mechanical monitorial method was condemned for failing to achieve mental and moral development of the young child.

(One curious feature of the Douglas infant schools was the fact that the one connected with St. George's, the place of worship for the wealthiest people in Douglas, paid its two mistresses a combined total of only £27, while St. Barnabas managed to pay £40 to its two teachers.)

SCHOOLS OF INDUSTRY

Even Mrs. Ward played a part in developing the variety of education offered in the Island by introducing to a number of areas the concept of the 'School of Industry'. In 'Reflections on the Education of Children in Charity Schools' the philosopher, John Locke, had advocated as early as 1697 that "working schools be set up in every parish, to which children of all such as demand relief of the parish, above three and under fourteen years of age, whilst they live at home with their parents, and are not otherwise employed for their livelihood by the allowance of the overseers of the poor, shall be obliged to come". Almost exactly a century later, William Pitt proposed that such an idea should become the law of the land. While this did not come into effect, the same year saw the foundation of the Society for Bettering the Condition and Increasing the Comfort of the Poor, which, in addition to such things as soup kitchens, savings banks and friendly societies, sought to spread schools of industry, where the sale of what the children produced covered the expenses of the schools and provided the children with meals. In some of the experiments in the late Eighteenth Century, the pupils even earned a small wage from their sewing, spinning, shoe-making, gardening and sundry other activities.[73] The 1809 Report of the Society showed that 20,336 of the children in receipt of parish relief attended such schools, a proportion of just under one in nine of the total of 188,794.

In the Island something of the same type of specialised school had already been established by Catherine Halsall in Castletown under her will of 1758, and by Jane Qualtrough of Kentraugh in the Parish of Rushen, where an advertisement of 1803 invited applications from women able to teach Reading, Sewing and Knitting, and offering a 'good house to live in' — a perquisite that a number of parochial schools could not offer.[74] Further advertisements of 1807 and 1811 reveal that the place of residence was also the place of tuition, and boasted four rooms. The salary was £8 a year, provided for after 1810 by a bequest of £100 in Miss Qualtrough's will of 1810.[75] But in addition fees were mentioned, showing quite clearly that this school cannot be put under the class of a school of industry, even if the subject matter was much the same.

It needed the arrival of Mrs. Ward before Schools of Industry proper were introduced into the social life of the Isle of Man, the first reference in the press being an announcement in the Advertiser in July, 1829, that a bazaar was to be held in Mrs. Dixon's Assembly Rooms, and a report a month later that over one hundred pounds had been raised.[76] The Manx Schools of Industry seem to have been confined to girls. An editorial in October, 1829, explained how the School of Industry for females of the lower order who could not afford to pay for instruction would be taught how to sew, knit and read. (On the mainland, while there would be always religious instruction provided, reading was in many cases considered an unnecessary extra.) The initial £109 raised was divided among six areas — Douglas, Braddan, Peel, Ramsey, 'the North', and German with Patrick. Thereafter funds were provided for the schools by sales of work, presumably by the pupils themselves, held from time to time. The role played by Mrs. Ward is revealed in the Rev. Thomas Stephen's Visitation reply of 1833, where he refers to the Patrick School of Industry under Miss Halsil, "founded by Mrs. Ward, the wife of the Bishop'. (The salaries paid were a modest four pounds a year.) Although directed towards a small minority of the population, these schools were a well known feature of the Eighteen Thirties. Their aims were extremely modest and belonged more to the fields of social engineering and economical local thrift than to any educational sphere of future import, but show again the increasing influence in Manx affairs of mainland movements.

Ward's episcopate had seen notable advances in education. Outlying areas of parishes had been provided with new schools under the National Society, where either there had been none before or parents had relied on private ventures, liable to be unsatisfactory, or ephemeral, or, most likely, both. In the towns purpose-built accommodation had been provided for the National Schools in Castletown and Ramsey, and an Infant School in Douglas. Ward had done what he could to help the parochial schools, although much remained undone. Perhaps most important of all, the wealth of the English Government had been tapped for the benefit of Manx education. 'The Stranger' marvelled at Ward's industry, commenting that many might have got immortality by half the amount of beneficial labour. "Strange to say, this ecclesiastical Hercules, who sows churches and ministers over the country like Deucalion would sow teeth, is scarcely thanked for what he has done." He might well with justice have replaced or supplemented the word 'churches' with 'schools'. Poor Bishop Ward's final months were spent in trying to prevent the annexation of the diocese to that of Carlisle, and his efforts finally succeeded in having this measure (which had already passed through Parliament), removed from the relevant Act. Sadly he died before the news of victory reached him. The tribute of Edward Wilson, preparing to go to Bath from King William's College, was justly deserved. "Poor Mona! She will not soon look upon his like again."

Ward's plans, however, continued to inspire imitation even after his death. J. T. Cregeen, writing to the Sun in November, 1838, thought that Cronk-y-Voddy, in the north of the Parish of German, needed an arrangement like that provided for Baldwin, Dalby and Sulby. There were thirty families lacking schooling, in an area long neglected, and he called on Bishop Bowstead to secure aid from 'the British Church Fund'. His claim of "Long neglect" was not really justified, as William Cowley had only left his school there for Malew Parochial School three years before. Nevertheless, his pleas did not fall upon deaf ears, and the new body, the Committee of the (Privy) Council for Education, gave £48.10.0 to supplement donations of £81, enabling a new school to be built in 1842.

A NEW DIRECTION FOR THE CLOTHWORKERS' SCHOOL

By 1840 the Philip Christian School in Peel had ceased to be the model of efficiency which had impressed the House of Keys Committee sixteen years before. Bishop Pepys, newly appointed as to the diocese, informed the Clothworkers' Company that the school was dilapidated, too small and very inefficient. The Vicar of Peel, John La Mothe Stowell, formerly of Douglas Grammar School and King William's College, declared in October, 1840, his intention of erecting a new school.[77] The probable reason for the timing of this decision was the news communicated by the Clothworkers' on September 12th that their letter contained the sum of £48, which was from now on to be the new annual sum from the rents of Lovell's Inn. £38 was for the school, and £10 for a pension for Thomas Quine. Initially, however, the Company made it clear that they were trustees only of the endowment, and disowned any interest in the erection of a new building. Pepys decided that the new school to be should be run in connection with the National Society, and proceeded to look for aid. A plot of land was donated by Edward Moore Gawne of Kentraugh, and in acknowledgment of this generosity, Gawne was elected as a Trustee at a public meeting at Peel on January 12th, 1842, together with the new Bishop, Thomas Vowler Short, Stowell as Vicar of Peel, the High Bailiff, Richard Harrison, and the churchwardens of German. There appears to have been some tardiness in claiming a Treasury grant, as a letter warned that it would be cancelled if not claimed by October, 1841. The National Society itself again explained that it could not make grants to the Isle of Man without being in breach of its charter which confined its financial aid to England and Wales.

The site was formerly conveyed on February 15th, 1842, on condition that £30 should be put aside for repairs. (Gawne, himself, laid down that it should be lent at 6% to William Kewley of Peel, but 5% would be accepted if the interest were paid within the month due.) As the whole of the Clothworkers' £38 was going to the master's salary this was a wise move, showing that some of the lessons of the past were being learned.

The Declaration of Trust signed on March 29th, 1842, stated that the school, to be known as 'Christian's National School' would be conducted "upon the principles of the National Society". The important effect of this was to change the school from one which had no official religious affiliations at all as far as denomination was concerned into one which was unequivocally Church of England. There was no mention at all of the Christian Endowment to avoid legal complexities.

The foundation stone was laid by Bishop Short on July 26th, 1842, and, conforming to the current Whitehall requirements of six square feet a pupil, had room for 165 pupils. It was hoped that this would meet requirements for many years to come. Some embarrassment was occasioned when the old premises were sold for £90, but the legal conveyance of 1688 could not be found for the purchaser so that he might show a good title to the property. The cumbersome solution was for the Vicar and Wardens to apply for an Act of Tynwald enabling them to convey the premises; this took until 1846 to effect, although the money was paid promptly at the time of the sale. With the Treasury Grant of £100 and income from the Clothworkers' Company of £130, the sale of the old school helped to cover most of the costs of the new buildings, estimated in 1843 at £352. There was an eventual debt of £53, towards which the Company made a gift of £20. The amount was not great, but the step was significant, for it marked a shift from the Company acting only as trustees of the endowment towards becoming again generous patrons of education in Peel beyond their legal duty. The new school was opened on June 27th, 1843, under William Cowley, whose leadership was to make the Peel School the outstanding example of elementary education on the Island.

OTHER DENOMINATIONAL SCHOOLS

During this period too, the Methodists felt moved for the first time to provide day schools, though whether as a natural progression from their Sunday Schools or deliberately to balance the National Schools is not clear. Although the Island had two official circuits as early as 1792, Methodists held a dual allegiance for decades, just as Wesley had intended, and continued to do so for some considerable time after English Methodists had broken completely with the Church of England. Lord Teignmouth observed that the Manx Methodists were the most regular communicants at the Church services.[79] Yet towards the end of Ward's episcopate, the town chapels for the first time began to hold services at times which clashed with those of the Established Church. As was to be expected, the town of Douglas was the location for the first venture, undertaken by Thomas St. Chapel and its daughter church at Well Road, opened in 1837 to relieve pressure. Well Road was used as the site for the boys school, under S. B. Moffatt as master, while Thomas Street served for the girls school under Mary Ann Hodgson, and the infants under Mrs. Watkins. The time between the decision to open (June 16th, 1841) and the actual opening date (July 19th) was short indeed, but as the chapels already had flourishing Sunday Schools in their basements, there was little that needed to be done in the way of setting things up for a day school, and certainly no delay caused in finding sites or premises. Luckily the Thomas Street logbooks of the Sunday Schools have survived, and in the early years provided information about the days schools too. The Infants School met in Thomas Street vestry until they were moved into a large room under the chapel in 1844, and took children up to the age of six. The rules drawn up asked for fees of a penny, or twopence if the child could write, only from those who could afford them, and insisted on clean and neat appearance. Pupils had to attend a place of worship, but there was no insistence that it should be Well

Road or Thomas Street Chapel. As usual, a ladies committee helped the general committee with girls and infants, giving instruction in sewing, and meeting with the general committee each quarter. Subjects to be studied included English Grammar in addition to the three 'Rs'. Holidays were a fortnight in the summer and at Christmas. Although the schools did very well in respect of numbers, numbers at the girls school and infants being given are 114 and 101 in 1843, they soon ran into financial difficulty, just as the National Schools in the towns had done. Debts mounted to £61, and the Committee sought to reduce the deficit by canvassing for more subscribers and by members going to the schools each Monday in the hope that some non-payers might be shamed into doing so.[80] But the same meeting suffered the embarrassment of receiving a request for an increase in salary from Moffatt, who had to be fobbed off with a promise to help as far as funds allowed. Two months later all children were to have their cases before the Committee to see if they were able to pay; if they could, they would be charged according to their time in school already. In March, 1844, Moffatt's extra five pounds was discussed, but put off for a further period of time, causing him to write a letter in which he pointed out that he was engaged with the distinct promise of a five pounds increase after a year if he gave satisfaction and the school prospered. He had given service for three and a half years, while the school had prospered and increased. (Moffatt clearly interpreted "prospered" as referring to numbers, while the Committee undoubtedly thought in financial terms.) School pence had brought in but £10 a year until the last six months had raised the sum to equivalent to £13 per annum. "In conclusion I am persuaded that every reasonable individual will consider £30 or £33 a year a very inadequate remuneration for discharging the arduous duties connected with such a responsible situation." Once again the Committee merely deferred to their next meeting — but the minutes of that meeting on May 30th made no reference to Moffatt's claim at all. It is unlikely that Moffatt ever secured his promised five pounds, for two years later his successor, Thomas Dewsbury wrote a similar letter, although in more wistful vein. He had been promised £40 a year, and he would like it to be fixed instead of having to wait for an increase in numbers. He was happy but underpaid; "I should like a little more encouragement." The November meeting, perhaps mindful of having lost Moffatt, agreed at their November meeting to his request, but did not make it official until their meeting of December 7th, in the meantime hinting that Dewsbury would find their decision satisfactory. Exactly how satisfactory he found it is not clear, for the next mention of Dewsbury came when, to the Committee's disapproval, he handed in his resignation at very short notice on June 2nd, 1847. Although as will be seen, £40 a year was well above the average for the Island, it was clear that competent masters were not likely to be satisfied with such salaries, while those who were satisfied were unlikely to be men of calibre. The point was perfectly illustrated by consequent events. John Morrison, a chapel member with a long connection with the Sunday School, was appointed on the same terms, first attending the school to improve in the system of teaching, and then in July being engaged for a month or six weeks' trial. (The same was arranged for Mrs. Watkin's successor, Ann Kneale.) The change was disastrous for Well Road, for by September numbers had plummeted so badly that total extinction was threatened. Even the Sunday School had collapsed and the Committee meeting of September 22nd felt no option but to give notice to Morrison, as a "change in mastership was unavoidable". Both sides were probably relieved when on October 8th, Morrison requested permission to leave immediately without working his three months' notice.

The pattern of public schooling in Douglas was also enriched by arrival in town of 'Kelly the Roman'. A local notable, Major Taubman, had given a site in 1814 to Fr. McPharlan, whom he had met in Ireland in 1798, and the Chapel of St. Bridget was built there, but not until the arrival of John Kelly with Fr. Gahan in 1823 was any serious educational work attemptd. A school was built the following year, a very mixed establishment apparently for Protestants as well as Roman Catholics, for all ages, with fees often paid in kind.[81] By 1836 the Roman Catholic community was strong enough to purchase a theatre, St. George's Hall, and convert it into a church, with the basement, just as with the Methodists, used as a school for Mr. Kelly. (A year later there was excited talk of a Jesuit College being built in the Island, but in the event it was established in North Wales and called St. Beuno's.) Kelly remained as master for many years, and his school, St. Mary's, was notable for the broadness of its curriculum.

There were thus some exceptions to the steady advance of Church schools, but only in and around Douglas: not until the Eighteen Sixties were non-Church schools founded successfully in any of the other towns. Thomas Street with Well Road and 'Kelly the Roman' school were very much the exceptions which proved the rule.

BISHOP SHORT — QUANTITY OR QUALITY?

Ward's successors, Bowstead and Pepys, were translated to the sees of Lichfield and Worcester respectively before they were able to make any significant impact on the educational scene of the diocese. However, the episcopate of Thomas Vowler Short (1841-47) was of major long-term importance, for it was during his tenancy of the see and owing to his interest that the Island's education was bound to that of England by new links which remain to this day.

Short had a very real interest in education, and much of his address to his clergy in the Island's Convocation was devoted to the subject. Before the development of the tighter links with England which were to lead to the eventual solution of the problem of schoolmasters pay and motivation, Short first looked to his clergy, as had Barrow and Wilson, insisting that they superintend the whole of the education of the parochial schools, and rebuking them for any failure to visit them. He warned that if they failed to keep a hold of the masters, it might take years to recover the lost ground. It was essential to win their hearts. (It was Short's explicit presupposition that the clergy could carry on education in all branches to a higher degree than could the master.) Part of the clergy's task was to turn information received in the schools into true knowledge, otherwise there might be many facts learned, but minds not opened. Short was well aware of the limitations of the monitorial method, unless it were properly followed up, and how it could merely be "An species of mechanical instruction, which is communicated by unenlightened teaching."[89] An appendix to his address, while basically on the running of Sunday Schools, revealed what Short had in mind, the continual asking of questions, both to enable the pupil step by step to grasp as far as possible by this method what the master wished to impart, and also to ensure that it was thoroughly digested. He returned to these themes in 1845. While he had no desire to return to the system whereby the clergy themselves were the masters, they should be the inspectors and superintendents of the schools. (This insistence on the supervisory role of the clergy explains the role given to them in the Act of 1851, to be discussed shortly, in an Island where the Methodists were now in a majority of among the population.)

Short seems to have had grave doubts about the wisdom of the policy of "filling in the gaps" in the country parishes, so enthusiastically undertaken by Ward. Having more schools assuredly did *not* mean that educational standards would improve. He much preferred to have just one good school in each parish, where all the neighbourhood would be educated, and a reasonable master retained. What had happened, however, was that land had been given and schools built in various parts of parishes, so that areas which could really only maintain one school, had several. Quarterage would give a good income in a populous neighbourhood but this was not the case in the Isle of Man in many parishes, and the building of local schools exacerbated the difficulties. For "a master who is fit to keep a good school, can elsewhere obtain a tolerable remuneration, and will not stay here unless he be tolerably paid." With more than one school per parish "the bodies of master and minds of children are famished and unfed . . . The people in general do not sufficiently value education to pay adequately for it, and in many cases the education offered to them is so bad as not to be worth paying for."

Undoubtedly, Bishop Short's distinct lack of approval for "Filling-in" explains why, compared with the Eighteen Thirties, there were so few ventures in providing remoter areas of parishes with National Schools. Apart from the establishment of 1842 of Barregarrow in the Parish of Michael, the only exception was the school founded at Foxdale, built in 1846 with the help of a Parliamentary grant of £100. The Foxdale School was almost a fortuitous by-product of the desire of the Rev. Benjamin Clarke of St. Mark's to build a separate schoolhouse

PRIVATE ELEMENTARY SCHOOLS 1820-1850
Very few of these schools covered the whole of the period. Standards would be generally very low, although at their best, such as at the Strang, these schools could form a valuable supplement to the 'official' schools.

for his chapelry. Faced with the task of collecting local contributions in the usual manner to balance his parliamentary grants, he displayed his initiative by casting his net as far as Liverpool, calling in December 1843, upon Mr. North, one of the owners of the Foxdale Mines, to seek contributions. The visit caused North to write to Bishop Short, stating that he now realised that property owners of all descriptions had duties as well as rights, and offered his help to the diocese. (Short appears to have been embarrassed by Clarke's ventures abroad, and wrote a marginal note that he must tackle Clarke "as to his going on begging.")[83] At first the help offered was directed towards pastoral rather than educational needs. Short suggested a Curate for Patrick would be welcomed, but the company proposed grants for three chapels of ease instead. A survey of miners revealed that Clarke had very few in his St. Mark's area, and even they were Wesleyan Methodists, and it was agreed in 1844 that a school or small chapel near Foxdale waterfall would be the best way to help the mining areas. In the meantime the existing schools would be helped in the Parishes of German, Malew, Marown and the Chapelry of St. Mark's to the extent of £100 per annum. The Bishop would divide the money between the schools, who received their portions on condition that free education was given to the miners' children.[84] The method adopted was for the various schoolmasters to send in their bills to the bishop for education given, the bishop then paying them directly. By August, 1845, a church for Foxdale had been ruled out as impractical, and attention narrowed to the selection of a suitable site for the proposed school. Distances from the various mines were carefully worked out, and a site considered to be eligible and central was selected by Short in consultation with two clergymen, Holmes of Patrick, and Christian of St. John's, at a meeting on September 4th, 1845.[85] The formal approval of the Mining Company was sought, and the piece of land at Ballamanagh purchased from Hugh Clucas of Peel for the nominal charge of five shillings, his only condition being the right to nominate four children to be taught free of charge.[86] The new school was, of course, to be carried on according to National Society rules. The Company gave £200 towards the erection and support of the school, but the royalties paid out by the Isle of Man Mining Company to Her Majesty's Commissioners of Woods, considered to be a possible source of further help, were not successfully tapped, despite a letter from the Rev. William Christian asking for aid. Nevertheless, the result of the Rev. Benjamin Clarke's initiative or impudence had been the first example on the Island of the co-operation in education of the industrial and commercial world, apart from the ancient link of the Clothworkers Company and Peel.

Two petitions from around this time give support to Short's general position doubting the wisdom of extra schools, unless like Foxdale, they were sure of adequate financial support. From the Parish of Lezayre, John Killey, schoolmaster of the Dhooar School asked Short for his aid, and his plight made even the parochial schoolmasters appear well off. The school "at the Dowa", in a very proper and convenient place for a School-house" according to the will of the donor, John Kneale, in 1813, had as its sole source of income, apart from quarterage, the interest on fifteen pounds left under Kneale's will. (He had actually left ten but given instructions that the money should be left to accumulate for ten years to increase the principal.) The Book of Charities noted the money had not been paid to the Vicar and Wardens of Lezayre as laid down, but mentioned Charles Howland as master there.[87] A letter from the Vicar, Henry Maddrell, once of Ramsey Grammar School, written in November, 1827, mentioned forty boys were taught at the "Dhooyer school",[88] but Killey's petition claimed his quarterage never exceeded five shillings a week, and the endowment was "quite inadequate to afford his subsistence"; neither had he the benefit of a house to live in. The Captain of the Parish and the four churchwardens vouched for the truth of his story. In similar vein, John Cawley of Sulby, told of the plight of the teacher at Kelly's Mountain School, where it was not possible for a qualified person to live on the five pounds from the Kelly lands. Apart from one Elizabeth Baunare, who had given general satisfaction, those filling in had not "been adequate to the wants of the children", and the school much neglected. Although the petition bears no date, it was again probably Short who was expected to conjure up an improved income, as the two petitions seem to belong to each other. (Dissatisfaction with masters was, of course, by no means confined to the non-parochial schools; the people of St. John's reacted to the news that they were to be among the recipients of the Mining Company's £100 a year by planning to raise a fund to pension off their Mr. Carrule if there were a prospect of obtaining a good master with the aid of the new income!).

Short's episcopate saw the end of the Royal Bounty for the parochial clergy, whose livings were now up to £150 a year. It was decreed from Windsor in December, 1842, that after the present incumbents left their livings, the Bishop should have the Royal Bounty at his disposal to help provide for the other clergy in the diocese. However, care was taken to insist that the schoolmasters who received payment under the Royal Bounty should decidedly not be deprived of their traditional income. Yet while Short could prevent the masters' situation being made even worse, there was no easy way to improve their lot, much less conjure income from nowhere to provide for remote underfunded schools outside the main parochial system, and not under the National School umbrella.

The Bishp had to accept the fact that extra schools had been built, and the financial problem of masters' salaries had no immediate answer he could provide. He therefore aimed at a quiet revolution rather than draconian measures. If he came across a master who was old and inefficient: "I have no right to turn him out, merely because he is inefficient.", yet he would not waste time on anyone who was not trying. His aim was to influence standards through the power of example. If the towns and threequarters of the parochial schools could be made efficient then a better tone would gradually spread to the rest. He stated that he had been trying already to improve existing schools, "trying to render those schools where I found tolerably efficient masters more efficient". If people would contrast the efficient and the inefficient, they would grow dissatified with the latter.

Educational reformers spread their methods partly by allowing others to see them in action. Lancaster's school in Borough Road has already been mentioned. Other famous early Nineteenth Century examples were Robert Owen's school at New Lanark, used not only for children's education, but also for evening classes and as a social centre for employees, and Thomas Wright Hill's School at Hazelwood, with its strange system of penal marks being collected for good work, which could be used to pay fines for bad work. Short wished that he had something similar to offer as a model school for others on the Island to copy, although, of course, he was offering no radical proposals himself. "I do not yet know of any school which I could exhibit as a pattern. There are several which are very respectable, but they are all wanting, either in instruction or method". He confessed that it was an uphill task to persuade schoolmasters that system and methods were vital.

Yet while there was no model school to train young masters, Short felt that progress had been made — "something of system has been introduced into all the schools". The use of questions to soften the mechanical harshness of the monitorial system had been generally adopted in the schools. Many had begun to use the class books of the Christian Knowledge Society and most were using maps and slates. (Short was actually too optimistic concerning these last matters, as a survey was shortly to reveal.) Despite his earlier reference to very bad schools, he was reasonably satisfied with the improvements in standard: "on the whole, the majority of them are carried on, on a better and more enlightened plane, though they are still far from perfection."

It was up to the clergy to see this progress was maintained, otherwise the schools would fall back into the "old do nothing routine". They were to ensure that the schoolmasters set down on paper their plans, and then carried them out. This would be the cure for the great want of system on the Island. A combination of frequent visiting and intelligent questioning would establish if real learning were taking place, and the scope should not be limited to religious subjects only. Short challenged his clergy, the great majority of whom were Manx natives, to demonstrate their patriotism through education which would determine the place of the Manx in the wider world. Ireland produced only labourers to occupy posts of drudgery, while Scotland "sends forth her sons to occupy stations of trust and emolument", their excellent education depriving Englishmen of these positions. Where in the order would the Manx take their place? The education given them on the Island would be the deciding factor.

Part of the system which Short wished to see employed was the accurate keeping of records. Even for the Sunday Schools he urged the keeping of Entrance Books, School Absence Books, and Class Absence Books. In his 1846 Convocation Address he stressed the importance of keeping statistics in general parochial life, including finding the proportion of those children who attended school in the parish compared with the population as a whole, and an all-Island survey was undertaken the following year.

CONCLUSION

By the middle of the Eighteen Forties, the provision of education at elementary level was very much superior to that of the start of the century. The number of places lacking easy access to a school had been markedly decreased, and in the towns the adoption of the new monitorial methods had enabled the numbers on the rolls of school to reach heights with which no single master using the old methods could have hoped to cope. Even if the movement was not quite the pioneering force it was on the mainland, the introduction and subsequent popularity of the Sunday Schools meant that a fresh emphasis was put upon the importance of being able to read the Scriptures. Despite some faltering starts, the notion of regular local subscriptions helping to aid building and maintaining town schools had become an accepted part of everyday life. The earnestness of Ward and Short contrasted strongly with the indifference shown by the Bishops since Hildesley towards education. Not only had the Island greatly benefitted from the grants given by the English treasury, but real encouragement had once more been offered to ministers and masters to apply themselves with renewed diligence.

Yet the reforms suggested by Short, while commendable in themselves, failed to tackle the root cause of weakness in the elementary system of the Isle of Man, which Short himself had diagnosed as well as others before him. The careful keeping of records, and the most diligent supervision by the clergy of the schools would still not attract men of ability and talent to teach in Manx schools unless something was done about their salaries. Internal encouragement might help the standards of the schools to some degree, but for a long term solution it took an invitation to England to reveal "a more excellent way".

RERENCES

1. H. C. Barnard, *A History of English Education*, p10.
2. *Ibid*, Feb. 7 1833.
3. *Northern Star*, May 6 1843.
4. *Manks Advertiser*, Oct. 10 1802.
5. *Ibid*, Feb. 19 1803.
6. *Notes for Autobiography*, AMW 221A.
7. *Manks Advertiser*, July 5 1821.
8. *Ibid*.
9. *Ibid*, Jan. 9 1823.
10. *Sun*, July 22 1824.
11. *Manks Advertiser*, March 29 1829.
12. BC 133.
13. *Sun*, Oct 11 1831.
14. *Advertiser*, Sept. 14 1830.
15. *Ibid*, March 31 1829.
16. Eric Midwinter, *Nineteenth Century Education*, 27.
17. Andrew Bell, *Experiment in Education 1809*, 62.
18. *Hansard*, July 11 1807.
19. Corston, *Life of Lancaster 1840*, 11.
20. Brian Simon, *The Two Nations and the Educational Structure 1780-1870*, 36.
21. *Manks Advertiser*, July 7 1810.
22. *Ibid*, Nov. 29 1810.
23. BC 116.
24. *Manks Advertiser*, June 8 1811.
25. *Ibid*, Feb. 2 1818.
26. *Ibid*, July 18 1818.
27. *Ibid*, April 30 1818.
28. *Ibid*, Dec. 28 1818.
29. *Sun*, May 18 1825.
30. BC 97.
31. *Manks Advertiser*, July 16 1838.
32. *Ibid*, Aug. 31 1820.
33. BC 119.
34. *Manks Advertiser*, Aug. 3 1826.
35. *Ibid*, Sept. 9 1826.
36. BC 119.
37. *Sun*, July 21 1829.
38. *Ibid*, Aug. 8 1834.
39. *Minute Book of Castletown National School*, MS 5668 **March 9 1822**.

40 *Sun*, Dec. 24 1822.
41 *Minute Book*, Aug. 4 1828.
42 BC128.
43 Robert Owen, *First Essay on the Formation of Character 3*.
44 Samuel Wilderspin, *On the Importance of Educating the Infant Children of the Poor*, 1823, 44.
45 H. C. Barnard, *Op. cit.*, 60.
46 *Manks Advertiser*, Sept. 2 1824.
47 *Ibid*, Oct. 26; Nov. 2 1830.
48 *Sun*, Oct. 7 1836.
49 *Manks Advertiser*, April 30 1808.
50 *Ibid*, April 30 1803.
51 *Ibid*, Dec. 17 1814.
52 *Ibid*, Jan. 18 1815.
53 *Ibid*, Feb. 4 1815.
54 *Ibid*, July 7 1822.
55 *Sun*, Sept. 28; Oct. 5 1822.
56 *Ibid*, Nov. 8 and 15 1833.
57 *Advertiser*, July 2 1834.
58 Hi William and Constance Radcliffe, *A History of Kirk Maughold*, 117.
590 MS 1980C June 25 1835.
60 Sir Llewellyn Woodward, *The Age of Reform 1815-1870*, 478.
61 *Sun*, July 14 1837.
62 Lord Teignmouth, *Op. cit.*, Vol. II, 251.
63 *Sun*, Dec. 16 1836.
64 *Advertiser*, March 14 1812.
65 Documents in private possession of Cowley family in Peel.
66 *Letterbook of James McCrone MS 1980*, June 11 1835.
67 *Castletown National School Minute Book*, March 8 1837.
68 *Sun*, May 19 1837.
69 *Advertiser*, Aug. 6 1838.
70 H. S. Hitchen, St. Barnabas Church, Fort Street, Douglas, *Centenary Souvenir 1832-1932*.
71 *Advertiser*, March 8 1837.
72 *Ibid*, May 7 1839.
73 H. C. Barnard, *Op. cit.* 8.
74 *Advertiser*, June 18 1803.
75 BC 132.
76 *Advertiser*, Aug. 25 1829.
77 MD 612 L/CVI Oct 18 1840.
78 *Ibid*, L/CIV.
79 Lord Teignmouth, *Op cit.*, Vol.II, 254-55.
80 *Thomas Street Sunday School Log Book*, Sept. 28 1843.

81 Rev. William Dempsey, *Pages from Manx Catholic History,* in 'Cathedral Record' Liverpool, March 1952, 88.
82 Bishop Short Convocation Address 1843, 11.
83 MD 612/13/1 Dec. 8 1843.
84 *Ibid*, 13/2.
85 *Ibid*, 13/11.
86 *Ibid*, 13/24.
87 BC 87.
88 MD 612 12/1.

CHAPTER TEN

ELEMENTARY EDUCATION 1847-1869
THE LEGACY OF JAMES KAY

In 1847 took place the most important single visit to the Isle of Man as far as education was concerned in the Nineteenth Century, for with him the Rev. Henry Moseley brought to the Island new ideas which would transform the standard of education and the status of the teacher both in the short and long term.

The source of the ideas was Dr. James Kay (1804-77), who after working as a doctor in the slums of Manchester had concluded that the real key to progress lay in education. Appointed as Assistant Poor Law Commissioner in 1835, he paid particular attention to the education of the poor, both in Britain and on the Continent. As a result he was invited to act as secretary to the newly formed Committee of the Privy Council on Education, set up by the Crown in 1839 "for consideration of all matters affecting the education of the people" and in particular "to superintend the applications of any sums voted by Parliament for the purpose of promoting public education." A letter from Lord John Russell in February 1839 mentioned that "among the chief defects yet subsisting may be reckoned the insufficient number of qualified schoolmasters, the imperfect mode of teaching which prevails in perhaps the greater number of the schools".[1] Apart from considering whether to make annual grants to the training colleges of two Societies, the new Committee or Board would "determine whether their measures will allow them to afford gratuities to deserving schoolmasters; there is no class of men whose rewards are so disproportionate to their usefulness in the community." From other legislation of the times the Committee borrowed the Inspector, whose role was partly to ascertain that grants given had been properly applied, but also embraced "a more comprehensive sphere of duty", including encouraging further local efforts, offering assistance to schools which did not receive public grants, and submitting reports on the state of particular districts as regards educational provision. By a Concordat of August, 1840, appointments of Inspectors were made in respect of National Schools only in liasion with the two Archbishops, and all reports were sent to the Archbishop and local Bishop as well as to the Committee.[2] Special emphasis was laid on the need for particular care to be taken about the children's religious development.

The Isle of Man, although independent of the Westminster Parliament, had received Parliamentary grants and formed part of the Province of York. In 1847 the Rev. Henry Moseley, M.A., F.R.S., who the previous year had been sweeping in his condemnation of moral degradation among the comparatively wealthy workers of Staffordshire, arrived on the Island to make his "Report on the Parochial Schools in the Isle of Man". The timing was fortunate as he was able to bring with him details of the newly sanctioned scheme for apprentice or "pupil teachers", the regulations for which had been approved as recently as December 21st, 1846. Earlier in 1838 Kay had secured a government grant to run a poor-law school in Morwood, South London, based largely on Fellenburg's 'Poor School' at Hofwyl in Switzerland, but also incorporating the use of "pupil teachers" whom he had seen at work in Holland and by whose use he aimed to get rid of what he called the "monitorial humbug" of the Bell and Lancaster methods. The long term aim was to provide schools with properly qualified teachers. The pupil-teachers' scheme was one way which he believed would benefit not only the teachers of tomorrow, but also the teachers already in the schools.[3] His ideas were accepted in principle at a meeting of the Committee of Council on Education in August, 1846, and the framing of suitable regulations put into motion.

Moseley's Report recognised the fact that the recent Minutes of the Committee would not, as he politely phrased it, have been generally circulated in the Island. He listed the factors that caused failure in education in the Isle of Man as elsewhere — inadequate knowledge on the part of the teacher, want of skill or zeal in imparting knowledge, inability of any teacher to cope with excessive numbers, and a lack of favourable public opinion regarding education among the labouring classes. Although addressed to the Lords of the Committee of Council, his report was clearly in reality for the Island's own consumption, the main points of Kay's scheme being carefully explained.

First was the encouragement of serving teachers with the chance to increase their salaries by as much as £30. A public examination by two of Her Majesty's Inspectors would, if successfully attempted, entitle the teacher to a Certificate of Competency, graded in three classes. Proficiency in Religious Knowledge, English Grammar, Geography, History, Arithmetic and Book-keeping, together with a knowledge of the elements of Mechanics, Geometry, Algebra, Mensuration, Land Surveying and Levelling would be expected. Each master was to submit the notes of a lesson, as it would be delivered; to give an account of the organisation of his school and its methods of instruction; to write an essay on some subject connected with the art of teaching; and to give a lesson in the presence of the Inspector, examining the children in the subject matter of the lesson. The list of subjects might appear daunting, but Moseley recommended simple guides and text books for some of the more abstruse subjects. While all would need a good knowledge of Scripture, including detailed knowledge of a Gospel, those in Church Schools would be expected to be thoroughly acquainted with church doctrine and the Catechism. As success would lead not only to a certificate, but more pay, self-education on the part of the masters would be encouraged.[4]

Further incentives were linked with the pupil-teachers. A master would receive £5 each year for training one, £9 for two, £12 for three and £3 per pupil-teacher thereafter. But the teacher must demonstrate to the inspector that he himself could pass the yearly examinations for teachers before he was allowed to take on any apprentices. In this way pupil-teachers would be prepared only by teachers who were preparing themselves.

The pupil-teachers themselves would be aged between thirteen and eighteen, respectable and healthy from disease or defect of limb. (The popular link of the lame and the schoolmaster, so damaging to the profession, was to be proved to be no longer applicable.) Candidates had to satisfy their clergyman as to their moral character, and the Inspector as to their knowledge. The requirements were fluent reading, neat writing, the ability to work out sums from dictation, some knowledge of geography, the analysis of parts of speech, and (if Church) a knowledge of the Catechism. All were to teach a junior class to the satisfaction of an Inspector, but girls in addition had to be able to sew and knit.[5] Once accepted, their subjects would be as their masters. (Moseley omitted to mention that their hours of instruction would be seven and a half a week, while they themselves would instruct for five and a half hours a day.) At the end of a pupil-teacher course, for those successful in obtaining an exhibition or "Queen's Scholarship" there would be paid maintenance at one of the training colleges, or Normal Colleges as they were called. The trained teacher would receive from the committee additions to salary when appointed to a school under inspection, amounting to £30 in the case of a teacher who had enjoyed three years of training. This would apply, however, only if the school provided a rent-free house and a further salary, equal to double the grant, and if the master kept his school efficiently and was of satisfactory character and conduct, including attention to duties. The government sought to help both "the future race of teachers" and those already engaged.

A master who worked his way to a First Class Certificate would earn an extra £30, and with three pupil-teachers his salary would rise by £42 — a very considerable financial inducement to make the best of himself, and at last offering real hope of curing the state of affairs in which

"No person, really qualified for the office of schoolmaster by moral character, mental energy, amiability of temper, and proficiency in all the elementary branches of education, together with aptitude in imparting knowledge, will doom himself to the worst paid labour and almost the least appreciated office to be met with in the country."[6]

Although these words were actually written of Welsh masters, they could be equally applied to the Isle of Man. Nevertheless the statement in the standard history of the Isle of Man by A. W. Moore that "judging by the report sent by the Rev. H. Moseley to the Committee of Council of Education (sic.) the state of education in Man was still far below the English standard"[7] is completely unjustified, Moseley's Report saying nothing of the sort. Perhaps Moore did not appreciate the extreme novelty of the ideas brought by Moseley, and assumed that the scheme of certificates for teachers, of pupil-teachers, and the financial incentives that went with them, was widely used in England, the Island having fallen behind the times. Indeed Moseley was very impressed with the progressive attitude concerning education enshrined in Manx Law. Since 1703 the Isle of Man had had on its statute book the legislation the English reformers were trying to attain: "The principle of 'State Education' appears to have received a legal recognition in the Isle of Man." Moseley was almost taken aback by such provisions as compulsory education, free tuition for the poor, charges fixed by law for those who could afford to pay, control of masters so that no-one could teach "whose qualifications have not been duly ascertained by a competent authority, and who has not been duly licensed, and the legal requirement that "a school shall be built and maintained in substantial repair, in every parish by assessment on the inhabitants." He concluded that "... The state of things which I have described is, in some respects, remarkable."[8]

Apart from this favourable framework for education, Moseley was further pleased by general attitudes: "there is a public opinion generally favourable to education, as well among the industrial classes as among the farmers." — a far cry from his experiences in Staffordshire. The majority of parochial schools were attended "by small Farmers and Tradespeople, as well as by Labourer (sic.) children." parents were keen, while the Manx children were "singulary apt, quick and intelligent, and fond of learning". A similar state of affairs had been found in Wales, with praise given for "natural ability and capacity", retentive memories, shrewdness "in catching an idea", and appreciation of education, although the teaching itself was dreadful and, to the fury of a nation, the Welsh language was blamed for alleged widespread immortality.[9]

Moseley believed that in the Isle of Man, given the advantageous framework of laws and attitudes, the only possible reason for education "falling short" must be "administrative neglect". The falling short lay not in comparison with England, but with the Island's own potential. The real cause of weakness, as obvious to Moseley as to others, lay in the low salaries paid to schoolmasters. yet in this era of self-help, the new scheme of incentives already outlined was designed to augment local effort, not to supplant it. A master could only earn his lowest level award of £15 if he were paid twice that sum from local sources. With some Manx masters earning only £12 a year, considerable improvement would have to be made to bring them up into a range where they could start to earn their increases by merit.

Moseley suggested two main reforms to achieve this end. The first involved action by the Island authorities, so that as well as providing a parochial schoolhouse as by the laws of 1704, they would provide a residence for the master. This too could be made a condition before the state would pay any augmentation. It "would constitute a perpetual endowment of the schools" if an act to this end were passed. Secondly the fees or quarterage last fixed in 1813 should be amended by a further enactment. Moseley did not favour payment per subject, which he felt tempted a master to cater chiefly for those who took most subjects and ignore those who took only a few and would pay little. Far better, he felt, to ask parents to pay a higher quarterage dependent on their station in society. He commended the system employed at King's Somborne in Hampshire, where farmers and tradespeople paid either ten or six shillings a quarter, and labourers paid between a penny and fourpence each week. By this means, in a rural parish of a thousand souls, no less than £124 was raised. Whatever they paid all the children received equal instruction. He felt sure that there would be no objection to a higher quarterage if a better education were assured. Once the salaries were raised sufficiently to attract qualified teachers, any failure in education, given the Manx educational framework, would be "Inexcusable".

The current state of affairs, even if nowhere compared unfavourably with the mainland, where the problems were as bad and probably worse, was very mixed. Moseley divided up the teachers on the Island into three groups. There were "no doubt some who are to be considered in every respect qualified for the office". He intended to return the following year to examine candidates for teaching certificates as well as prospective pupil teachers. Others could render themselves qualified if suitably motivated and encouraged in course of time, but a third group no motive could elevate. As it was, of the body of masters on the Island, "a large proportion are, I fear, to be considered inadequately instructed." In his work, Moseley had the aid of "A Satatistical View of the State of Education in the Isle of Man" furnished by the teachers to the Committee of the Isle of Man Educational Library earlier in the year.[10] This large printed sheet set out particulars of both Day Schools and Sunday Schools. Fifty two Day Schools replied to the request for information, and in column form was set out the name of the school and its teacher, the number of boys and girls, the numbers taught reading, writing, arithmetic, grammar, geography, history, composition, book-keeping and mathematics, the quarterage charged for each of these subjects, the salary, fees per annum, total income of the school, the number of children in the parish or district who attended no school, the number of families who could not afford to pay, the system of teaching, apparatus used and finally whether the teacher was wholly or only partly dependent on teaching. Fourteen declared that they were not dependent on teaching for their livelihood, but for differing reasons. Mr. Hudgeon of Quine's Hill, Braddan, claimed the independence brought by a pension of 10 pence a day, three pursued other occupations, while three others admitted they were obliged to follow other work. Miss Carran, of a Port St. Mary private school, kept a small retail shop, while the rest just declared themselves "not dependent on teaching" without further detail. Twenty two stated they used monitorial methods, some with a mixture of old methods too, while two claimed to follow the Glasgow method. The use of monitors did not, of course, automatically mean that a school was of a higher standard than one where they were not used, especially where numbers were low. More significant was the fact that exactly half of the 52 used no apparatus at all. Twelve used a blackboard, and twenty two made use of maps, including Mr. Thomas, of Glenmaye, who had only one map, of the Holy Land. With the exception of Miss Harrison of Balladoole, those who had blackboards also had maps. Andreas Parochial School and the Taubman School in Castletown were the only schools to have a globe. Four schools, all in the Douglas area, boasted two teachers. By far the highest income for any one school belonged to Douglas National School for Boys (£75), the salaries of the two masters, Messrs. Cretney and Fell. In the Castletown National School Mr. Kaye received the total annual income of the school £48.1.6. Of the old parochial schools, still with a basic salary of only £8.3.0., Malew received £25 extra in fees, totalling over £33, while Onchan seemed the lowest with only £13.3.6., (Jurby had no entry in the fees column at all, and no total income figure was given either.) Only six of the schools totalled over £40 a year, and four more exceeded £30. Thus only ten schools had a salary level at which the master would be eligible to receive government augmentation under the Privy Council Committee scheme. Eight schools did not even reach the level of £10 per annum. The average charge for reading was 1/- a quarter in Douglas, and 2/- outside Douglas, with an average of 2/- for writing and 4/- for arithmetic. Far and away the dearest school was one in Kirk Michael, (not the parochial school) with charges of 7/6d for reading and writing (each) and 10/- for arithmetic. No total was given, but the number of pupils was only thirteen. About twenty schools claimed to teach geography and slighty fewer history, although only Miss Gawne of Knocksharry, German, made any charge for doing so (2/6d for history). Seven schools offered book-keeping and eight mathematics, but the advanced nature of this work was reflected in the fees, apart from a school in East Jurby where Daniel Caley charged a moderate 2/6d a quarter. Mr. Cannell, at Andreas Parochial School, charged a full 15/- for mathematics, with the rest between 4/- and 7/6d., except for Mr. Teare, of Ballacross, in the same parish who charged 10/- for both book-keeping and mathematics. Interestingly four parochial schools — Braddan, Kirk Michael, Malew and Andreas — were among the schools offering these specialised subjects. However, to offer subjects was one thing; to have actual pupils was another. Mr. Cannell, of Andreas, with his high charge was the only school to have children studying mathematics, six in all, while the only pupils actually taking book-keeping were ten Douglas Roman Catholic boys at school under John Kelly. This school offered in fact the widest range of subjects for a mere penny a week.[8]

From the fifty two schools who made their returns, certain relative conclusions can be drawn, although sadly as a complete picture the Statistical View was spoilt by the large number of schools who did not co-operate. Twenty nine were named, together with the teachers, in a footnote, "besides a number of other Daily and Sunday Schools whose conductors could not be prevailed upon to furnish returns." No day school returns were offered by any school in the parishes of Bride, Marown or Maughold, although the Primitive Methodists in the last two places gave Sunday School returns. The Rev. G. S. Parsons, of Castletown Grammar School, and the Rev. E. Qualtrough may well have felt a little affronted in being asked to furnish statistics with elementary schools. The total number of schools on the Island vastly exceeded the eighty one mentioned — as has been seen earlier, there were dozens of private schools in Douglas alone, but not a single one featured either in the fifty two or the twenty nine. Where this survey is useful is in giving a rough guide as to proportions. Of the total numbers in the list of fifty two, boys outnumbered girls by 1,387 to 981. Tuition in reading (2,038 out of a total of 2,752), was twice as common as tuition in writing (1,193), or arithmetic (1,004), Geography (623) was studied by more than History (250), Composition (193) or even Grammar (309). Teachers earned roughly 60% of their income from salaries (£342) as opposed to fees (£255).

Another disappointment lay in the small proportion of those among the fifty two who essayed to answer the questions of how many children in the parish or district attended no school and how many families were unable to pay for the instruction of their children. No less than 34 contended themselves with "Not ascertained". In the cases where an attempt was made, the extent of the District was not clear. Did, for instance, the district of West Baldwin include or exclude the school of Mr. Callow at St. Luke's, Baldwin, who failed to send in a return? The answer would make a large difference in estimation of the proportion of children who did not attend school. With clearly defined boundaries the two returns mentioning the parishes were more helpful, together with Castletown. The masters of Lonan and Michael estimated that 100 and 200 respectively had no schooling, while the three Castletown replies concurred that 200 was the figure for their town, almost equalling their total of 206. However, this figure did not include Castletown Grammar which would include a goodly proportion of local boys, and Miss Finigan, who we know from the Book of Charities was the mistress of Catherine Halsall's School, with 40 scholars in 1829. When the private schools are taken into account, of which there were five in Pigot and Slater's Directory of 1843, the number not attending school there would be well under half the total. Similarly in Lonan the two schools sending returns totalled only 130 pupils, but there was no return from the National School under Mr. Cannon. Michael with 73 scholars only to balance 200 not attending and apparently no other schools left out would appear to be the exception, although it may be recalled that Mr. Cowen's fees were the highest on the Island for basic subjects. In Douglas, eight schools sent returns totalling 848, and without counting the private sector, another 250 at least might be added for St. Barnabas Girls School and the Wesleyan Boy and Girls School, judging by the returns of the other departments of these schools. With the population of Douglas somewhere between the 1841 figure of 8,647 and 1851 of 9,980, even the Island's largest town, where the rapidly growing population might easily outstrip the supply of places, showed a respectable proportion of the population attending places of education. It had been the belief of the Select Committee on Education of the Poorer Classes in England and Wales, who issued their report in 1838, that one in eight of the population should be attending school. Certainly compared with areas of the North of England, the Isle of Man was by no means lagging behind. In 1842 in the thirty two square miles of Oldham and Ashton, with a total population of 105,000, there was not a single public day school for poorer children.[11] Frederick Engels in Manchester three years before commented that "The few day schools at the command of the working class are available only for the smallest minority, and are bad besides."[12] The slogan of the French Jacobins that education ought to be "universal, compulsory, gratuitous and secular" had no fulfilment as regards the last in the Isle of Man where the Statistical Review recorded that ninety per cent of the schools were visited by the ministers, yet the first three, despite the obvious imperfections, remained in theory part of the law of the Isle of Man. Compared with the mainland, the Island had little cause to be ashamed, for its framework was better by far, and school lay within the reach of almost all, as far as both geography and finance were concerned.

Only in one important field could the Island possibly be accused of lagging behind. Lancaster had started at Borough Road in 1809 the first of England's teacher-training colleges, where expertise in the monotorial system might be acquired. The two societies had their central schools, regarded as model schools where would-be teachers might observe and learn their profession, while Parliament actually voted £10,000 in 1835 for a national college for the training of teachers.[13] This founded on religious problems despite high hopes in 1839, leaving Kay and a friend, E. C. Tufnell, to open their own training college, Battersea Normal College in 1840 with Kay himself lecturing on education, opposing fiercely the monotorial system inculcated at Borough Road. The Established Church was quickly convinced of the superiority of Kay's methods, and acted accordingly. In 1841 the National Society followed suit with colleges at Chelsea for men, and at Whitelands for women. By 1845 there were twenty two church training colleges, subsidised by government grants, and the National Society took over Battersea, promising to adhere to its original ideas. By 1861 there were thirty five, twenty five of them Anglican.[14] The Isle of Man, however, made no attempt to give this further training to its own teachers. In reality with a population of around fifty thousand, the Island was too small to support such an institution, even though the mainland colleges themselves only averaged about sixty students. From the start, Manx pupil teachers were forced to cross the seas to receive their advanced training. Important though the ideas were that Moseley brought with him, yet more generally important was the new linkage of the Isle of Man, through the inspectorate, with the standards felt appropriate in England. For the sake of imperial grants a certain amount of independence was sacrificed, but on the other hand it would be much harder for the Island to fall behind the mainland. There would be shortcomings in the arrangement, as for instance will be seen with the Revised Code of Robert Lowe, but in the long term the arrangement kept the Island abreast of things in a time of rapid change when standards and expectations were continuously being raised.

Bishop Eden sent a copy of the record to all his clergy. He thoroughly approved of the Inspector ruling on the efficiency of a master, and further supported Moseley in urging that the Kings Somborne concepts be adopted, believing that Manx farmers would pay 8/- a quarter. He thought that if the recommendation about masters' houses were given legal authority it would be an example to England. If this did not come to pass, the educational grants would be of little use. "We cannot expect to have good, skilfull and trained masters, unless we raise their position and give them not only convenient schoolrooms and appliances for teaching, but also sufficient salaries and comfortable houses of residence."[15] Although mainland churchmen tended to be highly suspicious of anything that smacked of interference, Eden recognised that private subscriptions would not provide the monies needed; "I cannot see my way out of the difficulty otherwise than by a small educational tax."

Even before any legislation was undertaken, the influence of Moseley's visit made itself felt. In February, 1848, the Managing Committee at Castletown National Schools told their secretary, James Gell, to write away concerning possible grants and requested a visit from one of Her Majesty's Inspectors. At the same time they made plans to provide the recommended houses for the master and mistress, and in May applied for aid in building these through the National Society. The detailed form which had to be filled in asked for information about the size of the school houses, the timetable, and the projected cost. The replies showed the school for boys to be divided into five classes. After singing and prayers from 9 a.m. until 9.15, all did writing except Class Three, who did reading and dictation. After fifteen minutes break at 10.30, Classes 1 and 2 did arithmetic, Classes 3 and 4 writing, while Class Five did spelling. All were catechised from 11.30 until the mid-day break. School resumed at 2 p.m. when Classes 1 and 2 did reading, Class 3 arithmetic, Class 4 reading and spelling, and Class 5 writing until 3 p.m. From 3.30 until 4.15 Classes 1 and 2 did arithmetic, Class 3 reading and dictation, Class 4 writing cards, and Class 5 spelling and tables. All did tables from 4.15 until 4.50 when the school day ended with singing and prayers. The girls school was also divided into five classes, but the first four did the same subjects, arithmetic after prayers, writing from 10.45 until 11.15 and reading until noon. Only Class 5 broke the pattern with their reading and spelling coming first. The afternoon was spent in sewing until 4.15 when the catechism was taught for half an hour, before final prayers and singing. In June the Committee made a further application, this time for help with the master's salary and for pupil teachers. Moseley himself did not return to the Island as he had intended at the time of his Report, but the Rev. M. Mitchell came as Inspector to view potential pupil teachers and candidates for the teacher's certificates. After a meeting with the management Committee in August, 1848, Mitchell recommended the Castletown National Schools should be allowed three boy pupil-teachers and one girl pupil-teachers, with others being allowed for Foxdale and Peel. One further result of the visit was the drawing up of fresh rules, with four hundred copies printed for distribution to parents. Included were provisions about compulsory attendance at Sunday School and the need for clean and neat appearance — "no finery will be allowed". Any parental complaints were to be made to the Committee, not the master, and the exhortation made that parents should see their children kept the Ten Commandments and were kind to animals. Mitchell commented that, along with Peel, the Castletown School was "very deserving of praise, for the efficiency with which they are carried out", but his successor, Kennedy, was less flattering, referring to Thomas Kay as "A middle aged man of moderate qualifications", and finding fault with his organisation of the school. It was clear that Manx schools were going to be scrutinized as they never had been before, and that a new era had begun.[15]

The Methodists too responded very quickly to the new ideas. The unfortunate experience with Morrison had taught a hard lesson about the desirability of competent masters and the folly of refusing to pay well enough to keep a good man. Although the Committee in November, 1847, rejected an applicant, Johnson, for Morrison's job from their short list because he demanded £50 a year, and appointed James Cannell on the same terms as Dewsbury and Morrison, they made it clear that "If he or the Girls School teacher wish further acquaintance with the system of teaching recognised by the Training Schools" — which the Committee deemed highly advisable — arrangements would be made. In order to avail themselves of the government grants to best advantage, the Committee decided in November, 1850, to consider making Thomas Street a mixed school. What pattern emerged is not clear from the minutes, but the suggestion in 'The Story of Methodism in the Isle of Man' that Well Road became a girls school and Thomas Street a boys school does not lie easily with the fact that masters were in charge of both schools.[16] There was discussion about the desirability of getting the new master for Thomas Street from one of the training schools, but eventually Samuel Parkin was appointed, despite admitting to the Committee

Committee that he was not a certified teacher.[17] James Cannell from Well Road, however, did depart for training at the Methodist College, the Westminster Training Institute, leaving a gap filled with the appointment of a Mr. Costain from Abbeylands. Costain was paid £40 a year, but Parkin applied successfully for an increase, and from January, 1852, was paid £70 a year, the Committee referring to the prosperous state of the school.[18] In the autumn of 1851, a quarterage charge of 2/6d had been imposed in addition to weekly fees. The pressures to conform to the new professional status of a certified teacher were still there, and eventually matters came to a head when Parkin flatly refused to go to London for "another examination" in November, 1852, although he was quite willing to be inspected with his school in Douglas. Parkin had already displeased the Committee with his cavalier attitude to their authority, having given the children holidays without their consent, and knew that an attempt to bring an Inspector across had been unsuccessful. The Committee of the Council for Education had proved reluctant to send an Inspector for single Methodist school, despite offers to pay his fare from Liverpool,[19] and the baffled Thomas Street Committee asked advice from the mainland Wesleyan Committee of Education. After first reducing Parkin's salary to £60 in December, 1852, on the grounds that help in the school was no longer given by his son, and that numbers had diminished, Parkin was eventually given notice, while £70 was offered to "a first rate teacher" who possessed a "government certificate of merit". (Parkin attempted to keep some degree of self-respect by handing in his own notice.) A Mr. Cranmore was appointed, but evidently failed to give satisfaction. By May a Mr. Lamplugh was temporarily running the school, while further advertisements for a "trained and efficient teacher" were placed. Cranmore was given notice, but did not deign to reply.[20] The school had fallen once again sharply in numbers, so that James Cannell, returning from training in London at the Wesley Normal Institute accepted a salary of only £20 with part of the school pence, the school being "in its present low condition". (The Douglas Methodist Schools, even if having their ups and downs, managed to survive, whereas a similar venture at Ramsey was less fortunate. Methodism in Ramsey in the Eighteen Forties was flourishing to the degree that even the Queen's Street Chapel with room for 450, the highest capacity for a chapel in the Isle of Man, was replaced by a new building in Waterloo Road, which held 750. The vacated premises in Queen's Street were intended to be utilised as a day school, but despite an opening in March 1850, the school was closed in the Spring of 1853. A fresh opening followed, but the premises were used in the week soon afterwards for a private venture school. The faltering starts in fact mirrored closely the early years of the National Schools in Ramsey, and not until 1874 was there a more setled Wesleyan School for Ramsey.) A much more ambitious curriculum now made its appearance with the commensurate additional fees; geography, history, art, book-keeping, mensuration, mapping, algebra, mechanics and even elements of natural philosophy made the range of subjects far wider than the normal run of elementary subjects, but fees for the more advanced went up to sixpence a week. Cannell had originally agreed to take the first 2d paid by pupils and only half of any amount above that, but first secured all the pence, and then threatened to resign unless he received the long promised £70. Some bargaining led to an offer of a guaranteed £60 in 1856, and after giving the matter a week's reflection, Cannell accepted, aware that the school had debts approaching a hundred pounds.[21]

The Island's only Noncomformist schools were thus well aware of the significance of the ideas brought by Moseley, and particularly with regard to the curriculum, were far in advance of the rest of the Island's schools, offering subjects that would normally be found only in grammar or 'middle' schools, or in private academies. Yet the legislation finally passed by Tynwald in its attempt to improve education in the Island must have been disconcerting to the Methodists, forming as they did by now a much larger proportion of the population than those members of the Established Church. It is possible that the original Bill was more liberal in its attitude to Nonconformity, for there exists in the Castletown National School logbook a Petition of April, 1849, protesting against the mixed Church/Dissenting schools contemplated, which it was feared would imperil the grants given by the National Society, confined to those who taught the principles of the Established Church. The Petition demanded alterations in the Bill, which may well have taken place for this was little cause for complaint by Churchmen as regards the eventual terms passed.

The legal consequence of Moseley's recommendations for the Island was the passing by Tynwald of the first major act concerning education since 1701, the Act for making better provision for Parochial and other Schoolmasters of 1851. The prologue referred to the legislation of 1704 and 1813, but pointed out that in some parishes the quarterlands did not all benefit from the existence of the parochial school, thus tending implicity to support the views of Bishop Ward as opposed to those of Short.[22] Many of the schools needed enlarging, and some had no residences for the masters, thereby rendering them ineligible for Parliamentary grants. (This was not strictly true; Moseley had suggested that it would be good if the Island legislature introduced such a rule, which would put the Island in advance of England in this respect.)

In line with current thinking, the Act sought to harness local interest, rather than impose anything from above. Consequently the adoption of the act was left to local areas. Ten or more cesspayers could petition the Bishop calling for a vestry meeting for which due notice was to be given, together with the Bishop's own permission. One potentially practical inclusion was the leave given for a district which might straddle several parish boundaries to take advantage of the Act. A majority at the vestry meeting was enough to levy a rate, with the accounts kept by the wardens; the maximum from each quarterland was fixed at £5.

The money so raised could be put to a wide range of uses, for schools, masters' dwelling houses if none sufficient were provided, for repairs and enlargements, for books and aparatus, or for salaries and retiring allowances for the old and disabled. Section 7 provided that for expenditure in excess of twenty pounds a year, money could be borrowed and then repaid under the act.

The traditional Church influenced in education, brought to the fore again by Bishop Short so recently, was most noticeable in the provisions of the Act. The incumbent was to be the chairman of the special Committee of five chosen annually to carry out the resolutions of the vestry. This Committee had the power fix suitable quarterages, appoint a ladies committee to supervise the education of girls and infants, and appoint the schoolmaster, although their decision in this last respect was subject to the Bishop's approval. Section 9 gave the Committee power to dismiss the master if there were complaints although this clause seemed unnecessary in the light of section 16 which made clear that tenure was decidedly not for life, but at the discretion of the Committee, referred to in the later clauses as the trustees. It was hoped that the common problem of a school's effectiveness being ruined by an inefficient master, whether through incompetence or advancing years, would be avoided in the future. While the local incumbent was obviously in a position of strength as chairman of the local committee, his power was considerably increased by Section 11. Part of this section very reasonably stated that National Schools would remain under National School rules, but the first part declared that the incumbent would also control religious education. This was somewhat surprising in an Island with so many Methodists, despite the fact that relationships were usually very good and free from the bitterness so prevalent on the mainland. By Section 18 buying and selling of land was permissible, but only if the formal consent of Tynwald were given, as of old in such cases. There had been no successful attempt outside Douglas, as yet, by any other denomination to set up its own schools.

The Isle of Man thus managed to put legislation through Tynwald permitting rate assisted education, while across the water in England equivalent schemes foundered still because of religious difficulties. It will be recalled that Whitbread's 1807 Bill seemed to undermine the Church influence in education, while Brougham's Parish School Bill of 1820 was rejected for the opposite reason, that it gave too many powers to the Established Church. The same see-saw continued decades later. Sir James Graham's Factory Bill of 1843 which contained proposals for the education of factory children between eight and thirteen was vigorously opposed for being far too Church-controlled. In common with the Manx Act of 1851 it made the appointment of masters in schools maintained by the rates subject to the bishop's approval, and put the vicar among the trustees, yet it went further in insisting the master be a member of the Established Church, made the wardens trustees too, explicity stated that the religious instruction would be that of the Church of England, as opposed to merely the incumbent being in charge, and laid down that the children would attend the parish church. A conscience clause allowing withdrawal from catechism and the church attendance totally failed to assuage Nonconformist objections, and despite further concessions, the Bill was dropped. By contrast the Eighteen Fifties saw a number of bills introduced into Westminster to establish secular schools, but Church and Nonconformists united to attack such proposals as Fox's Bill of 1850 which made no provision for the existing denominational schools. Bills of 1853 and 1855 proposed local school committees rather like those in the Manx Act of 1851, but such attempts as Sir John Pakington's Bill of 1855 to let local majority feeling decide the denominational colour of any new school failed to secure sufficient support to become law. While the Manx counterpart to the English Education Act of 1870, which eventually emerged after two-thirds of a century of debate, is usually considered to be the Manx Act of 1872, there is good ground for maintaining that in some respects at least, the Island equivalent in the Nineteenth Century ought to be considered the Act of 1851, twenty years in advance of the mainland.

The Manx Act also went some way towards curing the problem of poor salaries. Section 10 laid down a minimum of £30 for masters and £20 for mistresses, including quarterage, so that masters in addition to receiving an amount well above 1847 levels in most cases would also be in a position under Privy Council rules to augment this minimum by grants earned for training pupil teachers and by passing the teachers' examinations themselves.

Perhaps most important of all in the long term were the requirements of Sections 12 and 14, which stated that Committees would be bound by the terms laid down by the Privy Council in order to receive grants from Parliament, and that the schools must be open to the Inspectors within reasonable hours for such help. Although there had been a whole series of mainland developments copied in the Island in the course of the first half of the Nineteenth Century, any further improvements thought desirable by the Privy Council to raise the standards of education would automatically apply to the Isle of Man, if financial help was desired, as it certainly would be. Wherever in the Isle of Man the Act was adopted, there could be no possibility of standards slipping behind those of the mainland. A certain amount of independence was sacrificed in the legislation, but wise heads saw in this arrangement educational advantages as well as financial ones, and when in twenty years time the financial independence was regained, the ties with England about standards were clearly reiterated in the fresh legislation. For the first time, the educational systems of England and the Isle of Man were bound together, for good or ill, not only by influence, but by legal ties in an Act of Tynwald.

The full implications of the 1851 Act were not to emerge for another decade, when the ideas of Robert Lowe came into force. Until then there was a period of quiet consolidation, notably in respect of improvement of school premises, continuing the steady progress made in this respect under Ward, as has been seen, and during the Eighteen Forties too.

At Kirk Michael, a scheme of 1834 to sell the old schoolhouse and build afresh at Little Lough fell through as the site proved far too damp. Accordingly in 1839 the old site was taken back, and with the purchase of extra land the following year, a new school was erected in 1841, the Parliamentary Grant helping to the extent of £67.10.0. 1843 saw two major developments in the Prish of Malew, where the Vicar, the Rev. William Gill, was an enthusiast for education; "terrible for the schools" in the words of one of his parishioners.[23] Gill even managed, to the astonishment of Bishop Short, to persuade the National Society to reverse their policy on the Isle of Man and to make grants from the Society's own funds, as well as acting as agent for government grants.

The schoolhouse provided for the Chapel of St. Marks had received £30 from the Society as well as £70 Parliamentary Grant, the arrangements anticipating the recommendations of Moseley by including the provision of a schoolmaster's house. The Society provided the same amount for the new Parochial School in Ballasalla to supplement the local contributions and Parliament's £88. Sometimes the decisions taken by Acts of Vestry took quite a time to be given the formal consent of Tynwald. The sale by the Parish of German of its old schoolhouse and the erection of a new one near the master's house was decided in 1842, and approved in 1846.[24] At Onchan the Vestry felt in 1839 that the old school was not only small and out of repair, but unfavourably situated, and elected either to buy the old vicarage for a school or build a new one. Eventually in March, 1845, the Vicar and Wardens bought the old vicarage site for a school and master's house, and the Conchan School House Act of 1846 sanctioned the sale of the old school.[25] The time between the Santan Vestry decision of February 22nd, 1848, to buy an acre at Ballakissack for a new schoolhouse, and the Santan School Act of 1849 was much shorter, although it was laid down by the Act that the old school should not be sold until the new schoolhouse had been completed to the Bishop's satisfaction. This school was an ambitious undertaking in more ways than one. Its cost was unusually high at £419, and met from no less than six sources. From England came the grants from Parliament (£100) and the National Society (£30), and from the Parish donations of £148 and a gift of £20 from the Parish Friendly Society of £20 supplemented the sale price of the old school (£101). The remaining balance was £20 from the Commissioners of Her Majesty's Woods, Forests and Land Revenues, who managed the Crown property and revenues on the Island. Since the annual income for the Crown from this source already was nearing £10,000, the tiny amounts given to education could in no way be regarded as generous.

Apart from six of the ancient parishes having these improvements to the parochial schools, the Eighteen Forties also saw new developments in all of the four towns. In Douglas, St. Barnabas' Schools were enlarged in 1845, aided by a Parliamentary Grant of £85, just a fraction more than that given to the Castletown National Schools in 1849 to erect houses for the teachers, although in this case the National Society also gave £30. In Ramsey Bishop Auckland conveyed in November, 1849, "the commodious building in Church Street known as St. Peter's Chapel" to trustees for the education of the poor, the old premises of the National School to be sold and the proceeds applied to the benefit of the new.[26] By deed of August, 1850, Jane Martin gave an extra plot for the use of the school and eventually the sum of £420 was invested for the school in 1852. Under the 1850 Act, a local Committee consisting of the High Bailiff, the Chaplain and Wardens of Ramsey, and five elected members was set up to administer the school. As was only fitting for a National School, the master and mistress were required to be members of the Church of England. In Peel, it was noted that the Mathematical School in the Eighteenth Century had received Insular Government funds for a time: in the Eighteen Forties it received money from Parliament in 1847-48, its provision of education for ten poor scholars apparently overriding its status as a place of higher education not entitled to receive such funds. A fresh start as has been seen was also made at the Philip Christian School, but the story of this school, the jewel in the Island's educational system, deserves a place to itself as an illustration of how the Island could respond to the challenge of new standards and new methods.

The passing of the 1851 thus merely facilitated in respect of buildings a process of restoration and renewal which was well under way already. The statement in Moore's History, that borrowing powers under the Act enabled Committees to enlarge many of the schools and build houses for the masters,[27] might be misleading if the reader supposed that this were a new development emanating from the Act. As the implementation of the Act depended upon a majority vote to that end at a vestry meeting, it was entirely up to a parish whether the Act was used or not when the time came to think of school improvements, and not all parishes bothered to make use of it. By far the largest amount raised by assessment was at Jurby in 1860 to replace the old 1766 school. The total of £260 exceeded the Parliamentary Grant of £228, a further £100 being borrowed. At Patrick too the parish assessment of £147 made up a significant proportion of the cost of the new school on the Vicar's glebe in 1854, although appreciably less than the Parliamentary Grant of £200. However, when Rushen invoked the Act in 1858 the amount raised by assessment (£27) to cover the costs of the school, built on part of the

Ballachurry Estate sold by Thomas Gawne to the vicar and wardens, was trivial compared with donations of £226 and the Parliamentary Grant of £334. In 1855 Malew Vestry Meeting adopted the Act when part of the lands of Rushen Abbey was bought for an infants school, but this does not seem to have happened at Braddan when the 1815 school, although improved under Bishop Ward, was replaced by a new National School. The Society actually made no grant from its own funds, but the Parliamentary Grant of £344 in 1860 was the biggest yet received on the Island. (The Commissioners of Woods and Forests added their modest contribution of £25.) Nor was the Act invoked at Maughold, where private subscriptions were felt sufficient to provide the local share of costs for the new parochial school under the National Society. Elections to the Committee there, composed of five others in addition to the Vicar and the Captain of the Parish, were by those subscribing ten shillings a year. Those elected had to own property in Maughold and give at least one pound a year in subscriptions.[28]

Indeed the feature of the age was not so much the involvement of the wider community in education through payment of assessment, as the turning of the old parochial schools into unmistakably Church Schools through affiliation to the National Society. Strong links between the Established Church and the educational system had always been a traditional feature of Manx life, but what had been generally acceptable by custom appeared differently when given explicit legal terminology in the terms employed by the National Society. In the few cases of "in-filling" from this period, the new foundations were nearly all clearly Church of England, if not explicitly National Society Schools. In the ecclesiastical district of St. Judes in the old Parish of Andreas, for instance, the new school "for the children of the labouring or manufacturing or other poorer classes", to quote the usual formula, was affiliated to the National Society. (This school, erected in 1854, also relied on donations (£122) for the bulk of its funds and did not use the machinery for assessment.) At Derbyhaven in the Parish of Malew, where the Rev. Gilmour Harvey sold a house for use as a Church School in July, 1859, and the power of appointment and dismissal of the master lay in the hands of the Principal of King William's College, there was no mistaking the fact that the principles of the Established Church would be included as much as in any school with formal connections with the National Society. The same was true in the Parish of Braddan at Oakhill (1860) to the south of Douglas, and at Cronkbourne (1862) to the west, where William Fine Moore conveyed land so that the poor of Cronkbourne and Tromode might be educated in the principles of the Established Church. Only at Spoyt Vane in the parish of Michael where in 1860 part of the Ballaveigh Estate was conveyed for the purposes of a school does the strong Church connection seem to be missing. Where formerly schooling outside the parochial school system had been provided either by private individuals or by non-denominational endowments, these in many cases now had been replaced by overtly Church institutions, and the grip of the Church on education at elementary level appeared to be tightened as each year passed. This was true both of town and country. The four towns all had schools affiliated to the National Society although the circumstances were very different in each of them. In Castletown the old petty school had faded from the scene once the National Schools had their permanent building. In Douglas, as has been seen, the petty school element in the Grammar School perished with its closing in 1838, if indeed there was anything left. Certainly ever since the opening of the Athol Street Day and Sunday School, the old school was totally insignificant in the context of elementary education. Similarly in Ramsey, where the Grammar School was revived, the mantle of the old parochial school had fallen upon the National Schools, while at Peel, as has been seen, what was once an undenominational school was now very firmly part of the National Society. Methodist suspicion of Church pressure in the old parochial schools is well illustrated by the events of 1854 in the Parish of Rushen. A Methodist minister, George William Oliver, enquired of the Privy Council Committee if managers had the right to make all scholars attend the place of worship to which they, themselves, belonged. "Is this rule allowable", he asked in a letter of May, 1854, but found his general question would not be answered until he gave details about the offending school, which turned out to be Rushen Girls School. Rules drawn up in April, 1852, had stated that all children should walk with the mistress to the Church, and any wilfully breaking the rules would be expelled. Whitehall wrote to William Corrin, Vicar of Rushen, giving their opinion that such a rule would justify the establishment of a separate school for the persons aggrieved.[29] Corrin, however, assured the Committee that the rule was not applied if pupils lived over a mile from the school, and also "has never been, or is it intended ever to be applied to any child against the wishes of its parents or Guardians". The Committee in reply urged Corrin to acquaint Oliver of these facts, and suggested that in any such cases "the spirit of the legislation of 1851 should decide the question." After a period in the 1840's of hostility to government the Nonconformists soon realised the voluntary effort alone was quite unable to provide the education needed by the working class, and state aid lost its stigma. Certainly when the Methodists established their school in Peel in 1861, complete with schoolmaster's house, the grant of £395 in 1863 from Parliament was readily accepted. Rather more modest was the school in Greeba, between Peel and Douglas, opened in 1868 on land belonging to John Kelly, which received no such grant. Although a short-lived Wesleyan School had also opened in Ramsey in 1850 in Queen Street, there was no such venture in Castletown. While relationships between Wesleyans and the Church remained very friendly on the Island, with many having a leg in each camp, there were for the first time in the Island's history daily schools of different denominations in three of the towns, echoing the friendly rivalry long experienced in the sphere of Sunday schools.

The measurement of Island standards compared with those of the mainland ceased to be a matter of guesswork once the English inspectors extended their field to include the Isle of Man following the visit of Moseley. The Island was, of course, far too small to warrant an inspector for itself alone, and was given to the inspector of the Lancashire schools, by then usually classed among the best provided of English counties as far as education was concerned. Apart from a detailed report on each individual school, the inspectors also submitted general reports for their areas, published together with relevant new regulations and correspondence, as the Minutes of the Committee of the Council on Education for each school year. It is significant that in his report for 1855-6, the Rev. W. J. Kennedy made absolutely no distinction between the two areas under his supervision, when he looked back with some degree of satisfaction on how things had improved. In his own seven years of acting as an inspector he had noted how schools were better ordered and organised, better fitted up with books, desks and apparatus, and better taught on account of "the more general supply of well educated and duly competent teachers." He compared the new system with the old monitorial methods. Formerly there was a "large number of small ill-placed shapeless classes under the charge of a tribe of little monitors, between whom and their weary charges there was a constant squabbling, while the master in serene tranquility mended pens at his desk, although he now and again startled the disputants by sudden stentorian threatenings or by periodical smacks on the desk of the well known cane." Now there were well arranged classes, each under the master or an assistant master or apprentice, each with its own blackboard, maps and piles of clean and good books ". . . the schools under inspection in Lancashire and the Isle of Man, present a most pleasing contrast to those painful abodes of noise and dirt, and I may add of idleness and ignorance." Twenty years ago teachers were slovenly and careless about their own persons and their schoolrooms. Now there was order, cleanliness and tidiness, with reverence and obedience replacing quarrelling and positive disrespect alternating with sulleness.[30]

There were still obvious weaknesses. Too many schools were still confined in space, some without playgrounds, often ill-drained and ill-ventilated. Pupils rarely continued to study after leaving school — on the contrary they deteriorated for the most part. There was no stimulus to learn further, as the master imparted all, often 'skimming' over too many subjects. School life was short, with only 15% of the pupils in the combined areas staying more than two years at school. 46% stayed for less than one year, and 71% for less than two. The preponderance of Lancashire schools in these figures make any Manx conclusions of little worth. Kennedy expressed his own theories of four basic subjects, a language, drawing, arithmetic and music being quite enough for regular lessons, other subjects being touched upon in lectures, and attacked current notions of teaching 'facts'. The average salaries for the two areas reflect much higher amounts in Lancashire, for the average certificated master received £97, and the uncertificated £57, while the figures for mistress were £64 and £36 respectively. Kennedy regarded £70 with house as the minmum a certified teacher should receive. Although the inspectors from National Schools, in typical English compromise, reported to the Church concerning the religious education in the schools, and the Privy Council Committee concerning secular instruction, Kennedy saw the first need as being an educational rate. Only the Isle of Man was, of course, already entitled in law to take this action if a district so wished.

In this general report, only four schools were mentioned by name. A tiny place in Lancashire, called Shatterthwaite, for some unknown reason had an excellent school, but by and large Kennedy found the largest schools were the best, citing two at Rochdale and Lancaster as examples. The only reference to a Manx school was when Kennedy commented on the low standard of many Lancashire endowed schools: "deplorable and absolutely requiring some stringent remedy". The Island's only example of this type, the Christian School at Peel, was singled out by contrast as one which was "doing all that its means allow".[31]

A picture of how the Island compared with Kennedy's wider scale may be gleaned from the Report of the Island's own Diocesan Inspectors who for the first time in 1857-58 made the first general visitation of church schools, as opposed to clergy viewing just parts of the Island as hitherto. One church school was omitted owing to the prevalence of smallpox, but in the others 2,332 children were examined out of a total of 2,531 pupils in the schools. The links between quality of teaching and inspection by the government inspectors were manifest, and in several the teaching and discipline were fully up to what might be expected. The total picture was one of steady improvement, although work was hindered by irregularity of attendance, with children kept away on "trifling pretexts".

A rather poor report on reading, with 14 of 24 schools judged to be to unsatisfactory, appears not as damning when it becomes clear that the chief faults were found in delivery rather than in basic reading skills. Too rapid enunciation and careless slurring over of words may well have arisen from a desire to impress the inspectors with sheer speed. As far as writing was concerned, it was felt that teachers could superintend the formation of letters more closely than they did. The purchase by the masters themselves of properly ruled writing books was preferable to the children ruling rather badly on their own books of very inferior blank paper. However, when it came to arithmetic, the children appeared to have a natural aptitude, and were well taught, gave intelligent explanations of the principles and processes of their work. Only four schools made no attempt at Geography and Grammar, while 16 were found satisfactory. History was less popular, tackled reasonably well in twelve schools, but not attempted in thirteen. No school had ventured into the realms of Church History. Rather surprisingly, apart from the 23rd Psalm, there was very little knowledge of scripture by heart.[32]

The weakness of the Island as regards remuneration of teachers still continued. Only Peel with £106 equalled Lancastrian levels, while the average salary of £53 fell below even the average for the uncertificated teachers in Lancashire. The worst offenders were the parochial schools which had not compiled with the conditions necessary to them receiving aid from the Committee of the Council. In the North, Maughold still only paid the disgraceful sum of £15. The Diocesan Inspectors noted the correlation of good salaries and good tuition given to the pupils.

There was need of new buildings at Jurby, Lonan and Marown, although in fact only Jurby received a new building in the next few years, while the shortcomings at Braddan and Lezayre were about to be tackled. (As will be seen, in the case of Lezayre, this confidence was greatly misplaced.) The greatest barrier, however, to the improvement of the machinery of education was the difficulty in removing old and incompetent masters, who had been licensed by the Bishop. There was power of removal only where the 1851 Act had been adopted.

Despite the fact that his own clergy returns revealed that, at least in buildings, Dissenters outnumbered the Church by a ratio of three to one, Bishop Horace Powys stuck firmly to the unashamed connection of schooling with the Established Church, and dismissed too, the arguments of those who thought a little expediency could be used, so that making a "nominal sacrifice" by removing "precise expressions", the same indoctrination in Church principles could nevertheless be carried on. He stood out for the direct teaching of the Catechism, and indeed saw in education the chief instrument "of reuniting our people in the communion of the Church."[33] He drew a distinction between the Common Law which enabled assessment to be raised to build and maintain parochial schools, and Canon Law which gave the clergy a duty to enforce attendance. (This differentiation does not seem to receive any justification from the laws of 1703-4).

Bishop Powys in his Convocational Charges paid particular tribute to the work being done at the National School in Peel. Indeed as that school well illustrated, in its change from an institution of unspecified denomination to a decidedly Church school, the movement on the Island to explicit Church dominance of eduation, so too it showed the response of the Island at its best to the new opportunities opened up to teachers and pupils alike. Also as the rest of the Island found its links with mainland education increasing more and more, the same was found true of Peel's own special link with England through the Clothworkers' Company.

Despite the fact that the new 1842 building was intended to satisfy demand for many years, two factors helped to dash such hopes. One was the very success of the school. Numbers grew and put pressure on the accommodation. The other was a change in the requirements of the Committee of the Council on Education. It was decreed that each child should be allocated eight instead of six square feet, thereby reducing capacity considerably. It was recognised that an infants school was needed, and the people of Peel bestirred themselves, holding a Bazaar in August, 1848, in the grounds of Peel Castle, and raising nearly £147 as a result. Sadly this was one of the few occasions for such initiative, as the generosity of the Clothworkers' Company caused the belief to grow over the years in Peel that their own efforts were not really needed

Despite the HMI's report in 1851 that an Infants' School to "draft off the younger children" was a matter of urgency, it took until 1861 for the idea to become a reality. The Clothworkers' gave no direct help towards the building, and time elapsed while the bazaar fund increased through interest to a sum which enabled building to start. Robert Moore, the High Bailiff of Peel, and as such an ex-officio trustee, bought for £34 for the use of the school Halsall's House, which abutted inconveniently on the school premises, and this gift of 1851 was followed the next year with the donation of the adjoining plot by Thomas Cholmondeley. When in 1859 the next parcel of land was purchased from Henry Graves, it was felt that there was room and money to build a new school for the older children, leaving the infants in the 1842 building. After a lengthy correspondence with the Committee of the Council for Education, a school suitable for 254 pupils (at eight square feet per pupil) was approved, and a grant of £315 sanctioned in July, 1860. With the bazaar money and gifts now amounting to £291, there was a debt of only £25 on the total cost of £630. The debt rose when more land had to be bought from Graves to make an adequate playground, involving the expense of taking down and rebuilding the boundary wall. Incidentals such as the supply of gas and water, and the fine tablet to the Clothworkers' Company set up in the school increased the amount owed to £100. Moore set about raising from Peel the required sum. He pointed out that despite the National Society link, the school was open to all, with a free education provided for the very poor; that the last appeal for subscriptions was now nearly twenty years ago; that there was no call on Peel for any annual support; and that the school was an undoubted success. These last two points deserve a little elaboration.

After the buildings of the 1842 school, the annual income from the Clothworkers' contined to grow. The first increase was parhaps rather unfortunate, as it came from the stopping of Thomas Quine's £10 pension. The Company agreed with the Bishop in January, 1845, that Quine's behaviour had been such as to warrant the loss of his pension, and in December of that year put the £10 at the Bishop's disposal.[16] Bishop Short seems to have added the amount to the £38 going to the school, for when in 1850 the total annual amount received from rents rose to £66.10.0., £63 went to the school, while £3.10.0. was retained by the Company for any future emergencies. Although this was the legal consequence to the two-thirds rule, the Trustees of the school felt it fitting to call a public meeting at Peel Court House on February 23rd, 1850, and express grateful thanks not only for "the recent act of liberality" but also for the Company's "handsome and generous manner in the past". Whether this tribute was partly inspired by hopes of direct help towards the building costs on the horizon is difficult to say.[34]

There was also extra income provided from the use of the funds of Bishop Wilson's School for girls. In the codicil to his will of 1748 he had left fifty pounds for a petty schoolmistress in Peel. The Vicar and churchwardens of Peel, who had always acted as trustees of this fund, suggested while proposing the Infants' School in 1851 that it could be engrafted onto the Bishop Wilson School, and informally amalgamated with Christian's School. Wilson's fifty pounds Manx was worth only £42.17.2 in British money, but a five pounds legacy in the will of Leonora Munro was augmented by her executors to make the total fifty pounds British. No appointment as schoolmistress had been made for four years, so that the capital had been built up to £60. Moore thought that with some help from the Clothworkers' income, an annual sermon, schoolpence and subscriptions, there should be enough funds to pay a competent teacher. He suggested that a Committee of Ladies, elected annually from the subscribing families, should supervise the work of the Infants School.

Of the success of the school there could be no question. The independent assessment of the HMI's was invariably complimentary, to the master, if not to the conditions. The Rev. M. Mitchell in 1848 called it "An excellent school and very creditable to the master". His successor as Inspector, the Rev. J. W. Kennedy described Cowley in 1850 as "a painstaking deserving master" and the school as "thriving and creditable". In 1854 he commented that "the school continues to prosper under the assiduous teaching of Mr. Cowley". According to the Rev. William Bailey in 1857 "A better school does not exist in the Island than this: it reflects the highest credit upon the master, who labours under the disadvantage of a sadly contracted room.", while two years later Rev. N. Gream, M.A., described the school as "most excellent both in numbers and discipline, and also for instruction down to the youngest child." The Bishop was moved to write to Cowley, remarking that HMI's were not in the habit of giving undue praise. "I do not remember having ever read a report of a school so thoroughly satisfactory as this." The plaudits continued in 1860: "exceedingly well taught by Mr. Cowley" declared the Rev. W. Keenedy. By the time the new school was opened, 1,180 pupils had passed through Cowley's hands. He had produced the Island's first pupil teacher, and had trained 12 by 1861. Six of these had won Queen's Scholarships, which gave entry to a teacher's training college, with three of them obtaining First Class passes.[35]

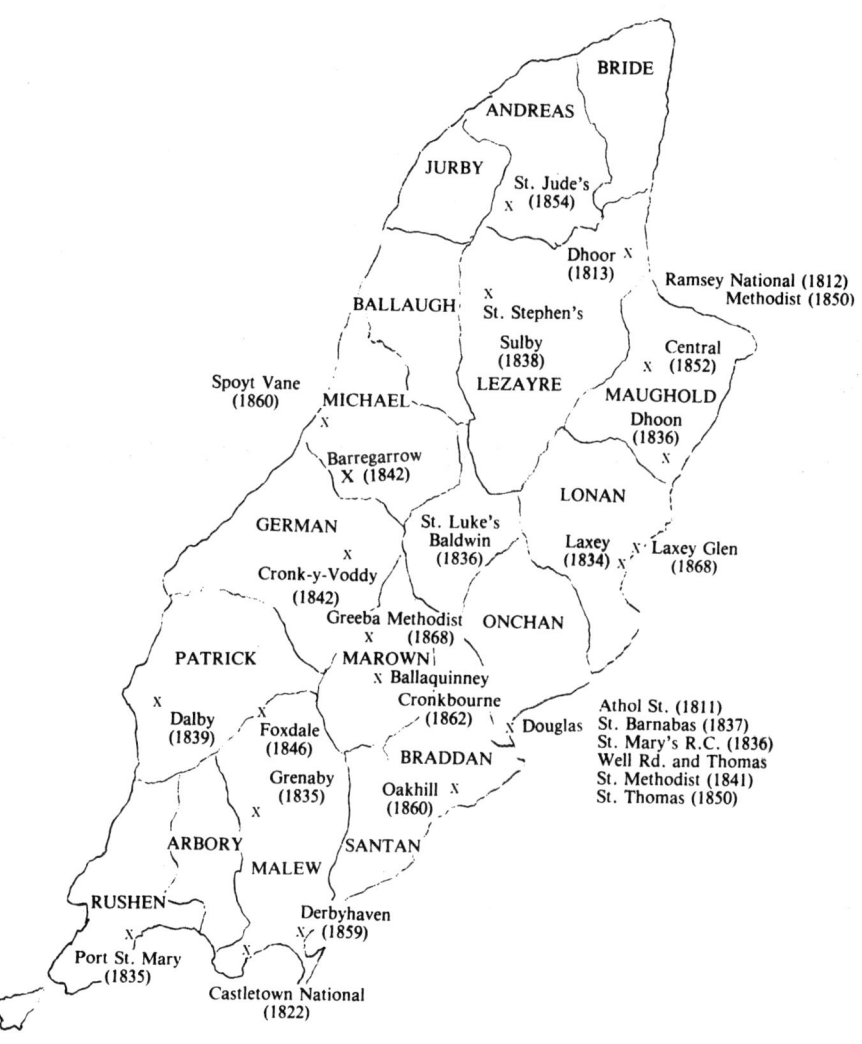

THE SURGE TOWARDS UNIVERSAL ELEMENTARY EDUCATION
NEW SCHOOLS 1800-1872

The opening of the 1861 school with its 'L' shaped plan, the two sides measuring 72 feet and 40 feet with a width of 18 feet, giving a total area of 2,025 feet, in addition to the 1842 school which measured 55 by 18, 991 square feet, went some way to helping the physical environment to match the excellence of the teaching. At a meeting to celebrate the opening of the new school, High Bailiff Moore revealed that he had it on the authority of the Inspectors themselves that Peel was the best of the Island schools, while the Island schools outshone their mainland counterparts. Peel, therefore, was the best school in the British Isles.[36]

Here then was the Island's outstanding example of the new ideas introduced by Moseley being put into practice in all ways. Cowley himself set a fine personal example, gaining his initial Teacher's Certificate in 1854, and gradually working his way up to the pinnacle of the First Degree of Merit in Division One by 1868. By the time of retirement he had not only trained nineteen Pupil Teachers but one of them, in addition to gaining a Queen's Scholarship, had passed the Matriculation Examination of London University. From definitely elementary routes, there was emerging a new path forward into advanced education, with the new methods of traiing proving their worth and extending horizons.

Where Peel led, others followed in taking advantage of the new opportunities. In the training college at Chester, for example, there were in 1859, former pupil teachers from Castletown National School,[2] Athol Street, Douglas,[2] St. John's, Port St. Mary, and one from Peel. Between them they held six first-class and two second-class Queen's Scholarships.

At less exhalted levels, the picture on the Island was very varied. A few miles away from Peel at Lezayre, there was a far different state of affairs. The inhabitants sent a memorial in August, 1863, to Archdeacon Moore, explaining that there had been an Act passed in 1857, which allowed a rate to be levied in order to pull down the old school and erect a new building. The rate had indeed been exacted, but absolutely nothing done. There was no parochial school at present, nor had there been one for some considerable time. "Education is much neglected and unattended to in the said Parish." There was a plea that the Act be enforced, and the old pressed into use until the new were completed. The Archdeacon duly made a visitation the following month, September, 1863. Only twenty attended the meeting. The rather feeble reason tendered by the incumbent was that a costly new burial ground had been purchased, and there were not enough funds left to build a school. All he could offer was the news that a schoolmistress was now teaching weekdays in the old and unrepaired school.[37]

Between the extremes of Peel and Lezayre, a more typical picture of the impact of the new ideas is to be found in an 1858 Report by the local Committee of Management at the National School in Castletown, showing that the way to higher standards could be paved with problems caused by the very acceptance of Committee of Council criteria. When a Miss Reid who only held the Certificate of the Irish Board of 'Education was apponted to Castletown Girls School, the Committee of the Council would not examine her for an English Certificate until she had taught the school for two years. Miss Reid resigned, and because there was no certificated teacher, the Pupil Teachers were not allowed to continue. They were also withdrawn at the Boys School, as Mr. Thomas Kay had not gained his certificate despite a long tenure. Government aid was thus lost to the schools, and the local Committee even debated not bothering with the new system and returning to the old independent ways. It was resolved, however, to retain the government links, and Mr. Kay resigned to make way for a certificated teacher, who, it was felt, would command a higher salary. (Kay had been master for seventeen years, and in recognition of past services was given £30 from the Committee of the Council and £35 raised locally.)[38] It was agreed that the old £40 with Royal Bounty, taken over from the defunct parochial school, would be augmented by half the school pence of the boys and the government capitation money paid for regular attendance, making a total of at least £65. In January Mr. H. Wyatt, a certificated teacher trained at Cheltenham, and Sara Clucas, an old St. Barnabas pupil-teacher trained at Warrington, were appointed. Unfortunately Wyatt resigned and was replaced by Mr. Geldard, a Skipton pupil teacher trained at Durham, not as well qualified as Wyatt, holding only a 3rd Division of the 3rd Class Certificate.

The Report also revealed the steady movement away from free schooling in the original charity schools, as it reported the decision to cut down the number of free places in each school to ten, the rest of the children either paying a penny a week or tenpence each quarter if they were presented by a contributor to the school funds of at least 5/-a quarter or, if they were not, twopence a week or 1/8d per quarter. This was to some degree forced upon the schools if they were to have the benefits of the new "capitation grants". These had been introduced after the failure in 1853 of Russell's bill to allow local rates to aid education: the Privy Council's Committee on Education had tried to achieve the same effect in rural areas by paying grants for regular attendance by pupils directly to the schools, and the scheme had been extended to the towns in 1856. The most useful extra sum of 6/- for each boy and 5/- for each girl who attended 176 days of schooling and paid at least a penny a week would supplement the school's income. The Castletown Committee stressed the importance of securing this income: at the moment average attendance among both boys and girls was only about two-thirds (79 of 119 on the roll for the boys, and 108 of 152 for the girls.).[39]

Already the role of the state was considerable. In theory merely aiding the voluntary work of the societies, in practice the English Government was paying the lion's share of educational costs, and things had come a long way since the early grants of the Eighteen

Thirties to aid building of schools. Income at Castletown from traditional sources, local subscriptions (£53), the annual sermon (£16) and school pence (£25), totalling £94, was now considerably less than the government grants for teachers, pupil-teachers and pension, at £121, even before capitation was taken into account. It is not certain if the paucity of the capitation earned at Castletown, a mere £8, was due to great irregularity of attendance or possibly the recent introduction of the system.

Castletown also illustrated the difficulty in the Island of extending specialised infants' education, which apart from the Wilson provision at Peel, was confined to Douglas and St. Mark's. The need for such education in Castletown had been pointed out by the HMI's in 1851, and the High Bailiff for the area had called a public meeting on December 2nd, 1851, to launch a subscription list to raise two-thirds of the £200 needed, the Committee of the Council being relied upon to provide the remaining third.[40] The venture was described by the Rev. Edward Ferrier as "a blessing to the little ones and to the parents in enabling them to pursue more unremittingly their daily toil." Money had already been donated, the Governor leading the way with ten pounds, yet the 1858 local report had to admit that no progress had been made.

The most important development in Manx education in the early Eighteen Sixties lay in the new structure of teaching in the schools. This was essentially a result of the recent ties with English education. By 1863 only three parishes, Marown, Bride and Ballaugh, had not been in receipt of grants from the English Parliament, which involved keeping in line with the rules and regulations laid down by the Committee of the Privy Council for Education. (The work of the Privy Council Committee was combined in 1856 with that of the Department of Science and Art, which came under the Board of Trade, to make a combined Department of Education, whose Vice-President was a member of the government of the day.) Whatever was decided in England would immediately effect the Isle of Man, unless the Island decided to abandon the links at great financial cost to itself. On the mainland there was a disquiet over the standards of education being achieved at what seemed enormous cost to the Treasury. The original grant of £20,000 in 1833 had risen rapidly, up to £541,233 in 1857 with another massive surge to £813,441 in 1861. A Royal Commission under the chairmanship of the Duke of Newcastle was set up "to inquire into the Present State of Popular Education in England, and to consider and report what measures, if any, are required for the Extension of sound and cheap Elementary Instrustion to all Classes of the People." The ten selected areas for investigation showed that there had been considerable improvement. 1 in 7·83 was now of the population was now attending school, compared with 1 in 14 or 16 in 1818, and the 1 in 21 in 1800.[41] While only 4·5 of children of school age received no education, the amount and value of their education was open to question. Elementary subjects were badly taught, and there was need to secure regular attendance and sounder teaching. Among their recommendations was the establishment of boards for local areas with the power to levy rates. This principle had long been established in Manx law since 1704, and given recent approval in the Manx 1851 Act, but the English Government flinched from unleashing yet another acrimonious round of disputes between denominations and secularists. However, the Report's recommendation that grants should depend on the proficiency of individual children in reading, writing and arithmetic very much appealed to Robert T. Lowe, the Vice-President of the Committee of the Privy Council on Education. "Hitherto we have been living under a system of bounties and protection. Now we propose to have a little free trade." The Education Department issued its Revised Code in 1862, and in a famous speech in February, 1862, Lowe informed the House of Commons: "If it is not cheap, it shall be efficient: if it is not efficient, it shall be cheap."

Elementary education in England, and in the Isle of Man too, would now be organised very systematically, with a series of 'standards' to be passed by children, who also were required to have made a certain number of attendances. If the child did not attend regularly, or failed his examination, he would not earn his grant for the school. The new arrangements had some merits. Teachers could not neglect basics for topics more interesting to themselves, and there was an incentive now to greater efficiency. The 'system' which Bishop Short had urged upon the teachers was now provided by the English Government. After entering school around the age of six, the child worked up to Standard Six around the age of eleven or twelve, when he was expected to enable to read a newspaper passage, write it down by dictation and do arithmetical problem of an appropriate difficulty. Brighter children advanced quickly, while the less intelligent might spend years trying to pass a single standard. Regular attendance earned 4/- for the school, and a pass in each of the three 'Rs' a further 2/8, a possible total of 12/- per pupil.[42]

Since a good grant meant prestige and more money to spend for the managers, this 'payment by results' dominated school life. Other varied work tended to be almost totally neglected, causing Kay-Shuttleworth to lament in his 'Memorandum on Popular Education' that "the Revised Code has constructed nothing; it has only pulled down." This overlooked the great improvement in attendance and basic subjects: the Newcastle Commission believed that not more than one-fourth of children received a good education at the time of their investigations. On the debit side, the search for economy had lead Lowe to withdraw the pupil-teacher grants to teachers, as well as their own payments for certification, so that there was less inducement to take on pupil-teachers. The result was a drop on their numbers by a third, and an increase in the size of classes, which in turn led to neglect of those unlikely to pass their examinations and earn grant school. In the Island, a school such as Santon had before the Revised Code a wide curriculum for its pupils. In addition to the three 'Rs', geography, history, scripture, mensuration, navigation and needlework for the girls found a place in the instruction given. But after 1862, teachers were reluctant to jeopardise the success hoped for in the inspector's examinations by spending time on extra subjects. To all intents and purposes the basic curriculum of reading, writing and arithmetic became the sole instruction of any elementary school. In efforts to ensure success, teachers resorted to having pupils learn their set reading books off by heart, while inspectors countered by asking for sentences to be read backwards, or by politely enquiring if the child could "do without the book".[43]

Yet all in all, the new links with the mainland had been most valuable to the Island. In purely financial terms, the insular schools had benefitted to the tune of nearly five thousand pounds in capitation grants, with £4,600 coming from the British Government to aid building and improvement of schools between 1834 and 1868. £824 had been given before the Committee of the Council was set up in 1839, and £3,776 afterwards. But ultimately of far greater importance were the new ideas. The surveillance of the experienced inspector replaced that of the local incumbent; provision of methods for the master to increase his salary by his own efforts had replaced reliance on totally inadequate ancient endowments; constantly rising standards of acceptable building and working conditions laid down in Whitehall replaced unsatisfactory premises: systematic, if rather soulless, schemes of education replaced the haphazard nature of much which had gone before. For such benefits, a certain amount of mechanical drudgery under the Revised Code was a small price to pay.

The new regime in Whitehall certainly did not impede the excellence of the education imparted at Peel, where Cowley continued to impress even more than previously, in the length of school life encouraged, and the excellence of his results under the new system. (Although slightly beyond the bounds of this chapter, his career will be followed to his retirement.)

The Inspectors were not without reservations from time to time. Kennedy's successor, the Rev. William Birley, thought in 1863 that the discipline was much improved, and the school very creditably instructed, but the following year said "the only weak point is discipline", otherwise there was the "customary success". In 1865 Augustus Hadley, while endorsing Cowley's certificate with "well taught in every respect" in his report thought that "more practical knowledge of the Scriptures is desirable." Yet on the whole the reports and endorsements were paeans of praise. "The tone, discipline and instruction in this School are all highly creditable to Mr. COWLEY'S management of it" (Hadley 1866). "The School continues to be distinguished by its good work and discipline, and by the proficiency and intelligence of its scholars" (J. W. Kennedy 1868). "Many of the children do wonderfully well in their sums and their writing and spelling. Out of 173 children examined in seven standards, there were extremely few failures of any kind. Of these 83 were examined above the third standard and there was no failure among them." Keenedy 1870). A shyness among the children at answering in 1870, and a weakness in needlework in 1873 were the only reasons for pejorative comment of any kind. Only towards the end when Cowley's health was breaking was there serious adverse comment. Hugo Wiggins in 1847 found discipline lax, room for improvement in the upper standards handwriting, and a failure to make sure that Standards 5 and 6 understood what they were reading. He found some of the blame to lie in the shape of the room, the 'L' not making for easy supervision, and recommended that an assistant master be employed. (It is an indication of rising standards of the period how the fine new school of one decade was considered the unsatisfactory premises of the next. This was the second time this had happened at Peel, and there would be yet a further example to come at the turn of the century.) The recommendations were duly noted, and a Mr. Fargher employed to help out Cowley, obviously to good effect, for the 1875 report praised "his promising exertions". Whether the weakness of 1874 had been eradicated is hard to tell. Possibly Alfred Percival Graves, knowing that Cowley was leaving on health grounds, dedicated that fault finding should not mar a valedictory tribute by Her Majesty's Inspectors. "... no school in England could show such a large per cent (45%) in the upper standards. An unusually large number of the children examined in the third and fourth standards have done the arithmetical problems." His final endorsement spoke of his forty seven years as a teacher, thirty two years at Peel, with his achievements "remarkable proof of his concientious energy and skill as a teacher and disciplinarian in spite of failing health. For this school is not only without its equal among the Boys' Schools in the Island, but is also distinguished beyond every school in England under the inspection of Government for the number and proficiency of its upper standards."[44] Praise indeed!

  The middle of the Nineteenth Century had been decades of great prosperity for the lead mines at Foxdale and Laxey,[45] and the provision of a new school for Laxey in 1868 saw the second involvement of an industrial enterprise in paying for a share of the cost. Indeed no Treasury money was needed, although the National Society gave £110 from its own funds. The Laxey Mining Company gave £339, to which was added £100 from the usually parsimonious Commissioners of the Woods and Forests. In recognition of their contribution, the Directors of the Mining Company and the Manager joined the local Church of England minister on the Committee in charge of the school. The Foxdale Mining Company appear to have made no such contribution to the enlargement of the National School there in 1867, but had kept up the generous sum of £100 each year to the upkeep of the school. A request that £50 of this be deducted from the royalties paid to the Commissioners of Woods and Forests had been made in 1851, and had met with partial success to the tune of £30.[46] Apart from the special grants made from time to time mentioned earlier, this £30, (kept from a meagre £10 to Noble's Hospital in later years) was the sole annual contribution to Island education and charitable institutions from mining royalties which exceeded £13,000 in 1866. However, events in the wider world were to render this potentially significant involvement of industry as of passing interest only.

CONCLUSION

The years 1847-1869 were a period of very marked progress for the Isle of Man as far as elementary education was concerned. The provision of new buildings was accelerated, and the dormant powers of the old 1704 Act given new life and direction by the 1851 Act expressly permitting the use of the rates for educational purposes. Most important of all, the low esteem given to the office of schoolteachers for a century and a half had been replaced by the recognition that teaching was worthy to be ranked as a profession, with financial rewards now at levels which would encourage a flow of trained masters and mistresses to pass on their knowledge and understanding to the rising generations. Much remained to be accomplished, but the path of progress was at the same time being cleared by other happenings.

For the end of the Eighteen Sixties saw three developments of great importance for education, one on the continent of Europe, one in England and one on the Isle of Man, although none was directly concerned with the subject. The Paris Exhibition of 1867 had revealed how Britain was failing to match the technical expertise of Germany, and how this superiority of German technical training had depended on their system of universal elementary schooling. The point was taken to heart by politicians such as A. J. Mundella as well as by British manufacturers and mine owners. Kay-Shuttleworth welcomed this new realisation by employers that a well educated workforce would help them fight off competition from foreign rivals, and their consequent demands for "A superior elementary education".[47] When the politician, W. E. Forster, made enquiries among Chambers of Commerce, the new importance given to education was most evident.

The widening of the franchise in 1867 had led to the same conclusions, although for different reasons. Robert Lowe feared that handing potential political power to ignorant men would obliterate itself. The only solution was "it will be absolutely necessary to compel our future masters to learn their letters", usually simplified as "we must educate our masters". No longer could reliance be placed on the voluntary system, the need was too urgent. Compulsory education was now "a question of self preservation". Kay-Shuttleworth, using the opportunity to attack the narrowness of Lowe's Revised Code, urged a wider education unity as the means to achieve the same desired end of a loyal, intelligent and Christian population. He too threatened the end of the capitalist system if the working classes obtained power without being educated to see what was in their own long-term interest. Even Edward Baynes, the leading spokesman for those who had once resented state interference in education, thought the matter was now one of "pressing necessity". Government action, with the Education Department under W. E. Forster after Gladstone's victory of 1868, was clearly imminent.

On the Isle of Man a couple of years earlier legislation had given to Tynwald limited control of the surplus revenue of the Island which had hitherto gone as profits to the treasury. The Governor retained a power of veto, as did the Treasury, but an element of 'Home Rule during pleasure' was obtained. As a condition for the Island's own use of its surplus revenue, the old House of Keys was virtually compelled to pass the House of Keys Election Act of 1866, which for the first time made them elected by popular vote, instead of remaining a classical example of the self-perpetuating oligarchy. The Island government was now to be representative, at least as far as the Keys were concerned, of popular feeling, and with a degree of control over its own finances it had not enjoyed previously under the British Crown (however far short this actually fell of what had been hoped, through the restraints placed upon it.) The possibility emerged of legislative independence in educational as well as other fields being joined by financial independence, so that the Island could loosen its financial bonds with Whitehall. At the same time, the impending changes in the structure of English education were not things that could be ignored, and it was clear that a new and exciting chapter in Manx elementary education was about to begin.

REFERENCES

ELEMENTARY EDUCATION 1847-69

1. Lord John Russell, *Letter Feb. 4 1839;* quoted J. Stuart Maclure *Educational Documents England and Wales 1816-1967.* 43.
2. *Order in Council Aug. 10 1840.*
3. H. C. Barnard, *Op cit.* 99-105.
4. Rev. H. Moseley, *Report on the Parochial Schools in the Isle of Man.* II.
5. *Ibid*, 12.
6. *Report of the Commissioners of Inquiry into the State of Education in Wales 1847.* 252.
7. A. W. Moore, *A History of the Isle of Man,* Vol. II. 674.
8. Moseley. *Op cit.* 18.
9. *Report of the Commissioners of Inquiry into the State of Education in Wales.* 309.
10. *A Statistical Review of the State of Education in the Isle of Man 1847.*
11. J. L. and R. Hammond. *The Town Labourer 1917.* 55.
12. F. Engels. *The Condition of the Working Class in England in 1844.* 110.
13. J. Stuart Maclure. *Op cit.* 45.
14. R. W. Rich. *The Training of Teachers in the Nineteenth Century.* 81f.
15. MS 5568. *Castletown National School Minute Book,* Aug. 25 1848.
16. *The Story of Methodism in the Isle of Man Interim Report 1971.* (Typed).
17. *Thomas Street Methodist Sunday School Minute Book,* Jan. 18 1851.
18. *Ibid*, Feb. 25 1852.
19. *Ibid*, Nov. 13 1852.
20. *Ibid*, Sept. 29 1854.
21. *Ibid*, October 15 1856.
22. *Statutes of the Isle of Man.* Vol. 2. 274.
23. A. W. Moore, *Manx Worthies,* 36.
24. *Statutes of the Isle of Man.* Vol. 2. 175.
25. *Ibid*, 155.
26. *Ibid*, 271.
27. A. W. Moore, *A History of the Isle of Man.* Vol. II. 674.
28. *Educational Endowments 1880.*
29. MD 716/117. *Letter of July 12 1854.*
30. *Minutes of the Committee of Council for Education 1855-56.* 354.

31. *Ibid*, 363.
32. *Report of Diocesan Inspectors 1857-58.*
33. *Bishop Powys Convocation Charge 1858.* E205/2/2/7.
34. Robert J. Moore. *Christian's Endowed School 1861.* D426/1/3(5).
35. *Ibid.*
36. *Isle of Man Times*, July 3 1861.
37. MD 612 20/16.
38. D426 IX. *Report on National Schools Castletown.* 1858.
39. *Ibid.*
40. D 426 IX. *Appeal for Infants School for Castletown.* 1851.
41. *Newcastle Report.* Vol. I. 87.
42. Stuart Maclure. *Op cit.* 70-72. 79.
43. *Ibid.* 81 for Matthew Arnold's Critique of the 'Effects of the Revised Code'.
44. Records of the Cowley Family in Peel.
45. A. W. Moore, *Op cit* Vol. II. 970.
46. William Cubbon, *Island Heritage.* 279.
47. Kay-Shuttleworth, *Social Problems.* 267.

INDEX

Academic School—30f, 68f, 185-6, 188, 194, 200, 209.
Academies—155f.
Adams, Williams—172.
Airey, Robert—176-77.
Aitken, Rev. Robert—158.
Allen, Rev. Henry—58.
Andreas School—18, 86, 88, 90, 95, 233-234, 241, 263.
Arbory School—49, 86, 239,241.
Aspinall, Susan—41.
Athol Academy—170.
Athol St. Day and Sunday School (Lancasterian school)—168, 222f, 226f, 263.
Athol, Dukes of:
James (1736-64)—53-5, 71-72.
John (1793-1830) 4th Duke—128-29, 132-33, 140, 156, 232.
Athol St. (private schools)—160, 161, 164, 166, 170-71.
Auckland Ld—167, 275 (see Eden Bishop 268).
Baldwin Chapel and School—237.
Baldwin East School—96, 239.
Ballasalla School—274.
Ballaugh School—12, 18, 88, 92, 233, 260, 283.
Ballaugh Village School—95.
Ballure Chapel—29, 48, 82.
Banks, William—17, 31.
Barker, John—115-116.
Barregarrow School—250.
Barton, J.—145, 163.
Barrow, Bishop Isaac—9f, 26, 28, 30f 43, 53, 208.
Battersea, Normal College—265.
Bell, Dr. Alexander—220, 225-226, 232.
Bennett, Hannah—28.
Bishopscourt—69.
Blundell, William—8.
Bounty, Royal—11, 15, 17, 20, 25, 47, 56, 284.
Braddan School—87, 96, 225, 232, 234, 239.
Bray, Thomas—70-71.
Bride School—18, 87, 88, 92, 232, 234, 240, 260, 283.
Bridgman, Bishop Henry—15, 28, 30, 69.
Bridson, Rev. John—118.
Brine, John—144.45.
Brougham, Lord—128, 191, 204, 232, 236.
Brown, Rev. E.T.—205.
Brown, Rev. Hugh Stowell—148, 208.
Brown, Rev. Joseph—14-141.
Brown, Rev. Robert—106, 145, 147, 198-200, 227.
Burgess, Bishop Thomas—183, 210.

Busk, Sir. Wadsworth—117, 138.
Callin, Ann—58.
Callister, Henry—80-81.
Cannell, James—270.
Cannell, John—149.
Carpenter, Dr.—243.
Castle Rushen—8.
Castletown Grammar School—26f, 67f, 139f.
Castletown National School—228-9, 241.3, 263, 266-7, 281-85.
Castletown Petty School—9, 20, 282.
Castley, Rev. Thomas—100-108, 197-198.
Certificated Teachers—261, 281-282.
Challenor, John—9.
Charities Book of—234f.
Charles II—11.
Charles, Earl of Derby—12, 53.
Chase, Bishop Philander—183, 191.
Chemistry—124, 166, 170.
Chevalier, Rev. Temple—191.
Cholmondeley, Frederick—70.
Cholmondeley, Thomas—17, 28, 33.
Cholmondeley, Thomas—79, 105.
Christian, John—19, 29.
Christian, John (Vicar of Marown)—89.
Christian, Margaret—51.
Christian, Nicholas—87, 104, 106.
Christian, Philip—22.
Christian, William—22.
Circulating Schools—62.
Clarendon Commission—197, 201.
Clothworkers' Company—22.
Cochrane, Governor Basil—74, 100.
Colquoun, Rev. J.—144, 159, 164.
Comenius, James—10.
Coolingen—79, 119, 123.
Corlett, Rev. henry—96, 118.
Corrin, Caesar—139.
Corteen, Robert—157.
Cosnahan, Julius—107.
Cowley, William—241, 280-81, 285-86.
Crail, James—147.
Craine, John—57.
Crellin, Rev. John—122.
Crescent Academy—169-171.
Crigan, Bishop Claudius—87, 108, 121, 139.
Cronkbourne—274.
Cronk-Y-Voddy—241, 245.
Cubbon, Sir. Mark—123.
Cumming, Rev. J. G.—204.
Curghy, John—42.

Dalby—238, 240, 261.
Darling, Horatio—22.
Dawson, Lt. Governor—116.
De Ruvignes, H.—171.
Denton, Thomas—34.35.
Derby, Earls of:
    James I (1627-51)—8, 9.
    Charles (1660-72)—12, 33.
    James II (1702-36)—53, 72.
Derbyhaven School—274.
Dhoor—252.
Dickson, William—76.
Dixon, Robert—193, 204, 207.
Dodd, John—131f.
Douglas Petty School—9, 18f, 29, 75.
Douglas Grammar School—74f, 109-11, 144f.
Dove, Hester—176.
Drummond, Archbishop—87.
Drury, John—90.
Dublin, Trinity College—30, 34.
Dutton, Misses—165f.
Dykes, Robert—42.

Eden, Bishop—266.
Education Acts 1703-4—37f, 261.
    1813—231.
    1851—269f.
Ellerslie—59.
Enquests—21.
Eyreton—158-59.
Examinations, public—121, 160, 169.

Fairplay, Peter—137.
Fannin, Peter—157.
Fairfax, Thomas—9, 16.
Ffarand, Peter—7.
Farrar, F. W.—205-6.
Feltham, John—124.
Ferguson, Robert—14.
Fitzsimmons, Rev. William—105, 114, 120.
Fletcher, Robert—19.
Forrester, Walter—176.
Foster, Bishop—8.
Fowler, Thomas—205.
Fox. Robert—14. 17.
Foxdale Schools—239, 250-1, 286.
Frankland, Samuel—27.
French—120, 160.

Garvin, J. A.—164.
Gawne, Edward Moore—246.
Gell, John—110.
Gelling, Rev. James—131f.
Gelling, Rev. Samuel—148-9.
Geneste, F. D. P.—146-7.;
Genkins, David—28.
George IV—188.
German, Parochial School for—233, 272.
Gill, Rev. John—89-90.
Glasgow Method—241.
Glenmaye (Glenmoij)—240.
Gostwike, William—33.
Gouge, Thomas—61.
Graham, John—42.
Grenaby School—239.
Gunn, Angus—147, 163.

Haining, Rev. Samuel—158, 216.
Halsall, Anthony—77.
Halsall, Catherine's School—94, 264.
Halsall, Henry—35.
Hampton Court—164.
Hans, Nicholas—113.
Hardwick, Lord Chancellor—85.
Harrison, Vicar-General—16, 18.
Harrison, David—118.
Haskins, Joseph—121, 124, 129, 131.
Hastings, Lady Elizabeth—55-6, 61, 85.
Heterick, Robert—118-9, 136.
Heywood House—164.
Hildesley, Bishop Mark—81, 85f, 217.
Holt, Gilbert—28, 35.
Horner, Governor—72.
Horrobin, Archdeacon—71.
Horton, Governor—52.
Howard, Rev. Thomas—123, 147.

Imeson, Christopher—144.
Impropriate Fund—11, 18, 85, 92.
Industry, Schools of—244.5.
Infant Schools—229-230.

James, Earl of Derby—8.
Jeffreys, Ld-Chancellor—53.
Jones, Griffiths—62.
Jordan, W. K.—8.
Joughin, James—95
Jurby School—85, 88, 92, 95, 232, 239, 293, 273.

Kay, James—260, 267, 290.
Kay, Thomas—281-2.
Keble, John—9, 29, 69.
Kellett, Henry—172.
Kelly, Fr.—249.
Kelly's School—96, 252.
Kennedy, Rev. W. J.—276-78, 285.
Kewley, Rev. John—144.
King William's College—187-210, 242.
Kippax, Archdeacon—76.
Kissag, John—52.
Knipe, James (the elder)—80.
Knipe, James—80.
Knox, John—10.

Lace Family—31.
Lake, Bishop—20, 23.
Lampeter, Joseph—220, 267.
Lancasterian School (see Athol St. School)
Langley, Matthias—8.
Lawrence and Imeson—145.
Laxey School, 189, 239, 286, (1868).
Leach, A. F.—151.
Legh, Peter—70, 100, 140.
Levinz, Bishop Baptista—20, 24-25, 29, 43, 44, 47.
Levinz, Sir Gresswell—24.
Lezayre School—18, 49, 86, 90, 233, 234, 278, 281.
Lhiaggyn the—96.
Libraries—68.
Locke, John—69.
Lonan School—12-13, 86, 88, 95, 232, 234, 239, 264, 278.
Looney, Thomas—49, 67.
Lowcay, Henry—28, 34, 70-71.
Lowe, Robert—268, 273, 284, 288.

MacCawell, Hugh—7.
McCrone, James—236, 241.
McHutchin, John—187-8, 196.
McMullen, J.—172-3.
Macquyn, Luke—7.
Maddrell, Rev. Henry—123, 129, 130, 253.
Makon, James—71.
Malew Parochial School—14, 18, 88, 232, 234, 240-1, 274.
Manx Language—81, 86f, 217.
Mark, Richard—176.
Marown School—20, 86, 88, 92, 232-3, 239-40, 264, 278.
Mason, Bishop—87, 118.
Mathematical Schools—112.

Mathematical School, Peel (see Peel).
Mathematics—69.
Maughold School—18, 92, 93, 234, 236, 264, 274.
May, Edward—164-65.
Melbourne, Lord—177, 192, 196.
Michael School—14, 18, 86, 89, 240, 263-4, 274.
Methodist Schools—284-9, 263, 267-68.
Milton, John—30.
Moffatt, S. B.—248.
Moore, A. W.—13, 168, 262.
Moore (Deemster), Charles—32.
Moore George—112, 115, 117, 119, 139.
Moore, Rev. James—112, 115.
Moore, John—133-4.
Moore, Phil(ip)—75, 78.
Moore, Rev. Philip—77, 88, 94, 107, 109-110, 114.
Moore, Robert—279.
Morrison, John—249, 269.
Moseley, Rev. Henry—258f, 277.
Murray, Bishop George—129, 132, 218, 232.
Murray, Governor James—73.
Murray, John—76.
Murrey, William, 110.
Mylrea, Archdeacon , William—117, 139.
Mylrea, David—182.
National Society—22, 270f.
Natural Philosophy—69.
Nelson Edward—14.
Newcastle Commission—283-85.
Norris, Deemster—15.
Nosson, Edward—19.

Oakhill—164, 274.
Oates, William—119.
Oddfellows' Hall—171.
Onchan School—49, 86, 88, 233, 239, 263, 272.
Ormande, James, Duke of—31.
Owen, Robert—254.

Parkin, Samuel—268-69.
Parr, John—29.
Parr, Rev. John—114.
Parr, John (Vicar-General)—19.
Parr, Bishop, Richard—8.
Parr, Robert—8.
Parr Thomas—20.
Parsons, Rev. George—143, 183, 196, 204, 226, 229.
Patrick School—20, 49, 88, 92.
Payl (Pully), Bishop Richard—7.

Peel Clothworkers' School—9, 14, 23f, 60-61, 133, 230, 246f, 278f, 285.
Peel Grammar School—78-79, 111-121, 130-138.
Peel Mathematical School—111-121, 130-138.
Peel, Sir Robert—129, 133, 143, 185, 187, 189-90, 205.
Philips, Alfred—203.
Philips, Bishop John—10.
Philips, Rev. Thomas—129, 158, 176.
Philpot, Rev. Benjamin—174, 183, 230, 239.
Port St. Mary School—238.
Postlethwayt, Malachi—155.
Powys, Bishop Horatio—278.
Preceptors, College of 171-172.
Presentments—20, 44.

Quakers—17.
Qualtrough, Jane—95.
Quayle, George—132.
Quayle, Robert—59.
Quayle, Alderman William—77.
Qualtrough, Miss Jane—244.
Qualtrough, Rev. Joseph—145.
Quilliam, Margaret—208.
Quine, Thomas—134, 279.
Raikes, Robert—215.
Ramsey School—9, 14, 28-29, 79-82, 122-123, 129-130.
Ramsey National School—225-6, 233, 274.
Ramsey Methodist School—268, 275.
Ready, Governor John—199, 204.
Richmond, Bishop—105.
Rimmer, William—163.
Robinson, Samuel—14.
Robinson, Rev.—20, 77.
Ross, Professor William—70, 72-74, 100, 103.
Ross, Grissel—103.
Royal Bounty—252.
Rushen School—50, 88, 93, 219, 234, 239, 264, 275, 277.
Rushen Abbey—33, 166, 275.

Sacheverell, Governor William—25, 70.
St. Barnabas Schools—243, 265, 272.
St. Bees School—156.
St. David's College, Lampeter—183, 188, 209-210.
St. John's—57.
St. George's Church
St. Mark's—96, 251-2, 272.
St. Mary's R.C.—249, 263.
Santan School—12, 20, 234, 238, 272.
Scottisk Education—10, 43.
Secker, Archbishop—106.
Shaw, Lt-Governor Alexander—120.

Shaw, John—33.
Short, Bishop Thomas—204, 247, 250f.
Smelt, Lt-Governor Cornelius—140, 184f.
Smith, Governor Edward—116.
SPCK—61, 68.
SPG—68.
Statistical View (1847)—262.
Steuart, Col.—185-85.
Steele, Alexander—169.
Stephenson, John—116.
Stephenson, Richard—27.
Stowell, Rev. Hugh—111, 122, 136, 141, 150, 160, 193, 216, 223, 227, 233, 234, 240.
Stowell, John—119-120, 156.
Stowell, Joseph—107, 111, 120-121, 129, 137, 150.
Stowell, John de la Mothe—147-8.
Stowell, Misses—166-167.
Stowell, William—148.
Stowell, William Hendry—146, 208.
Sulby School—51, 238.
Sunday School—215-220, 264.
Sutherland, Patrick—170.

Taubman, John—103.
Taubman's School, Castletown—94, 263.
Tear William—60.
Thimbleby, Rev. Thomas—141-3, 183, 228.
Teignmouth, Ld—193, 196-197, 202.
Thompson, Peter—8.
Thomas Street Methodist School—247-249, 267-269.
Tompson, R.S.—107, 139, 197.
Training Colleges—265.
Trimmer, Sarah—221.
Tynwald—3, 43.

Ulster Schools—123.
Urquhart, Archdeacon William—20, 24.
Villa Marina—165, 166.
Vincent, W. A. L.—8, 26.
Visitations—62-63, 89f.
Waldron, George—76, 105.
Walker, William—48, 71, 76.
Ward, Bishop William—183-205, 236f.
Ward, Mrs.—244.
Watterson, John—42.
Wattleworth, Samuel—25.
Welch, John—237.
Well Road Methodist School—247-9, 267-68.
Whitehouse, Rev.—100.
Wilderspin, David—229, 242.
Wilks—73, 79, 89, 101, 105.

William IV—190.
Wilks, Col. Mark—107, 120, 124.
William IV—190.
Wilson, Edward—191f, 197.
Wilson James—204.
Wilson Richard—116-117.
Wilson, Bishop Thomas—41-63, 70-82, 86.
Wilson, Dr. Thomas—60, 104.
Wilson, Bishop Wilson's School—280.
Woods, Rev. Thomas—81.
Woods, Rev. John—35, 50, 53, 81.